the Heretics

by
Walter Nigg

Edited and translated by Richard and Clara Winston

Dorset Press • New York

Originally published in German as
Das Buch der Ketzer.
Copyright 1949 by Artemis Verlag AG, Zürich.

This edition published by Dorset Press
a division of Marboro Books Corporation,
by arrangement with Alfred A. Knopf, Inc.
1990 Dorset Press

ISBN 0-88029-455-8

Printed in the United States of America

M 9 8 7 6 5 4 3 2 1

*Do not think that heresies
could have arisen
from a few beggarly little souls.
Only great men have brought forth heresies.*

—AUGUSTINE

Translators' Note

By arrangement with the author, the work presented here is an abridged version of Das Buch der Ketzer *(Zürich: Artemis Verlag; 1949). All the chapters of the original are included, in shortened form, except for two chapters dealing with Gottfried Arbold and Gotthold Ephraim Lessing, which have been omitted entirely.*

Contents

the Heretics

Note

All quotations from the Bible are from the Revised Standard Version of the Bible, copyrighted 1946 and 1952 by the Division of Christian Education, National Council of Churches of Christ in the United States of America. Used by permission of Thomas Nelson & Sons, New York, N.Y.

In keeping with the practice of the Bible and many religious books, pronouns referring to the Deity are, because of their frequency, not capitalized.

INTRODUCTION

Heresies on Heretics

In his short story, "After the Ball," Leo Tolstoy tells of a young man who attends a gay party. All evening the guests dance and apply themselves to the champagne. The belle of the ball is a colonel's daughter, a charming girl in a white dress with pink sash, toward whom the young man has romantic feelings. After the party the lovesick young man cannot sleep, and in his stimulated, happy state he goes for a stroll through the city as dawn is breaking. In the course of his wandering he passes by a barracks and becomes involuntary witness of a punishment: a Tartar deserter who has been recaptured is being "beaten through the ranks"—made to run the gauntlet. As he stumbles forward, he pleads again and again: "Brothers, have mercy on me! Brothers, have mercy on me!"

Suddenly the young man recognizes the father of the pretty girl, who toward the end of the ball had delighted all the guests by dancing a mazurka with his daughter "in the old style." Now, with the victim's back already a bloody pulp from the ordeal, the colonel orders "fresh sticks." The young man flees from the place. But the horrible scene remains with him, and his feelings for the belle of the ball have vanished. The story closes with the remark that this incident caused the life of the young man to take an entirely different direction.[1]

This story of Tolstoy's—an instance of the greatness of his art—has an inner meaning that reaches into the realm of religion. Though any overt reference to God is absent from it, it affects the reader like a Biblical vision, reveals to him one of the profoundest of truths. The problem of reality's many levels is laid bare in all its mystery, and the interconnections between different strata of reality are suggested. In the story Tolstoy shows two utterly different kinds of human reality, which are separated from one another by a deep gulf and yet are also strangely related. It would be a serious error to think of the one reality as true, the other false.

On the one hand reality is represented as a gay ball at which the mazurka is danced and champagne drunk. Wonder and rapture surround this festive scene. Let us not underestimate it; it occupies considerable space in man's mind. It should not be dismissed out of hand as illusion and deception. The ball has its beauty, even though its glitter may serve only for ostentation and effect. The charming girl in the white dress and pink sash represents a reality whose value cannot be denied. History can also be regarded as such a pageant.

How strangely does this festive reality contrast with that dark side of life which the young man encounters by chance:

---

[1] Leo Tolstoy: "After the Ball," in Avrahm Yarmolinsky, ed.: *A Treasury of Great Russian Short Stories* (New York: The Macmillan Co.; 1944), p. 570.

the human experience conceived as a "running the gauntlet." The curious links between these two realities are among the most incomprehensible phenomena of human life. For there are people who can gaily dance a mazurka, and a few hours later can order a man to be beaten mercilessly. The character of the girl's father is proof of the many-layered reality which extends deep into the nature of men—and only makes the enigma more perplexing.

These philosophical observations, then, are inherent in a simple story. They are also inherent in the history of Christian thought. Strange things are revealed when we turn our eyes from the bright pageants of history to the events that lay behind them. The grim ordeal of those who had to run the gauntlet may be equated with the theme of heresy: a drama of tremendous scope, and one which has been more or less deliberately slurred over in histories of the West. Few persons have ventured to deal with those dark events which took place in the wings, amid scenes of surpassing cruelty. We would rather not think of the frightful indictment contained in the history of heresies; we shy away from the sight of such brutality. We do not read these annals for fear of running into things which would rob us of our sleep. It is far pleasanter to dance the mazurka than to stand in a square at dawn and watch the heretic beaten to death. And yet the story of the heretics contains truths which inescapably confront man with the Eternal.

The Tartar deserter is at a disadvantage from the start because no one asks him why he tried to run away. Must his reasons necessarily have been dishonorable ones? In similar fashion, there has been a failure to question the heretic, whose suppression was also brutal and complete.

The view that heretics were wicked men whose fate need not concern the Christian has been widely propagated. For centuries heretics were defamed in every possible way. The aim has always been to spread a forbidding and repulsive picture of heretics. In ecclesiastical history the mere charge of heresy proved to be a potent weapon with which to cut down an opponent. The heretic was portrayed as a person infected with spiritual leprosy, one who seduced good men to evil, someone who had given his soul to the devil. A heretic was capable of any crime. By such means, the heretic was discredited in advance, so that his doctrines could never gain ground. Such views of the heretic have persisted down to the present time. Even in twentieth-century works on secular history we can find such comments as this: "Heretics were individuals with a tendency to be know-it-alls." [2]

But who is responsible for this caricature of the heretic? Is he not like the officer who calls out, when the Tartar is already half dead: "Fresh sticks!" Or, to drop our figure of speech, has not the caricature been drawn by the parties who emerged as victors from the ecclesiastical struggles? The historical works which show heretics in so unfavorable a light were mostly written by these victors, by those who carried the field. Naturally, they have been at pains to show that their victory was desired by God; understandably, they have devalued everything that might throw some question upon their legitimacy.

The heretic is not a new phenomenon; he appeared early in the history of Christianity. But the old questions he tried to answer are not outmoded; rather, they must be asked afresh. From time to time certain recurrent problems have to be discussed again, nor do we necessarily arrive at the same results as an earlier age. When we take up the problem of heresy in the twentieth century, we do so from premises different from those of the second century. The many-leveled conception of reality, the possibility we now admit that history may be as much a running of the gauntlet as a festival, also casts the story of heresy in another light.

In an age like the present, which has known such vast spiritual upheavals, we are well equipped to understand this trend which earlier ages named as heresy. We can, perhaps, enter into the nature of the heretic's attitude. We can, perhaps, feel our way into the seditious thinking of the heretics, acquire a sense of

[2] Ricarda Huch: *Römisches Reich deutscher Nation* (1934), p. 202.

the heretic point of view, the heretical experience, and the heretic's force. At bottom there is something heretical merely in an agonized contemplation of the seamy side of life. Once we begin to focus our attention on that, we can easily drift onto forbidden paths and catch glimpses of uncanny things which are usually carefully hidden.

People, after all, are not interested in the revelation of truth. Pascal expressed this in that terrifying sentence which comes to mind again and again whenever we think of the fate of heretics: "Earth is not the home of truth; unrecognized, she wanders lost among men." [3] If we are going to examine the problem of heresy, our first requirement is the spiritual readiness to set forth on an unfamiliar road that leads into unknown territory. A love for outsiders is called for, and an unabashed fondness for the outlaw. To be sure, there is a certain danger in tracing the destinies of heretics. The story of heresy is not the best fare for immature or unstable minds. Along with mighty truths we shall have to discuss diabolic temptations which demand critical thought and the ability to make distinctions. Here is the place to cite the words of Gideon: "Whoever is fearful and trembling, let him return home." [4]

In order to establish our new approach, let us in all deliberation postpone examining the question of the origin of heresy. Naturally enough, this question has consistently preoccupied the minds of Christians. During the first centuries of Christianity, heresy was regarded as a fall from orthodoxy provoked by the devil. Satan, it was said, had crept into the ranks of the Christians and inveigled some to belief in false doctrines.

In thus attacking the question from a metaphysical point of view, the early Christians certainly gave it depth. But in proposing such a genesis for heresy, the question was closed as soon as it was opened. If the heretics were creatures of the devil, they had to be seen as ugly and horrible. Having assumed Satanic inspiration behind heresy, a Christian could not listen to the

---

[3] Blaise Pascal: *Pensées*, Fragment 843.
[4] Judges vii, 3.

statements of the heretics. He closed his mind in advance to any understanding of the phenomenon of heresy.

Another theory had the virtue of being less arbitrary. This was the patristic explanation of heresy as arising out of the doctrines of Greek philosophy—the wisdom of Hellas being regarded, of course, as error. In the light of the intellectual history of the Early Church we must admit that there is a strong element of truth in this thesis. Heresy represented the corruption of Christianity by Greek philosophy. But the theory fails altogether to account for the medieval heretics, who in most cases lacked the slightest knowledge of Greek philosophy and who were impelled by motives entirely different from those of the earlier heretics.

In more recent times, students of the subject have explained heresy as the outcome of quarrels between the majority and the minority within Christianity, the victorious majority ultimately branding the defeated minority as heretics.[5] This explanation, too, is upheld by correct observation and historical probability. Its great defect is its shallowness, for it ignores the large complex of historical and philosophical questions. It takes the view that orthodoxy or heresy was decided historically more or less by chance—a concept which the religious mind finds unsatisfactory.

The origin of heresy cannot be explained by a simple formula, for the forces that gave rise to heretics were constantly changing. The question of origins cannot be answered in any summary fashion, and we will therefore do well to table it, and not place it at the head of our story of heresy.

Of far more importance to our new examination of the problem is the perception that heretics may not be ruthlessly detached from the body of the church. That is, we must comprehend that heresy is a necessary component of the life of the church. As a Christian religious philosopher of the rank of Leopold Ziegler has put it: "As for heretics and teachers of erroneous doctrine, let us not forget that they are necessary for

[5] Cf. W. Bauer: *Rechtgläubigkeit und Ketzerei im ältesten Christentum* (1934), pp. 2 f.

8

the tradition, so that it will remain in flux and not congeal into rigidity." [6] It is wrong to think of the heretic as merely in opposition to the church. Rather, he must be conceived as a supplement to it. The church and the heretics form a far more vital union than either are willing to admit. In recognizing this we are not trying to braid together the two strands of heresy and orthodoxy into one. Rather, we are making the point that heresy was there from the very start.

The idea that Christianity was unified in the beginning, and only afterward split up, will not stand the test of history. Rather, we find the epistles of Paul already discussing various currents within the early Christian communities—which is not surprising, given the multifarious world in which the Gospels made their appearance. It was always a desire of Christians to attain unity, but they were never destined to do so. Moreover, the church has always been responsible for the rise of heresy in its midst, for heresies almost invariably arose from some neglect of truth on the part of the church. Whatever the church may say, it cannot deny that it had some responsibility in the birth of various heresies.

Within the church the message of the Gospels has repeatedly been subject to falsification, degeneration, and obscuration, and for this reason the heretics have performed a needed function. The emergence of heresy would spur the church to the self-criticism which alone could act as a rejuvenating force. Christianity today needs this more than ever. Even the Catholic view, after all, holds that "the heretic still stands upon the ground of Christian belief"—though not with both feet.[7] The church and the heretics are manifestations of a single world of the spirit. Both must be regarded as emanating from a divine reality, each having a specific function to fulfill. It will not do, then, to set our sights upon that "ultimate passing beyond the concepts of orthodoxy and heresy" which Nikolai Berdyaev has called for.[8] Our aim in embarking on a re-evaluation of heresy is to discover

[6] Leopold Ziegler: *Menschwerdung* (1948), II, 191.
[7] Josef Brosch: *Das Wesen der Häresie* (1936), p. 68.
[8] Nikolai Berdyaev: *Orient und Okzident* (1936), Heft I, p. 13.

what in heresy may be pertinent to our own urgent spiritual problems.

Our starting point must be: In what does the essence of heresy consist? What makes the heretic? Is it disobedience to the church, defiant rebellion against the truths of the Bible, some cunning sophistry which lures men to their ruin? These are oversimple formulations. The genuine heretic is impelled by other motive forces, which cannot be summarized in a brief phrase. The heretic cannot be reduced to a stereotype; to try to do so does violence to his subtle psychology, which spans and includes large contradictions. Heresy is a richly variegated phenomenon, assuming different forms in every century. Since the views of heretics have been different, the type of the heretic cannot be reduced to a common denominator.

Bernard Shaw in *Man and Superman* has said that every truly religious man is a heretic, and therefore also a revolutionary. Like most Shavian dictates, this is an exaggeration. Yet it contains much truth. Certainly we must concede that many religious men are heretics. The heretic has this in common with the prophet and the saint: that he is religiously alive, filled with Christian dynamism, and prepared to sacrifice everything for his faith. He is the extreme antithesis of the indifferentist, or of the person whose central concern is ecclesiastical diplomacy and policy. The heretic is in deadly earnest; he does not straddle the fence. He courageously accepts the consequences of his actions. His fervor can teach us the meaning of loyalty to truth. We may even say that the heretic embodies the religious spirit in concentrated form. The principles of Christianity take first place with him; to these he subordinates everything else.

This statement applies to almost all the significant figures among the heretics, and of course these alone deserve a place in a book like this. The historian must be aware that there were also pathological troublemakers among the heretics. But they are not key figures and need not be discussed—all the more so since space in any case makes us selective. Only the great heretics are significant, those who represented vital religious feeling, and such passionate personalities are to be found in all periods of history. With their religious fire they often set whole generations ablaze. These men and women were filled with a Christian fervor which places them among the outstanding religious figures in history. When we assemble the members of this Christian opposition and survey them in their whole range, we have an extraordinarily impressive spectacle. Viewed all together in this way, the religious significance of heresy can be fully grasped. In sum, the heretics afford us a new insight into the Gospels.

The religious "outsiders," which is what the heretics were, represent a different conception of Christianity. It is essential to understand this; what we say in the following pages depends upon a proper appreciation of this truth. Heresy has nothing whatsoever to do with hostile assaults upon the Christian religion. Rather, heresy is Christianity, Christianity felt to its fullest intensity. To be sure, the heretic advocates a view of Christianity different from that of the victorious churches. We might put it that he attempts to bring to the fore the *other side* of the Gospel. Whether this other view is inferior, equal, or superior to that of the church is a matter of evaluation which need not be discussed for the present. Nevertheless, it can no longer be denied that this view springs from the essence of Christianity and has been acquired by sincere struggle.

Now, there are a multitude of conceptions of Christianity, both individual and national forms. The Gospel cannot be forced into a single mold which alone is regarded as valid. Such spiritual regimentation would directly violate the words of John that in the Father's house there are many mansions. To be sure, not all the conceptions of Christianity have equal value, but they all have a function to fulfill. As against a narrow and dogmatic outlook, we must emphatically insist upon this broader view of Christianity, which is more in keeping with the notion of many-layered reality. It, too, has its validity, and leaves space for the development of still unrecognized forces.

The heretics, then, represent a repressed interpretation of Christianity. They are the vanquished who were left lying on the battlefield. This misfortune cannot be considered a verdict on the merit or lack of merit in their views. Only too often in ecclesiastical history the profounder conception has been worsted because the time was not yet ripe for it. Victory must not be identified with truth! In the course of history, movements representing a false claim to truth have frequently won at least initial victories, and much time has passed before defeated men have been vindicated. History often goes off the rails for a time and makes mistakes which are later corrected. This book proposes to make one such revision and bring to light suppressed potentialities in Christianity. Out of the history of the heretics there emerges a buried truth which unexpectedly begins to glow with new radiance. Spiritual problems can never be settled by violent measures—that is one of the lessons of this history. Unresolved problems come to life again in the story of heresy. Prematurely suppressed questions rise to the surface; questions not answered in the past call for renewed examination. The unresolved problems are of greater importance to the history of Christian thought than those which can be written off as finally solved. The heretics' special contribution to church history is to be found in their incessant endeavors to advance the other, the overlooked and misunderstood conception of Christianity. Their place in God's great cosmos must no longer be denied them, for they, the runners of the gauntlet, are as much creatures of God as their opponents, the dancers of mazurkas.

By their courageous and heroic advocacy of the other conception of Christianity, the heretics often became great precursors of new ideas. To be sure, not all heretics can be regarded as pioneers. Among them were some who argued the rights of tradition and took a conservative stand against the currents of their times. But many heretics were avant-gardists who lent a new forward impetus to the spiritual life of Christianity, thereby saving it from petrifaction. With their dynamic drive they often sped far ahead of their contemporaries, advanced into novel and at first sight frightening realms, and discovered religious values wholly unknown before they came upon the scene. This constructive activity is one of the greatest aspects of heresy. As mighty warriors for truth, the heretics often formed an intellectual elite, and for that very reason were beyond the comprehension of their contemporaries. With their passionate religious longings they felt dissatisfied with existing beliefs, and found themselves opposing the dead hand of tradition. But their contemporaries regarded them as reckless innovators who in their tempestuous drive broke down the sheltering sea walls, letting in terrible floods.

And they were that. As a rule, heretics are religious revolutionaries whose activities are far from harmless. They do not think in collective or authoritarian categories. They examine things independently, intrepidly, and are wholly free of the widespread but pernicious tendency to be always joining the majority. They are people who subscribe to the seldom-obeyed words of the Bible: "You shall not follow a multitude." [9] Among the heresies which must be said about the heretics, then, is this: the heretics were truly creative people who produced new and imperishable religious ideas. In spite of the initial vexations which are inevitably connected with new ideas, Christianity cannot do without them.

In their whole bearing as religiously vital people and pioneers in Christian thought, the heretics resemble the saints. This resemblance can at times become so strong that it is difficult to tell the two apart. Heretics and saints are alike in their overstepping the limits of everyday Christianity. But while in both types the religious current flows in the same direction for a while, it forks at a decisive point into two widely diverging streams. The most striking difference is in their attitude toward the church. For the saint, piety toward the church is too precious to be abandoned, and he therefore ultimately submits to the will of the church. He is a patient sufferer; humble submission is one of the most authentic characteristics of the saint. The heretic is too militant to make this submission. It is incompatible with his nature. Fighter that he is, he must rebel against the church's

[9] Exodus xxiii, 2.

authority and insist upon his own convictions. He would rather forfeit the community of the church than renounce his own views, and thus he enters upon the thorn-strewn path of open revolt. The heretic's life almost always becomes a tragedy.

This rebellion, so essential a part of the heretic's life, is not undertaken merely for the sake of insurrection. Nor does the heretic cling to his position out of sheer self-righteousness. Rather, he sees ultimate truths at stake, truths which have been given to him and which he does not dare betray lest he be unfaithful to the grace which has been bestowed upon him and hence unfaithful to himself. Out of this sense of religious mission has sprung the amazing ethic of heresy, which refuses to yield in spite of the cruelest measures against it. The heretic places his religious conscience above the authoritarian claims of the representatives of the church. As a rule, this decision for conscience has not been made easy for him. Terrible struggles must have raged in the souls of a good many heretics. Church circles would speak somewhat less scornfully of the heretics if they would only devote a little imagination to visualizing the spiritual situation in which these religious rebels found themselves. The heretic knows himself to be dependent upon God alone; he knows that he must obey his conscience. From the Christian point of view, this attitude is irrefutable.

Yet this fidelity to God and his own conscience was always viewed as disobedience to the church, and the heretic was punished by being expelled from its communion. All heretics have been marked men, outlaws cast out from society. Hence they cannot be measured by ordinary standards. These persecuted people often took unspeakable burdens upon themselves for the sake of God's truth. They were condemned to run the gauntlet, as those on the seamy side of life must be, and for that reason they often cried out in their pain: "Brothers, have mercy on me." But the brothers had no mercy. Rather, they shut their minds and hearts against them. The old documents often reveal an incomprehensible callousness on the part of Christians. It is saddening to consider the frightful punishments meted out to all who deviated from the doctrines of the majority. But this sadness is illumined by a strange inner light, for the heretics remind us of the words of the New Testament: "All who desire to live a godly life in Christ Jesus will be persecuted." [1] The Christian who triumphs and wins prestige is no longer walking in the way of the Gospel. In the eyes of genuine Christianity, all worldly success would be suspect. One of the most difficult questions is why the Gospel can be victorious in this life only through defeat; the answer is hidden in the event on Golgotha.

Heresy is a poignant illustration of this truth. It presents the sublime story of persecuted truth—one of the noblest spectacles upon this earth. The bloodied pages of the story of heresy tell a tale of martyrs within Christendom. With their heart-rending readiness to suffer, the heretics represent a continuation of the Passion of Christ, which will go on until the end of the world.

The staggering idea that the evangelical story of the Passion goes on into the Christian era can be comprehended only in terms of a mysticism of suffering; it cannot be understood rationally. It springs from the deepest reaches of Christian feeling. Christianity was unable to remove suffering from the world, but it has shown suffering in an entirely new light. It has elevated suffering for the sake of truth into something divine. Being "beaten through the ranks" for Christ's sake is a disgrace only in superficial terms; viewed from within, it is a mark of nobility. The Passion is the true path to the Eternal. In inexpressible pain, man encounters God. Christianity first taught humanity how to suffer properly—by linking the endurance of pain to the heavenly powers. Before Christianity, no one understood that. The story of the persecuted heretics leads directly to the heart of Christianity. It presents the unfathomable mystery: burned at the stake, the heretic rises to Paradise in the leaping flames and shares in the Eternal Glory!

[1] II Tim. iii, 12.

1

The Father of Heresy

Simon Magus

The father of all heretics—this is the title Irenaeus gives to Simon Magus in his book against heresy.[1] This Father of the Church contended that all heresies derived from Simon Magus, who should therefore be detested by all right-thinking Christians. Irenaeus' view was adopted by Eusebius in his *Ecclesiastical History*, with the result that Simon was ever afterward considered by the Early Church as the "first author of all heresy." [2]

---

[1] Irenaeus: *Against Heresies*, III, Preface.
[2] Eusebius: *The Ecclesiastical History*, II, xiii (London and New York: Loeb Classical Library; 1926), I, 139.

To be called the father of a great movement is a distinction accorded only to a person of unusual stature. This is the only testimony of his importance that we have, for few reliable accounts of this Christian heretic of the first century have come down to us. Moreover, these accounts were written neither by himself nor his disciples. They derive exclusively from his adversaries, who had axes to grind. The scattered references cannot easily be assembled into a coherent picture; they are as perplexing as a jigsaw puzzle. Simon's true aims have only been hinted at in Church tradition; only the outlines of his mysterious figure glow dimly in the darkness. His personality remains an enigma, leaving ample room for guesswork. Yet the fragmentary allusions do permit us some shadowy notion of Simon's intentions.

Simon bears the surname of Magus, "worker of magic." The epithet is a warning to the historian to proceed with caution, for the magical approach to the world defies rational interpretation. The "Wise Men" of the East seem to have known secrets which remain closed to modern man—and Simon was such a "wise man." The Samaritans said of Simon: "This man is that power of God which is called Great." [3] Such a judgment was not passed on many. In the oldest account (in the *Acts of the Apostles*), Simon is described as an uncanny magician who "amazed the nation of Samaria." This remark is a significant one. Simon had awakened amazement in men, and that emotion is the first step of the ascent into the spiritual world. His contemporaries sensed in Simon an ability denied to ordinary mortals. The ancient world still believed in magic, and belief in mysterious forces and the gifts of the spirit is not alien to the New Testament. We remember the Gospel of Matthew, where three magi from the Orient were the first to be aware of the birth of Christ and to follow the star until they came to the stable in Bethlehem. But while primitive Christianity accepted the magical approach to the cosmos, in the course of Christian history magic fell into disrepute, and the use of it came to be regarded as sinful. Only a few thinkers later made the necessary distinction between white magic and black.

[3] Acts viii, 10.

17

According to the *Acts of the Apostles*, Simon Magus was converted to Christianity. When Philip preached, "Simon himself believed" and accepted baptism. Doubt was soon cast on the sincerity of Simon's acceptance of Christianity. It was said that he had hypocritically pretended conversion. But such a view reveals little faith in Philip's knowledge of human beings. It is related, after all, that after baptism Simon remained constantly at Philip's side. And later, when Simon became embroiled in conflict with the other Apostles, he expressed a genuine religious spirit. According to the account in *Acts*, Peter cursed Simon, who humbly replied: "Pray for me to the Lord that nothing of what you have said may come upon me."

Thus Simon was undoubtedly Christian—and here we have the first instance of the essentially Christian nature of heresy. The question remains: What was Simon's conception of Christianity? Certainly he did not take its tidings in the same sense as the Apostles. But the difference between his conception of Christianity and that of the Apostles does not make him a man of impure motives.

Simon had another connection which antedated his relations to the Christians. He came from Getthon in Samaria, where he had entered the religious school founded by Dositheos after the death of John the Baptist. Simon then went to Alexandria to study Arabic-Jewish magical medicine. From this fact, the third-century Church Father Hippolytus inferred that Simon had been close to "dark Heraclitus"—that subtle philosopher of whom Nietzsche wrote so ecstatically. According to Hippolytus, Simon taught that Infinite Force was the principle of the universe. Hippolytus quotes him as writing: "This is the book of the revelation of the voice and the name by knowledge of the great Infinite Force. Therefore it will be sealed, hidden, veiled, and placed in the space where the roots of the universe are found." [4]

Whether Simon actually wrote a work entitled "Great Annunciation," which abounded in such phrases as "roots of the universe"—strange echo of Empedocles—must remain an open

[4] Hippolytus: *Refutation of All Heresies*, VI, ix.

question. At any rate, we have only the extracts given by Hippolytus, and he is quoting from a book issued by second-century "Simonians." What is significant for us in Hippolytus' extracts is the conspicuous influence of Greek philosophy. If we may judge Simon by his later disciples, Simon was a student of Hellenistic thought. He was the first Christian to attempt to form a bridge between Christianity and Greek philosophy. This was Simon's original heresy, for which he was to be so reviled. Yet, ironically enough, this was an undertaking which, in the course of the church's history, would be imitated by countless Christians who did not realize that they were treading on heretical paths.

This tie with Hellenism explains Simon's concern with the myth of Helen. Helen, of course, was the symbol of earthly beauty. Simon, however, seems to have linked her in curious fashion with the idea of redemption. According to Irenaeus, Simon called Helen "the mother of all" who had passed through many incarnations. "Thus she was also in the body of that Helen who was the cause of the Trojan War. In her migration from body to body she suffered new shame in each, and at last ended in a public house. She is the lost sheep." [5]

This statement throws some light on the deeper meaning of Helen for Simon. The term "lost sheep" leads us back to the Gospel again. Simon's Helen is of course equivalent to the repentant Magdalene. However, she meant far more to him; she was the symbol of wisdom itself brought down from heaven. Temple prostitute and Phoenician madonna, she was to Simon a figure of mythic proportions exiled from the celestial realm of true being to this world of shadows, where she was kept prisoner until such time as she could begin her return journey. Helen is one of the prototypes of man in search of redemption. Her fate is meant to be understood as the story of a soul; in the course of her transmigrations a heavenly consciousness frees itself from the unworthy fetters of matter.

Most Christians were not receptive to such mythic ideas. Their attachment to the symbols of their own faith was too pas-

[5] Irenaeus: op. cit., I, xxiii.

sionate and too literal. They were conscious only of the breath of an alien spirit and felt Simon's work to be competing in a highly undesirable way with their own spreading of the Gospel. Whatever the patristic literature tells us about Simon must be read in the light of this antagonism. The accounts of the Fathers were meant as indictments, not as objective descriptions. The early Christian writers were determined to root out Simon's influence. Thus Simon was represented as *the* false apostle who sought to spread his false doctrines throughout the world. Such is the picture drawn in the Pseudo-Clementines (writings attributed to St. Clement). According to Clement, who wrote in the late second century, Simon Magus followed at Peter's heels only because he wanted to refute Peter's evangelical message with his own proclamation. The two men were said to have engaged in endless disputations lasting for days, with Simon pluming himself on his own cleverness. Peter could not answer him, he gloated, because he was only teaching things long familiar to the unreasoning common folk, whereas he, Simon, was proclaiming a new message. Simon's divergent doctrine was referred to by the Apostles as "shameless." As time went on, he was painted as a pseudo-Messiah and even as the Antichrist himself. More and more dreadful stories were told of the erstwhile magician, and his doctrines were cast in the most unfavorable light. Thus the image that has come down to us of Simon is distorted beyond recognition. The early writers accused him of being a charlatan who could nevertheless fly through the air, make gold, and conjure spirits—who, in short, was a personification of Satan himself. Their immoderate slanders demonstrate their utter failure to understand Simon's deeper intentions. Most libels in history are symptoms of incomprehension. A good example is the mockery of Simon's Helen myth by Tertullian, a third-century Father of the Church.[6] So much abuse has been heaped upon the "father of heretics" that we feel it necessary to sift over the sources and discover what the historical Simon was really like.

[6] Cf. Tertullian: *On the Soul,* xxxiv.

We are told in *Acts* how Simon, converted, offered Peter a sum of money if he would acquaint him with the secret of transmitting the Holy Spirit by laying on of hands. Horrified by this proposal, Peter replied: *Your silver perish with you because you thought you could obtain the gift of God with money! You have neither part nor lot in this matter, for your heart is not right before God. Repent, therefore, of this wickedness of yours, and pray to the Lord that, if possible, the intent of your heart may be forgiven you. For I see that you are in the gall of bitterness and in the bond of iniquity.*[7]

This incident was enough to indict Simon in the eyes of all Christians. His offer had not been understood as the Hellenistic custom of offering to pay compensation for a shared secret. Rather, Simon was considered so corrupt that he attempted to buy spiritual gifts with money—introducing Mammon into the things of faith. Deep into the Middle Ages the horror of this offer remained, so that the immoral practice of buying ecclesiastical offices was termed simony. Thus the name of Simon was preserved as denoting one of the worst of the abuses within the Church. The fierce curse uttered by Peter echoed down the centuries, and was heard again in Dante's words: "Oh Simon Magus! Oh ye his wretched followers, who, rapacious, do prostitute for gold and silver the things of God that ought to be the brides of righteousness."[8]

Not only had Simon wanted to mix God and Mammon, but he was also accused of a depraved way of life. According to Justin's account "a certain Helen went about with him in those days, after having formerly abandoned herself in a house of ill fame. She is now called by his disciples his first Idea."[9] This damsel was reviled as a shameless slut whom, moreover, Simon had lured away from his teacher Dositheos and taken into his own possession. In keeping with this immoral conduct, the religious community which he had founded was likewise charged

[7] Acts viii, 20–3.
[8] Dante Alighieri: *The Divine Comedy,* translated by Charles Eliot Norton (Boston; 1892), Vol. I, Canto xix, p. 97.
[9] Justin: *Apology,* I, xxvi and lvi.

with sinful practices. *Their secret priests therefore serve the lust of the senses and practice magic with all their might, employ conjurations and spells, concoct love potions and methods of seduction, and engage in dream-interpretation and dark prestidigitator's arts. They also have a statue of Simon in the manner of Zeus and one of Helen in the manner of Minerva, and worship them. They call themselves Simonians, after the author of this accursed heresy. What is falsely called Gnosis took its beginnings from him, as can be learned from their own statements.*[1]

Even worse tales are spread by Hippolytus, who connects the Helen myth with sexual excesses. His story is that promiscuity was rife in Simon's sect, since his followers held the view that: "All earth is earth, and it does not matter where one sows, so long as he sows; indeed, they hold themselves blessed on account of community intercourse of the sexes, for they say that it is perfect love. . . . They say they will not let themselves be dominated by an imagined evil, for they are already redeemed."[2]

Such slanders inevitably brought Simon into the gravest disrepute with all upright Christians, for very few of them had sufficient critical intelligence to see that these tales should not have been taken at their face value. We find similar tales throughout the literature of the church. The heretics were always being discredited on moral grounds.

As father of all heretics, Simon is said to have crowned his misdeeds by blasphemous arrogance. Intellectual pride was, after all, the original sin of which our first parents had been guilty when they hearkened to the serpent, who promised them that they could be like God. Simon Magus, too, it was charged, had not contented himself with appearing as an emissary of God; he had averred that he himself was the highest divinity. "Now this man, who was glorified like a god by many persons, taught concerning himself that he had appeared among the Jews as the Son, had descended in Samaria as the Father, and come to the

---

[1] Irenaeus: op. cit., I, xxiii.
[2] Hippolytus: op. cit., VI, xix.

other nations as the Holy Spirit." [3] Since the basic religious attitude of humility was completely lacking in him, we are told, he had encouraged people to worship him as God, and the Romans had honored him by a statue. "This statue, stands in the River Tiber between two bridges and bears the Latin inscription *Simoni deo sancto*," writes the second-century Father of the Church Justin.[4] In saying that Simon wanted divine honors for himself, Justin was making much of the heretic's blasphemous *hubris*. But the charge will not stand examination. In 1574 a statue was in fact dug up from the Tiber island at the very spot mentioned by Justin. It proved to be a statue of the ancient Sabine god of oats, Semo Sancus. Evidently Justin had been misinformed, or had leaped to a wrong conclusion, and Irenaeus took over the false story of the statue without checking. Thus the charge that Simon encouraged people to worship him as a god becomes questionable, and Justin's mistake serves only to cast doubt on the entire legend.

A horrible end is supposed to have overtaken Simon, in just punishment for his *hubris*. The story goes that the magician, having followed the Apostle Peter to Rome and preached his nefarious doctrines there, at one point boasted that "if buried alive, he would rise again on the third day. After his pupils had dug a grave at his command, he ordered that he be buried in it. They did as they were commanded; but he has not yet reappeared to the present day, for he was not the Messiah." [5] According to another tale, Simon Magus possessed the supernatural power of being able to fly up into the sky. Peter, however, when he saw "Simon rising to celestial heights on the pinions of magic, hurled him down and laid him low by depriving his magic spells of all power." [6]

The propagandistic intention of this tale is obvious; the inci-

---

[3] Irenaeus: op. cit., I, xxiii.
[4] Justin: op. cit., I, xxvi and lvi.
[5] Hippolytus: op. cit., VI, xx.
[6] Ambrose: *Exameron*, IV, viii, 33.

dent is nothing more nor less than Simon's damnation. The heretic cannot be allowed to have a peaceful death like a pious Christian. His end must necessarily be a horrible one, and serve as warning to all Christians to shun such paths of error.

Despite all the distortions in Christian accounts of Simon Magus,[7] there is no denying his historical existence. If we study the tradition from *Acts of the Apostles* through the Pseudo-Clementines, from Justin, Irenaeus, and Hippolytus to Ambrose in chronological order, we observe a pattern of ever-increasing calumny which serves as an instructive example of how a heretic was "fictionalized"—that is to say, how new features were ever being added until the portrait had achieved the desired degree of villany. The farther we move from the actual historical figure, the more detailed is the information we are offered about Simon. Ultimately, truth and fiction become inextricably confused. This process of negative myth-making goes on until the historical personage has been more and more stripped of his historically demonstrable features. In the end it is scarcely possible to refer these features to a particular person or country. Every conceivable heretical trait has been projected upon this one figure until he serves as the personification of heresy itself. Thus Simon Magus became the archetype of the heretic, a convenient embodiment of the incomprehensible phenomenon of heresy.

The process in itself is one which should be appreciated in its full importance. Here were consistent forces at work under the surface of Christianity, providing a solution for the whole problem of heresy, in that a single figure could be made accountable for the troublesome phenomenon. "Thus Simon became the whipping boy for everything that could not be attacked under its true name."[8] When the Irish monks showed themselves stubborn and clung to their tonsure in the face of new directives from Rome, it was said that this mode of wearing the hair was derived from Simon Magus. So effective a portrait has been

---

[7] Cf. Hans Waitz: *"Simon Magus in der altchristlichen Literatur" in Zeitschrift für die neutestamentliche Wissenschaft und die Kunde des Urchristentums* (1904), pp. 121–43.
[8] Wolfgang Schultz: *Dokumente der Gnosis* (1910), p. lviii.

forged of Simon Magus that no one down to the present day has ventured to rehabilitate him.

The meagerness of genuine source materials, of course, puts limits on any such effort. Nevertheless we sense that the Simon Magus behind the legend must have been a personality of some majesty. Who was he really? To this day no one can say with any definiteness. The historical veil cannot be pierced. Yet, as one of the first Gnostics, the historical Simon might be called an early Christian Faust. This, perhaps, is the best way we can approach this mysterious man, and at the same time understand the great horror he aroused in the Christians. But the very things which induced shudders in the early Christians are precisely the things which make Simon alluring to the modern mind. His exploits in magic accord with the Faustian character, and his myth of Helen is a logical part of the whole. Simon represented a conception of Christianity radically different from that of the Apostles. His philosophic interest in establishing a connection between Christianity and Hellenistic wisdom must be regarded as intellectual boldness of a rare order. Such aspirations mark Simon's as a truly Faustian nature. The striving, struggling man who wishes to enter into relations with higher worlds is perhaps truly "the father of all heretics." For he, like Faust,

> *möchte wissen, was die Welt*
> *im Innersten zusammenhält.*

Rembrandt, in his well-known etching, created a portrait of Simon Magus which will stand as an eternally valid symbol of all such deeply brooding spirits.

2

The Birth of Religious Philosophy

The Gnostics

Early Christian tradition tells of John the Apostle once going to a public bath in the city of Ephesus and there encountering the Gnostic Cerinth. Horrified, John immediately left the place, crying out: "Take care, the baths will collapse because the enemy of truth is in them." [1]

Whether John, that disciple who lay upon the Lord's breast, actually behaved in this manner, need not be discussed. But even if this incident is more legendary than historical, it conveys the horror the early Christians of the Church felt toward the Gnostics,

[1] Irenaeus: op. cit., III, iii.

whom they regarded as enemies of truth. So strong was this feeling that they imagined the activities of such men would bring about the collapse of the world order, and they were afraid even to be in their proximity, let alone debate with them. This horror of Gnosticism has remained almost unchanged down to the present day among adherents of the Church.

This attitude was not altogether unfounded. It is difficult today to obtain any clear picture of the Gnostics as individuals, but there is no doubt that they were persons who could frighten pious Christians to the depths of their souls. Their revolutionary doctrines show them as men of unusual capacity for thought and passionate emotion who dared to venture upon paths sown with perils. Possibly they had a poor grasp of the realities of the world, but they had highly original minds, the determination to achieve a rounded philosophy, and the courage to attack the most difficult problems.

When, after many centuries, Christianity had lost its dread of the Gnostics, it began to treat them contemptuously as a reactionary movement and to condemn them as a belated blossom on a withering tree. The labyrinthine ideas of the Gnostics were regarded as excesses of eccentricity, the untrammeled play of morbid imaginations. But such a view does not do justice to the hidden light of Gnosis, which radiates a great sanctity. Gnosis has preserved "whole layers of submerged religious ideas and views in rigid, petrified form." [2] It represented a movement which was in fact older than Christianity. Nor should its archaic character mislead us into overlooking the novel and original concepts born from the attempt to syncretize Oriental and Hellenistic with Christian elements. Although the whole system has been dismissed as outmoded and decadent, the time has come to recognize that it also included new beginnings, creativeness, growth, and potentialities for the future. [3] We discover that there was a Gnostic Age in which a new sense of the cosmos was born out of apocalyptic ideas, reached its climax in the second century, and

[2] W. Bousset: *Hauptprobleme der Gnosis* (1907), p. 8.
[3] H. Jonas: *Gnosis und spätantiker Geist* (1934), p. 73.

27

revealed tremendous creative force. Clement of Alexandria, a Father of the Church who in some respects stood close to these heretics, was one of the first to recognize their importance: "For in the doctrines of the schools of heretics, in so far as they have not become totally obtuse . . . are to be found many things which, dissimilar as they appear, agree in category with the Wholeness of truth." [4]

The basic problem around which these heretical thinkers circled was the contradiction of *gnosis* and *pistis,* knowledge and faith. The heretical element appears in the consistency with which these men sacrificed faith to understanding. But the original contradiction has nothing to do with the modern tug-of-war between knowledge and faith. The modern age, in which technology has taken the place of metaphysics, scarcely finds room in its weary agnosticism for understanding a movement whose supreme efforts were bent upon achieving metaphysical understanding. Nevertheless, we must do our best to apprehend what the Gnostics meant by knowledge. The Gnostic strove for insight, not for that abundance of knowledge which loads upon a man the burden of knowing many things with which he has no inward relation. Gnostic understanding had little to do with the intellect. It is quite wrong to term the Gnostics the rationalists of the second century—modern conceptions of rational knowledge are strictly out of place here. The Gnostics practiced, in contrast to rectilinear logic, a form of circular thinking whose content can only be conveyed in figurative language.[5] The knowledge they sought was of inner truth related to the soul of man. Understanding of a sort irrelevant to man's soul did not interest them; they were concerned only with that sacred knowledge which is illuminated by the Logos. In this search for knowledge of inner concern to man lay the timeless value of Gnosticism; in the crisis of modern scientificality, the Gnostics still have something to say, can still point a way.

In the Gnostic view, sacred primal knowledge rested upon

---

[4] Clemens Alexandrinus: *Stromata*, Book I, xiii, 57.
[5] Cf. H. Leisegang: *Die Gnosis* (1924), pp. 9 f.

revelation. Jesus had initiated the Apostles into a secret tradition which was passed on by the Gnostics, likewise in secret. Their enemies in the Church had no admittance to these esoteric circles and for this reason had inadequate and often altogether erroneous conceptions of the Gnostic movement. The Gnostics strove to be seers in the sense that "the true Gnostic knows all and embraces all, for he has a certain grasp even of those things which are unclear to us." [6] Gnosticism embodied the spirit of searching and striving; according to the Gnostic work *Pistis Sophia,* Jesus said to his disciples: "Do not leave off searching day and night."

As "knowers" the Gnostics had an extremely gloomy view of the cosmos. They radically rejected the world. Not even the spectacle of nature could bring joy to the hearts of these men. They saw a sinister law operating in nature; indeed, they were the first to see nature as embodying a diabolic principle. For centuries afterward Christianity proved unable to liberate itself from this fundamentally anti-natural view initiated by the Gnostics. The Gnostics shuddered at the eternal silence of infinite space; the mute universe frightened them. To the Gnostic mind, man was enclosed in a terrible cosmic shell composed of a mingling of light and darkness, from which he could find no escape. "Who has cast me into the suffering of the worlds, who has placed me in this evil darkness?" the Gnostic asked, and in heart-rending words he lamented his alienation, loneliness, and weary wanderings in this dark world. In the Gnostic view, earthly existence was anxiety and dread, error and curse, horrible sleep and stupefaction, intoxication and self-forgetting. The decadent world has been engendered by the "wine of ignorance." All material things had arisen out of despondency and despair; spirituality, obsessed with fear and longing, could never rise up sufficiently to overcome the superior power of the dark forces. Gnostic accounts of this terrible world anticipate all of modern pessimism, although Gnosticism never wallowed in descriptions of the seamy sides of life. The Gnostics themselves knew what

[6] Clemens Alexandrinus: op. cit., Book VI, viii, 68.

real suffering was, and consequently the soul of any man who has languished in similar darkness will respond to the Gnostic creed.

The novelty of this pain-wracked view of the world, within the intellectual atmosphere of antiquity, can be fully grasped only when we consider it in terms of the Old Testament view. According to the Old Testament, after God had created this world he pronounced upon it the majestic verdict: "And behold, it was very good." [7] From the vantage point of this Biblical attitude, Irenaeus was shocked by the Gnostic rejection of the world: "If, therefore, anyone should declare that what the Father of the universe planned and preshaped in his mind just as it was created was the fruit of error and the product of ignorance, that is a great blasphemy." [8] The Greeks, too, were convinced of the eternal harmony of an ordered cosmos, and glorified it in words of praise. Plotinus could not understand how anyone could revile nature, instead of regarding her with religious awe. He cried indignantly to the Gnostic thinkers: *Whosoever reprehends nature does not know what he is doing or how reckless he is in his impertinence. Such reprehensions come about because many men do not know the law of succession from first, second, third, etc., down to last; because they do not know that things must not be reprehended because they are worse than the first things. Rather must one patiently accept the laws of the universe, and direct oneself onward and upward toward the first things, refraining from the fabrication of gaudy imaginary terrors.* [9]

But the mood of Gnostic pessimism was destined to become a permanent part of human thought. Centuries later the old debate was re-enacted in Schopenhauer's pessimism and Hegel's optimism, each side claiming that it alone revealed the truth.

Modern pessimism, as expressed in the literary works of the Swiss Nobel Prize winner Carl Spitteler, makes a sick God responsible for this evil world. The Gnostics attempted to deal with this question in a less drastic fashion. Since a sick God is not

[7] Genesis i, 31.
[8] Irenaeus: op. cit., II, iii.
[9] Plotinus: *Enneads,* II, Book IX, xiii.

God but a grotesque caricature, the Gnostics placed the blame for this cruel world in another quarter. The Syrian Gnostic Saturninus held that angels had made this imperfect world, and man as well.[1] Other Gnostics postulated a Demiurge who had engendered this abortion of an earth. In any case, to the Gnostic mind the true God could not be charged with responsibility for what Heinrich von Kleist calls the "brittle constitution of this world."

This explains why these heretics did not feel that their furious contempt for the world was blasphemous. Their denunciation was in no way addressed to the Supreme Being, and consequently they did not need, like Ivan Karamazov, to respectfully send back their ticket of admission. They were challenging the dark intermediaries who had committed the crime of setting up so painful a world as this. The Demiurge that they had postulated was an excellent answer to the eternally burning problem of theodicy (vindication of God's justice) which was one of the fundamental themes of Gnosticism.

The "unknown God" to whom Paul alluded in Athens [2] is the closest thing to the Gnostic concept of God. The thinking of these heretics revolved around this unknown God, who was antinatural as well as supernatural. No faintest breath of pantheism affected their thinking. This supreme God could only be described by circumlocution, in grand negations, because he was unknowable, unnamable, inexpressible, incomprehensible, formless, boundless, and nonworldly. In their passion for superlatives they even spoke of the "non-being God." Stammeringly, they found unusual words, such as only truly religious men seek, to describe their unknown God.

However, when the Gnostics differentiated the supreme God from the Creator of the world, they found themselves caught in an absolute metaphysical dualism. On the one hand there was an entirely supernatural God who represented absolute Good and was blissfully unconcerned about the world; on the

[1] Galatians iii, 19.
[2] Acts xvii, 28.

other hand, totally opposed to him was matter, existing from eternity and representing evil.

Although they acknowledged the evils of the world and believed that God was indifferent to it, the Gnostics did not condemn man to hopelessness. They offered a sure path out of the dreariness of this world. Their various cosmogonic speculations restored light to the darkness and pointed out the way of overcoming this metaphysical dualism. For the Gnostics evolved a profound doctrine of "eons," by which they meant emanations from God. These emanations flowing from God were not to be understood as divine attributes. To speak of "attributes" of God implies an abstractness that was alien to the symbolic thinking of Gnosticism. Rather, the emanations were actual forces and divine persons in whom the Deity unfolded his being. We must imagine them as divine streams flowing out of the overbrimming vessel which is the Deity. The greatest of these emanations was the figure of Christ, whom they conceived as surrounded by a tremendous light-force and pouring out unimaginable joy. The Gnostics attributed the decisive role in the cosmic process to Christ—with the result that the Christian eon was set apart from all others. Christ represented the turning point in world history. He had at last succeeded in smashing a breach in the terrible shell encapsulating this world.

We see, therefore, that the Gnostics assigned a significant part in their system to Christ. Certainly these heretics did not bypass him. Their image of Christ, however, differed sharply from that of the adherents of the Church. According to Carpocrates, Jesus was made "to flee the angels who were forming the world, to pass through all the things of the cosmos, and afterward, liberated in all things, embracing in love that which is equivalent to him, to return to it." [3] The Gnostics made a sharp division between the heavenly Christ and the earthly phenomenon of Jesus of Nazareth. The true Christ, they contended, has no bodily form. The Gospel traditions of the historical features of Christ are meant to be interpreted symbolically. According to

[3] Schultz: op. cit., p. 158.

Valentinus, who was perhaps the most important of the Gnostics, "Jesus ate and drank in special wise, without giving forth the food again." [4] The second-century Gnostic sect called Ophites— "serpent worshippers"—took a similar view: "The greatest error that arose among his disciples was their thinking that he rose again in his earthly body." Following this idea through, the Gnostics were led to assert that Jesus had not suffered at all on the cross, but that Simon of Cyrene had been crucified in his stead "while the true Christ, laughing, made off." [5] Redemption, then, was the gift of the heavenly Christ alone.

The sect called Docetae held that Christ's body had been only a phantom. Thus the Docetic conception stood opposed to the incarnation of the Word, a central doctrine in the Christianity of the Church. The first epistle of John launches an attack upon Docetism in the words: "By this you know the Spirit of God: every spirit which confesses that Jesus Christ has come in the flesh is of God, and every spirit which does not confess Jesus is not of God." [6] We understand the meaning of such statements only if we are aware of the fierce struggle the Early Church was waging against Docetism, for it regarded this doctrine as a challenge to the reality of redemption. But this pronouncement by no means disposed of the whole problem of Docetism.

In the first place, Docetism must not be dismissed as a mere whimsy on the part of a few visionaries. One might imagine so when one comes upon certain Gnostic comments to the effect that a finger could be thrust through the entire body of Jesus without encountering resistance, because the body was only illusory. But for the Gnostics such a point was highly important, flowing as it did from their metaphysical dualism. If matter was to be regarded as evil, a product of the Demiurge, Christ could not be burdened with a material body, for then he would not have been able to accomplish the redemption from matter. Underlying Docetism was the idea of the absolute superiority of spirit over

---

[4] Clemens Alexandrinus: op. cit., Book III, vii, 59.
[5] Schultz: op. cit., p. 57.
[6] I John iv, 2–3.

matter. We may say, if we wish, that the Gnostics solved the problem wrongly; but we must be impressed by the keenness with which they posed this significant problem as a subject for discussion. Docetism addressed to the Christians this highly important question: "Is man in truth and originally his body, or ought he to regard his body as the mere mirror and resonator of his illimitable spiritual life?" [7]

The basic motif of all this intellectual effort was a keenly felt longing for redemption. Gnosticism was distinctly a redemptist religion. But in their idea of redemption the Gnostics were again at odds with the Church. They regarded redemption as primarily a cosmic event whose outcome was liberation from matter. In the Gnostic view, man is an intermediary being, partly enslaved by matter and partly composed of light substances from the upper world. The celestial Christ redeems man from this painful mixed condition. The Gnostics hailed this discovery with the greatest joy.

We can measure the importance of Gnostic philosophy by its capacity to forge a new interpretation of history. If a movement is really opening a new era, it must also be able to consider the past from a changed perspective. The truly heretical attitude of the Gnostics appears most markedly in their view of history, which involved so thorough a reassessment of all values that it threw the Church Christians into a panic. Moreover, the Gnostics deliberately opposed their revolutionary interpretation of history to the official one.

Profound problems were brought to light in the course of the Gnostics' laborious wrestling with their theological view of history. The boldness of their interpretations emerges in their totally novel interpretation of the figure of Cain. This archetype of the outlaw, whom the Creator had condemned to be "a fugitive and a wanderer on the earth," was no longer conceived as an accursed fratricide. Rather, the Gnostics linked him with the similarly persecuted Redeemer. They did not do this for the fun of flouting conventional views. Rather, they meant to defend one

[7] Eugen Heinrich Schmitt: *Die Gnosis* (1903), I, 255.

who had fallen into disfavor with the cruel Creator. Thus Gnostic rebellion against the Creator-God logically led to a radical reversal of previous historical judgments. From their defense of Cain, moreover, they went on to defend all the other rejected and unfortunate persons in Scripture. The Gnostic thinkers came to the rescue of the Sodomites, Esau, the "sons of Korah," while they rejected Abel, Enoch, and Noah. They even justified Judas Iscariot. According to the Gnostic view, he had betrayed Jesus only in order to bring about the redemption. These supposed villains, the Gnostics argued, were in fact serving as instruments of the higher principle.

Thus the Gnostic heretics recognized these despised characters as men of their own kind. They, who were denounced as heretics, took sides with those in the past who had been similarly defamed. By this reasoning, the branch of the Gnostics who called themselves Ophites even paid reverence to the serpent. In the myth of the fall of man this reptile was cursed. But, the Ophites asked in all seriousness, did it really betray man? Was not the serpent the means for bringing Adam and Eve a gift which they had not possessed? Was not truth on its side? Such philosophical considerations led the Ophites to regard the serpent as a divine being because it first conferred knowledge upon man, and was thus responsible for knowledge of the higher mysteries. Did not even Jesus call upon his disciples to become wise as serpents? In this manner, the Gnostics sought out hidden meanings in the Scriptures which justified their own revolutionary revisions. By their unusual exegeses Gnostics became the models for all subsequent oppositional interpretation of the Scriptures.

Gnostic ethics were likewise a violation of traditional views. Since the Gnostics felt themselves the Elect of God, they presumed to solve the problems of ethics in a novel fashion. To be sure, not all men were capable of proceeding along this royal way, but only, as the Gnostics proudly declared, "one out of a thousand and two out of ten thousand." The Gnostic movement produced two diametrically opposed ethical attitudes.

One branch of Gnosticism advocated a strict asceticism, the

extirpation of all sensuality, in order to attain likeness to Christ. Sexual intercourse was absolutely forbidden. These Gnostics ruled out marital relationships even for the purpose of begetting children. There was no point to reproducing the human race, since the result was only the propagation of misery. These Gnostics cited the answer Jesus had given to Salomé's question: "How long will death reign?" Jesus had responded: "As long as you women bear children." [8] This fierce hostility to the body was again founded upon their view of the evil character of matter. Evil was a physical quality inextricably bound up with matter.

The greater number of the Gnostics belonged to this school of thought. The broad masses of the populace, however, could not follow along with this stern rejection of all sensual pleasures. The Church's polemics against the Gnostics frequently focused upon this extreme asceticism, which the Church viewed as exaggerated and unnatural.

For us, however, it should become evident that the Gnostics were people of unusual fiber. The sternness of such asceticism is a sign of the serious character of this movement. There is an element of profound truth in its doctrine of renunciation. The Church itself could not bar it completely. Monasticism took up these ascetic tendencies, and they have returned again and again in the history of Christian thought, for all that they originated in a heresy.

The antithetical ethic—unlimited freedom—also had limited acceptance, and was in fact advanced only by a small group of Gnostics. Their enemies charged them with a craving for sin which would lead to the undermining of all morality. But we must be cautious about accepting such judgments; the Gnostics were the victims of a vast amount of calumny. There must have been some instances of immorality among them. That could scarcely be otherwise, given the climate of decadence in the great cities of the age. But the Gnostics did not, as a movement, partake of the vices of disintegrating classical civilization.

Nevertheless, a group extolling libertinage did exist among

[8] *Neutestamentliche Apokryphen*, ed. E. Hennecke (1904), p. 23.

the Gnostics, a group which took pride in its disdain for traditional moral concepts. "Despising the powers of the world" was a favorite Gnostic phrase; it amounted to a declaration of war upon the Creator of the world. Clement of Alexandria tells of a school of heretics whose head declared "that he would combat lust by enjoyment of lust." [9] According to Carpocrates, "good or evil exists only in the opinion of men, for no man's life leads to gratification unless all that opposes him is eliminated." [1] Here was a libertinage which boasted of its freedom from all matter. Occasionally it directly glorified pleasure as a divine phenomenon and exalted lust as the bond between all created things. Sin was to be banished from the world by releasing and exhausting men's sensual appetites—a tempting doctrine.

Here again we see the revolutionary character of Gnosticism, and can understand the moral indignation felt by many in the face of an ethical system that turned all ordinary principles topsy-turvy. The representatives of the official Church were horrified. But the small group of libertine Gnostics remained undisturbed by this reaction, for the rebel always takes pride in giving offense. Rather, they regarded their superiority to good and evil as the patent to nobility of a new type of man who "offered up the flesh to the flesh and the spirit to the spirit." [2] Carnal pleasure, they maintained, in no way compromised their purity, any more than gold falling into filth was less gold.

Behind this libertinage was a fundamental question that was seldom understood, and yet calls for discussion: What does freedom mean in reality? Does the good consist *only* in the moral imperative? Has the man who has become conscious of his divine nature in Christ any need to consider other authorities lying outside himself—outside, that is, his own divine nature?

In the Gnostic view, pure knowledge had value solely as a form of preparation for the practice of religion. To this end the Gnostics inaugurated a number of mystery rituals. Secret conse-

---

[9] Clemens Alexandrinus: op. cit., Book II, xx, 117.
[1] Schultz: op. cit., p. 158.
[2] Irenaeus: op. cit., I, vi.

crations and sacraments formed the core of Gnostic mysticism. The Gnostics felt that the practice of these mysteries enabled them to unite with the Deity. The sacrament of baptism in particular served to bring about union with the Deity, for it involved "merging with, becoming one with the divine element of water, partaking of its purity, its vitality, its redemptory powers." [3] The Gnostics made a great deal of the sacrament of unction. As for the sacrament of the Eucharist, it was performed by the Ophites in a unique fashion. They heaped loaves of bread on a table and had a snake, which they venerated as a sacred animal, crawl among the loaves.

The climax of Gnostic mysticism was the sacrament of the bridal chamber, which was held in ceremonially furnished rooms. In the mystery of the bridal chamber the Gnostics claimed that they experienced supernatural union with the Deity, an experience that could not be expressed in words. Upon entering the chamber the initiates addressed the deity: "We must join in oneness. First take grace through me and from me. Adorn Yourself like a bride who awaits her bridegroom, so that I shall be You and You shall be I. Let there descend upon Your bridal chamber the seed of light. Receive from me the bridegroom and take him up and let Yourself be taken up by him." [4]

There is a profound religious impulse, ordinarily misinterpreted, underlying this mystical identism. It utilizes excessively daring phraseology because it aims at the Highest. The idea behind mystical identism—to enter into as close a communion as possible with God—is certainly praiseworthy, despite the danger that man, having attained this intimacy, will overstep the boundaries of reverence. It is not by chance that bridal mysticism has undergone such elaborate development in the history of Christian thought. Here is an image which continues to express the burning longings of religious man.

Taken as a body, these Gnostic theories represent nothing less than the birth of religious philosophy. Although condemned

[3] Bousset: op. cit., p. 280.
[4] Irenaeus: op. cit., I, xiii.

as heretics by the Church, the Gnostics were in fact the first religious philosophers. To be sure, they ventured into dangerous territory, and climbed to altitudes where unpracticed thinkers could easily be overcome by giddiness and plunge into the abyss. *The best approach to the systems of the Gnostics is to regard them as magnificent allegory in which ideas of profound speculative importance were cloaked in forms not necessarily essential to them. In many passages we strongly sense symbolic meanings. Here the Gnostics themselves could not have meant their ideas to be accepted literally. They considered such statements as mere image of a poetic or mystical order.*[5]

The Gnostics approached the inner meaning of Christian symbols by way of religious philosophy. In so doing they initiated an effort that has continued ever since. All believers who seek an intellectual foundation for their faith necessarily engage in religious philosophy. The Gnostics did not lack for successors. From Valentinus and Basilides, a direct line leads through the Cabalists, Böhme, Novalis, Schelling, and Hegel all the way to Soloviëv.

In underlining their role as religious philosophers, we have by no means said all there is to say about the complexity of Gnosticism as a phenomenon. It must not be forgotten that Gnosticism is older than Christianity, so that its origins cannot have been purely Christian. The Gnostics owed much to both Hellenism and Orientalism; they also contributed many Jewish elements to the stream of Christianity. As philosophers they were not averse to assimilating components from many religions. Since each Gnostic system includes pagan, Jewish, and Christian elements, the question arises: What proportion of each? One of the major problems of the Gnostic religious philosophers consisted in fusing the non-Christian with the Christian ideas. They hoped that by making use of the pre-Christian religions they would arrive at a true conception of Christianity. For they regarded Christianity as the perfection of those things for which paganism and

[5] F. C. Baur: *Die Christliche Gnosis* (1835), p. 239.

Judaism had already prepared the way. This syncretistic spirit of Gnosticism led to the "acute Hellenization of Christianity."

The Gnostics found numerous statements in the New Testament that accorded completely with their own doctrines. Jesus distinguished between those to whom it was given to know the secrets of the kingdom of heaven and those to whom it was not given.[6] Thus the Gnostics found a model for their own differentiation between two classes of people. Likewise, Jesus' accusation that the Pharisees had "taken away the key of knowledge"[7] was felt to be a confirmation of their own excursions into religious philosophy. The epistles of Paul also abounded in phrases which they could hail as akin to their own ideas. They made a Gnostic conception out of Paul's distinction between the natural man who does not receive the gifts of the Spirit of God and the spiritual man who judges all things but is himself judged by no one.[8] Paul frequently made use of the term *gnosis*.[9] It may be said that the great Apostle was a major influence on the Gnostic movement as it evolved into its Christian form. The religious philosophy of the Gnostics and the Pauline interpretation of Christianity display a greater kinship than is generally acknowledged.

Of course there are many passages in the New Testament which directly oppose Gnosticism. Some of these were outgrowths of the struggles between the Early Church and this, its most dangerous rival. The warnings to Timothy to avoid "what is falsely called knowledge" (*gnosis*)[1] and to have nothing to do with "silly myths"[2] are products of a later period. The pastoral letters contain unmistakable attacks upon the Gnostics, and therefore express the increasing antagonism between the growing Church and Gnosticism. For the latter exerted a seductive attraction upon many Church Christians and threatened to overwhelm the primitive communities. Thus the Gnostics were early

[6] Matt. xiii, 11 and Mark iv, 10–12.
[7] Luke xi, 52.
[8] I Cor. ii, 14–15.
[9] I Cor. viii, 1; xii, 8; xiv, 6.
[1] I Tim. vi, 20.
[2] I Tim. i, 4 and iv, 7.

regarded as heretics, and the Church came more and more to think of them as the most dangerous of enemies, worse than the pagans with their persecutions. The fiercest of disputes broke out between the Church and the Gnostics, disputes whose violence we can hardly imagine today. In patristic literature, however, the scars the Church carried away from these almost incessant controversies can be plainly seen. Both sides felt that they had been touched upon vital nerves. For, after all, ultimate truths were at stake. There was not room for both to live peacefully side by side; one group had to yield to the other, especially since the Gnostics "claimed to form the true pneumatic [i.e. spiritual] church." [3] The details of this embittered struggle cannot be described here; indeed, many of these details remain obscure. But it is clear enough how the contest ended. Although the Gnostics had already attained "half a victory" within Catholicism,[4] the passionate combat led ultimately to their expulsion. The Church cast them out as heretics and destroyed their writings. As a result of this ruthless procedure, all that remains of the immense body of Gnostic literature are some pitiable fragments. Present-day scholarship must lament this destruction; nevertheless, it was what the primitive Church had to do. For had the Church not taken such action, it would in turn have been driven to the wall by the Gnostics.

The early Christians made a grim analogy between Gnosticism and an orchid: "It is the most beautiful of all flowers, but poisonous serpents lurk at its root." [5] When we study this religious philosophy we will no doubt find that it must be purified of a good deal of dross. But it can no longer be kept under a ban. Here is the verdict of Leopold Ziegler, who speaks of the Gnostic schools as "heresies which fought the young Church to the hilt, and from their point of view had to fight, although at bottom they are less heterodox than the orthodox tradition itself. Today we may, indeed we must, concede that these so-called

[3] R. Seeberg: *Lehrbuch der Dogmengeschichte* (1920), I, 270.
[4] A. Harnack: *Lehrbuch der Dogmengeschichte* (1909), I, 250.
[5] Georg Koepgen: *Die Gnosis des Christentums* (1939), p. 334.

heresies illuminate many things that are otherwise confusing." [6]

The old Gnostics proposed stirring questions which, as Nicolai Berdyaev says, must not be repressed as impermissible.[7] For the Gnostics were filled with a vigorous philosophical craving to clarify for themselves the origins of the universe. There is something deeply moving about their ever-renewed attempts in this direction. Their intuitive statements sprang more from the heart than the brain. We might look upon these early Christians as fellow pilgrims on the road to a Christian *gnosis*—a goal still to be won by striving.

Origen

"There are eunuchs who have made themselves eunuchs for the sake of the kingdom of heaven." [8] This mysterious saying of Jesus seemed to have made a deep impression upon one young man named Origen. He promptly translated word into deed, and unmanned himself, thus anticipating the practices of the Russian Skoptsy. Even Eusebius, who venerated Origen, was horrified by this action. It had sprung, he said, from an "immature and youthful mind," and the great Church Father himself had later called it a misunderstanding.[9] In modern times Origen's self-emasculation has been analyzed as an example of morbid over-excitement betraying pathological tendencies.

No one is going to recommend that this bloody self-mutilation be imitated. Neither can we dismiss it as the act of a "frenzied follower in the festival procession of the Syrian goddess." It is an act whose meaning is not so simple. (Modern historians, by the way, have tried to assert that the story is a slander invented by Origen's enemies.) What must have taken place in this man's soul before he chose this radical fashion of following the saying of Jesus! Evidently Origen thought it impossible to carry his body with him into the spiritual life. That is, indeed, a far more diffi-

[6] Leopold Ziegler: *Überlieferung* (1936), p. 319.
[7] Nicolai Berdyaev: *Die Philosophie des freien Geistes* (1930), pp. 332 f.
[8] Matt. xix, 12.
[9] Eusebius: op. cit., VI, viii.

cult problem than people imagine. From the Neo-Platonic school of Ammonius Saccas, Origen took over the view that the body is the antagonist of the spirit. We can only wonder whether Origen's terrible act of self-emasculation proved helpful to him in his spiritual quest.

In any case it is plain that the person who committed such an act upon himself was no ordinary man. Only an extraordinary man is capable of such grim resolution. In this man lived a fiery spirit, before whose greatness we can only bow down. "He has the most comprehensive and perfect of minds"; "a man who struck out on so many new paths must be forgiven for having sometimes gone astray." Such are the verdicts of orthodox Catholics.[1]

Born in Egypt about A.D. 185, Origen was a unique and superior personality. The first historian of the Church said of him: "The life of Origen seems to me to have been praiseworthy from the cradle, as it were."[2] He seems to have been animated by a fierce determination to exceed himself and to take the Gospel seriously, allowing himself no compromises whatsoever. For he refused to preach to others when he did not abide by his own teachings. In him, theory and practice matched. He fought his need for sleep, and chose the bare earth for his bed. For many years he renounced shoes entirely and abstained totally from wine. The purity of his life was such that it silenced all reproach. Truly, "there have been few Fathers of the Church whose lives have left an impression of such purity as that of Origen."[3] He thirsted for martyrdom, and in his old age suffered cruel persecution for the sake of the Gospel. He was thrown into prison, fettered with a heavy iron collar, and at last stretched on the rack. He ended his life, therefore, as a Christian martyr.

Oddly—and this should be emphasized—for all his ascetic practices, Origen did not have the strait-lacedness that usually accompanies asceticism. Rather, he represented a rare union of austerity toward himself and liberality toward others. By no

[1] Viller-Rahner: *Askese und Mystik in der Väterzeit* (1939), p. 74.
[2] Eusebius: op. cit., VI, ii.
[3] Harnack: op. cit., I, 651.

43

means inclined to escape from the world, he was able to say: *Holiness must be sought not in a single place, but in acts and life and conduct. If these are godly and if they are conceived in obedience to the commandments, you will be serving the Word of God even when you are at home, even when you are in the market. Why do I say at the market?—even when you sit in the theater, do not doubt that you are in a holy place!* [4]

His searching mind was receptive and free from bias. "For he taught us to seek wisdom by perusing all existing writings of the old philosophers and poets, as far as our strength enabled us, not excluding anything," one of his disciples recounts.[5] Modern biographers, too, conclude that "a holy gravity and sincere worshipfulness, an enthusiasm for the Gospel which generally characterizes only those suddenly converted in mature years, a passion for knowledge and a world-forswearing, unwavering faith formed the inner core of his nature." [6] Origen embodies all that is most glorious in Oriental devoutness; we may say of him what he himself said of the Fourth Gospel: that its meaning could be grasped only by one who had himself lain upon the bosom of Jesus.

At the age of eighteen, he assumed charge of the school of catechists in Alexandria, and remained at its head all his life. As leader of this school his influence was so great that he succeeded in winning over to Christianity much of the cultured society of his time. In his teaching Origen followed the model of Socrates, subjecting his pupils to the most rigorous cross-examinations, in order that they might make their positions logically impregnable. An inspired teacher, he aroused a true love of knowledge in his pupils. They learned, moreover, that "no one can understand a prophet if the spirit active in the prophet does not itself confer understanding of his words." [7]

Through his teaching Origen became the founder of Biblical

---

[4] Origenes: *Geist und Feuer, ein Aufbau aus seinen Schriften,* ed. H. U. von Balthasar (1938), p. 68.
[5] Gregorius Thaumaturgus (St. Gregory): *Panegyric on Origen,* chap. xiii.
[6] E. Redepenning: *Origenes* (1841), I, 190.
[7] Gregorius Thaumaturgus: op. cit., chap. xv.

science. But he spoke Biblically of the Bible, not with that pedantry which can be the death of the spirit of Scripture. We can almost hear the sparks crackling in his remarkable exegeses. He brings to light many secrets which lie hidden in Scriptural texts. For he regarded them as ciphers which called for an allegorical interpretation. Where other commentators scrutinized them for fine points of grammar, Origin cast on them the bright light of spiritual insight.

It may be that Origen carried his allegorical interpretations too far. But this method had already been employed by Paul and thus has considerable validity, however much its detractors may spurn it as "Biblical alchemy." Even as a boy Origen had not been "satisfied with reading the sacred words in a simple and literal manner, but sought something further, and busied himself, even at that age, with deeper speculations, troubling his father by his questions as to what could be the inner meaning of the inspired Scripture." [3] To Origen, the historical episodes of the Bible represented symbols for events in the celestial worlds. Thus, he took Jesus' entry into Jerusalem as symbolizing the entrance of the Logos into the soul. When Jesus had cried "Woe to the scribes," he had meant to denounce obstinate clinging to the letter of the Bible. The Apostles, Origen argued, had communicated only the essentials, not the whole truth. The enlightened Christian was supposed to penetrate to the more hidden tradition which Jesus had imparted only to a few.

The crowning feature of Origen's bold doctrine was that even the New Testament did not contain the conclusive revelation of God. The four Gospels alone did not contain all the mysteries of the faith. They only suggested to Christians the "shadow of the secrets of Christ." The New Testament must be regarded as the gateway to the eternal gospel whose *pneuma* could not even be expressed in letters of the alphabet.

In this proclamation of the eternal evangel Origen went beyond the official view of the Church and in essence anticipated the ecstatic Joachim of Floris. Like this Calabrian abbot, Origen

[3] Eusebius: op. cit., VI, ii.

drifted, with his whispers of an eternal gospel, upon that prophetic track which leads into the land of heresy.

While Origen's enigmatic references to the eternal gospel remained unnoticed, other points of his became famous. Thus, he set up three categories of Scriptural meaning: the literal (*somatikos*), the moral (*psychikos*), and the mystic or pneumatic. Here we have the key to any deeper understanding of Origen. In his conception of Christianity he took over the Gnostic view of two classes of believers, the average Christians and the pneumatics. But the Gnostics conceived the difference as a fundamental cleavage. Origen, always seeking harmony, considered these classes as stages. This apparently simple modification represented a stroke of genius, for it showed ordinary Christians an ascending staircase toward an electness they must all aspire to. At the same time, they would need illumination from above in order to make the ascent.

The lowest step was the traditional faith of the masses. Origen did not despise their crude beliefs. Christ had come for the little ones also, and the piety of the common people was altogether sufficient for salvation. Belief in the letter of Scripture formed the foundation for the ordinary member of the Christian Church. Origen made himself the champion of this simple faith when, in his *Eight Books against Celsus*, he undertook the defense of this lowest stage of the concept of Christianity. Although this apology established Origen's fame within the Church, we must nevertheless ask whether the author fulfilled the requirements of a genuine defender of the Christian religion—one of the most difficult of offices. Was not Origen rather practicing that ambiguous art—as Job puts it [9]—of speaking for God falsely and deceitfully? Let us leave this question open, for it is a difficult one to answer. There is, for instance, Origen's preface in which he admits his own misgivings about such polemics. It runs counter, he says, to the conduct of Jesus who "was silent when false witnesses spoke against him." [1] He feared that his *Eight*

[9] Job, xiii, 7.
[1] Origen: *Contra Celsum*, translated with an Introduction and Notes by Henry Chadwick (Cambridge: Cambridge University Press; 1953), p. 3.

Books against Celsus might "weaken the force of the defence that is in the mere facts, and detract from the power of Jesus." [2] Jesus accepted the contumely of being disbelieved and did not shield his face from the shame of being spat upon. Was it right, then, to produce a voluminous, learned work in order to refute an opponent?

This polemic contains a great deal of dross, and like all apologists Origen resorted to arguments which would not hold water. But he remained too aristocratic to become spiteful, and honorably stood ready to "freely acknowledge the excellence of any truths" in the statements of Celsus. [3]

The second stage consists in examination of the philosophical questions involved in the faith. Origen's teacher had been Clement of Alexandria, one of the greatest of the Greek patristic writers, and he was therefore well equipped for just such an enterprise. Whereas the earlier Christians considered it inadvisable to enter the literary arena, Clement—as Overbeck has determined—was the first to take this step, thus becoming the father of that line of "writers who did not want to be writers." [4] Clement in his *Miscellanies* had spoken of the distinction between esoteric and exoteric teaching. He himself practiced a curious kind of obscurity. He wove his secret doctrine into his works, masterfully concealing it in casual remarks. At the same time he was not excessively afraid of error; he stated that "we must err frequently if we seek to be noble men." [5] Through the tutelage of Clement of Alexandria, Origen was helped to climb to the second stage: Christianity based on a foundation of philosophy. The base was broadened without dilution of the religious substance. Under the influence of Clement, Origen learned to transcend his fear of pagan thinking—a fear so strong in his early days that it had led him to dispose of his secular library. Later on, however, he ceased to regard philosophy as an enemy. Instead, like Justin, he came

---

[2] Ibid., p. 4.
[3] Ibid., VIII, 76.
[4] F. Overbeck: *Über die Anfänge der patristischen Literatur"* in *Historische Zeitschrift* (1882), p. 447.
[5] Clemens Alexandrinus: op. cit., Book V, xiv, 140.

to see it as another road leading to God. Origen followed in the footsteps of Paul, who in his address in the Areopagus paid due respect to the intellectual background of his listeners and did not hesitate to use a phrase like: "as even some of your poets have said." [6] Following the example of the Apostle, Origen endeavored to be a Greek to the Greeks. He studied Greek philosophy principally in order to be better able to preach Christianity to educated pagans. He endowed philosophy with a religious function, and taught that it was the necessary second step in the spiritual progress of the Christian. But the study of pagan philosophy had a profound influence upon Origen's own thinking. Far more than he acknowledged, it changed the very fabric of his mind and transformed him into a philosophizing Christian. "For a great number of years he continued to live like a philosopher" and "in his opinions about material things and the Deity he played the Greek." [7] Not that he had become unfaithful to Christianity— Origen was and remained a Christian, passionately attached to the religion. He lived and moved and had his being in the Bible, which forever occupied his thoughts. But he also saw the greatness of the Greek world. Through Origen, the Greek spirit poured in a torrent into the Church, and would never afterward be expelled.

Origen went about this appropriation of Hellas with wise discrimination. "For philosophy is neither opposed in all things to the law of God, nor equivalent to it in all things," he held. [8] He believed in an eternal primal Reason; Christianity was not the sole revelation of truth because God had inscribed truth in the heart of man. It would be a mistake, however, to identify his religious philosophy with Neo-Platonism. It would be equally wide of the mark to consider his book *On the Principles* as a work of ecclesiastical dogmatics. In it he several times stated emphatically that "all these are not dogmas, but merely questions and suggestions." [9] He expressly declared that he wished to leave his

[6] Acts, xvii, 28.
[7] Eusebius, op. cit., VI, iii and xix.
[8] Origenes: *Geist und Feuer*, pp. 302–3.
[9] Origenes: *Über die Grundlehren*, ed. K. Schnitzer (1835), p. 83.

statements to be "freely reflected upon by everyone." And he added: "I advance these arguments not as doctrine, but only that they may be submitted to free examination." [1] This was the language of the philosopher of religion, not of the ecclesiastical dogmatic. Origen consciously undertook the task of constructing a Christian philosophy, a task that has lost none of its urgency to this day. In so doing he laid the foundation for a new structure which aroused mistrust in many men of little faith. Yet it is one of the grandest structures in existence. The sum total of his achievement made Origen the creator of Christian humanism, whose underlying religious idea is "the unity of the divine and the human." [2]

The philosophical Christian, which Origen had become when he reached his "second stage," can also look upon heretics with different eyes. Naturally Origen took a position against heresy, and as head of the catechetical school he was often faced with the necessity of refuting heretical errors. But he was particularly sensitive to this whole matter because he was in constant peril of becoming a heretic himself. In the end, he did not escape this fate. Origen may be called the heretic in patristic garb.

Origen's public attitude toward the heretics was an exemplary one, free of spite and blindness. With an amazing openmindedness he would examine and analyze the various heretical views in a manner that was scarcely possible to any of his contemporaries. He could say: "The heretics are, to be sure, on the 'way,' but not on the one guided by the Lord, rather upon one which has been twisted by the Evil One. They turn to right and left, for they are not content with mere faith; it is true that they think more deeply, but not more truly." [3] But in the last sentence he gives himself away. Beneath the temperate tone is a sympathy, even an admiration, for dangerous lines of thought.

This Father of the Church was conscious of the part which heresy played in the dynamics of the faith. He pointed out that philosophy necessarily gave rise to differing schools. "Sects in-

[1] Ibid., p. 137.
[2] Redepenning: op. cit., II, 314.
[3] Origenes: *Geist und Feuer*, p. 143.

49

evitably came to exist, not at all on account of factions and love of strife, but because several learned men made a serious attempt to understand the doctrines of Christianity." [4] With his intellectual alertness Origen made every effort to investigate these various opinions among professors of Christianity, since in his opinion "a man who looks carefully into the sects of Judaism and Christianity becomes a very wise Christian." [5] Such a statement could be made only by a man who did not follow the teachings of the Church blindly, but had the inner clarity to attribute positive values to heresy. In keeping with this attitude, he was quite free of hatred of heretics. "Those who have understood the sayings 'Blessed are the peacemakers,' and 'Blessed are the meek,' would not detest those who debase Christian doctrines, nor would they call people who are in error Circes and cunning seducers." [6] Origen did not feel himself too superior to learn from the heretics. "All his opponents are also his forerunners." [7] For he frequently learned important things from them, and was more dependent upon them than he admitted to himself. "The surprising parallel between Origen and the system of Valentine" has always struck students of the religious philosophers.[8] Origen was an excellent advocate of the principle that in order to expose the falsehood of an intellectual movement one must be ready to pay due respect, first, to whatever truths it holds.

The third and highest stage of spiritual progress is reached by the pneumatic Christian who possesses true knowledge, *gnosis*. To Origen the word *gnosis* had no obnoxious sound; indeed he placed divine knowledge as far higher than mere faith. He defined true *gnosis* as "perfected faith" which "rightly remains hidden from the great majority." His religious philosophy differed only by degrees, not in principle, from that of the Gnostics. Together with Clement of Alexandria he laid the basis for a Christian Gnosticism—a glorious scheme which, unfortunately, his followers

[4] Origen: op. cit., III, xii, p. 136.
[5] Ibid.
[6] Origen: op. cit., V, lxiii.
[7] Harnack: op. cit., I, 652.
[8] W. Völker: *Das Vollkommenheitsideal des Origenes* (1931), p. 119.

among the Fathers of the Church failed to develop. What he envisioned was a different kind of Christianity, much broader in its
foundations, which "in all freedom would make everything the
object of its investigation and would enrich itself with all intellectual goods." [9] His Christian *gnosis*, however, could only be
imparted by illumination. Only one who had been struck by this
sunbeam of revelation was entitled to call himself a pneumatic
possessing insights into the ultimate ground of existence. Only the
"eye of the soul" can witness the struggles of the superhuman
spiritual powers; ordinary men know nothing of these. Origen
drew an extraordinary picture of the pneumatic Christian. The
ideal he arrived at was a stirring one. He enjoined his Christian
to be "inured to suffering and all misfortune, firmly armored by
inner order and equilibrium, and finally blissful and like unto God
in truth." [1] He who possessed stoic firmness and unshakable
serenity in the face of all the vicissitudes of life would be allowed
to partake in the vision of divine glory. This was a bridal mysticism akin to that of the Gnostics: the soul seeks spiritual marriage with the Logos.

There was boldness, excessive boldness, in Origen's Logos
mysticism; it was sustained by a religious ardor that could spring
only from speculative vision and not from historical knowledge.
Origen's way of life must be understood in terms of this mystical
ascent of the soul; he was possessed of that fervent love of God
which he considered a divine gift, not something that man could
achieve by effort. According to Origen, the pneumatic Christian
enjoyed a sublimity and inner richness which came about from
his intoxication with divinity.

Origen's mysticism reached its peak in his paeans on the
birth of Christ in the soul of man, and on inward, wordless
prayer. He called Christ the Perfect One, but did not reserve this
appellation for Jesus of Nazareth alone. "Knowing that Christ has
come, we see that because of him there have been many Christs
in the world, who like him have 'loved righteousness and hated

---

[9] Gregorius Thaumaturgus: op. cit., chap. xv.
[1] Ibid., chap. ix.

iniquity.'"[2] Origen, then, was the first to voice the profound idea that every pneumatic Christian becomes a Christ. It is an idea that borders on heresy.

To the Christian who has reached the mystical pneumatic stage Origen assigns a cosmic vision of enormous range. He spiritualizes all of Christianity; even the second coming of the Lord will not be an outwardly visible event. God is the Incomprehensible, surrounded by darkness, not to be grasped by any human reason. Confronting God is man, whom Origen calls a microcosm: "Understand that you are a second world in small, that within you there are sun and moon and stars as well."[3] The history of the cosmos consists of a succession of eons in which souls ascend and descend. Once we have grasped the principles of this elaborate spiritual ballet, *we will be astonished at how much likeness there is in the whole. There is a specific fundamental idea which everywhere recurs: the idea of the education by Providence of fallen rational beings. This is what Origen is really interested in. To him God is above all the Great Teacher who in every possible way guides and educates souls so that they may be led back to their heavenly origin without forfeiting their right of free self-determination.*[4]

The divine pedagogic plan operates both for individual men and for the entire universe. The way to God is the great theme of this cosmic, Christ-centered vision. "Everything, in fact, is here graded upward, everything directed toward *ascensiones in corde;* everything turns from the misted lowlands to the radiant light of Tabor, to transparency of garments, to illumined clouds from which the voice of revelation resounds."[5]

In Origen's conception, the purifying ascent does not end with death, but continues after it. The soul leaves the place of purification when the purpose of betterment has been accomplished; punishments do not last forever.[6] But the completion of

[2] Origen: op. cit., VI, lxxix, p. 392.
[3] Origenes: *Geist und Feuer*, p. 66.
[4] H. Koch: *Pronoia und Paideusis, Studien über Origenes und sein Verhältnis zum Platonismus* (1932), p. 18.
[5] Origenes: *Geist und Feuer*, p. 22.
[6] Cf. G. Anrich: *Clemens und Origenes als Begründer der Lehre vom Fegfeuer*, in *Theologische Abhandlungen für Holtzmann* (1920), pp. 97–120.

redemption will not come about until all souls have ultimately found salvation and become as angels. Even for the devil, the way back to God is not cut off. He too will not remain Satan forever. All created beings ultimately return to God, whose infinite mercy will overcome the very last negations. Thus Origen capped the whole development of primitive Christian eschatology with his doctrine of apocatastasis.

Few doctrines have been subject to more misunderstanding than that of apocatastasis: Origen's grandiose finale to the course of the cosmos. This was no question of a dogma to which another dogma might be opposed. Undeniably there was a dangerous element inherent in the idea of the restitution of all things. It threatened to deprive earthly life of its unique and decisive character and to persuade men into indifference. Apocatastasis cannot be preached to the frivolous-minded. Yet it is scarcely fair to ridicule the doctrine of restitution as an invention of the over-sentimental, as Augustine did in his polemic against Origen.[7] Origen saw apocatastasis as a profound mystery visible only to the pneumatic Christian who has reached the third, highest stage. Universal salvation is no arbitrary human theory; an all-merciful God has revealed it to man. Hope for the "restitution of all things" derives from the New Testament,[8] although Scripture also speaks of the "unquenchable fire."[9] In the Bible two differing conceptions of this subject are to be found; to human reason these appear contradictory and incompatible. The question therefore is: Which of the two antithetical concepts is accepted by the Christian? It is difficult to understand how the great majority of Christians so easily submit to the idea of an everlasting hell, without seeming to recognize the horrible vindictiveness that underlies such a conception. Origen did not deny hell, but he questioned that there could be an eternal hell because eternity could be an attribute only of God. Moreover, it was spiritual torment for him even to think that hell could be eternal, for that would have meant the triumph of Satan.

Origen could not bring himself to grant Satan any such vic-

[7] St. Augustine: *The City of God*, XXI, xvii.
[8] Acts iii, 21.
[9] Mark ix, 42–7.

tory. He wanted nothing less than to reconquer hell for God. The deeper meaning of his doctrine of apocatastasis, which has been scarcely understood, was nothing less than a tremendous struggle against eternal damnation, waged in defense of divine mercy. The idea of endless hell preyed on the mind of this Alexandrian religious philosopher. The fate of the damned preoccupied him incessantly, and thus he was led by his own temperament to emphasize the New Testament doctrine of the restitution of all things, culminating in that universal salvation which to this day remains the strength and the glory of Oriental Christianity.[1]

Origen's effort to redeem hell was one of the most moving and most Christian acts in the whole history of the church. He represents that alternate conception of Christianity which takes no joy in a blessedness based upon a contrast with the torments of the damned. It is food for thought that theologians should have condemned such a Christian for saying that there was hope for the damned. For his Christian heart had grasped that profoundest truth of God, that Golgotha does not end until the last soul has been rescued from the bowels of hell.

Origen's doctrine has found some defenders in the Western as well as in the Eastern Church. Among these were such men of God as Christoph Blumhardt the Younger, who wrote the truly Christian words: *To set up a hell in which God no longer has any say to all eternity, is to abolish the entire gospel. We must fight to the last breath, to the last drop of blood, so that the whole of heaven, the whole earth, the whole world of the dead, comes finally into the hand of Jesus. If we must abandon hope for a single man, for a single region, there remains an intolerable burden of death, a burden of woe, a burden of night and darkness, and in that case Jesus is not the light of the world.*[2] Men may not set limits to God's mercy; his love pursues lost souls even into the flames of hell.

In his religious philosophy Origen had clambered to heights

[1] Cf. Friedrich Heiler: *Urkirche und Ostkirche* (1937), pp. 237 f., and Nicolai Berdyaev: *Von der Bestimmung des Menschen* (1935), pp. 357 f.
[2] In Eugen Jäckh: *Blumhardt Vater und Sohn* (1925), p. 264.

to which the Christian masses were unable to follow him. The Church drew back in alarm from his system of universal salvation, which so dangerously teetered on the border of heresy. Even more alarming was Origen's Platonic conception of the pre-existence of the soul and of knowledge of divinity as a form of recollection. Origen's own bishop felt uncomfortable in the face of a Christianity leading to such heights, whose loftiest regions he himself could not reach. What men cannot grasp, they reject, and often begin to hate. Such was the psychological response Origen's theories evoked. Soon his enemies were more numerous than his many friends. Even during his lifetime there began to be complicated intrigues against him. He had destroyed the whole of sacred history by his symbolic conception, his enemies said.

Seeing that people in Alexandria were turning against him, Origen voluntarily left the city. After his departure an assembly of bishops raised charges against him, ruled that as a eunuch he was unworthy of the priestly dignity, and excluded him from the Alexandrian Christian community. During the bloody persecution of Christians under Emperor Decius in A.D. 250, he was arrested, imprisoned, and maltreated. A few years later he died, probably from the consequences of this experience. But even after this virtual martyrdom, the hatred and calumny did not cease. From decade to decade the attacks upon Origen as a wicked heretic mounted. He was charged with having used philosophy to undermine Christianity. Methodius of Olympus spoke of Origen's blasphemies. The less the Christians understood his religious philosophy, the more recklessly they tended to speak of him in terms such as those employed by Epiphanius of Salamis: "Origen the visionary who far preferred to introduce into life the products of fantasy than the truth."[3] He was branded the "pagan of pagans."[4]

In this mania for denunciation the Greek monks took the lead, although their ideal of piety had been predominantly formed by Origen. They repaid their teacher with base in-

---

[3] Epiphanius: *Ancoratus*, chap. liv.
[4] Braun, ed.: *Persische Märtyrer-Akten* (1915), p. 239.

gratitude. Pachomius, the founder of cenobitism, abhorred Origen as a blasphemer and apostate. He advised his brothers to take no notice of the "foolish babble of Origen," and "testified before the face of God that every man who reads Origen and accepts his writings will fall into the pit of hell" [5]—that selfsame hell from which the Alexandrian had attempted to save Christendom. These fanatical monks represented his Christian Gnosticism as a grave temptation, a corruption of the old simplicity of the Church's doctrines. Origen was pictured as a man who had trusted too much in his genius, who had arrogantly sought to be cleverer than others and had wantonly abused the grace of God.

After a desperate defense on the part of his adherents, Origen was finally condemned. In 543, at the instigation of Emperor Justinian, a synod at Constantinople pronounced the anathema upon Origen, and the Fifth Ecumenical Council of the year 553 condemned his doctrines as erroneous. This was one of the most fateful events in the history of Christian dogma. For even in the judgment of a Catholic scholar, after the Church's condemnation of Origenism "everything became narrow, one-sided, dogmatic and self-righteous; optimism and cosmic breadth had vanished." [6]

Nevertheless, the majority of Christians accepted this verdict. Only a few isolated individuals in the course of history refused to acquiesce in this dark outcome. In the Middle Ages the sensitive twelfth-century mystic Elisabeth of Schönau was troubled by the question of whether this great teacher of the Church had been saved or not, and the answer was given to her in a vision: "You must know that the errors of Origen sprang not from wickedness but from the excessive zeal with which he bent his mind to the depths of his beloved Holy Scripture and sought to peer too closely into the divine mysteries. Therefore the punishment which he endures is not severe." [7] But the voice of this nun did not suffice to break down the wall of misunderstanding which had

[5] Athanasius: *Life of Pachomius,* chaps. xi and xxxvii.
[6] Koepgen: op. cit., pp. 323–4.
[7] Öhl, ed.: *Deutsche Mystikerbriefe des Mittelalters* (1931), p. 138.

surrounded the works of Origen since his condemnation. Even Luther was hostile to that "excellent learned man" because he had first introduced the "game" of allegory; and Baronius saw Origen as no more than an outlawed heretic. Reformation and Counter-Reformation agreed in their disdain for Origen. His name remained suspect, that of an outcast heretic.

But in spite of this odium, Origen's doctrines could not be killed. Traces of his work could not be expunged from the writings of the Church Fathers. His noble mind had created too magnificent and unique an intellectual system for him ever to be consigned to oblivion. His spirit proved to be stronger than all condemnations. Repeatedly, his Biblical commentaries were consulted and his sermons secretly pillaged. In 1700 Gottfried Arnold dared to come forth and admit his spiritual kinship with Origen. But only in modern times was the ban totally broken; only in modern times has there been a change in Christian thinkers' judgment of Origen. Catholic theology cautiously began reassessing the Alexandrian philosopher, overlooking as far as possible his dangerous extremes. Hans Urs von Balthasar has declared in unmistakable terms: "While the vessel was shattered into a thousand fragments and the master's name stoned and buried deep beneath the ground, the fragrance of the chrism arose and filled the whole house. No thinker of the Church has been so invisibly omnipresent as Origen." [8] Origen's vision, whose greatness we have only been able to suggest, cannot be set aside. He remains the immortal philosopher of religion who taught men's souls the way to ascend, who preached universal redemption and restored the eternal evangel. To have been once struck by the rays of his light is to be forever enraptured by this creator of Christian Gnosticism. Origen first established that Oriental spirit of devoutness whose attraction is so strong that many profess: "Better to err with Origen than to be right with the others." [9]

---

[8] Origenes: *Geist und Feuer,* p. 13.
[9] Vincent of Lerins: *Commonitorium,* chap. xvii.

3

The Exposed Conspiracy

+ +

Marcion

The figure of Marcion haunts patristic literature, wandering about in a curious twilight. Nowhere can we see it with the clarity that the contemporary mind demands. But it reappears again and again, casting an uncanny spell upon the reader.

Marcion was pursued with savage hatred by the venerable Fathers of the Church. So early a writer as Polycarp hurled at him the terrible words: "I know you, you Firstborn of Satan." [1] And Irenaeus called him "the devil's mouthpiece." [2] Tertullian

[1] Irenaeus: op. cit., III, iii.
[2] Ibid. I, xxvii.

compared him to a raging beast and Cyril of Jerusalem spoke of him as the "mouth of godlessness." Marcion was regarded as the arch-heretic after Simon Magus, the personification of evil whose name alone made Christians shudder. Many good Christians were said to have fallen prey to his pharisaical hypocrisies. No vituperation was too strong for the representatives of the Church to apply to Marcion.

The passionate opposition alone suggests the unusual importance of this heretic. And the supposition is confirmed by later writers. Clement of Alexandria called him a giant, and Origen praised his fiery spirit. Marcion has likewise been termed a religious genius of "grand simplicity, profound piety and trenchant intellectual keenness," "the greatest heretic who ever emerged from Christianity," a "unique phenomenon, quite inimitable, who verged on bizarreness and monomania." [3]

The personality of Marcion remains obscured in the semi-darkness of primitive Christianity. But his bold thinking, his inexorably consistent logic, and the consuming fire of his religious intensity have acquired new meaning for the contemporary world. According to Leopold Ziegler his example serves to show how *heretics have repeatedly intervened in all the intellectual developments of the Occident, interrupting and twisting them, forcing them into blind alleys or even literally destroying them, frequently shaking the Occident to its foundations and imperiling its continuance. On the other hand, however, a mild doubt arises as to whether Marcion was really a heretic at all, or whether he did not on the contrary in some points surpass the Church itself in genuine orthodoxy.* [4]

Almost all the details of Marcion's life are unknown, and it is therefore impossible to trace his religious development. He came from the port city of Sinope on the Black Sea. Tertullian, in his passionate polemic against Marcion—which is one of our principal sources of information on this heretic—made an interesting attempt to explain the whole man in terms of his birthplace.

[3] Egon Friedell: *Kulturgeschichte des Altertums* (1936), pp. 6, 7.
[4] Leopold Ziegler: *Überlieferung*, p. 409.

Given the inhospitable region and the wild barbarism of its inhabitants, Tertullian says, it is not surprising that Marcion should come forth with such revolutionary views.

Born around the year 85, Marcion grew up in Christianity, for he was the son of the head of the Christian community in Sinope. Since Marcion was a shipbuilder by trade, he must have been comparatively well-to-do. He traveled from Asia Minor to Rome, where he was accepted into the Christian congregation. Upon his entrance he presented the Roman community with a considerable sum of money, and tried to win it over to the novel views he had meanwhile conceived. The year of his death is unknown. There is no reason to credit Tertullian's remark that Marcion repented on his deathbed. His sect, though denounced for heresy, survived for centuries, which can be explained only by assuming that the founder remained steadfast in his beliefs. Moreover, it has long been a favorite tactic of the Church to claim such deathbed recantations for heretics.

At some time in his little-known life there occurred a decisive experience which Marcion himself summed up in the ecstatic cry: "O wonder of wonders, ecstasy, power and amazement— there is nothing that can be said about the Gospel, nor thought about it, nor can it be compared with anything else!" [5] This one sentence expresses the rapture with which the Gospel inspired Marcion, and gives a hint of his interpretation of it. Marcion had seen the white radiance of the coming kingdom of God expressed in the tidings of Jesus. He felt that the beatific experience of the Gospel could not be expressed in words, and that this ecstasy was what really mattered. As long as a man can speak eloquently about the Gospel, he has subjected it to the avaricious grasp of his intellect and has not been lifted above himself. To Marcion the Gospel was an incomprehensible miracle, and this mute astonishment shows what a religious breakthrough he himself had experienced. This is the key to his religious ideas, and not his relationship to the Gnostics, which is as yet unclear. To be sure, the patristic writers always classified him with the Gnostics. But this

[5] Harnack: *Marcion, das Evangelium vom fremden Gott* (1921), p. 81.

merely means that they failed to understand the nature of the man. Marcion was more concerned with the tidings of salvation than with mythological speculations about cycles and eons. Although there were some points of contact between Marcion and Gnosticism, it may equally well be said that he stood in direct antithesis to the Gnostics.

The Gospel figure of Jesus Christ was central to Marcion. It is far from true that he proclaimed a Christianity without Christ. On the contrary, the personality of Jesus was of vital importance to him; he felt deeply the uniqueness and incomparability of Christ and of Christ's tidings of God. For God Marcion coined the expression "the Stranger"—a phrase so characteristic of Marcionate doctrine that Adolf Harnack entitles his book on Marcion "the Evangel of the Stranger God." By his recurrent use of "the Stranger" this second-century Christian was attempting to express precisely what Rudolf Otto in the twentieth century sought to bring back to the consciousness of modern man in his phrase "the wholly Other." [6] To both men the *mysterium tremendum* arouses in amazed man a sense of absolute estrangement. And it must be said that one of the profoundest religious truths lies hidden in the mystery of strangeness and in the inexplicable radiance of the divine.

According to Marcion, the stranger God descended with great suddenness upon this world. Marcion put great emphasis on the unexpectedness of this event—such emphasis that he lost all interest in the tradition which prepared the way of the Lord. The gospel of the stranger God, he said, brought tidings altogether new, not at all based upon prophesies. Here was a view directly opposed to Solomon's statement that there is nothing new under the sun; rather, Marcion's idea paralleled the Buddhist "that which no one had ever heard before." Marcion regarded Christianity as absolutely new.

The essence of the stranger God is merciful love. There is no wrath in him at all; he condemns no one. God is incomprehensible *agape*. This insight, which thoughtless repetition has un-

[6] Cf. R. Otto: *Das Heilige* (1919), p. 28.

fortunately reduced to a banality, was for Marcion so overpowering a vital experience that he could scarcely find words to express it. Marcion manifested his uncommon understanding of divine love by the way in which he contrasted it with justice. Justice, too, is an important matter. But love is more important, superior to justice, and Marcion's subtle religious sensibility recognized the tensions between love and justice. God redeems men not in the interests of justice, but out of his incomprehensible love. "Redemption redeems so completely that nothing whatever is left of the old; it makes everything new down to the ultimate ground of things. Hence, everything that has previously existed becomes null and void, for redemption is redemption not only from the world but from its creator and lord also." [7]

Marcion's gospel of the stranger God was indissolubly linked with his rejection of God as creator of the universe. Like the Gnostics, he was disturbed by the imperfections of this world. The senselessness of its institutions seemed to him revolting, and he regarded nature as the product of an evil power. How could anyone think that this wretched, stupid place swarming with noxious vermin could have been created by a loving God?

Marcion likewise regarded man, whom the creator of the world had brought into being, as a wretched creature in his weakness, helplessness, and mortality. He considered human reproduction a repulsive act, which made man like the beasts. "In the womb a foetus coagulates out of horrible materials of generation, is nourished for nine months by the same filth, comes to light through the genitals, and is fed and raised by a buffoonish process." [8] Finally man sinks into the grave as a cadaver, thus completing the proof of his nullity. According to Marcion, all of creation is a miserable tragicomedy for which only its creator can be blamed. Hence the creator of this world cannot possibly be identical with the good God, the stranger. All through Marcion we find this protest against creation. Although his thought was in keeping with the Gnostic spirit of his times, his wild words about this

---

[7] Harnack: *Marcion,* p. 138.
[8] Ibid. p. 145.

world are reminiscent of Ivan Karamazov's diatribes—so difficult to refute. With true heretical fervor he rebelled against the
existing order, and in the invective he hurled against this
world he anticipated the whole of modern pessimism.

This attitude toward the world included rejection of the Old
Testament, whose God had created this earthly existence. The
more Marcion elaborated his interpretation of the new gospel, the
more clearly it seemed to him that the Christian message was incompatible with the Old Testament. *Marcion's revaluation of
the Old Testament, which involved renunciation of it, cost him
dear; he was able to arrive at it only at the price of intense pain.
For he had to consign to the flames what he had hitherto adored.
And along with the Law he was forced also to condemn the
Prophets and the Psalms, which yet contained so much that
seemed to coincide or to prepare the way for the evangel. Error!
Error! Even the sublimest and most consoling words must be
mere sham and deception! Even in them could be detected,
though in disguise, the fearful countenance of the cruel creator
of the world.*[9]

As Marcion saw it, the God of the Old Covenant was merciless, stern and cruel, full of passion, fanaticism, wrath, partisan-
ship, pettiness. His justice was purely formalistic: an eye for an
eye and a tooth for a tooth. His self-contradictions and weaknesses, his vacillations and his morally questionable commandments had to be rejected. Marcion's criticism culminated in his
demonstration that the Old Testament God had been an instiga-
tor of wars, a breaker of promises, and a master of malice. Marcion regarded him as an enemy.

Tertullian quite properly saw that this antithesis between the
stranger God and the Old Testament creator constituted Marcion's fundamental idea. "The separation of the Law and the
evangel is Marcion's peculiarity and his main work." [1] In stressing
the conflict, this heretic was choosing his side on a question
which has been discussed throughout the history of Chris-

[9] Ibid. pp. 28, 29.
[1] Tertullian: *Against Marcion*, I, xix.

tianity. It testifies to his profound understanding of Christianity that he was concerned not merely with the confrontation of good and evil, but with a far more subtle antinomy: that of merciful love as against chastising justice. The just man—not the sinful man!—was according to Marcion the true enemy of the Gospel. It is patent that in arriving at this conclusion the great second-century heretic was taking up one of the most significant sayings of Jesus. Christ's invective against the righteous pharisees had been little understood until Marcion grasped its essence.

The average member of the Christian communities appeared to be unaware of the difference between the Old Testament and the Christian concept of God. From this Marcion concluded that a great conspiracy against the truth must have taken place very early in the history of Christianity. Even the twelve Apostles had not understood Jesus correctly, and afterward the Christian fellowships had been infiltrated by those men whom Paul denounced as false apostles and false brethren.[2] These must have falsified the entire Gospel, acting as instruments of the evil powers who were seeking to destroy the revealed truth. According to Marcion, this carefully concealed event was the most fateful in the history of Christianity, for it turned everything into its opposite.

Once he had come to this conclusion, Marcion no longer had a day's peace. Henceforth he regarded it as his great mission to expose this abominable act and to arouse a complacent Christian world.

This idea of conspiracy was Marcion's undoing. It was what made a heretic of him. Of course he did not think of himself as a revolutionary bringing dissension into the Christian fellowship. On the contrary, he felt he understood true Christianity, while the acknowledged Church with its corrupted version of Christianity was an assembly of plotters who employed cunning means to undermine truth.

It was a sweeping accusation, and one which made any devout member of the Church shudder. Yet we cannot dismiss it as

[2] Galatians ii, 4 and II Cor. xi, 13.

the product of pure fantasy. There was an element of truth in Marcion's charge, although the form in which he cast it was untenable. During the second century Christians had in fact made compromises; their Christianity was no longer so radical as it had been. Most Christians failed to notice this deterioration, but Marcion had absorbed the Gospel with such ecstatic intensity that he did. Between the message of Jesus and the official Christianity of the second century a decisive break had occurred, which could perhaps never again be mended. The modern historian speaks of this break as "development"; Marcion called it a conspiracy.

When Marcion had recovered from his initial consternation at the adulteration of the religion, he felt called upon to expose the criminal conspiracy. Unmasking the plotters became the great aim of his life, a task at which he labored with bitter passion.

To weed out the falsifications of the conspirators, he attempted a critical sifting of the Gospels and the Apostolic letters. Thus Marcion was led to subtle textual criticism. The foundation of New Testament textual criticism, without which serious scientific theology is unthinkable nowadays, must therefore be credited to a heretic. And indeed the odor of heresy has clung ever since to textual criticism. According to Tertullian. Marcion was "the first improver" who fancied that he should correct the "corrupted gospel." [3] Irenaeus calls him the first man who made so bold as "to prune" the Holy Scriptures.[4]

Of the four Gospels, Marcion outrightly rejected the Gospel of Matthew with its constant references to the Old Testament; likewise the Gospel of Mark because it preserved too few of the sayings of Jesus. The Gospel of John, with its statement that "salvation comes from the Jews," was also contaminated. He therefore recognized only Luke's Gospel as genuine. But even here he detected traces of the conspirators' activities. He set about the laborious task of excising these falsifications in order to arrive at the original version. A similar process proved necessary with the

---

[3] Tertullian: *Against Marcion*, xiv, iv.
[4] Irenaeus: op. cit., III, xii.

Epistles of Paul, for he saw at a glance that the pastoral letters could not be genuine. The other ten letters likewise required sharp censorship, chiefly deletions; Marcion reduced the Epistle to the Romans by half. This was necessary because he would not put up with any allegorical interpretation.

Marcion completed this laborious textual criticism by drawing up a canon consisting of the Gospel of Luke and the ten "censored" letters of Paul. In making this canon Marcion thus opened the way to the creators of the New Testament. The importance of his effort cannot be overemphasized, for up till then no such collection had ever been made. The basic idea for the eternal Book that has given consolation to innumerable human beings was, thus, first conceived by a heretic!

It is, of course, true that scattered writings had earlier been used in divine services. But Marcion was the first to compile them into a single testament. Replacing rather than merely supplementing the Old Testament by a new one was an act of boldness of which only a heretic would have been capable. The fact is that Marcion's situation forced him to take this course. Since he had been led to reject the Old Testament, he had to provide the Christian community with a new sacred book from which it could derive edification and guidance. The Church could not, of course, adopt Marcion's version as it stood, for it was marked by his obsession. But once he had assembled his testament, the official Church was under a strong compulsion to undertake a collection of its own, one far more inclusive, which it could set alongside of the Old Testament.

Marcion felt, however, that his work on the Bible was only one blow in the battle against the conspirators. He held that the Church no longer understood the fundamental principle of the Gospel, since it merged evangel and the Law into one, instead of cleanly distinguishing the two. Thus it had relapsed into Judaism and was obscuring the light of the stranger God. In order to put a halt to this unfortunate development before it went farther, a different kind of activity was needed, a thoroughgoing—and the word cannot be avoided—reformation. The shipowner from

Sinope appointed himself the first reformer of Christendom, and it is in this light that we must regard his activity. It would be false to present him as the founder of a religion; he never made any such claim. Nor did he assume the authority of a prophet or apostle. His sole mission, as he saw it, was to expose the conspiracy and recall Christianity to the true gospel of the stranger God.

Marcion did not succeed in putting his views across. The resistance was too great. Like most such efforts to renew the spirit of Christianity, Marcion's reform also failed of its purpose. Instead of the hoped-for transformation within the Church there took place a regrettable separation from the Church. Although Marcion repeatedly cited Luke's words regarding the "good and the bad trees,"[5] and constantly warned against pouring "new wine into old wineskins,"[6] his preachings had little effect. Instead, his doctrine aroused fierce disputes within the Roman community. The upshot was that he was expelled from the fellowship in the summer of 144. The money he had presented to the community was returned; all ties with him were cut, and Marcion was driven out as a heretic. Such was the disastrous end of his efforts to recall the Church to the original Gospel. The expulsion "was an impressive proceeding, probably the first of its kind in Rome. It will remain forever memorable that at the first Roman synod of which we have any knowledge a man stood before the presbyters trying to elucidate the difference between the Law and the Evangel, and declaring that their Christianity was Judaistic."[7]

After his expulsion, Marcion set about founding a new church. Although by this time already of advanced age, he promptly began organizing and propagandizing. The new church's profession of faith was contained in Marcion's *Antitheses*, a work which has unfortunately been lost and which can no longer be reconstructed from the few preserved fragments.

---

[5] Luke vi, 43.
[6] Luke v, 37.
[7] Harnack: *Marcion*, pp. 24, 25.

Valentinus, a Gnostic who was at Rome at about the same time as Marcion (middle of the second century), had founded a Gnostic school; now Marcion deliberately set up a heretical church as a rival to the official one. It became clear even to his opponents that Marcion represented not merely a group, but a firmly established church. Naturally enough, this rival enterprise evoked the wrath of the official representatives of the Church, and they rained down slanders upon Marcion. According to Justin, by about the year 150 Marcion's doctrine had already spread among the entire human race, and according to Tertullian Marcion's heretical seed had sprouted all over the world. In the following period Marcionite churches were erected everywhere, in city and country. The services were distinguished by simplicity and steered away from all mystifications. Hierarchy was unknown; laymen could function as priests, and even women could administer baptism.

The Marcionite church differed widely from the Church in its morality, in a way which testifies to the ethical earnestness of the founder. Perhaps not many of the faithful could muster up the fortitude for its rigorous asceticism. Fast regulations forbade members of the church meat and wine. It was required of all believers that they be prepared for martyrdom, and indeed we read frequently of Marcionite martyrs. Sexuality was absolutely banned. Marcion forbade his believers to marry, and those who were already married had to pledge themselves to strictest continence in their marriages. Since Marcion aimed at radical abolition of all sensuality, he baptized only the unmarried, or those married persons who were living apart. Once Christians had become sons of the Highest, all physical sonship had to cease. Marcion's whole ethical system represented a fantastic repudiation of materiality. Given such anti-erotic principles, Marcion's church was in the long run at a disadvantage as against the official Church. Nevertheless, it held its own into the sixth century.

Anyone with a degree of open-mindedness must see the tremendous divine drama contained in Marcion's message. His image of God is formed by Christ, and is anything but a God who operates from without. In Marcion's picture of God, there is a struggle within the Deity: the tendencies of power and of love clash harshly, almost destroying the whole idea of God by the force of their impact. The arch-heretic of the primitive Church was thus caught up in a divine maelstrom that threatened to destroy him. Only profoundly religious men are so possessed by the question of the divine nature that everything else seems unreal to them. Anyone approaching Marcion after having read the early Christian apologists might well say: *Here at last is someone who understood how absolutely new the message of Christianity is—someone at last who saw where, in the final analysis, the new element lay. . . . More than any other of the theologians of the second century Marcion understood that love must be regarded as central to Christianity. He proclaimed forcefully that God is love and nothing but love. . . . He saw clearly that the Christian community in God is by its innermost nature not a community of law but a community of love.*[8]

Marcion had come to this evangelical understanding of Christianity because of his closeness to Paul. Marcion's contemporaries, like Justin Martyr and the Shepherd of Hermas, had scarcely been touched by the real spirit of Paul. It often seems as if second-century Christianity had ceased to understand its greatest Apostle and was in danger of forgetting him. Marcion, on the other hand, seems to have been deeply impressed by Paul, and to have drawn conclusions from this encounter with the man who said to King Agrippa: "I was not disobedient to the heavenly vision."[9] In Marcion, too, we can feel something of the heavenly vision that had overwhelmed Paul. He struggled with the spirit of Paul as did few Christians of the primitive Church. Nevertheless, there is Overbeck's comment: "No one ever understood Paul, and the only one who did understand him, Marcion, misunderstood him."[1] This remark is no mere bon mot. Rather, it sums up the situation perfectly. We need only add that since Marcion further progress has been made in the misunderstanding of Paul!

[8] A. Nygren: *Eros und Agape* (1937), II, 124, 125.
[9] Acts xxvi, 19.
[1] Overbeck: *Christentum und Kultur* (1919), p. 218.

As an ultra-Paulist Marcion truly enunciated an unweakened Gospel. He understood faith as an inner transformation. Like the Apostle to the pagans he illuminated the stringency and unconditional character of the New Testament's tidings. But his was a rigid Paulinism, unleavened by dialectics, tending toward a one-sided consistency and therefore terminating in a blind alley. Probably Paul would have gestured despairingly at this continuator and violator of his doctrines, and would have said: Far be it from me! Marcion, however, did show that Paul was far subtler than modern men are inclined to think. Fichte, Lagarde, and Nietzsche, in their distaste for the Apostle, have led many to ignore the brilliant rays of evangelical light underlying Paul's rabbinical formulas. Yet the modern religious thinker should hearken to Albert Schweitzer's excellent summation; Schweitzer has called this Apostle "the patron saint of thought in Christianity."[2] Thanks to his reversion to Paul's interpretation of the Gospel, Marcion was immensely far ahead of his theological adversaries. He had penetrated to religious depths unknown to them.

Nevertheless, the power of Marcion's tidings of the stranger God is greatly reduced by his hostility to the Old Testament. This rejection of the Old Testament must not be equated with modern, racist anti-Semitism. If Marcion had been racist, he would not have been able to assign so important a place to the Christian Jew Paul. Marcion's antipathy was a religiously based anti-Judaism. The early Christians' appeal to the authority of the Old Testament was not a matter of Jewish eggshells still clinging to newly hatched Christianity. The Old Testament contains a revelation of God of timeless validity. Undeniably, there are also elements of questionable religious content in the Old Testament canon. But that simply means that we must differentiate among the various components of the Old Testament. It must not be taken as an indivisible whole—and strangely enough, this is an idea that has not penetrated deeply enough into the consciousness of religious men. But to abandon the Old Testament entirely would be to cut off the roots of Christianity. Marcion's diatribes

[2] Albert Schweitzer: *Die Mystik des Apostels Paulus* (1930), p. 366.

against the Old Testament produced an intellectual cleavage; what belonged together was wrongly separated. Whatever may be said about Jahve, even the most unbiased and critical of Church historians has stated: "The God of Christianity is the God of the Old Testament." [3]

The Fathers of the Church likewise had right on their side when they opposed Marcion's libeling of the world. Marcion's references to the terrible cruelty of nature contain an element of truth. But he overlooked the fact that this is only one aspect of nature; there is also another side. He also did not consider that creation cannot be judged by purely human categories. Tertullian hit the mark when he commented in his *Against Marcion:* "A single flower, I mean only a wildflower, not even a cultivated one, should have taught him otherwise." [4] Clement of Alexandria likewise found this devaluation of nature incomprehensible. Did not Marcion, like any other man, "make use of created foods and breathe the air of the Creator of the world"? [5] Yet this fierce adversary of the Creator did not see the flowering countryside, nor the work of art that is a bird's nest. He shut his eyes to the glorious world of God which the Christian regards with religious reverence. Instead, he whipped himself up into a blind hatred for the universe, and reserved a special brand of crude vituperation for the mystery of connubial relations. Marcion contributed greatly to that unfortunate movement within Christianity which set Christians at odds with divinely created nature, of which the realm of Eros is a part.

The most unacceptable aspect of Marcion's ideas was his metaphysical dualism. The attempt to reconcile negation with God is in itself a questionable enterprise which calls for utmost caution. But instead of bowing to the ultimate perplexity that attaches to this problem, Marcion was unable to brook such religious resignation and attempted to solve the quandary by his doctrine of two gods. Tertullian's sarcastic polemic against Marcion

[3] Overbeck: *Christentum und Kultur,* p. 266.
[4] Tertullian: *Against Marcion,* I, xiii and xiv.
[5] Clemens Alexandrinus: op. cit., Book III.

is directed chiefly against this disguised polytheism, which indeed casts doubt upon Marcion's Christianity. This dualism, an outgrowth of the excessively rigid consistency of his thinking, gravely lessens the value of Marcion's magnificent concept of the stranger God. For polytheism contradicts the essential nature of God.

In making this criticism, are we passing a final verdict upon this arch-heretic and dismissing him? Not at all. But his case brings out the necessity for discrimination in our estimates of heretics. Since truth and error are mingled in their thinking, we must be prepared to affirm and to deny them. Marcion was a profoundly religious soul who saw everything under the aspect of religion. His opponents would have it that he was not sincere, and in this they were profoundly unjust to him. If we take a closer look at this man, we cannot help feeling his inner force, and we see why he wielded such power over his followers. In their pictures they showed him sitting at the left hand of Christ, while the place on the right was reserved for Paul. They reckoned their calendar from the day that Marcion had broken with the Church.

In the judgment of an objective historian, it is "patent that his interpretation of Christianity is one of the most remarkable and original in the whole history of Christian thought." [6] In religious vigor he may well be compared with Origen and Augustine. Moreover, Catholicism owes much to Marcion in that it was built up in conscious opposition to him. It likewise took over some fundamental ideas from him. "There is a greater difference between Christianity before and after Marcion than between the Occidental Church before the Reformation and after the Reformation." [7] Marcion became a heretic out of religious conviction, not, as the Church Fathers claimed, out of malignancy. We shall observe the same process taking place again and again in the history of heresy.

[6] G. Aulén: *Das Christliche Gottesbild* (1930), p. 60.
[7] Harnack: *Marcion*, p. 247.

+ +

4

The First Fighter Against Heresy

+ +

Irenaeus

The heresy of the second century can be compared with a raging
mountain stream. It swelled like a torrent and threatened to carry
away everything in its path. The Church could not stand idly by,
watching this terrifying process. It was imperative for it to oppose
heresy, to check the onslaught. The men who undertook this task
are called the heresiologists. By no means intolerant fanatics,
these men are as important to the history of heresy as they are to
Christian thought, for they show the phenomenon of heresy from
its reverse side.

The most important heresiologist of the Early Church was

Irenaeus, Bishop of Lyon. He was born in Asia Minor about A.D. 140. As a boy he had known Polycarp of Smyrna, the disciple of John, and had listened raptly to the former's tales of the post-apostolic age. Thus a last dim ray of that fading era fell directly upon him. Although Irenaeus stands at a distinct distance from primitive Christianity, remnants of the archaic period can still be observed in his work. He possessed considerable general learning; his culture was not confined within the boundaries of Christianity. Thus he knew Homer and Plato, Hesiod and Pindar, although he had no strong attachment to Greek philosophy.

From Asia Minor he removed to eastern Gaul, where he became a presbyter and, with his congregation, bore the brunt of the severe persecutions of Christians in Lugdunum (Lyon) and Vienne. His noble behavior during the crises won him, after the death of Bishop Pothimus, election as the bishop's successor. In the dispute over the date of the paschal fast, which developed between the Roman and the Asiatic churches, Irenaeus did not simply side with the Bishop of Rome. He took an independent and mediating position. According to a legend which, however, arose much later, he is supposed to have found death as a martyr during the persecutions under Severus in the year 202.

Irenaeus was a likable person, although compared with his contemporaries, Tertullian and Clement of Alexandria, he can scarcely be called the greatest theologian of his age. His strength lay in his moderation. All excess and fantasy were alien to his practical disposition. Sobriety was the foremost characteristic of this righteous man, though it did not keep him from believing fervently in chiliasm (the doctrine that Christ will reign for a thousand years on earth). "Like Polycarp, Irenaeus was a peace-loving soul who was most disinclined to cause division for the sake of minor differences." [1] With his conciliatory temperament, he tried to compromise interchurch disputes, as indeed a priest should. There was nothing of the gloomy fanatic about him; he was no bloodthirsty battler of heresy who took joy in the annihilation of heretics.

[1] H. Ziegler: *Irenäus, Der Bischof von Lyon* (1871), p. 20.

The Bishop of Lyon wrote a book, *Against Heresies,* for which he is remembered to this day. For the period it was a great achievement, although it was by no means a coherent piece of work. Written around A.D. 190, the work has come down to us only in a Latin translation of the third century. Reading it, we may well believe the author's apology that he was "unaccustomed to writing." In spite of its faults, however, it is an interesting work, one which we will not be likely to lay aside in boredom. It is the oldest heresiological work that has been preserved, and contains a mine of material for the historian of heresy. The first part presents the heretical doctrines, which are then refuted in a second part. "But in order to convert them we must know their dogmas or tenets precisely, for it is impossible to heal a sick man if we do not understand his condition," was Irenaeus' principle.[2] Many of the statements of the heretics have been preserved for posterity only in the summaries given by Irenaeus. For example, our knowledge of Gnostic doctrines derives mostly from his book.

Irenaeus' work might be called a plan of campaign directed against the rising tide of heresy. The book cannot be evaluated merely as historical writing. For Irenaeus neither wrote it *sine ira et studio,* nor was he intending a scholarly investigation of his subject. It is distinctly polemic—and what an irony of history it is that so mild and balanced a man as Irenaeus should have been the one to usher in the polemical era of Church history.

Irenaeus made his intention plain in his foreword: he would write an "unmasking and refutation" of the heretical doctrines.[3] His idea was to confront all the internal enemies of the Church. "We want not only to show the beast but to wound it from all sides," he declared.[4] And he picked no small enemy, for he had the insight to recognize Gnosticism as the major intellectual movement of his time. Its colorful and melancholy mythology represented the gravest challenge to the official Church, for it shook all the historical foundations of Christianity and made short

[2] Irenaeus: op. cit., IV, Preface.
[3] Ibid., II, Preface.
[4] Ibid., I, xxxi.

work of the specific doctrines. Irenaeus regarded Gnosticism as a terrible snare; he literally implored his readers to beware of the Gnostics. Even where their "speech is similar to that of the believers, they mean dissimilar, nay, contrary things." [5] The Gnostic distinction between psychics and pneumatics represented, he held, a fearful pitfall. He warned his readers not to stumble into it. It was incumbent upon him, he felt, to expose all the cunning devices of the Gnostics.

Irenaeus' great disputation has rightly been called a struggle between myth and the Word of God. Compromiser though he was, the Bishop of Lyon never sought to weld these two by some supposed synthesis. In his struggle against heresy he recognized no compromises. Yet he did not forget the heretics as human beings, and expressly included them in his prayers: *We, however, pray that they may not linger in the pit which they have dug for themselves . . . but may abjure the doctrine and leave the shadow, so that they may be reborn while there is yet time and may be converted to the church of God. This we implore for them, and love them with greater profit to them than they believe they love themselves. . . . Therefore we will try not to falter, but will hold out our hand to them with all our strength.* [6]

It would be unjust to the Bishop of Lyon to call this statement hypocritical, for he undoubtedly meant it with all his heart. In his prayers for the heretics, he hoped to mobilize the heavenly powers for the struggle to overcome heresy.

Nevertheless Irenaeus' feelings against the Gnostic heretics were often too strong for him. He called them "bad interpreters of the good words of Scripture," [7] and ridiculed their arguments as "hollow fantasies" and "old wives' tales." [8] He spoke of the "cunning of their conduct and the malice of their error," and charged them with "obvious falsifications" in their interpretations of Scrip-

[5] Ibid., III, xvii.
[6] Ibid., III, xxv.
[7] Ibid., I, iii.
[8] Ibid., I, iv and viii.

ture." [9] He compared the heretics with "serpents who seek to twist away in all directions." [1] He also sought to discredit them morally, accusing them of licentious excesses: "Not to all, but to many this Marcion has given love-potions and magic draughts in order to involve their bodies also in shame; these people admitted it after they had been converted once more to the Church of God; they said their bodies had been misused by him and that they had loved him in abominable sensuality." [2] The heretics, Irenaeus flatly declared, were resisting their salvation from sheer obstinacy. Then again he tried to make the heretics ridiculous, mocking the way they "curl their eyebrows, shake their heads and declare that this passage in Scripture has a very profound meaning and that not everyone could understand its profundity, therefore silence is highly important to the wise." [3]

But whether he prayed for his enemies or made them the butt of his anger, Irenaeus always proved to be a skilled and keen thinker. Through his polemics he delivered more rigorous blows against the Gnostic heretics than Plotinus was able to do from the point of view of Neo-Platonism. Irenaeus did his best to keep the discussion centered upon the major questions; he never bogged down amongst inessential marginal comments. Moreover, he was clever at picking out the weak spots in Gnosticism; he hammered away powerfully at these spots. From the standpoint of the Church, the great flaw in the Gnostic system was the Gnostic concept of God. In view of the nature of this world, there is much to be said for the doctrine of the Demiurge. Suppose, in the end, it is right? Yet to distinguish between God and the Creator of the world leads inevitably to polytheism. And Irenaeus was a convinced champion of monotheism. In his refutation of the heretics he returned again and again to this question of the One God, laying the greatest stress upon it. The Gnostic heretics, he said, had been guilty of a caricature of the Christian view of God. According to Irenaeus, they were committing a horrible blasphemy.

[9] Ibid., I, ix.
[1] Ibid., III, ii.
[2] Ibid., I, xiii.
[3] Ibid., IV, xxxv.

Contrary to what they claimed, the same God spoke in the Old Testament and the New. He quoted the bold statement by Justin: "I would not believe even the Lord Himself if he had proclaimed any other God than the Creator." [4]

Irenaeus exposed the overt or covert anthropomorphism of the Gnostic ideas. He was able to do this only because he himself was sustained by a profound consciousness of God's existence. He was not merely repeating theories he had heard from others. Had that been so, he could not have set forth so succinctly the fundamental principle of all religious insight: "Without God it is impossible to know God." [5] He admonished his fellows to consider, in thinking about God, the limits of all human knowledge: "Out of his own nature man does not see God." [6] The Creator is incomprehensible, he said, and cannot be reached by reason alone. As the Logos he is, to be sure, reason, but unlike human reason. All conceptions of him are inadequate. "In his greatness, therefore, we cannot know God, for it is impossible to measure the Father. In his love, however, which leads us to God through the Word, we shall, if we obey him, understand better and better that God is so great and has decided, chosen and adorned everything by himself." [7]

Having reached this insight, Irenaeus could well feel that he had won the first round. A triumphant note enters into his writing. But one battle was not enough; he attacked the enemy from all sides, determined to unseat him. The Docetism of the Gnostic heretics offered Irenaeus an equally vulnerable point. The idea that Christ's appearance had been in a phantom body was shared by almost all the Gnostic thinkers, for it was indissolubly connected with their condemnation of matter as evil. Irenaeus contended that this view attacked the very root of Christianity. If Jesus had suffered and died only in appearance, and if in reality Simon of Cyrene had been crucified in his place, then the whole redemption of man had taken place only in appearance.

[4] Ibid., IV, vi.
[5] Ibid.
[6] Ibid., IV, xx.
[7] Ibid.

In making the point that Docetism invalidated the reality of redemption, Irenaeus once more smashed victoriously through the Gnostic line and administered a serious blow to his opponents. He followed through in order to demonstrate the untenability of the whole Gnostic rejection of matter. Matter, he held, was not something bad to be shunned, but a creation of God which had its own purposes. "The perfect man," he said, "is the intimate union of the soul, which receives the spirit of the Father, with the flesh, which is created in the image of God." [8]

A curious reversal of fronts comes to light in the course of this argument. In modern times Christianity has constantly been reproached for unnatural hostility to the body and excessive concentration upon the hereafter. Yet in the second century, as we see, official Christianity entered the lists as the conscious defender of the body against the Gnostic antimaterialists. Clement of Alexandria, too, had strongly defended marriage, and as against the Gnostics, Irenaeus may be termed the successful advocate of the physical world. This defense of the body against the Docetist doctrine of "appearances" deserves the highest praise, and should instruct us not to fall into the reverse of the common error and seek right always on the side of the heretics.

In his incessant struggle against heresy Irenaeus remembered that an opponent cannot be defeated by a merely negative argument. Refutation alone convinces nobody. A superior truth must be offered in place of mere rejection. Thus his opposition to the Gnostics spurred Irenaeus into formulating his own doctrines. He did so with remarkable success. Irenaeus' theology was by no means fragmentary in character; it was organized around a central religious idea.

"His fundamental idea is that of the union of all things in Christ, which springs from Ephesians 1, 10. But he frames it rather in the manner of John the Evangelist; what leads to perfection is an all-comprehending recapitulation." [9] To the arguments of the heretics he opposed his Christology: a remarkable doctrine

[8] Ibid., V, vi.
[9] N. Bonvetsch: *Die Theologie des Irenäus* (1925), p. 98.

of recapitulation which sets a unique significance upon the person of Jesus. The curious idea of recapitulation expresses Irenaeus' own personal view, which was later taken up and formulated most pregnantly by Athanasius. Christ, as Irenaeus put it, "recapitulated everything in himself." [1] Christ, that is, "comprehended within himself the long evolution of man in that he became man by incarnation and in this condensation gave us salvation, so that in Christ we might regain again our likeness to God, which we had lost in Adam." [2] In other words, Irenaeus says, Christ became like us in order that we might become like him. Thus he viewed the historical process as a story of salvation.

Irenaeus supported his key concept—that God became man in order for us to become divine—in a twofold manner. He countered Gnosticism's speculative religious philosophy with the Word of God as it is found in Scripture—the Old as well as the New Testament. Thus he set up a firm standard by which men could think and live. The Bible was the sword of the Spirit to Irenaeus; he used it constantly in his struggle. Of course it was an ambiguous weapon, since the heretics likewise appealed to Scripture. But they did violence to the Bible, Irenaeus contended, with their audacious allegorical interpretations. By such methods they could prove anything imaginable. He was outraged by the arbitrariness of allegory, and returned to the subject again and again.

Ironically, Irenaeus himself was guilty of the very fault for which he castigated the heretics. He too employed Scripture allegorically in that he conceived the Old Testament typologically. By this method he found in it everything he needed for his purposes. Indeed, every approach which sets out to find a particular doctrine in Scripture consciously or unconsciously depends upon reading allegories into Scripture. In this respect Irenaeus stood upon the same plane as the heretics he hated, although he would not admit it to himself. Nevertheless, Irenaeus was a far more vigorous Biblical theologian than the Gnostics. A mystical ferment was at work in his Biblicism. His doctrine of the divine Word was

[1] Irenaeus: op. cit., IV, xxxviii.
[2] Ibid., III, xiii.

impregnated with the spirit of John the Evangelist: "Thus the Word of God, which dwelt in man, made man capable of understanding the Father, and became the Son of Man so that man would accustom himself to receive God and God would accustom himself to dwell in man after the wish and will of the Father." [3]

Irenaeus supplemented his appeal to Scripture with his reliance on tradition. The Bishop of Lyon was the first great theologian of tradition in the history of Christianity. He first insisted upon the immense value of tradition, without which there can be no religious continuity. In asserting the validity of tradition, he was in direct opposition to Marcion's doctrine of the stranger God who suddenly descends upon man without previous warning. The idea of religious tradition can be carried to excess—as for example when Leopold Ziegler declares that a kernel of revelation underlies every tradition—but if taken reasonably, there is great validity in the concept that due respect must be paid to tradition. Modern man with his conscious or unconscious principle of revolution all too often lacks that respect.

Yet even this second pillar of his system was not as firm as Irenaeus had hoped. For the Gnostics likewise could appeal to tradition, the secret tradition which, they maintained, Jesus had communicated only to a few. This postulate of a secret tradition allowed the Gnostics to make a good many assertions which could not easily be refuted. Irenaeus consciously opposed to them the traditions of the Church, which were subject to confirmation. To his love of tradition we owe the famous list of the Bishops of Rome which is found in his book, and the argument that these bishops were the rightful guardians of the true ecclesiastical tradition.

Irenaeus' emphasis upon a fixed ecclesiastical tradition marked a turning point in the history of the Church. Thenceforth the enthusiasm of the primitive Church faded. Doctrinal tradition became more and more important; in cases of doubt it was consulted for decision, and it became the regulatory principle of the Christian path to salvation.

[3] Ibid., III, xx.

Through his concern for Scripture and tradition, Irenaeus became the typical ecclesiastical theologian and the first to devote
consistent thought to the nature of the Church itself. He saw the
Church as the preacher of truth. "The preaching of the Church is
invariable and constant." [4] It is impermissible "for petty and insignificant reasons to cut the great and glorious Body of Christ
into pieces." [5] The doctrines of the Gnostic heretics were so subjective that no two or three of them would have the same answers
to any given religious question. The Church, on the other hand,
had a universal answer binding upon all. To live outside the
Church, Irenaeus maintained, was to put oneself outside the pale
of truth. To see at what point the Church took on an important
role within the history of Christian thought, we must study Irenaeus. He was one of the major proponents of churchliness in
primitive Christianity, and he deliberately extended the claims
for the Church. Only the rock of the Church, he held, could act as
an adequate breakwater to the ruthless tides of heresy. Again and
again Irenaeus extolled the unity and universality of the Church.
So early, then, the Bishop of Lyon set down the basic principles
of what was later to be the Catholic Church.

In keeping with this belief in the function of the Church, Irenaeus became one of the first theologians of authority, thus opening a path which was later trodden by almost all churchmen. But
this first appearance of ecclesiasticism must not be admired uncritically. We also have to ask: What was lost as a result? Was
Irenaeus' ecclesiasticism pure gain? Was his conception of the
Church purely religious, or did it not have certain political overtones? [6] One statement of his is highly significant. "Every church
must agree with the Roman Church because of its special precedence," he wrote bluntly.[7] Almost every ecclesiastical theology
came to this conclusion, insofar as it was thought through consistently—which was not always the case, to be sure.

[4] Ibid., III, xxiv.
[5] Ibid., IV, xxxiii.
[6] Cf. Wolfgang Schmitt: *Die Kirche bei Irenäus* (1934), p. 109.
[7] Irenaeus: op. cit., III, iii.

Thus the stalwart fighter against heresy made the salvation of man dependent upon acceptance of a specific dogma of the Church. The mistake, here, was to overestimate the intellectual element in religion. Since he put great stress upon the authority of tradition, he introduced an external principle into Christianity. In place of freely operating grace, a universal regulation was substituted. In spite of his chiliasm, Irenaeus imperceptibly put aside the primitive Christian expectation of the coming of the Kingdom. He substituted the ideal of the spreading of the Church: a process fraught with enormous consequences.

In all studies devoted to the Bishop of Lyon, Irenaeus is regarded exclusively from the Church's point of view. Hence it is only fair to turn the matter around for once, and to consider Irenaeus as the heretics might have seen him. From the point of view of a historian of heresy there are a number of questions which cannot be evaded.

One significant question concerns Irenaeus' sources, for on these his reliability rests. Who were his informants? Had he personally known any of the Gnostics? Irenaeus claims that he had "many conversations" with the heretics.[8] But this statement is open to doubt, for he lived far from the centers of such religious movements. On the whole it must be concluded that he depended upon mere hearsay, and was only too willing to believe evil gossip. According to his own testimony, he also went to the trouble of collecting the writings of the heretics.[9] But this could have been true only to a limited extent. In all probability he had at his disposal no significant original writings, for what he cited are only untrustworthy fragments which had been passed on in the Church without examination from generation to generation. In any case Irenaeus was not the man to know how to sift texts critically, just as he did not distinguish, in connection with the Gnostic systems, between original doctrines and later modifications. It is generally assumed that he utilized the now lost work of Justin against the heretics, and that this anti-Gnostic work pro-

[8] Ibid., II, xvii.
[9] Ibid., I, xxxi.

83

vided him with his major source of materials.[1] There can be no doubt that Irenaeus' sources were not of the best. In this respect his writings do not deserve the reputation for authority which has so readily been given them for centuries.

Even more crucial is the question: Did Irenaeus understand the heretics? Had he been just to their efforts? Was he right in holding that the essence of heresy was blasphemy? The answer must be no. We need only consider Irenaeus' foreword to his first book, in which he writes: "For all these reasons I considered it requisite to reveal their wonderful and profound mysteries, which cannot be grasped by all people since all people have not yet gone out of their minds." [2] That is, the Bishop of Lyon is saying that the Gnostic writings make no sense except to those who have lost their reason. Irenaeus disregards the New Testament phrase concerning "folly in Christ"; obviously he does not consider himself a person without reason, and this one sentence is an inadvertent confession that he is writing on a subject which exceeds his grasp.

His discussions of the heretics are accordingly unfair. He does not reproduce the Gnostic line of argument, but is always taking sentences out of context. For that reason his account often sounds like a caricature, and he regards the magnificent Gnostic systems only as "products of fantasy" full of "high-sounding phrases." [3] He breaks into mocking laughter at the persons who "give credence to these gray myths." [4] All his expositions are made with the aim of unmasking and refuting dangerous heresies. Since he made no effort to understand his opponents, he never asked himself: Are not the Gnostics for once right in regard to this and this point? Did not they recognize at least part of the truth? What can we learn from them? How did the Gnostics arrive at their ideas? Is everything in their doctrine wholly alien to Christianity, or are they not sometimes striving toward the same goals?

[1] Cf. R. A. Lipsius: *Die Quellen der ältesten Ketzergeschichte* (1875), p. 63.
[2] Irenaeus: op. cit., I, Preface.
[3] Ibid., I, i and iv.
[4] Ibid., I, xvi.

All such questions were far from Irenaeus' mind. It did not occur to him that the Gnostic speculations could possibly mean anything different from what he assumed they meant. The Bishop of Lyon was unfortunately not one of those rare persons who tries seriously to understand alien ideas. He never considered the possibility that metaphysical questions can be answered in different ways. He had not the remotest conception of the needs from which the Gnostic systems had sprung. In his militant opposition to Gnostic dualism he failed to observe that the Gnostics, too, were striving to bridge the gap between God and the world as men know it. He himself saw no need for the philosophical labors of the Gnostics. As far as he was concerned the matter was finished as soon as he had demonstrated Gnostic dependency upon Greek philosophy. Scathingly, he wrote: "They even collect the utterances of the philosophers who know not God." [5] He took it for granted that philosophers had missed the road to truth.

Irenaeus not only lacked the slightest understanding of Gnosticism, such as Clement of Alexandria and Origen had indeed had, but he also knew nothing about Christian Gnosticism. For that reason a number of the profounder questions are not even mentioned in Irenaeus' work. He regards it almost as *hubris* to discuss metaphysical questions. *Irenaeus attacks the weak sides of Gnosticism accurately and with good arguments, but he does not understand the connection of the whole movement with the strivings of the age or with the movements within the Christian church itself. He fights against symptoms and leaves the real seat of the evil untouched. He demonstrates the errors in individual doctrines and in the method of proof, but he mistakes the deepest meaning of the whole movement, and hence its justification. He regards heretical Gnosticism as a deadly foe and not as what it in fact was, an outgrowth of a misguided but in itself perfectly justified impulse which was likewise felt in the Catholic world.* [6]

In his struggle against heresy Irenaeus introduced a task

[5] Ibid., II, xiv.
[6] Ziegler: op. cit., p. 86.

which henceforth was to be a permanent concern of the Church. He had many successors, although none of them can be compared with him in originality. Hippolytus (first half of the third century) wrote a *Refutation of All Heresies,* a work that was only rediscovered in 1842 in a monastery on Mount Athos. Hippolytus, too, proved to be a vigorous and sharp-tongued fighter against the heretics. Since he traced all heresies to origins in Greek philosophy, his work has a remarkable coherency and consistency.[7] Epiphanius (c. 315–403), too, participated in the battle against heresy with his *Panarion* ("Medicine Chest"). According to his own account, in his youth a Gnostic sect attempted to win him over with sensual seductions. This equivocal contact with the Gnostics made his reporting no more reliable, and he seems not to have had the slightest understanding of the Gnostic symbols. He is quite merciless in his treatment of his opponents, and his uncritical book cannot be remotely compared in quality to that of Irenaeus, whom, incidentally, he pillaged along with Justin and Hippolytus.

The fierce campaign that the Church Fathers waged against the hydra of heresy had a dual outcome.

In its struggle with this internal enemy, the Church certainly accomplished one thing: the almost complete liquidation of the heretical literature of the early centuries of Christianity. The writings of the heretics were systematically and ruthlessly destroyed. For this reason it is difficult today to form an accurate picture of the early Christian heretics. The documents are missing; we have nothing to go by but the inadequate and unreliable accounts of the enemies of heresy. What we have are only occasional quotations which the heresiologists were obliged to cite in order to refute them. For the rest, nothing but fragments are left. The contemporary historian stands before a heap of rubble.

Nevertheless, the heresiologists did not succeed in overcoming heresy. Hippolytus was right when he compared heresy to the legendary hydra. As soon as one head was cut off, a new one grew in its place. For all the fierce assaults, for all the fair and foul

[7] Hippolytus: op. cit., I, xxvi and V, vi.

means used against it, the monster of heresy remained invincible. It arose in another form, ready to renew the battle. All efforts were in vain because the Church had set itself an impossible goal. Christianity cannot exist without heresy because a variety of possible interpretations are inherent in the nature of the religion. Heresy remained undefeated, and will remain undefeatable in all time to come.

5

The Tragedy of the Apostate

+ +

Emperor Julian

The Church divides heretics into three groups: apostates, schismatics, and teachers of heterodoxy. Whether these categories cover all the nuances of heresy is open to question. But for convenience we may tentatively accept the classification, so long as we keep in mind that behind the categories lie the destinies of human beings who once staked everything on their religious convictions.

From olden times those who fell away from the Church were regarded as persons who had committed a breach of faith. The apostates were always persecuted, within the Christian community, with the most savage hatred. A renegade was never conceded legitimate motives; his wickedness could only be explained as godlessness. In the minds of the representatives of the Church, a man who had fallen away from the revealed truth necessarily exposed himself to the wrath of God, and this wrath would be sure to descend upon him, even if only at the end of his life. It followed that every apostate must meet a painful death as the due punishment for treachery.

But if we see what was really involved in apostasy, we see that it was a positive stand rather than a negative one. The so-called apostate was not a traitor to his old faith so much as he was the convert of a new one. In most conversions a large number of imponderables are operative, many of which can scarcely be named. Complex and painful family relationships and joyful affinities to new friends often exercise a considerable influence. The break with a religious community is seldom undertaken frivolously. There is nothing superficial about it, as there is in the case of men who subside into religious indifference—which has nothing to do with conversion. Apostasy, however, is usually the outcome of a spiritual development extending over a considerable time, something that shakes the personality to its depths. First the apostate is overcome by the dreadful thought that he may be on the wrong path. It is like feeling ice giving way underfoot. A religious struggle rages in the soul of such a man. He is forced to ask himself again and again: Shall I take the step from this religious community to that other one? Is such a parting in keeping with truth?

The struggle may go on for many months of sleepless nights and torment-ridden days. But a psychic compulsion drives the individual in one particular direction. He undergoes a religious drama within his soul of which outsiders have scarcely any conception. All the while he knows that the act he is contemplating, though it may mean the attainment of new light for him, will be felt as shameful defection by the community he abandons. Consequently, apostasies are always accompanied by unfortunate side effects; loving relationships invariably change to hatreds. Yet apostasy is a fate which descends upon some persons for inexplicable reasons, just as others are inexplicably spared the ordeal.

The most vivid historical example of apostasy, and of the tragedy connected with it, is to be found in the life of Emperor Julian, who has gone down in history as "the Apostate." We are fortunate in possessing considerable source material on Julian's defection, so that we can form a good picture of the spiritual process as it took place in his case. Julian, in fact, is one of those personages of late antiquity whose very appearance has come down to posterity. Gregory of Nazianzus, who met Julian in Athens in the latter's younger years, stressed his "abnormal conduct," his "twitching shoulders, restless eyes, excited glance, nervous gait, and faltering speech." [1] But this is actually a malicious caricature. Julian had one of those attractive sensitive faces which are often seen in the aristocratic classes of an overripe culture. He was of medium height, well proportioned, with expressive eyes in which the fire of enthusiasm glowed frequently. His conduct was of a friendly simplicity that won him much sympathy, so that he enjoyed great popularity among the soldiers. His friends were deeply attached to him, for Julian was a person who could give love and arouse it.

Julian was brought up as a Christian. His mother died shortly after his birth. When Julian was six (A.D. 337), there took place on the orders of Constantius II a bloody palace slaughter, such as occurred more than once at Byzantine courts. Julian's father, eldest brother, uncle, and several cousins were among the victims of the massacre, while he himself was spared because of his age. The recollection of this day, the savage cries of the murderers and the shrieks of the murdered, the sight of his closest relations lying in pools of blood, was stamped forever upon the mind of the frightened child, causing irreparable damage to his psyche. His youth was lived under the fearful shadow of Constantius, although the devastating effects of the trauma were to emerge only much later in his life. It is incomprehensible that his churchly enemies should have obstinately overlooked the in-

[1] Gregory of Nazianzus: *Second Invective against Julian,* chap. xiii.

credible crime that had been committed against Julian by an emperor who called himself Christian. Not a single bishop uttered a word of protest or a call to repentance for this hideous butchery.

As an unwanted relation, Julian was kept far from the court and raised in the mountainous district of Cappadocia in "glittering slavery." During this period he was tutored in the Christian religion. After he had received baptism, he was required to attend Christian worship. "Julian passed clear-eyed through his Christian phase, and realized with remarkable perspicacity what means were at that time most effective in spreading the new doctrine."[2] He even received consecration as a member of the lower clergy, and participated in the activities of the Christian community, serving as a lector.

Julian did not actually suffer under this instruction, although it was of an authoritarian cast and the most innocent questions of his speculative mind were rigorously discouraged. Most of all, his Christian tutors had no knack for communicating the religious enthusiasm which might have kindled the young man's soul. In the sober Christian education he received, there was little that was ardent or joyful. Julian encountered not a single Christian of stature who might have made him feel the charismatic forces of the Gospel. Not a single Christian teacher could reveal to him the uniqueness of the person of Jesus.

The second phase of Julian's life was marked by a spiritual influence of the sort he had looked for in vain among the Christians. His tutor Mardonios found it easy to win the future emperor's youthful mind for the intellectual world of the Greeks. The wonderful tales about the gods sounded powerful echoes in Julian's soul. Before long the land of the Greeks filled not only his mind but his heart with longing. For Julian's temperament was that of an enthusiast. The Homeric cosmogony met the needs of his receptive spirit. With a fervor verging on worship, Julian read the classical writers. The happiest period of his life was that spent in his beloved Athens, devoted to his studies, in the immediate vicinity of the ancient sanctuaries. His enthusiasm for Greece

[2] J. Bidez: *Julian der Abtrünnige* (1940), p. 41.

mounted to sheer intoxication. Certainly his passion for the beauties of Hellenism can be called romantic; certainly he saw greater beauty in Hellas than was actually there. The light of transfiguration played over a Greek world that had already vanished.

The genuineness of Julian's romantic attitude is evident in the existential character of his experience with Hellenism. He did not take the view of a modern philologist toward Hellenism, for whom Greece merely provides interesting texts which are grist for his scholarly instincts. Rather, Julian really believed—as did Hölderlin fifteen centuries later (and the belief is crucial)—in the reality of the gods. He did not regard them as poetic fictions. His churchly enemies, in their hatred for him, refused to see that Julian possessed a remarkable capacity for devotion, a piety that would have shamed many a Christian. He himself once confessed: *From my childhood on there lay deep within me an infinite longing for the radiance of the god; from childhood my inner being mounted toward this ethereal light, so that I not only craved to gaze fixedly upon it, but also went out into the cloudless, starry nights, forgetting everything around me and losing myself in the beauties of the heavens. If anyone spoke to me, I did not hear him; if I did anything, I was not aware of it . . .*[3] This is the language of a deeply spiritual temperament.

Upon rising in the morning, Julian said his prayers. To be worthy of the gods, he imposed upon himself an austere, ascetic life. He was one of the chastest of men. His devout Hellenism has been called by Bidez in his fine biography "a kind of pagan Catholicism."[4] Julian wanted to live constantly in the presence of the gods. And when, with ecstatic fervor, he opened his heart to Greek religion, he suddenly felt a call of the gods which transformed faith into vision. Like a flash of lightning he was struck by a ray of illumination which lighted the darkness of his longings. He had been touched by the world soul as it lived and had its being in the magic of the sun's rays.

[3] J. Geffcken: *Kaiser Julian* (1914), p. 7.
[4] Bidez: op. cit., p. 272.

All of Julian's later actions can be explained by this mystic "call." It was, along with the bloody events he had witnessed in childhood, the most important event of his life. As a result of it, he came under the sway of Maximos of Ephesus, who introduced Julian into the mysteries of the Mithras cult. Maximos was primarily a theurgist who believed he could summon the gods by conjuration. He exerted an unfortunate influence in stimulating Julian's interest in divination, so that Julian's religious development degenerated in the direction of superstition. But the decisive experience of the vision remained with Julian: he believed that he had been commanded to return to the old gods. When he raised his hands to the sun god, it was an act of religious obedience to a divine injunction.

Julian's return to the old gods meant, of course, apostasy from Christianity. In entering the Mithras cult, Julian had to abjure the Christ to whom he had once vowed fidelity. But like all converts, he did so with the conviction that he was moving forward toward truth, not falling away from it. Jubilation drowned out all stirrings of conscience. In parting from Christianity, Julian felt not the slightest sorrow. What troubled him was the necessity of concealing his change of religion. For the time being he had to hide his apostasy under a mask of dissimulation. Secretly, he worshipped in his new faith and felt all the zeal and joy of the new convert. Only his closest friends were aware of this fervent love of the old gods.

Julian has been criticized for this dissimulation and accused of insincerity. But such charges are unjust. With his frank nature, it was hard for him to play a double game. But for personal and political reasons he was forced to conceal his defection. The emperor was a Christian, and in any case had little trust in him. Julian would only bring martyrdom upon himself if he admitted his change of faith. We cannot impugn his character because he followed the course of prudence. Julian was no saint; he had his faults and his weaknesses. The young man was not free of vanity, and he was not the brilliant philosopher he thought himself. But he was honest, and his reversion to the gods of Greece was a step undertaken in deadly earnest. He was determined to live a life worthy of their commands. Thus he banished all luxury from his personal life, and would rise soon after midnight in order to devote himself to his studies.

The third phase of Julian's life was marked by his public profession of paganism. In so doing he became the victim of an inner conflict which heightened the tragedy of his life. The abandonment of one religion for another is a step that few people can manage without severe psychic damage. Most converts are overstrained by the effort. To mask their state of exhaustion, they develop the so-called convert mentality, usually an unpleasant one. Since religions cannot be changed like a piece of clothing, unresolved remnants of the old remain attached to the psyche. The renegade seldom frees himself completely of his old beliefs, although he tries to make it seem that he has done so. Often he feels the need to revenge himself for all the years in which, as he now believes, he was being cheated of the truth. He thinks he has a score to settle with his former coreligionists who now revile him as an apostate. Resentments build up. In Julian, too, this disagreeable attitude of the apostate can be observed at work.

Constantius died suddenly, and Julian found himself the rightful successor to the imperial throne. At this point his conversion ceased to be a personal matter, of concern to himself alone. At the same time the reasons that had compelled concealment dropped away. He now made his personal concern an affair of the empire. In his unexpected ascension to the throne, he saw an obvious sign from the gods, which imposed an obligation upon him. This sense of mission grew with each passing day. It seemed to him that the Christian religion had sickened the Roman Empire, and that the sun god alone had the power to restore it to health. With typical convert's zeal, he was sure that the return of the gods was the panacea that would revive the glory of the ancient empire. It was his destiny to restore the gods to the nations that had lost them.

Thus Julian became the first person to strive for a renaissance of paganism—an attempt that was henceforth to be made repeatedly in the course of history. He reopened temples, and such was his zeal that he lent a hand in the actual labor, carrying wood himself, slaughtering the animals, fanning the sacrificial fires. He virtually transformed the imperial palace into a temple in which he felt himself to be primarily high priest and only secondarily emperor. He did everything in his power to bring about restoration of the old religion, and to this end was even prepared to learn from the Christianity he had renounced. *As imperial high priest of a renewed cult, Julian was forever instructing his band of priests to practice the charity and love of neighbor which he himself had learned at the side of his first teachers. In his "encyclicals" he declared that all men are brothers who should love and help one another, that the hungry should be fed, the naked clothed, even though they be enemies, prisoners, or condemned men.*[5] What Julian envisioned was a pagan theocracy under the headship of a priest-king.

But Julian did not content himself with furthering the cause of paganism and assigning a preferential position to his adherents. His original ideal had been one of religious tolerance, but he was not able to hold to this for long. At first, to be sure, he proceeded cautiously. He was determined not to renew the persecutions conducted by the earlier pagan emperors. For he was well aware that these persecutions had strengthened rather than weakened Christianity. He was not going to make the same mistake, and as Gregory of Nazianzus put it, "grant the militants the honor of martyrdom." [6] His approach was more inconspicuous and subtle. His first measure was aimed at cutting Christianity off from the world of culture. Christians were no longer permitted to hold positions as rhetoricians and grammarians. Their sons were excluded from all "instruction in poetry and philosophy." [7] The treasures of Greek thought, Julian contended, should not be available to those who condemned them as a tissue of diabolic inventions.

He also dismissed Christian soldiers from his army. These

---

[5] Ibid., p. 40.
[6] Gregory of Nazianzus: *First Invective against Julian,* chap. lviii.
[7] Theodoret: *Ecclesiastical History,* III, viii.

measures bore down heavily upon cultivated Christians, and were felt by them as bitter insults. Julian also retracted all the privileges which Constantine had showered upon the Church. The Christians found it hard to part with these, for they had already grown accustomed to their worldly goods and high positions. Julian commanded that they return the temples and works of art which they had stolen from paganism—again a grave embarrassment to them. Although he carefully forebore from shedding Christian blood, his cunning policy of humiliation and exclusion had worse effects than direct persecution. His attacks on Christianity by indirection proved far more detrimental to the Christians than open battle would have been.

To undercut the Christian influence still further, Julian used the power of the pen. His pamphlet, *Against the Christians,* which had been lost, was reconstructed from fragments in the last century. In it he represented Christianity as a "deceitful doctrine of the Galileans" and "an invention of man, the product of maliciousness." Paul, he said, had surpassed the "jugglers and charlatans of all places and all times." Julian took issue with the Old Testament concept of a jealous God, and commented on the story of Genesis: "If all these stories are not myths whose core is mystical speculation, then these stories about God are packed, at least in my estimation, with blasphemies." [8] He also critically examined the tradition of the Gospels—incidentally noting thus early the difference between the synoptic Gospels and the Gospel of John. Julian's *Against the Christians* is no masterpiece. It never rises above the level of pamphleteering. Impelled to settle accounts with his earlier religion, the Apostate plunged all too readily into a marsh of petty spitefulness.

Nevertheless, Julian's indirect assaults upon Christianity might have become a serious danger to the Church if they had gone on longer. But Julian was inwardly a far from harmonious personality. In addition to his activities as a religious restorer of the past, he was also anxious to win military laurels. He prepared a campaign against the Persians to recover the provinces that had

[8] Neumann, ed.: *Kaiser Julians Bücher gegen die Christen* (1880), p. 6.

been lost under his predecessors. When he set out with his army, he burned his ships behind him, and soon found himself in so grim a predicament that death came as a relief. Whether Julian invited death by rushing into the midst of a skirmish without his armor, or whether—as the pagans maintained—he was assassinated by a Christian soldier hired to do so, is a question that cannot be answered.[9] It is known on unimpeachable authority, however, that after receiving his death wound he chatted composedly with his friends, made no protest against his fate, and dropped away gently into his last sleep amid philosophical discussions of the future lot of the soul. Death came to him when he was barely thirty-two.

The Christians' response to his death was a flood of vituperation. During his lifetime they had not dared openly to oppose the emperor. Now, however, that the hated enemy was out of the way, Ephraim the Syrian sang paeans of rejoicing at the death of the "accursed man," and Gregory of Nazianzus denounced him as the "murderer of Christ" and "hater of God" who had been "less the instrument of his own ideas than the plaything of the devil."[1] Julian was compared with Pharaoh, Ahab, and Nebuchadnezzar; it was hinted that the corpse of the traitor should be torn to pieces, and that his "filthy tomb" should be desecrated, which it was.[2] The representatives of Christianity scarcely did themselves honor as they voiced their "joy at the death of the miscreant."[3] The distorted image of Julian created by these Christian polemical writers persisted until August Neander published his epoch-making book on Julian in 1867.

From this distance in time we can form a relatively objective image of this man who was one of the last religious pagans. Julian represented a historical phenomenon that can be regarded from a number of angles. From the Christian point of view, the hatred which was poured out upon him was disproportionate. He was

[9] Cf. Theodoret: op. cit., III, xxv.
[1] Gregory of Nazianzus: *First Invective against Julian,* chaps. lxviii and lxxxv.
[2] Ephraem Syrus: *On Julian the Apostate,* Carmen III.
[3] Theodoret: op. cit., III, xxvii and Gregory of Nazianzus, op. cit., chap. xlix.

more to be pitied. The Christian should regard the moving tragedy of his life with sadness and pain. It would have been strange indeed if, after the terrible experience of his youth, Julian had remained true to Christianity. What must have taken place in the soul of this young man when the Church silently passed over the brutal murder of the boy's entire family? What picture of Christian freedom must he have had when, through no fault of his own, he was forced to spend his entire youth in exile, with his Christian tutors as virtual jailers? Why should he have been intellectually attracted to a Church which was shot through with bitter rivalries and a mania for discovering heresy everywhere? What impression must have been made on a sensitive boy when Christians committed the worst of crimes against each other? The spectacle of the Church in the post-Constantinian age, a Church racked by disputes over Arianism, was one of hopeless ugliness. These dissensions must have aroused in Julian a repugnance toward the doctrine and barred him from any inner understanding of the Gospel.

The tragedy of Julian's life also has a historical aspect which must be emphasized. He entered upon the stage of world history at a time when the contest between the proud gods of Olympus and the humble carpenter's son had already been decided. Julian refused to admit this fact; he could not accommodate to the changed times. With his conservative disposition he refused to understand that Christianity had begun a new era in the history of mankind.[4] In this, the opportunist Constantine showed himself more intelligent than Julian, though his mind and spirit was of a far inferior order. As a romanticist Julian thought he could turn back the wheel of history—an effort that has always proved to be impossible. From the start he was fighting for a lost cause, and his reign could not be anything but a brief intermezzo. All his efforts were doomed to failure for historical reasons. They were undertaken by a man who had appeared, tragically, at the wrong hour. That is why his whole religious policy has the air of a strange relapse into a bygone era. Julian attempted the artificial

[4] Cf. A. Neander: *Über Kaiser Julian und sein Zeitalter* (1867), pp. 32, 35.

galvanic stimulation of a corpse, and in doing so he failed to revive the eternally valid values of Hellenism, but concentrated on the mantic elements. Yet this revival made clear even to the simplest how superior Christianity was to outmoded superstitions. Julian missed the command of the hour; he remained unaware of the true tasks of his age. That is one of the harshest judgments that can be passed upon a man who has taken an important political role in history. According to legend, Julian died with the words: "Thou hast conquered, O Galilean," upon his lips. This is probably sheer myth, for we have trustworthy accounts of the emperor's last hours. Nevertheless, this cry would sum up the lesson of his life—an example of the way legends express the inner truth of events far better than any historically accurate report.

There remains, finally, a theological problem to be discussed in connection with the tragedy of Julian's life. The relationship of the Gospel and Hellas had not been solved, within the Church, ever since it was first made a problem by the work of the Gnostics. Most Christians despised Hellenism as sheer paganism. This is understandable in view of Greek polytheism, but not in view of the great achievements of the Greeks in philosophy and poetry. Moreover, the rejection of Hellenism was not carried out with any consistency. The Christians appropriated the formal elements of Greek thought as they found these in the schools of rhetoric. They had no scruples about such borrowings. But as far as the substance was concerned, they would have none of it. All the noble qualities of the pagans were dismissed as mere glittering vices. This adoption of the formal elements accompanied by an absolute rejection of the substance was a questionable procedure, since the shell and kernel of an intellectual movement can never be separated so cavalierly. Christianity was destined to pay for its indifference to the proposals of Clement of Alexandria and Origen, who had attempted syntheses of Christianity and Hellas. There were a few like the noble Synesius, who upon being elected bishop declared that he intended, in the conduct of his Christian office, to remain faithful to the Hellenic heritage. But such men were exceptional. The representatives of the Church were for the most part blind to the grandeur of Greek religious history. They lacked the intellectual superiority and the spiritual breadth to perceive Hellenic thought, too, as part of the Word of God. Such unsolved problems always have fateful consequences in the history of ideas, as Julian's conflict vividly demonstrates.

In view of all these things, the tragedy of Julian's life becomes a reproach against Christianity itself. Instead of reviling this apostate, it would be more useful to reverse the traditional way of thinking about him. Every apostasy, in the final analysis, addresses a question to Christianity: Did the apostate fail to find what he sought in the fellowship he abandoned? Was his apostasy a sign that an unsatisfactory situation had developed within the camp of the Church? For men do not, as a rule, abandon a vital community. Such questions arise not only in the case of Julian. In the face of the conversion of a man like Angelus Silesius, Lutheranism has equal reason to examine its conscience. The same may be said of Anglicanism when a John Henry Newman is converted to the Catholic Church. Every apostate is a debt that Christianity has failed to pay. For these debts it is thrown into the spiritual debtor's prison, to which the words of Jesus apply: "You will never get out till you have paid the last penny." [5]

[5] Matt. v, 26.

+   +

6

The Rent Tunic of Christ

+   +

From Montanus to Donatus

In the Gospel of John a scene of rare symbolic force is mentioned. After the soldiers had crucified Jesus, they took his clothes and distributed them among themselves. But when they came to his tunic, they found that it was "without seam, woven from top to bottom; so they said to one another, 'Let us not tear it, but cast lots for it to see whose it shall be.'" [1] What the rude soldiers were loath to do, the schismatics were guilty of, according to the Church's view. The heretics who received this name—which goes back to a remark of Paul's [2]—were those who without

[1] John xix, 23–4.
[2] I Cor. xii, 25.

compunction tore the seamless tunic of Christ, which symbolizes Christianity.

It was the problem of Christian ethics that drove the schismatics into conflict with the Church. Ethical questions ordinarily sound tedious—all the more so since ethics has made only slight progress since Aristotle and the average man thinks that he knows quite well what he ought to do. But this is a deception fostered by the textbooks of ethics. In reality, ethical considerations are always of enormous interest: the question of acting rightly reaches to the very depths of man's existence.

Christianity began by subscribing to the strictest ethics, as the New Testament eloquently testifies. The upright ways of the early Christians stood out in glorious contrast to the moral decay of the Late Roman Empire. The Christians made it clear by all their actions that they had nothing in common with the decadence of the classical world, but were on the contrary a new people who belonged to the future. The ethics of Jesus was based upon imminent expectation of the coming of the kingdom, and upon the Apostles' possession of the gift of the Holy Spirit.

Once the Christians ceased to be a small flock, the situation changed. With constant increase in their membership, Christian morality could no longer be maintained at its original high level. A visible slackening in the realm of ethics became apparent. And as soon as Emperor Constantine opened the floodgates and the masses of the people poured into the Church out of sheer opportunism, the loftiness of the Christian ethos was done for. Church discipline could no longer deal so sternly with the overwhelming forces of secularization. The Church had to draw its lines more flexibly, and ethics underwent a profound modification. From that time on, stone after stone crumbled away from the structure of Christian morality.

Many Christians were shocked by this slow degeneration, and were by no means willing to make their peace with it. They wished to remain unconditionally loyal to the original Christian ethos. They bitterly protested against the laxity which was invading the Church. Nor was it mere virtuous conduct that the schismatics clamored for. Their ethic was still that of primitive Christianity; it involved a strong insistence on sanctity. But sanctity is a straight, hot flame that leaps up out of numinosity. In the ordinary communal life of men, it is only a disturbing factor. This emphasis upon the ideal of sanctity within the Church is a manifestation of the heretical temper as much as, if not more than, differences over theology. Ethically, the heretic inclines toward supreme achievements. Such high ideals ill suit the aims of the Church insofar as the Church aims to embrace the largest possible number of people. The charges of immorality so often hurled at the heretics usually sprang from the fact that members of the Church felt unable to live up to the heretics' ethical demands and countered by imputing corrupt motives to them. For it was usually the heretics who took the more rigorous view on moral questions. That is plainly to be seen in the history of the schismatics from Montanus to Donatus.

Tradition has preserved few clear traces of the personality of Montanus. He lived in the second century and came from Phrygia, a fact which has been used to explain the entire character of the movement. Whether Montanus had formerly been a pagan priest is uncertain—nor would it have affected the nature of his subsequent activities as a Christian. Of far more importance was his ecstatic temperament. Montanus was a visionary, and the prophetic visions he experienced were destined to leave their mark upon Christianity. In addition to the two virgins, Priscilla and Maximila, whom he numbered among his followers, he was joined by the disputatious Tertullian, a man who, in his uncompromising conception of Christianity, might be called the Kierkegaard of the second century. Tertullian, who fought heresy so passionately, had the misfortune to become a heretic himself in the course of his struggle.

The essence of Montanism was a call for the revival of primitive Christian enthusiasm. Montanus embodied the spirit of militant prophecy which a lukewarm Christianity had already lost. For Montanus claimed that he himself was the paraclete (advocate or comforter) predicted in the Gospel of John, and that he had new revelations to make which surpassed the old. The fullness of the Gospel would be revealed no longer in the past, but in the present and future. In the Gospel of John, Christ had said mysteriously: "I will pray the Father, and he will give you another Counselor, to be with you for ever."[3] Montanus boldly asserted that these words had been fulfilled in himself. Thus he became the advocate of continuous revelation. The outpouring of the Spirit was no longer to be understood as a unique event which had taken place once in the past and then ceased to occur. Rather, he argued, it was going on all the time, for such a view alone was in keeping with a living conception of the Gospel. Here was a radical departure from the conservative interpretation of the Church's pentecostal doctrine.

The new prophecy consisted in the announcement that the world was soon to come to an end. In this ringing of midnight bells to warn that the kingdom of God was on hand, Montanus wished to arouse a sleepy Christian world. To be sure, the Church at that time had not yet openly abandoned its expectation of the imminent coming of the kingdom. Still, that element had imperceptibly receded into the background. Montanus revived these hopes and fears, for he himself lived in a racking expectation of the end of all things. The joyous frenzy incited by Montanus roared like flame through the Christian world.

In regard to dogma, the paraclete communicated no new revelations. The Montanists took the orthodox view on Christological questions, as even their opponents had reluctantly to admit. Montanism had but slight interest in speculative questions of doctrine. Instead, Montanus put forward disciplinary ideas that arose out of his eschatological theses.[4] According to the Montanist view, the Christian must reform his life because the New Jerusalem was about to descend and its outlines were already visible on high. The utmost must be demanded of the Christian, so that he would pass the test which lay awaiting him.

[3] John xiv, 16.
[4] Cf. N. Bonvetsch: *Die Geschichte des Montanismus* (1881), pp. 81 f.

On such grounds Montanus drew the line in ethical questions far more strictly than did the Church in the second century. He called for Christians to become once more the band of saints of which the Apostles had written.

Montanus' first strictures concerned marriage. He did not reject marriage, as Marcion had done, but imposed severe limitations upon it. According to Montanus, Christians may marry only once. A second marriage after the death of a spouse is regarded as "successive" bigamy, equivalent to sinful concubinage. Distaste for connubial pleasures led to the glorification of virginity as the true moral ideal. Montanus held that the time for marriages was over in any case, since, with the world about to end, reproduction of the human race should cease. The Montanists' tremendous hatred of the flesh tells us a good deal about the state of mind in which these enthusiasts lived. For them, asceticism was the height of voluptuousness.

Montanus also attempted to introduce new fast regulations directed against the pleasures of the palate. Several days of each week and whole sections of years were to be periods of fast during which the Christian must demonstrate his self-conquest. In the matter of fasting, the Montanists were extremely rigorous; they fought all relaxation and demanded that Christians make real and painful sacrifices for the sake of sanctity.

The third Montanist reform concerned martyrdom, which was glorified as a goal to be sought. Montanists would not condone taking flight from persecution. Prudence, they said, was equivalent to denying the religion. "Do not wish to die in beds, nor in childbearing, nor of weakening fevers, but in martyrdom, so that he who suffered for you may be glorified," Tertullian urged the Montanist Christians.[5] And indeed the Montanist church was blessed by an unusually large number of martyrs who ardently shed their blood for Christianity.

The fourth reform dealt with stricter Church discipline, so that all tendencies toward slackness would be nipped in the bud. Sins must be earnestly condemned, and the sanctity of the Church

[5] Tertullian: *De Fuga in Persecutione*, ix.

as a whole must not be tainted. In the case of mortal sins, absolution was to be withheld. The struggle against sin was waged with fanatical fury. The Montanists would not yield an inch on the field of ethics. "All or nothing" was their proud watchword. They would have the Church become in truth a community of saints, the pure bride of Christ going forth to meet her Lord. And this sublime ideal was to be obligatory upon all Christians without exception.

The emergence of the Montanists threw the Church into a grave crisis, for it was faced with a fundamental choice. Could Christianity return to its earlier form, which may be called that of a holy community, or was it to continue on its course of adapting to the world? After a fierce internal struggle the Church decided on the second course—which indeed the trend of history prescribed. This decision was not easy for the Church to make. But to maintain its position in the world, it had to reject Montanism, seductive though this doctrine was. Montanus came forth with his prophetic preachings soon after A.D. 155, and as soon as the Church had recovered from its initial consternation it launched a counterattack. It branded the Montanist paraclete a pseudoprophet. Around A.D. 177 the Montanists were expelled from the Church. Thus a first and irreparable rent had appeared in the seamless tunic of Christ.

Along with the Montanists the Church banished the prophetic spirit from its purview, at the same time launching a vigorous literary rebuttal of the Montanist arguments. In these Church writings the Montanists are called schismatics. Yet they were not the ones who made the break, for according to the account of Eusebius, it was the Church which excommunicated these advocates of early Christian sanctity, and set them down as heretics influenced by the devil.[6] Since the Montanists were continuators of primitive Christian ecstasy, the Church, by excluding them, was condemning its own past. The institutionalized Church had pronounced against the free operation of the pneuma—a fatal decision, and one of tremendous signifi-

[6] Eusebius: op. cit., V, xiv.

cance, though few have seen this. Yet that decision has to be annulled to some extent if there is to be any meaning to the prayer for the coming of the *creator spiritus*.

Since the ethical demands of the Montanists had gone unanswered, they were soon brought up once again by Hippolytus. This man had made a name for himself as a follower of Irenaeus in the struggle against heresy. Once more it is difficult to form a rounded picture of his personality. It has been said that Hippolytus was "undoubtedly the most learned man of the Roman Church, and of the West in general."[7] Soon after his death a statue was erected to him, a homage that was paid to no other Father of the Church. Hippolytus, too, was an ardent chiliast who like Montanus was convinced that the end of history was at hand. This had a strong influence upon his ethical ideas. In his case, too, the ideal of a community of saints led him into conflict with orthodoxy.

According to the early Christian view, baptism brought with it a forgiveness for all previous sins. In regard to the sins a Christian committed after baptism, the distinction was made between venial and mortal sins. Unchastity, apostasy, and murder were counted among the mortal sins. All three were considered unforgivable. The severity of this doctrine was ameliorated by Callistus, a man with a colorful past who had worked his way up from slavery to a position of respect. Although he had been at times involved in dubious financial affairs, the ambitious Callistus succeeded in 217 in having himself elected Bishop of Rome. In order to secure the favor of the Roman community, he soon mitigated the strict rules of penitence, which to his mind no longer corresponded with the spirit of the times. He was particularly lenient toward the sins of unchastity, so common in society. "Callistus also permitted women of high rank to have lovers after their choice, whether slave or free, and to regard such as their husbands without proper marriage."[8] By measures such as these, the bishop made himself popular with his flock. A realist, he

[7] J. Döllinger: *Hippolyt und Kalistos* (1853), p. 100.
[8] Hippolytus: op. cit., IX, xii.

pointed out that the superhuman ideal of a pure community could not in the long run be put into practice in this earthly world. For support of this novel conception of the Church he cited the Biblical words: "Let the weeds grow together with the wheat." [9] Noah's Ark, as Callistus interpreted it, had been a parable of the Church, for both clean and unclean animals had been given space in it.

As a man devoted to an austere ideal, Hippolytus protested against this new viewpoint, thus demonstrating that in some circumstances heretics could stoutly defend the conservative tradition. He declared that the forgiveness of sexual offenses was impermissible, and charged Callistus with directly fostering adultery. Callistus himself, he said, was a man "experienced in evil and skilled in leading astray." In his indignation Hippolytus overlooked the fact that Callistus was by no means the first to uphold the principle of unlimited forgiveness of sins. This mild outlook had its precedents in the Eastern Church.

Although the struggle was conducted with a good deal of venom on both sides, Hippolytus' position on the matter must not be regarded as stemming from mere personal rivalry for the episcopal seat. An objective problem of considerable significance was at stake, one that persists to this day in modified form. Here two fundamentally opposed conceptions of the Church were clashing. Hippolytus was concerned for the ideal of the sanctity of the Church, which to his mind was inextricably linked with the moral purity of all its members. The toleration of mortal sins in its midst endangered the entire flock and made it impossible to speak of the Church as the stainless bride of Christ.

The Roman community divided on this question. The split became inevitable, although we have no certain knowledge whether Hippolytus actually permitted himself to be elected antibishop by the minority.[1] In any case, the result was a separation within the Roman community which lasted for some time. The seamless tunic of Christ had been rent a second time. Hip-

[9] Matt. xiii, 29.
[1] Cf. G. Fricker: *Studien zur Hippolytfrage* (1893), p. 30.

polytus was forced into the role of schismatic; henceforth this intrepid battler against heretics himself became a member separated from the body of the Church. He now discovered that not evil motives but on the contrary the purest intentions might lead a Christian into the heretic camp.

Banished to Sardinia, Hippolytus soon succumbed to the unwholesome climate. Just before his premature death he became reconciled to the Church. Thanks to this last act, Hippolytus was entered into the roll of the saints because of his bloodless martyrdom in Sardinia. A heretic saint is a striking phenomenon and once again demonstrates how closely the two paths impinge upon one another. But even the canonized heretic could not halt the further secularization of the Church. Hippolytus' lofty ethical ideals shattered against the realities of daily life and survive only as a longing which to this day stirs the hearts of many earnest Christians.

The story of the presbyter Novatian might be regarded as a recapitulation in a related key. Like Montanus, Novatian came from Phrygia and had formerly been an adherent of the Stoic philosophy. Novatian was a high-minded person who conceived of his conversion to Christianity as a radical break with the spirit of the world. He had little understanding for weaker natures and regarded the Church as a pure community of saints whose sanctity he considered gravely threatened by the treatment of apostates. In the course of the bloody persecution under Decius, not all members of the Church were heroic martyrs who died for the Gospel. There were also many Christians who were weak and renounced their faith. After the end of the cruel persecution many of these apostates asked to be received into the Church again. A violent discussion raged within the Church over these requests. In view of the large number of *lapsi* (lapsed Christians), as the apostates were called, some method had to be found for granting them forgiveness. At last remission of the sin of apostasy was made dependent upon a long period of penitence. The rigorists were strongly opposed to this, demanding that the

Church adhere to the old practice of regarding apostasy as an unforgivable mortal sin.

The disputes reached a climax when Cornelius, advocate of the lenient view, was elected Bishop of Rome in 251. Novatian opposed this election, whereupon Cornelius promptly excommunicated him at a synod, despite his reputation for personal integrity. Novatian, however, had a fairly sizable following within the Roman community, and his excommunication produced a new schism. In the ensuing years the Novatian church spread to most of the larger cities of the Empire. One element in its favor was its appeal to tradition against the new principles of leniency in the question of apostasy, for there was strong feeling on this matter. As late as the fourth and fifth centuries Novatian communities existed in all the provinces, despite the fact that they were persecuted by the Christian emperors. But they were doomed by the spirit of the age and eventually died out.

A schismatic movement that became a major threat to the Church was Donatism, one of the most interesting phenomena of the Early Church. However, here again it is most difficult to draw up a coherent account of this movement, since none of the original sources has survived and all later documents are products of the opposing party.

A minor event appears to have provoked the Donatist schism. After the death of Bishop Mensurius of Carthage in 311, a deacon named Cecilian was elected to succeed him. The community split over this election, chiefly because of Cecilian's opportunistic, progovernment policy, his imperious manner, and his lack of moderation toward those who disagreed with him.[2] Apparently Cecilian was also lukewarm in his Christianity, for he forbade Christians to visit their brethren who had been imprisoned. For this cowardly conduct the resistance group despised him. But Cecilian's faults alone would not have sufficed to stir the whole Donatist movement to activity. More than one cleric had already erred in the direction of arrogance and

[2] Cf. D. Völter: *Der Ursprung des Donatismus* (1883), p. 117.

shallowness without producing schisms. This time, however, the excitement was great because Cecilian was suspected of being a *traditor*. This was the term for those who during the persecution had surrendered the Holy Scriptures to the pagan authorities. Such an act was regarded as a variety of apostasy. In a country so intensely Christian as North Africa then was, it was considered an unforgivable offense. A man guilty of such a crime seemed to the Carthaginians unworthy of the office of bishop. Moreover, a number of traditional customs had gone unobserved in the course of Cecilian's overhasty election.

As a result of all these dissatisfactions, the more serious-minded Christians elected for their bishop the lector Majorinus, concerning whose character little is known. He was consecrated by the Numidian bishops. With this counterelection, the schism became an accomplished fact. The discussions that followed did not succeed in patching the new rent in the tunic of Christ. The damage proved to be irreparable.

The schism was intensified when the party of rigorists, after the death of Majorinus, succeeded in electing as bishop the vigorous Donatus. Donatus lent great impetus to the movement, which henceforth took its name from him. The opposing party accused Donatus of wishing to raise himself above his colleagues, and of regarding himself as more a god than a man. But such slanders were always thrown about freely during the factional struggles. It may well be that Donatus was not free of vanity and arrogance. Certainly he was a man of extraordinary talent and passion. He towered above his coreligionists in learning and intelligence. He must also have possessed that power of persuasion which is encountered in so many heretics. Donatus appears to have been a born ruler; he knew how to make the best use of his superior gifts. It is not for nothing that the epithet "the Great" was attached to his name—a rare event among ecclesiastical personalities. His followers venerated him with boundless enthusiasm, calling him "the pride of the church of Carthage, the man with the glory of a martyr." [3] So powerful was

[3] F. Ribbeck: *Donatus und Augustin* (1857), p. 120.

his charismatic personality that he was even reputed to be able to perform miracles. With his gifts of eloquence, Donatus so stirred his adherents that they were ready to go through fire for him. Even Augustine called him a "precious stone," for the brilliance of his writings. Regrettably, all the works of this great schismatic were ultimately destroyed.

The schism in Carthage was no tempest in a teapot. Donatism was primarily a protest movement [4] in defense of the sanctity of the Church, although the Donatists did not go so far as their schismatic predecessors in demanding complete purity on the part of their members. Reality had demonstrated that that ideal exceeded human nature, and so it was therefore no longer advocated with the same stringency. The Donatist Christians were prepared to make concessions to human weaknesses; like the main Church they absolved their members for sins of unchastity and readmitted lapsed Christians. But—and here we see in adulterated form the old spirit of the schismatics—they insisted that at least the clergy observe purity. The priest had to be free of mortal sins, for otherwise his sacramental acts lost their validity. This demand for purity on the part of those holding ecclesiastical office was the central concern of the Donatists. *For a church which tolerates deniers and traitors in its midst cannot possibly be the true church of Jesus Christ; hence it cannot possess the true sacraments. The validity of the sacraments and of every ecclesiastical act therefore not only depends upon the worthiness of the servants who administer them, but also is destroyed if they are administered in a church which does not excommunicate clerics suspected of having denied the faith.* [5] Only a clergy free of mortal sin could be in possession of the Holy Spirit and therefore effectively administer the sacraments. Communion and baptism received from an impure priest would not, in the Donatist view, confer any divine force.

Thus the sanctity of the church became dependent on the sanctity of the clergy. This idea, of key importance to the

---

[4] Cf. E. Altendorf: *Einheit und Heiligkeit der Kirche* (1932), p. 120.
[5] Ribbeck: op. cit., p. 105.

medieval heretics, had its birth among the Donatists. It raises an extremely interesting problem which cannot be taken lightly. A morally corrupt priest is certainly an offensive sight, and the Church does not deny it. But the Church could not make the effectiveness of the sacraments depend upon the worthiness of the officiating priest. The Church agreed that the priest ought to be pure, but it held that, even if he were not, the sacraments he administered remained effective. The sanctity of the Church could not be allowed to become dependent on human idiosyncrasies; it had to rest on the objective foundation of the proper institutions. In the official view of the Church, the true giver of the sacraments is Christ; the priest serves only as Christ's deputy. Had it not been for this principle, the Church could not have survived the grave corruptions of the papacy in the tenth and fifteenth centuries.

The Donatist movement spread through all of North Africa and grew into a dangerous rebellion within the Church. "It is not fitting," the Donatists declared with that spiritual arrogance so characteristic of separatists, "that the sons of the martyrs and the spawn of *traditores* should assemble together." [6] Inevitably, the Donatist clergy fulminated from their pulpits against the slackness of the Church. They even forbade their followers to associate with the others.

Donatism was seriously compromised, as well as significantly furthered, by its connection with the Circumcellions. We cannot ascertain from the sources if there was an internal bond between Donatists and Circumcellions. If there was, it would mean that the Donatist schismatics also proposed a new social ethic, though in inchoate form. The Circumcellions are generally depicted as a savage band, the terror of all honest folk. Probably they were guilty of some excesses, as might be expected of a revolutionary religious movement of peasants, erupting out of the unhealthy social conditions of the times. Apparently the Circumcellions wished to transform the relations between the classes. They provided the Donatists with welcome auxiliary forces, lent

[6] Ibid., p. 441.

113

impetus to the Donatist movement, but at the same time brought it into disrepute. For the followers of Cecilian raised the cry that the movement was a threat to public safety and so appealed to the emperor. And Constantine was forced by the steady spread of the schism to intervene.

The emperor, who approached the problem politically, was incapable of understanding the Donatists' religious concern. He regarded the whole affair as mere theological disputatiousness, and brusquely ordered the Donatists to conform. But the schismatics would not dream of sacrificing the sanctity of the church to an imperial ordinance. They refused to yield. Angered, Constantine sent soldiers against the Donatists. This use of the imperial military forces only strengthened the Donatist party, for now those who had fought for purity of the clergy were joined by those who were the foes of any alliance between church and state. In the Donatist view, the Church by its submissiveness to Constantine had made itself a prostitute practicing shameful whoredom with the state. Donatus cried out to his opponents within the Church: "What business has the emperor with the Church?" It was a highly pertinent question, and has remained so. These heretics were the first Christians in the history of the Church to advocate the significant principle that the state must not intrude itself into ecclesiastical affairs. Their insistence on this was one of the profoundest insights that posterity owes to these schismatics, and one that remains valid to this day. Wherever the state has tried to impose one of its rough and ready solutions upon intrachurch problems, the result has been bad.

The rod of iron with which Constantine lashed the Donatists produced numerous martyrs, which merely intensified the already strong veneration for martyrdom within the sect. Firmed by suffering, Donatism underwent enormous growth. Ultimately the Donatists attained a majority among the Christians in North Africa.

At last the emperor realized that a schismatic movement had to be dealt with in a manner different from the treatment of rebellious nations. What was called for was theological discussion, not military repression. The subsequent discussions extended over a period of nearly a hundred years, during which a large number of synods took place between Donatists and representatives of the orthodox Church. Since the Donatists attacked only the constitution but not the dogma of the Church, they received on the whole friendly treatment, once the period of military repression had passed.

The discussions reached a significant turning point around 417 when Augustine took part in them on behalf of the Church. The Bishop of Hippo honestly endeavored to meet the Donatists on a Christian plane. He was earnestly concerned to negotiate, for he hoped to be able to convince the schismatics by arguments out of Holy Scripture. The Donatists, to be sure, confronted him warily, all the more so since they did not regard such debates as the true way to settle ethical controversies. And their suspicions proved to be somewhat justified. For in discussions Augustine could display his intellectual superiority, putting the Donatist clerics at a disadvantage. His questions were blunt and discomfiting. Referring to Jesus' parable of the weeds among the wheat, he asked: Is Donatus the reaper? Is the time in which the Donatists have broken with the Church the time of the last sifting? Augustine's point—that it is impossible to make a sharp distinction between good and evil in this world—was hard to refute.

Protracted though they were, these religious discussions led to no result. In the course of the disputation Augustine finally called the Donatists people who had cut themselves off from the Body of Christ. Naturally enough, his opponents took this for an insult. And suddenly Augustine lost patience. For he discovered that all his eloquence and keenness of intellect made no difference, that religious convictions can scarcely be affected by logical arguments, for they are rooted in irrational soil. When his passionate discourse rebounded uselessly from the Donatists' obstinate negations, Augustine gave way to anger. He violated the spirit of tolerance, and called for forceful measures to bring these stubborn opponents to heel. Although this outburst is

psychologically understandable, the subsequent theological justification of this resort to force had extremely fateful consequences.
Augustine had maintained that no one should be forced to believe
against his will. Now the great thinker abandoned this principle
and expressly demanded that the Theodosian laws against heresy
be applied to the Donatists. The schismatics were to be fined,
their churches closed, and they themselves sent into exile.

Augustine had an uneasy conscience about this, but reassured himself by a Biblical parallel: the Church was free to
proceed sternly against the godless, since Jesus had made use of
a scourge to cleanse the Temple. Now Augustine scrambled to
find arguments in favor of force: *The wounds of a friend are
better than the kisses of an enemy. To love with sternness is
better than to deceive with gentleness. It is better to take bread
from the hungry if, sure of his food, he despises justice. God has
treated us similarly. In Luke 14, 23 it is written: "Compel people
to come in!" By threats of the wrath of God, the Father draws
souls to the Son. Just as Sarah persecuted Hagar, so may the
Church persecute the Donatists. What did Elias do with the
priest of Baal? Did not Paul, 1 Tim. 1, 20, deliver some to Satan?
Psalm 2 is a command to the kings to help the Church . . .*[7]

It was one of the darkest hours in the whole history of
Christian thought when Augustine, that noble God-seeker and
fervent mystic, set forth the terrible principle: *Cogite intrare*—
compel them to enter. Seldom has a more dangerous slogan
crossed the lips of a Christian, and that he was one of the great
and illuminate Christians made the matter even more tragic and
the guilt graver. For Augustine had earlier insisted that heretics
must be treated with gentleness. Now it was as though the sun of
the Gospel had ceased to shine and the shades of night had
descended upon the Church. From now on, any dissent within the
Church could no longer be adjudicated peacefully. Augustine
devised a good many more questionable arguments: that God did
not wish the Donatists to perish outside the pale of the Church;
that at times it is well to coerce people to accept the truth; that

[7] Cf. Augustine: *Letter to Vincentius,* No. xciii.

he was interested in the Donatists' souls, not their money, and so on. But the fact remained that in issuing the watchword, "Compel them to enter," the greatest of the Fathers of the Church had almost committed treason against the Gospel. Whatever we may say to excuse Augustine, the sword had been drawn from its sheath. All those instrumental in the ferocious suppression of the heretics in the Middle Ages could call upon the authority of St. Augustine—could and did. The violence and cruelty unleased by this one man was beyond measure. The slogan, "Compel them to enter," remains the ugliest stain upon the great teacher's repute, and no explanations can wash it away. Here was a fateful fork in the road, and Augustine took the wrong turning. Because of this decision—and his pseudo-Christian justification of war was part of it—we have to condemn at least this aspect of Augustine's thought. The Donatists were right when they pointed out that Jesus had sent forth fishermen but no soldiers.

Augustine's counsel was followed, and the attempt was made to exterminate Donatism root and branch by brute force. Ruthless measures succeeded where argument had failed. The strength of Donatism was broken by the power of the sword. The sparse remnants of the Donatists who survived the rule of the Vandals in North Africa were finally wiped out by the advance of Islam.

The schismatic movements raise a number of significant questions. In a sense, the schismatics may be regarded as the radical Pietists of the Early Church. They cannot be simply dismissed as visionaries committed to an excessive idealism which does not properly belong to Christianity. It is somewhat too facile to dismiss a whole historical movement with the epithet "visionary." The schismatics were never that. It is in the nature of religious feeling that it be experienced with subjective intensity. There is something dubious about religious feeling which is not. Yet Christianity includes objectivism and subjectivism, and both must be given their due.

The one great failing of these heretics was their curious

pedantry and legalism. With their stringent ethic, they were all inflexible rigorists. But the Gospel is not rigoristic. Montanus, Hippolytus, Novatian, and Donatus superimposed one dangerous doctrine upon the New Testament. To say that there is no remission of sins after baptism negates the Christian tidings of the immeasurable love of God. The schismatics did not perceive that a loving attitude toward sinners could arise out of boundless mercy as well as out of frivolity. Novatian was sterner toward the apostates than Jesus had been toward the Peter who thrice denied him. In his battle against Callistus, who would have absolved sins of unchastity, Hippolytus never recalled the words of Jesus: "Let him who is without sin cast the first stone." The schismatics did not take the Gospel attitude toward sinners.

But this point aside, we can only admire the Christian earnestness which gave a heroic tone to the ethical system of these schismatics. To them Christianity was still something intimately bound up with life, a creed which required man to surpass himself. The last embers of pneumatic primitive Christianity still glowed in their hearts. The schismatics were all maximalists, demanding the ultimate and the highest. Maximalism is an important strain in the history of Christian thought. Most saints were maximalists, for Maximalism alone counteracts the tendency for morality to degenerate into insipid lip service to virtue. The Church herself has never taken a stand in principle against maximalism, and in fact has let it flourish freely in monasticism.

The deepest problem posed by the schismatic movements is that of the pure community of God. Here were people who sought to realize the idea of a sinless church—certainly one of the sweetest dreams ever dreamed upon this earth. This thoroughly religious wish for a sinless church cannot be a matter of indifference to any Christian who professes the Apostle's Creed: "I believe in one Holy Christian Church." To be sure, both Montanus and Donatus considered the sanctity of the church to be founded upon the ethical purity of its members rather than upon the invisible presence of Christ. And though it has been shown that a pure community of the faithful, no matter how high it sets its standards and how heroically it tries to meet them, cannot prevail in the long run of history, still it is good for Christianity to recall the challenge of this demand at frequent intervals. For the call to holiness is a check against ignoble lapsing into an easy life wherein man's heavenly destiny is forgotten.

Yet the sublime ideal of a holy church resulted in a rending of the seamless tunic of Christ. The goal could be attained only at the price of schism. The image of the undivided garment of Jesus is more than a mere metaphor. There is something essential there, and the lament that the garment has been torn must not be taken lightly. To understand the depths of this matter we must know what it means "to feel with the Church." Cyprian's essay on *The Unity of the Church* conveys some idea of the consternation felt by the Fathers of the Church when the schismatics rent the holy tunic of Christ. *Everyone who parts from the Church and unites himself with an adulteress, who excludes himself from the promises of the Church and abandons the Church of Christ, will not be rewarded by Christ. He is a stranger, an enemy, an unholy one. He who does not have the Church for mother cannot have God for father. . . . He who does not cling to this unity does not obey God's law, does not keep his belief in the Father and the Son, and has neither life nor bliss.*[8]

Since separatism remains a recurrent phenomenon to the present day—with modifications, in the political field as well—it is instructive to consider the early Christian dissident movements in detail. In almost all of them, problems which arise in our own day are already anticipated. Thus, the reflective individual is faced with the question: Which is better, to remain in a community that is unsatisfying in a religious and ethical way, or to leave it? Remaining in the community has the merit, of course, that one may be able to exert some influence upon its future development. One pays a certain price for this advantage—one must abandon one's purity of principle. Is the game, then, worth the candle?

[8] Cyprian: *The Unity of the Church*, chap. vi.

It seems impossible to settle the problem conclusively. A strict concern with sanctity rends the unity of the Church, whereas extending the Church and preserving her unity invariably results in diminished holiness. Sanctity and extensiveness are scarcely reconcilable in this earthly life. A holiness which will not imperil the unity of the Church must be a holiness conceived in religious, not merely ethical terms. To the truly religious eye, it will be evident that a community composed of heterogeneous elements can never attain the same ideal the individual approaches only by incessant spiritual effort: the goal of perfection demanded in the Sermon on the Mount.

+ +

7

Error as a Way to Truth

+ +

It must have been a lively scene at the Council of Ephesus in 449, when the discussion became so inflamed that the delegates went at one another with clubs, until one party held the field and could enforce the decree it desired. Fanatical bands of monks terrorized the assembly of Church notables, and sailors staged a street demonstration in favor of the councillors. There were other tumultuous scenes in which the envoys from Rome were set upon and soundly thumped. With good reason Leo the Great described it as "The Robber Council." Nor was this the only one of its kind. There were other councils at which the Church Fathers became so incensed that they hurled the Bible at each other's heads.

So savage were the doctrinal struggles of the Early Church that many people find themselves repelled by all those conflicts and their outcomes. The dogmas, too, seem dead and dreary, and to modern men as incomprehensible as a chemical formula to the non-chemist. The whole story of the old doctrinal disputes has become a closed chapter of Church history to the contemporary Christian. He regards them as useless bickerings over microscopic distinctions, whereas in fact the deepest questions of human life were involved. We must try to see the issues locked within these formulas. As for the rancors and animosities connected with the disputes, these are mere dust on the road kicked up by men striding toward eternity. Few ideas in history were fought for with more fervor than the dogmas of the Early Church.

From the very first the Church was faced with the task of establishing dogmas. For Christianity abounds in problems more hinted at than answered in the New Testament. Its doctrine did not spring full blown with its inception. Many questions did not come to light until centuries after the time of the Apostles. Thus the doctrine underwent an evolution which necessarily led to the formation of dogmas. True, the Church did function for some time without dogmas. Nor can we say that Christian dogmas were formulated merely as an adjustment to the situation resulting from the non-arrival of the Second Coming. The impulse toward dogma-making lay within the Christian cause itself; it sprang from a need for intellectual clarification. And that need was felt throughout the Christian populace. If elaborating dogmas had only been the pastime of a few disputatious clerics, the marketwomen of Constantinople would not have taken so lively an interest in the matter.

The impassioned and necessary growth of dogma in the Church must not be considered in terms of a rigid pattern. In his endeavor to explain the inexplicable, John Henry Newman stated that error is in many cases the only way to truth.[1] A strange but telling insight is contained within that statement; it holds the key to an understanding of the historical process. What Newman

[1] J. H. Newman: *Die Kirche* (ed. Karrer; 1945), I, 308.

is asserting is the same as what was expressed by one of the profoundest Christian thinkers when he said that here on earth "every single thing is partly true and partly false," and that human beings possess "both truth and goodness only mixed with falsehood and evil." [2] Truth and error pass into one another as do day and night at dusk. We can find no truth which does not contain an element of error, and there exists no error which is not a harbinger of truth.

Recognizing this, we look quite differently upon the "false teachers"—the third group, after the apostates and schismatics, into which the Church divided heresy. The so-called false teacher who stuck by his views after a council had ruled against them must no longer be regarded as an obstinate, unrepentant scoundrel. As has been mentioned, these councils were occasions where the majority brutally suppressed a minority. With the best will in the world, the defeated party could not accept the council's decision as some divinely ordained truth. They had to abide by their views for conscience's sake, even if it meant being charged with heresy. Loyalty to the defeated cause was not mere disobedience to the Church. The heretics had the courage to swim against the stream, whatever the cost.

It would require a history of dogma to deal with the bewildering array of theological disputes in which the Early Church engaged. Not all the disputants were heretics, by any means. Out of the large number of "teachers of false doctrines" we shall discuss only two who carried out that vital function of stimulating the formation of dogma.

Arius

As soon as we begin to investigate the man who stirred up the fiercest dogmatic struggles in the Early Church, we come across the surprising fact that Arius was among other things a writer of verse. His songs of sailors and millers were sung by the

[2] Pascal: *Pensées*, Fragment 385.

people. Unfortunately, only a few fragments of his chief work, the *Banquet,* have come down to us. These, written in a facile style, tell little of the nature of the book. His enemies reviled this work and insinuated that its author participated in "drinking bouts" at which he jested and sang. Arius' followers, on the other hand, thought very highly of the *Banquet,* wherein, they claimed, God is glorified as an inexpressible Being to whom nothing may be likened.

While Arius was not without his share of pride and obstinacy, he was certainly no monster. His African birth may possibly account for the violence of his disposition. He is described as a person of tall stature and engaging manner whose face, however, always looked a little melancholy, as is often the case with men of poetic endowments. Emperor Constantine, too, remarked on the nuance of sadness in Arius' expression. His monklike garments were in keeping with his ascetic principles and strict conduct of life. In Alexandria he enjoyed great popularity among both ascetics and women. Whether in his youth he was taught by the martyr Lucian and attended the rationalistic school at Antioch remains uncertain, but it is highly probable.

As so often in history, in the case of Arius a small cause produced a great effect. In the year 319 Alexander, the Bishop of Alexandria, was delivering a lecture to a group of clerics. He asserted that a Oneness was present in the divine Trinity. In the subsequent discussion Arius contested this view, arguing that if the Father had begotten the Son, he who had been begotten had a beginning, and therefore there must have been a time when the Son did not exist. This view of Arius was not new; he was only expressing what many more radical theologians of the time thought. Bishop Alexander, however, would not tolerate contradiction from a subordinate, and sharply commanded him to withdraw his opinion. Arius believed that a man could not divest himself of his convictions on command—and the great debate was launched.

Very likely personal tensions and the fiery dispositions of the two men contributed a good deal to the sharpening of the dispute. But rivalry and emotionality are not sufficient explanations. A real problem was at stake, which at that time had not yet been clarified. Let us try to feel the full weight of the metaphysical question posed: "The Father begot his only begotten Son before aeonic times, through whom also he created the aeons and the universe. The Son was begotten before time, was made and created before the ages; not that he existed before he was begotten, but that he alone was begotten by the Father apart from time and before all things else." [3] In these and similar statements of Arius, living thought seems to be buried in Byzantine formalisms. Yet for the Christians of that age these words had life; only to the modern sensibility do they appear calcified. If we break the shell and penetrate to the kernel, we soon discover that behind the involved and abstruse problems of whether the Son is coeternal with the Father and whether he was brought forth out of nothingness there lies the never-ending question: What do you think about Christ?

What definition is given of the Son of Man? It is the central question in all understanding of the Gospel. This was why all Christendom was set aflame.

Bishop Alexander quickly lost his temper and wanted to be done with the whole debate. Arius was to be removed from office as a Presbyter of the Church and excommunicated. This first public humiliation poisoned the air and gave the conflict a disastrous turn. A campaign of slander was launched against Arius. He was pictured as the third great heretic after Simon Magus and Marcion, and branded a sophist, a hairsplitter, a deceiver, a man who concealed his true opinion and spoke other than he thought. "Haughty, avaricious, lustful" were only a few of the insulting adjectives hurled at the heretic. [4]

Athanasius, the great Bishop of Alexandria, took a leading part in this campaign of slander. Yet it can be said that without Arius there would have been no Athanasius; for in this theological battle what was called the error of Arius proved to be the in-

[3] G. Pfannmüller: *Jesus im Urteil der Jahrhunderte* (1939), p. 104.
[4] Athanasius: *Against the Arians*, I, vii.

dispensable step to truth. But Athanasius could not see the problem in this light. From all we know about Athanasius, he was an ambitious man, with a good deal of vanity and a weakness for flattery. He had made up his mind that Arius was an agent of corruption and error, and never tried to understand the basis for his argument.

Since the nucleus of this dispute was the problem of Christ, the quarrel spread over ever-widening areas. Soon there was not a city or a village in which the relationship of God and Christ was not being discussed with bitter intensity. Families divided on the question; riots raged in the streets. Christians plunged into brawls for the sake of the divinity of Christ, and the pagans made fun of them in the theaters. Emperor Constantine saw himself obliged to take part in the dispute, although it seemed to him a useless one which dangerously threatened his political interest in the unity of the Church. On the other hand, a pretext to intervene in the internal affairs of the Church was welcome, and he therefore called a council to arbitrate the quarrel.

The Council of Nicaea, which assembled in June 325 in the magnificent halls of the imperial palace, is usually celebrated as one of the glorious events in the history of the Christian Church. Bishops who but shortly before had been persecuted traveled by imperial post, and the emperor came forward to meet them with the most flattering courtesies. He kissed the scars of the martyrs who were present, and himself presided as chairman over the proceedings. This was the first triumphal public spectacle of the Church, and it must have made a deep impression upon all those partial to pomp and circumstance and to the sight of bishops in their full regalia. But regarded realistically, the glittering colors of the first ecumenical council fade somewhat. Even in those days genuine Christianity was rather with Anthony in the desert, not with those who entered the emperor's palace in silks and brocades.

As at all councils, the question of organization played a great part, and brought the busybodies to the fore. Once the discussions started, it frequently happened that the participants threw their episcopal dignity to the wind and shouted wildly at one another. The Fathers at the council were concerned neither for mutual understanding nor the practice of Christian brotherhood. Their maneuvers were directed toward improving their own positions of power. There was little of that higher outlook Paul expressed when he said: "What then? Only that in every way . . . Christ is proclaimed, and in that I rejoice." [5] Diplomacy was wielded like a weapon, and intrigues often replaced intelligence. There were so many ignorant bishops that one participant bluntly called the council "a synod of nothing but blockheads." [6] The Arian bishops relied upon their skillful tactics, while the adherents of Athanasius hoped to win advantages by their boisterous conduct. Opinions clashed sharply, but the followers of Arius were in the minority. Finally the faction in the middle offered a compromise formula stating that Christ was "one in essence with the Father." Of course, this had the defect of having been originally a Gnostic phrase, and one which had no precedence in the Bible. However, that seemed all right to Constantine. The conservative party saw to it that the compromise statement was salted with a few anathemas against the Arian theology, and finally, with pressure from the emperor, it was adopted. Constantine, who treated religious questions solely from a political point of view, assured unanimity by banishing all the bishops who would not sign the new profession of faith. In this way unity was achieved. *It was altogether unheard-of that a universal creed should be instituted solely on the authority of the emperor, who as a catechumen was not even admitted to the mystery of the Eucharist and was totally unempowered to rule on the highest mysteries of the faith. Not a single bishop said a single word against this monstrous thing. The same Church which had effectively defied the iron regime of Diocletian supinely yielded to the command of his successor, who struck at its vital nerve in a wholly different way from the outward violence of persecution.*[7]

[5] Phil. i, 18.
[6] C. A. Bernoulli: *Das Konzil von Nizäa* (1896), p. 15.
[7] E. Schwarz: *Kaiser Konstantin und die christliche Kirche* (1913), p. 141.

Arius did not cut the kind of figure at the council that might have been expected of the originator of the whole dispute. Only at the end did he come to the foreground, but not as a participant with the Fathers in discussion. The council held his view to be unadulterated error, containing not a spark of truth, and therefore decided to crown its work by issuing a formal condemnation of Arius, since he had refused to sign the profession of faith directed against himself. He was pronounced an accursed heretic. People who owned his writings were ordered to deliver them up on pain of punishment. Arius himself was banished to Illyria. He went into exile without complaint, and it is worth remembering that in this struggle it was Arius who became the persecuted one, suffering for his religious convictions. Since the emperor declared that the decisions of the council were laws of the empire, to side with Arius henceforth became a crime. These measures, it was hoped, would soon destroy the Arian heresy. But such hopes proved a fatal illusion. Violent repression as usual accomplished the opposite of its intention; in the case of Arius it served to spread rather than crush the heresy.

The Nicene Council had failed to recognize the true situation within the Christian world. Since too narrow a majority had tried to impose its rule by force upon too large a minority, the victory rested upon a weak foundation. Countermoves against the decisions of the council were led by Eusebius of Nicomedia, a clever politician with Arian leanings. Eusebius had signed the Nicene creed against his convictions; now he applied himself to revising the policy which he had abetted through weakness of character. Through the emperor's sister, whose spiritual adviser he was, Eusebius succeeded in bringing about a reversal of policy. Constantine was chiefly interested in peace within the Church, and he therefore wished to reconcile the offended Arians. The emperor's intervention resulted in 330 in the recall of Arius. After some hesitation, Arius obeyed the invitation and went to the court of Constantine, where he was received graciously. But when the emperor commanded that Arius be restored to his priesthood, Bishop Athanasius had the temerity to refuse. Someone whom a council had condemned as the author of heresies could not be taken back into the fellowship of the Church, Athanasius declared. The reconciliation sought by the emperor failed once more; the factional struggle continued and became intertwined with political disputes. Within ten years Arianism gained the upper hand, was proclaimed truth, and the opposing party condemned as advocates of error. In 335 it was Athanasius' turn to go off into exile.

The rehabilitation of sorely tried Arius, however, was frustrated at the last moment, and his life came to so surprising an end that no novelist could have invented anything more grotesque. When he arrived in Alexandria, to assume his office once more, a great hue and cry was raised by the orthodox Christians, imploring God to avert this evil from his church. Only too soon were they to rejoice that their prayer had been heard. On the eve of his reinstallation, Arius and his friend Eusebius of Nicomedia were walking about the city. Arius suddenly felt unwell and had to go to a public privy. While his servant waited outside the door, Arius, within, fainted and, like Judas Iscariot, was riven internally. His bowels poured out of him, his liver emerged, covered with blood, and then, suffering the most violent pain, he discharged his heart, the seat of all his wickedness. To crown these horrors, Arius' whole body became thinner and thinner until at last the heretic fell through the opening of the privy into the sewer beneath.[8]

This was the repulsive story which Athanasius circulated after the death of Arius. What it tells us of the character of Athanasius is not to his credit. Moreover, the lurid fiction did not have the desired effect. Rather, the sudden death of Arius just before his restoration to office gave rise to the suspicion that he had been poisoned by someone of the orthodox party. Athanasius himself admits that his party publicly rejoiced over the death— indicating to what an ethical low these Christians had fallen through their doctrinaire struggles.

It scarcely matters whether or not the unhappy Arius really

[8] J. A. Stark: *Versuch einer Geschichte des Arianismus* (1785), II, 101 f.

did fall into the *cloaca,* or whether this was only a bizarre fantasy of his opponents. For in the memory of Christians this myth attached itself to Arius. From an illustrious figure, he sank lower and lower. Like Joseph of the Old Testament, Arius was cast into the pit by his brethren.

But since the nastiness of the legend reflects less upon him than upon his opponents, the time has come to lift Arius from the sewer in which he has been immured for nearly 1,600 years. This man who became a heretic only because he earnestly concerned himself with Christ is worthy of closer examination.

As Herman Kutter has put it: *The whole process of dogma-formation in the church is in reality nothing but the attempt to comprehend the divine phenomenon of Jesus after the fact, that is, after human intellect had once again usurped the place of the Spirit of God. Naturally, all that comes out is a series of incomprehensible statements whose logical absurdity nevertheless embodies the perception that in speaking of Jesus we are speaking of God.*[9]

The problem Arius posed was not one of mere theological cavil totally removed from true Christianity. Behind the formulas "of similar substance" and "of the same substance" is concealed one of the most significant questions that Christians ever had to wrestle with. In spite of the clumsy slogans in which the dispute was couched, the eternity of Christ was at issue. The theologians of the Early Church tried to form a clear conception of Christ, but none of their formulas fully satisfied the Christian world. This is understandable, for the figure of Christ can never be fully interpreted; the discussion has no end. Arius was a man struggling to achieve an understanding of Christ, and his doctrine therefore inevitably contained both truth and error. We must be on guard against seeing the question in the light of later ideas. Arius is all too easily misunderstood by modern critics and regarded as a forerunner of deism. But Arius did not argue for a historical Jesus as against Athanasius' metaphysical Christ. That question did not exist for Arius.

[9] H. Kutter: *Not und Gewissheit* (1927), p. 139.

Arius fell into error through his own division of soul, which caused him to make of Christ a supernatural person who nevertheless was not supernatural. His rationalistic temper prevented him from going all the way into metaphysics. Mystery was alien to him, and consequently his Christianity lacked depth. Arius attempted to solve the Christological problem by proceeding from rational premises. It is an effort that has been repeatedly made throughout history; evidently it corresponds to some deeply rooted need of men. But the Gospel is by its very nature irrational and defies any attempt to master it by reason. Arius failed to see the unfeasibility of the logical approach, and that is probably the greatest weakness in his system. His efforts were doomed to failure, for to prove by logical formulations what is beyond logic is bound to lead into a network of contradictions. Such contradictions are to be found throughout Arius' arguments. Arianism is an impossible attempt to unite the opposing Christologies of Origen and of Paul of Samosata. For this reason the Arian Christ impresses one as a regrettable hybrid, for he is at one and the same time called a creature and the Creator of the world. A Christ who was not eternal and yet existed before all time began becomes a demigod, which is to say a contradiction in terms.

But this error too was not sheer error; it aimed at truth. What Arius was saying was an aspect of the truth, and should at last be recognized as such. Arius was fighting to keep monotheism from sinking into ditheism. He opposed the metaphysical exaggeration of Christ which infringed upon the singularity of God. To maintain the oneness of God, no absurdity in the matter of Christology was too great. With intense fervor he advocated an almost Jewish monotheism. Let us remember that it is possible to protest out of the deepest religious spirit against exaggerated development of the Christological process.[1] If Jesus is elevated too far into a superhuman realm, too wide a gulf arises between him and the Christian believer. What Christ thereby gains in sublimity he loses in vitality. After Arius, the overemphasis upon

[1] Cf. C. Blumhardt: *Ihr Menschen seid Gottes* (1928), p. 192.

the divinity of Christ acutely imperiled the idea of the imitation of Christ which is essential to Christianity. Arius was very anxious to stress the imitation of Christ, a theme which is easily thrust into the background by one-sided emphasis upon Christ's function as Redeemer. And here Arius was right, and saw clearly that this eternally valid truth was endangered by dogma. At a much later age Kierkegaard recognized the same peril, and in this respect the Dane served a function similar to that of Arius. "By dogmas," said Kierkegaard, "we shield ourselves against everything that with some degree of truth could be called a Christian exemplar." [2]

Since the error in Arius proved to be a way to truth, his efforts did not fade away without leaving a mark. His enemies tried to represent his sudden death as a sign of divine punishment. The Arians lost no prestige as a result of it, and the struggle continued with as much vehemence as before. The dispute went beyond the person of Arius, who had only started the ball rolling. We cannot here devote space to the further history of Arianism, which its enemies unjustly represented as poorly disguised paganism. But Arianism was by no means a small sect. Favored by Emperor Constantius after 355, it grew into a great church which claimed that it alone was the true church. One of the less amiable attributes of Arian Christianity was the readiness with which it accepted subordination to the state.[3]

Arianism was also the first Christian faith of the converted Teutons.[4] Bishop Ulfilas was an Arian and spread the Arian version of Christianity among his Goths. Among the Arians were such tolerant Christians as Agilas. Gregory of Tours told Agilas the story of Arius' death as proof of the invidiousness of the doctrine. To this Agilas replied quietly: "Do not defame a doctrine which is not your own. We, for our part, although we

---

[2] Sören Kierkegaard: *Angriff auf die Christenheit* (1896), p. 269.
[3] Cf. Heinz Giesecke: *Die Ostgermanen und der Arianismus* (1939), pp. 57 f.
[4] Cf. H. von Schubert: *Das älteste germanische Christentum oder der sogenannte Arianismus der Germanen* (1909).

do not believe what you believe, do not revile you. For we see that it is not a crime to believe one way or another." [5]

Pelagius

Around the year 400 Pelagius appears out of obscurity, arriving in Rome, where he stayed till the sack of Rome by the Goths in 410. Probably Ireland was his home, but the circumstances of his early life and education are unknown. Pelagius was a monk, though not a priest. He had not, however, joined any monastic group, nor did he live as a hermit; this was nothing extraordinary in the pre-Benedictine age. Carefully dressed and erect of bearing, Pelagius aroused respect in the capital. His gentle nature, his peaceful disposition and quietly superior intellect, soon won him many friends in the city. He had a logical mind, practically inclined, with a strong distaste for farfetched speculation. Consequently, he was not at all drawn to the mystical side of Christianity. Calm and sober, he was averse to all excess.

With his high moral character Pelagius was shocked by the corruption of the Eternal City. He was disturbed by the religious indifference of many Christians, by the superstitious ceremonialism and the theological contentiousness he found in Rome. Zealously, he set to work preaching against the lukewarm morality that had entered so many Christian circles. Soon the stricter Christians were flocking to his sermons. At the same time he avoided all disputatiousness, posed no theses, and did not attempt to set himself up as a teacher.

In his struggle against the declining morality of Roman Christendom, Pelagius made the significant observation that the degeneration could not be ascribed to the decay of the Empire, which at that time was undergoing its last agony. Moral decline,

[5] A. Helfferich: *Der westgotische Arianismus und die spanische Ketzergeschichte* (1860), p. 49.

Pelagius held, was indirectly fostered by the doctrine which stressed man's redemption through Christ too exclusively and ignored man's own efforts. The view that doctrine could encourage religious indifference was unprecedented, and is thus worth examining more closely.

First of all there was the concept of infant baptism which explained this sacrament as essential to the remission of sins, rather than for sanctification in life. Pelagius could not feel that newborn children really had sins which had to be remitted by the baptismal waters. This question of infant baptism, however, was only a springboard for Pelagius to attack the still more difficult problem of original sin on which it was based. Once again Pelagius judged this question in the light of Christians' conduct, and was thereby led to reject original sin. Here as always his concern was Christian practice, which he saw endangered by false theory. To his mind there was no sin which the parents of mankind had passed on to all their descendants. To be sure, Adam's disobedience had injured man, but only as a bad example. Death, Pelagius held, is a natural event and not the punishment for the Fall. Sin is merely a flaw of the will. The idea of sin attaching to man by his nature seemed to Pelagius self-contradictory. Sin, he argued, is not born with man, but is committed by him in his life.

In taking this position, Pelagius fought against lukewarm morality. The problem of freedom of the will is obviously intertwined with the question of sin. Pelagius wrote: "In the freedom to choose good or evil lies the pre-eminence of the rational soul. In this lies the honor of our nature and its dignity. Therefore the best receive praise and reward. There would be no virtue in him who perseveres in the good if he had not had the possibility of going over to evil." And with a holy earnestness he cried: *We gainsay the Lord when we say: it is hard, it is difficult, we cannot, we are only men, we are surrounded by weak flesh. O blind folly! O unholy recklessness! We accuse God of a double ignorance: that he appears not to know what he made, and not to know what he commanded, as if he were forgetful of human weakness whose Author he himself is, and had imposed upon man laws beyond his capacity.*[6]

Pelagius was outraged by the view that man ought to have been made so that he could not sin. To maintain this, Pelagius held, was to ascribe the responsibility for sin to God himself. Nevertheless, Pelagius declared, serious endeavor to practice virtue is impossible without the assistance of the Holy Spirit. He never denied the necessity of grace. Grace equips man with freedom of the will. In Pelagian doctrine, the importance of Christ consists in his teachings and his example. We must always keep in mind that Pelagius' ideas on original sin and freedom of the will were always inspired by a practical desire for moral reform.

Augustine took issue with these views of Pelagius. We can be sure that the great African Father of the Church did not do so out of contentiousness, but because he saw truth gravely imperiled.[7] Augustine's conception of the Gospel was, in keeping with his whole spiritual development, totally different from that of Pelagius. Had he not written in his autobiography: "Give what you command, and then command what you will"—an utterance which Pelagius questioned. Augustine, on the other hand, held that Pelagius' doctrine narrowed the field for the operation of grace. Infant baptism, Augustine contended, had exactly the same purpose as baptism of adults, namely, remission of sins. Every man brings the corruptness of his nature into the world with him, so that it is impossible for him not to sin. Original sin is passed on by means of sensual pleasure in the act of generation. Through the sin of Adam, man's freedom of will has been entirely lost. Given his present corruptness, man can desire only evil. If he occasionally commits good acts, this is only the work of grace, which is irresistible. From eternity God freely decided to give bliss to a few, the rest of mankind being subject to damnation. For these few alone Christ has come into the world.

[6] G. F. Wiggers: *Versuch einer pragmatischen Darstellung des Augustinismus und Pelagianismus* (1833), I, 125.
[7] Cf. H. Reuter: *Augustinistische Studien* (1887), pp. 4 f.

Thus Augustine was the renovator of the doctrine of predestination which had already been developed by Paul. These ideas were diametrically opposed to those of Pelagius, and Augustine made this known in the sharpest manner.

Pelagius went to Africa to discuss the matter personally with the great Father of the Church. Just once these two great men confronted one another face to face—and we can only wish we knew more about the meeting. At that time Augustine still spoke with respect of his opponent, of whom he had heard much praise. He himself called him "our brother." But soon the fundamental antagonism between their viewpoints put an end to this truce. Once again Augustine took the convenient course of denouncing adversaries as heretics—as he had done with the Donatists. The topic was discussed at a number of councils in Africa, and under the pressure of Augustine's overriding authority Pelagius was condemned. In addition, Augustine treated all followers of Pelagius as heretics, although he had earlier refrained from going so far. Thus the man who had been fighting for the purity of Christian morals found himself excommunicated. It is understandable that henceforth he became more and more averse to Augustine's arguments. He found them mere pretexts for failure to fulfill the Commandments.

Depressed by his experiences in Africa, Pelagius went to the East, where he succeeded in winning a number of bishops over to his cause. In negotiations at Diopolis the charges against him were quashed. It is a moot question whether he recanted with mental reservations or whether he trimmed his doctrines to some extent in order to win favor from the eastern bishops. It is true that these were emotionally somewhat inclined toward the side of Pelagius. But they did not shoulder his cause, even though they recognized that in the matter under dispute Augustine had represented novel views, while Pelagius had merely given a sharper formulation to traditional conceptions. Historians of the Eastern Church do not so much as mention the dispute. Pelagius went on to Jerusalem, where he is said to have been expelled from the city because of his doctrines. Where he went thereafter is uncertain. The time and place of his death are unknown.

With the passing of Pelagius a powerful spiritual drama came to a temporary end. Modern man is sometimes apt to regard original sin as an outmoded problem in theology. What, however, did Pascal say but: "Undoubtedly nothing offends us more than this doctrine. And yet without this obscurest of all mysteries, we are the greatest of enigmas to ourselves." [8] The question of original guilt—which is also implicit in Greek tragedy —reveals itself to every man who has glanced into the abysms of life. Nor can we deny that evil must have a supernatural foundation, for it exceeds the scope of human reason. Augustine, too, had considerable difficulty accepting the "immoralism" of the Bible. The Bishop of Hippo would by far have preferred a world in which the sun does not set upon good and evil alike, but shines only for the good. But Augustine did not decide the matter according to his personal preferences. He bowed before the incomprehensible mysteries, and did not close his eyes to the eternal antinomies. His religious conscience compelled him to take arms against a merely moral conception of Christianity, which reduced the Gospel to intolerable shallowness. For Augustine still had a living awareness of Paul's imperishable paradox, that man must create his salvation in fear and trembling, although it is God who produces in him both the desire for salvation and the perfection of it.

In spite of all this, we cannot dismiss Pelagius as a superficial thinker. Quite understandably, his views were eagerly taken up and warmly defended by rationalists in all ages. Yet, although Pelagianism bears a certain resemblance to Stoicism, it must not be equated with pure moralism. Pelagius was not trying to attain man's independence of God; he was not trying to forge an autonomous human ethic, despite the fact that his doctrine has so often been taken in this light. A ray of truth had fallen upon Pelagius, and the viewpoint he presented had a special function

[8] Pascal: *Pensées*, Fragment 443.

to fulfill in an age of decadence. For Pelagius fought for the immeasurably precious good of man's freedom. That freedom cannot be surrendered without loss of human dignity. History has always bitterly avenged the denigration of human freedom. Unless man's freedom to make his own decisions is recognized, he is reduced to a mere marionette. According to Pelagius, the Creator conferred moral authority upon man, and to detract from that authority is to cast doubt upon man's likeness to God. Certainly the Irish monk had no idea that in defending man's freedom of will he might be minimizing the role of grace in favor of a self-glorification of man. Rather, he was aware of the sluggishness of the human heart; he wanted to cut away the excuses which are repeatedly used to justify ethical slackness. By insisting on practical Christianity, he was attempting to close off all roads of escape to shirkers, to make their responsibility clear to them. Man, he held, was a born sophist, always inclined to excuse himself and place the blame for his inadequacies upon God. Pelagius was determined to make such alibis impossible. Endlessly he called upon the neglectful Christian to work for his salvation, not rely exclusively upon the Redeemer. In this endeavor Pelagius was only following a consistent course of Western theology since Justin. Augustine was wrong in accusing him of radicalism. Pelagius' heresy was based upon a long and honorable tradition.

Because this was so, and because it contained elements of truth, Pelagius' doctrine could not be suppressed. Crushed by the weight of Augustine's authority, it was revived during the fifth century and in the modified form known as Semi-Pelagianism was discussed at the councils of Orange and Valence in 529. Semi-Pelagianism sought a middle road between Augustinism and Pelagianism; it accepted a weakened freedom of the will, but would not allow that this freedom had been altogether abolished. This new middle-of-the-road doctrine was eyed mistrustfully by Augustine's followers. New struggles ensued, which ended once more with the victory of Augustinism.

Even this second condemnation did not succeed in finally destroying the ideas of Pelagius. Having been expelled through the Church's front door, they cheerfully returned at the rear. In the Eastern Church the weight of opinion was in any case strongly on Pelagius' side, and Pelagianism was belatedly taken into the Occidental Church in the guise of the sixteenth-century Jesuit doctrine of Molinism. Down to the present day Semi-Pelagianism is advocated from many a pulpit. As Pascal so profoundly said, men are by nature Pelagians and become Augustinians only through grace. It is as we have so often stated: certain elements of truth cannot be suppressed; the Church may brand them as heretical, but again and again they force their way to recognition in one way or another.

It is a sign of the heretic's sensitivity to decisive questions that Pelagius should have made freedom of will the central issue of his doctrine. Since those faraway days this question has never ceased to be discussed, for it is one of the great metaphysical themes of the West. Its very insolubility has stimulated philosophical minds to attack it repeatedly. It is impossible to think about life without raising the question of freedom of the will. Yet despite all the passion with which the debate has been conducted, the most that can be done with this problem is to ask certain questions and make certain assertions. No dogma can be formed to deal with it. It is the same with the question of original sin. In neither case has anyone arrived at so clear and incontrovertible a solution as to justify anathematizing the opponent. There is truth in both negation of and affirmation of the will's freedom, and for this reason the one view never succeeds in overcoming the other. Negation of freedom has rational comprehensibility on its side; affirmation has the allure of metaphysical profundity. The Christian finds it hard to see how man can remain free since God after all predetermines everything. There is nothing in the Bible by which to judge whether Augustine or Pelagius was right. This being so, the intellectual struggle between these two men continues within the Christian community, figuratively, down to the present day. Scripture contains statements which can be understood only in terms of freedom of the will, and other statements which unequivocally deny that freedom. This ambiguity in the Bible greatly complicates the question, as Erasmus and Luther were later to discover in their great dispute upon this problem—a dispute reminiscent of the clash between Pelagius and Augustine. The relationship of human freedom to divine grace cannot be ultimately decided, for it is an unfathomable mystery.

Can it be said that at the end of the great Arian and Pelagian disputes truth had triumphed and error lay defeated at its feet? Hardly—although the victorious majority had indeed brutally crushed the minority. The Church might contend, in self-defense, that it had to come to some decision. If it were not to be reduced to a mere debating society, it had to clarify its dogmas. If everyone upheld his own views, a babel would ensue which would leave everyone in doubt. For the Church it was a necessity to speak in unequivocal language, to state bluntly what it thought right and what wrong. This is the great value of ecclesiastical dogma: a clearly delineated system is provided, and everyone knows exactly where he stands.

But a price is paid for this achievement. The victory won by the Church in these doctrinal struggles proved to be fraught with new dangers. Refusing to admit that religious problems could be considered from more than one point of view, the Church councils insisted with unparalleled obstinacy upon a monistic interpretation of Christianity. All Christians with other ideas were condemned as heretics. Granted the inextricable mingling of truth and error in this world, this meant that a part of the truth was inevitably lost. And with such an attitude, Christianity proved incapable of solving the problem of minorities. It would not brook any opposition within its ranks. Such a position has always proved unfruitful. And the consequences were disastrous. The Russian Christian Nikolai Berdyaev has summed up the unfortunate result in these words: "For the first time in the history of civilization, Christianity began to judge every idea from the point of view of orthodoxy or heresy, and thus set a tragic example of the collectivist mode of thinking." [9] Collectivistic thinking is an atrocious idol even in ecclesiastical matters, a Moloch to which many Christians were ruthlessly sacrificed. No amount of coherence in the Church's world-view makes up for the loss. When modern man groans under the yoke of collectivistic thinking in the totalitarian state, it must be remembered that the Church long ago provided a terrible example. She took the lead in teaching compulsory unity of thought as something divinely desired. The totalitarian state has only been her docile pupil in thought control.

If Christians claim the freedom to oppose all forms of intellectual slavery, they must first of all utterly renounce the collectivistic mode of thinking in their dogmatic disputes. It will no longer do to brand those who disagree as dangerous heretics. Rather, the sincerity of their dissent must be recognized. The heretical point of view must be regarded as a needful corrective to the doctrines of the Church—that, indeed, is our aim in recording the history of heresy. Not until the Christian has fought his way through morasses of prejudice to such a view will he be on the way to truth. Only by acknowledging the value of heresy can Christianity solve the great task with which it is confronted: to establish universal unity. Universal unity and collectivity are not the same thing; they are as different as day and night. Collectivism apes universal unity, it is a means of enforcing a solution from below, whereas universal unity is grace itself descending from heaven to earth. This kind of unity alone can solve the perplexing problem of the individual and the community. True universal unity can be attained only by way of freedom, by eschewing all coercion of men's hearts. Only thus can a new future for Christianity dawn.

[9] Berdyaev: *Wahrheit und Lüge des Kommunismus* (1934), p. 66.

8

The Loneliness of the Heretic

In the northern Europe of the Early Middle Ages, the primary energies of the Church were still being devoted to the Christianizing of the various German tribes. The appearances of heresy were quite sporadic, for heresy always supposes a fairly discriminating intellectual life, and its subtle problems tend to be unreal for men of a missionary era. Heresy as we know it gathered to a flood only in the High Middle Ages.

The heretics of the Early Middle Ages were so far in advance of their times that their contemporaries could not comprehend them. They were totally isolated in a spiritual sense from their fellows. There are few persons in history who lived in such inner solitude as the heretics of the Carolingian age. But what need has a man for community if his religious convictions suffice him? None of these men complained, as other thinkers have done, about the incomprehension of the populace, for they were well aware that their situation could not be otherwise. The heretics of the Early Middle Ages found their isolation fruitful because they lived in true communion with the Eternal.

Gottschalk the Monk

In Carolingian times the protracted struggle between the Franks and the Saxons came to an end. Christianization had not been a matter of religious conviction; it was imposed upon the Saxons by their Frankish conquerors. Baptism had, fatefully, been made the sign of submission. The Church was needed to give the empire of Charlemagne its necessary unity; the emperor followed a policy of state Christianity, and tried to incorporate the Saxons into that empire. The Saxon leaders were unwilling to accept Christianity on such terms—this must be said to their credit. The grim struggles between Franks and Saxons formed the background of Gottschalk's childhood.

Lonely, never understood, Gottschalk's life was consigned to almost complete oblivion. Few people have ever heard his name; fewer still have much of a conception of him. Only a tiny group of scholars have attempted to assign him his proper place in the history of the Church. No chronicle contains any detailed account of him, and only a few fragments of his works have been preserved—everything else was destroyed. Once again, as so often, we can form a picture of his character, vigorous, direct, and typically German, only from the statements of his adversaries. There is enough, however, to show us that Gottschalk sacrificed his whole life for his religious conviction. At the same time the fate of Gottschalk augured ill for those who might follow in his footsteps. The fate of independent thinkers in the coming centuries was foreshadowed by the treatment given to this brooding mystic who was so brutally silenced.

Gottschalk was a rare phenomenon for those primitive times: a man whose religious life had a pronounced personal character. Nordic and introspective, he was filled with an unwavering consciousness of the reality of God. He had experienced God directly and had no need of intermediaries. Consequently Gottschalk was scornful of the priests. This immediacy of experience with the divine is movingly expressed in one of the few poems of his that have been preserved:

> *What command dost thou give me, O infant Boy,*
> *What demand dost thou make, O infant Son,*
> *That I am compelled to sing sweet songs,*
> *That, exiled, I sail through a sea of wrongs?*
> *O why, why should I sing to thee?* [1]

Given such highly individual devoutness, conflict with the Christianity of his times was fairly predictable. The circumstances of Gottschalk's personal life sharpened the clash.

It began with Gottschalk's dramatic struggle with his monastery. Gottschalk was born a few years after Charlemagne's coronation as emperor on Christimas Day, 800. The son of a Saxon count named Berno, Gottschalk was early orphaned, and at the age of five was given to the monastery of Fulda for education. As his knowledge of the patristic writings and the artistry of his own poems prove, he was well instructed at Fulda. Since he was the heir to a considerable fortune which the monastery could well use for its ambitious building projects, the youth was forced by his abbot to become a monk. Gottschalk's entry into the order meant that his entire property went to the monastery.

Compulsory tonsure was a violation of the rule of Benedict. Gottschalk felt the monastery's action was illegal. He was also certain that nature had not destined him to be a monk. He did not want to spend his life behind walls. Monasticism required a vocation, he believed; since he had never heard the "call," he could not find peace in the monastic cell. His whole nature

[1] F. Wolters: *Hymnen und Sequenzen* (1922), p. 69.

craved freedom, and he was also shocked by the crassness of his superiors, for it was evident that the monastery was interested only in his property and not in his soul.

When Gottschalk came of age, he demanded his release and the restitution of his property. When both requests were refused, Gottschalk began a protracted struggle for freedom and justice. He waged his campaign with extraordinary persistence and without assistance from any quarter. Gottschalk appealed to Saxon law; the abbot rested his case on canon law. Gottschalk made the point that Emperor Charlemagne had expressly forbidden involuntary tonsure. The abbot rejoined that according to canon law parents had the right to consecrate their children to God. As a matter of fact, the young Gottschalk had been placed in the monastery by his kinsfolk, not his parents, but the abbot refused to admit this difference.

The Saxon monk now lodged a complaint against his abbot with Archbishop Otgar of Mainz. At a council in Mainz in 828 the case was heard. Gottschalk passionately declared that he was a free Saxon and that the abbot had no right to treat him like a purchased slave. The council decided that Gottschalk should be released, but refused him the restitution of his property. This self-contradictory verdict satisfied neither party. Gottschalk appealed. Since he was concerned for a principle of justice, he demanded not only freedom but the property that legally belonged to him. At the command of Louis the Pious, the matter was discussed again at Worms the following year. There is no record of the decision of the synod of Worms. Curiously, Gottschalk is found the following year staying as a monk at the monastery of Orbais in northern France. From this we may infer that the decision at Worms had gone against him and that his abbot got rid of this unruly monk by shipping him off to France. But Gottschalk was not the man to submit to an unjust decision. He considered his fight a holy struggle for freedom and right, and the more the ecclesiastical powers conspired against him, the more resolutely he pressed his cause.

It may be said that sooner or later every man is the victim of some outrageous injustice, and that this is no justification for moving heaven and earth; that to fight on so stubbornly is crankiness and reveals a lack of Christian humility. Certainly this criticism can be made against Gottschalk. But the greatness of this Saxon monk lay in his ability to raise his personal misfortune into the suprapersonal realm. Gottschalk sought and found consolation and support in a doctrine which, it is true, made him a first-class heretic without his having intended any such outcome. The center of gravity in his conflict shifted; his struggle for justice proved to be only the prelude of a second battle which was to be of far more importance for the Church of his age.

Gottschalk ultimately found his comfort in the doctrine of predestination. This was no mere exercise in theology for him. He saved his soul by coming to believe that his fate had been prepared by eternal decree. His tormented heart found peace in Augustine's conception of dual predestination. In his credo, which he derived from Augustine, Gottschalk stated: "As immutable God before the Creation of the world by his grace immutably predestined all his elect to eternal life, so he also equally immutably predestined all the wicked, upon whom on the Day of Judgment the divine punishment will be visited for their evil ways, to their merited eternal death." [2] Divine salvation was confined to the elect; even Christ's sacrifice on the cross would affect these alone. The Saxon monk envisaged God as an eternally unchangeable will. God had predestined all that is and shall be before time began. This did not mean, however, that God was the author of evil. According to Gottschalk, God foresaw which men would of their own accord live a sinful life, and determined in advance their just retribution. Thus his doctrine of predestination led Gottschalk to the problem of free will, which he too was unable to settle in a satisfying manner. According to his paradoxical view, from the viewpoint of God there is no human freedom of will, because of predestination, but man nevertheless bears the full responsibility for his acts.

[2] In A. Freystedt: "*Studien zu Gottschalks Leben und Lehre,*" *Zeitschrift für Kirchengeschichte,* 1898, p. 3.

Failing to win the monks of Orbais to these doctrines, Gottschalk escaped from the monastery. Thus he gained his freedom at last, though illegally. Henceforth he led a life of wandering—far more congenial to his restless spirit than monastic contemplation. He turned up in northern Italy, where he preached to the populace and started a movement. With his fiery temperament and extraordinary oratorical gifts, he won many followers. As an itinerant preacher at the head of a band of disciples, he went everywhere proclaiming the doctrine of dual predestination. The populace took to his ideas; the clergy was consistently inimical. But poor Gottschalk was evidently not "predestined" to be a popular leader; he was banished to an island in the Mediterranean. The exact circumstances are unknown, as are the details of his later activity in Dalmatia.

In 848 Gottschalk suddenly reappeared in the territory of Mainz. A synod was being held in the presence of King Louis the German and his doctrines were being discussed. The former monk had the opportunity to confront his opponents face to face and to defend his views in an impassioned theological duel. But the contest only deepened his isolation. He found no sympathizers at the synod. His courage and eloquence were of no avail, and the majority pronounced against him. In spite of his appeals to the authority of Augustine, he was declared a heretic and commanded to return to the abbey from which he had fled. The following year Gottschalk appeared at the synod for the second time. The opposition was led by his first abbot, Rabanus Maurus, now Archbishop of Mainz, who saw to it that the verdict was even harsher than it had been the year before. The second verdict called for severe whipping for escape from the monastery, expulsion from the priesthood for obstinate heresy, and life imprisonment in a monastery cell. The assembled bishops and abbots hurled themselves at the poor culprit. According to a contemporary account *in an unheard-of scene of godlessness and cruelty the unfortunate was beaten to the ground with scourges and blows of the fist until, half dead, he was forced to throw into the flames of a fire the book in which he had inscribed sentences*

147

from Scripture and the Holy Fathers, the which he had collected to read to the council. This he was made to do with his own hands, and the book was burned to ashes in the fire.[3] The ferocity of this treatment was felt to be an unwelcome novelty since "in former days heretics had been overcome with words and disputations." The minutes of the sentencing were kept secret, but Gottschalk was thrown into the prison from which he did not emerge alive.

Nevertheless Gottschalk continued his heroic struggle. He spurned all offers of alleviation of his imprisonment. He wanted no mercy springing from pity; he demanded right and justice. Since he was not forbidden to write, he composed a new credo which expressed his views in ever sharper form. He offered to submit voluntarily to a trial by ordeal in order to demonstrate the truth of his beliefs. He was prepared, he said, to enter four tubs of boiling water. But his proposal was scornfully rejected as the braggadocio of a new Simon Magus.

For many years Gottschalk pined away in his prison. In the end the authorities prohibited him from writing; this, it was thought, was the only way to silence him. He bore this additional repression also, never wavering in his conviction that his creed was right, that God had predetermined the destiny of his elect from all eternity. For almost twenty years Gottschalk was buried alive in his prison. During this long loneliness not a single friend was admitted to his cell. But not even utter isolation broke his steadfastness. With magnificent fidelity to his creed he patiently endured his hopeless situation. At last Gottschalk fell ill. When the archbishop learned that Gottschalk was on his deathbed, he ordered that a moderate profession of faith be presented to him for him to sign, so that he might depart at peace with the Church. But even in the face of death Gottschalk refused to recant. True to himself to the last breath, he declared: "I would sooner die a thousand times for the truth than once submit to a lie." Still unbowed, Gottschalk died in 869, a glorious example of heretical steadfastness.

[3] In Dinkler: *Gottschalk der Sachse* (1936), p. 18.

The Church has never made Augustine's doctrine of pre-destination its own in anything like the manner in which this son of a people barely emerged from paganism passionately espoused that doctrine. Involuntarily we draw back from the arbitrary Deity whom Gottschalk preached; on the other hand, we can also feel the power of such an image of an all-devouring divine reality. Gottschalk himself, in his own words, felt that he had been "taught, inspired, armed, wonderfully and mercifully aided by the truth." And he therefore felt obliged "to believe the truth in secure, defiant and upright loyalty, to hold bravely to it and patiently to defend it." [4] Gottschalk's doctrine of dual pre-destination—which anticipates the whole of Calvin—is certainly a noose that closes around man's throat and makes him gasp for air. Yet it is impossible not to be swayed by the majesty of his concept of God. In Gottschalk God is seen once more as that Being into whose hands it is terrible to fall, the sovereign Lord whose decrees are made by standards totally different from those of hapless little men.

However it may go against our grain, there is an undeniable element of truth in the doctrine of predestination, the kind of truth that has prompted the modern religious philosopher Ernst Tröltsch to remark: "There is no getting away from it: Election, grace, predestination, selection are all-important. . . . Grace and election are the secret and the essence of history." [5] We are forced to recognize the immeasurable religious force contained within a doctrine of predestination that is not conceived me-chanically. Without that force, Gottschalk could never have endured his solitary lot for so many years. Jesus and Paul, Augus-tine and the Reformers, have elucidated the truth of predestina-tion. It is one of the most profound and consistent of efforts to grasp the world in purely religious terms. According to the doc-trine of predestination, the single significant factor in the uni-verse is the will of God, unlimited in its sovereignty; compared to it, men are nothing. The idea of election is indeed an insult

---

[4] In H. von Schubert: *Die Geschichte des deutschen Glaubens* (1925), p. 57.
[5] E. Tröltsch: *Der Historismus und seine Probleme* (1922), p. 101.

to human reason, and yet it is not easy to contradict Pascal's: "We understand nothing of the works of God if we do not assume as a premise that he wished to strike some with blindness and illuminate others." [6]

The principal significance of Gottschalk consists in his renovation of Augustinism, which has remained one of the most vigorous ferments in the history of Christian thought. The Saxon "really understood Augustine, looked into his heart, whereas others merely copy him to the letter." [7] But the rebellious monk did not realize that the Church had never taken over the whole of Augustine. Gottschalk had, indeed, stumbled into a curious situation. For everything that the Church had insisted on four hundred years earlier, everything it had then been Pelagian heresy to deny, was now anathema. As later happened to the profoundly religious Jansenists, Gottschalk was made a heretic for holding the same beliefs which had made Augustine a saint. In appealing to Augustine he was undoubtedly in the right, and the Church of his time in the wrong. He demonstrated that the great African had been not only the celebrated Father of the Church, but also the ancestor of many heretics. In his study of the Saxon heretic, Dinkler writes: *Gottschalk's labors in theology were critical of the Church, not destructive of the Church, for his truth about God's omnipotence was intended neither to defame nor to cozen the Church, but to help her find her way back from an erroneous path to the true Christianity of the Gospel. In condemning Gottschalk the Church pronounced sentence upon herself.*[8]

Johannes Scotus Erigena

According to a legendary account, John the Scot was murdered by his disciples within the holy precincts of a church. They stabbed him through the heart with penknives and styluses. The story does not say who incited the young monks to kill the

[6] Pascal: *Pensées,* Fragment 566.
[7] H. von Schubert: *Die Geschichte des deutschen Glaubens,* p. 57.
[8] Dinkler: op. cit., p. 40.

heretic. But for several nights after his death a heavenly light is reputed to have shone above his grave. Since this would occur only in the case of saints, he was revered as a martyr.

This legend reflects the ambiguous impression the personality of Erigena made upon his ninth-century contemporaries, who regarded him now as a heretic, now as a saint. John was an Irishman; in those days the Irish were universally called Scots. The Irish Church was notorious for its independent spirit, its reluctance to adhere to Roman practice. John the Scot manifested a good deal of that spirit of obstinacy which survives to the present day among the Irish.

Erigena was a man of unusual learning. In addition to Latin, he knew Greek—a rarity at this time. This early medieval Faust seemed so miraculously learned that people were actually afraid of him. In philosophical powers he towered over Boethius, Cassiodorus, and Bede.

At the beginning of the forties of the ninth century John the Scot came to the court of Charles the Bold in France, one of the centers of the short-lived Carolingian Renaissance. The king made him head of his Palace Academy and invited him to his table, where the Irishman could display his sparkling wit. This extraordinary man moved among his contemporaries like a Humanist ahead of his time. Yet the end of his life is lost in the same obscurity as its beginnings, adding to the mysterious aura around this man.

In the abbey church of Malmesbury stands a pillar bearing the inscription: "Johannes Scotus, who translated Dionysius from Greek into Latin." This single sentence sums up his contribution to his times. For Erigena's primary achievement was his translation of Dionysius the Areopagite, through which he was to wield far greater influence than through his original works. The translation, made at the king's request, has its linguistic flaws, but its significance for the Middle Ages was enormous.

In modern times the writings of Dionysius have been greatly devaluated since it has been demonstrated beyond doubt that he was not the same Areopagite who is referred to in the seventeenth chapter of *Acts*. But to prove what he was not is scarcely to solve his mystery. Dionysius remains an enigmatic figure, a glimmering of whose true countenance has only been seen in modern times by Hugo Ball.[9] The High Middle Ages, on the other hand, placed the authority of Dionysius next to that of the Apostles. Yet both scholastics and mystics owe their knowledge of this unique hierarchical thinker to the work of a heretic—a fact usually passed over in silence.

How much would have remained in embryo in the intellectual life of the Middle Ages but for this heretic's labors. Erigena's translation built a bridge between late classical Neo-Platonism and medieval Christianity. The result was not a corruption of Christian thought, but a profitable enrichment of it. Wherever traces of Neo-Platonism are to be encountered in the Middle Ages, they all indirectly go back to Erigena, who inoculated this vital serum into the corpus of medieval Christianity. He was the indispensable intermediary who brought mysticism to life once again. By his translation Erigena handed to coming centuries the cup from which the medieval mystics drank that ecstatic draught which works like an elixir upon the religious soul and communicates a foretaste of eternal bliss.

The Middle Ages understood and appropriated this part of Erigena's achievement. But, strangely enough, they did not at all comprehend the Irishman's further work, which sprang forth out of the translation like a plant from its seed. The applications which Erigena made for himself of the Areopagite's *On the Divine Names* and *On the Celestial Hierarchy* were not accepted with the same grateful spirit. The Irish philosopher's ideas derived from Greek thought, and this was so alien to the Latin churchmen of the time that they drew back in horror.[1]

Erigena turned the mysticism of Neo-Platonism in an intellectual rather than a spiritual direction. Out of Neo-Platonic building blocks he erected a unique structure of his own. His

[9] Cf. H. Ball: *Byzantinisches Christentum* (1923), pp. 61 f.
[1] Cf. H. Dörries: *Zur Geschichte der Mystik, Erigena und der Neuplatonismus* (1925), pp. 10 f.

book, *On the Division of Nature*, was a brilliant continuation of the ideas of Dionysius within the framework of medieval thought, the product of a master philosopher. According to Hermann Kutter this work "anticipated the philosophy of Hegel" and makes for "uncommonly enjoyable reading."[2] The lengthy book is written in the form of a dialogue between teacher and pupil—the latter taking more than a purely passive part. The dialectical exchange gives life to the frequently difficult discussion.

A preliminary chapter is devoted to the relationship between reason and authority, and in treating of this Erigena at once reveals his heretical point of view. Reason and authority, he argues, are only two different forms under which the same truth is communicated. However, he assigns priority to reason. *Reason teaches us this too, since authority has proceeded from true reason, not vice versa reason from authority. For every authority which is not approved by true reason appears feeble; on the other hand, true reason, because it rests soundly and immutably upon its own strength, needs no enforcement on the part of any authority; for true authority appears to me to be no other than the truth found by reason.*[3]

Though Erigena always spoke of the Fathers of the Church with reverence, he did not hesitate to reject the views even of Augustine if he considered this necessary. His arguments on the question of reason and authority, which is of such vital importance to the history of heresy, are not free of contradictions, for on the one hand he advocated humility in belief and on the other hand spoke with a proud self-assertiveness. The bold Irishman must be regarded as the founder of speculative theology in the early Middle Ages. He regarded true philosophy as true religion. It has been said of him that "he may claim the honor of first having expressed clearly the inner unity of philosophy and theology."[4] The idea of the union of Christianity and reason became the fundamental principle of all metaphysical speculation.

[2] H. Kutter: *Not und Gewissheit* (1927), p. 174.
[3] Erigena: *On the Division of Nature*, Book I, chap. lxix.
[4] Theodor Christlieb: *Leben und Lehre des Johannes Scotus Erigena* (1860), p. 112.

In Erigena's ingenious system, such speculation circles around a single problem.

In the center stands God, who is the unity of all being. Creator and creature, God and the universe, are different only formally, not substantially; the being of both is identical, for both are the divine Being. God alone is all in all. He is the principle, the center and the goal of the established universe. Again and again Erigena stresses the same idea: it is God who makes everything and who is made in everything; he is not any one thing, neither this nor that, but everything. Appearing in everything, he fabricates everything and becomes everything in everything and returns to himself, casting everything back into himself; yet while he is present in everything he does not cease to be above everything. God is both creator and creature, the beholder and the thing beheld, time and space, essence and substance of everything that exists. Erigena found he could express his stammering comprehensions of God only in a series of great paradoxes: "God is not the whole of the created world, nor is the created world a part of God, just as the created world is not the whole of God nor a part of the created world." [5] Since all beings exist through him, God likewise exists in things. He must be sought there, for he approaches man only in and through things. Throughout his cosmology, Erigena strongly emphasizes the connection of God with the world. The world was created in order to reveal God's nature. The meaning of the entire evolution of the universe is the praise of God's goodness.

Erigena's ideas should not be characterized as pantheistic, although they do easily give rise to this misunderstanding. If there is anything of pantheism in them, it is of a highly curious sort, constantly cross-fertilized by a firm theism. For Erigena not only tells us that God becomes known in the world and is its whole being, but also that he is outside of it, above it, and nevertheless in it and in himself, and furthermore that God is wholly present in the totality of his creation as well as in each of its parts, and yet at the same time remains whole in himself. Terms like "pan-

[5] Erigena: op. cit., Book II, chap. i.

theism" must be used cautiously in any case, for not much is gained by such labels which do not do justice to nuances. Erigena, in keeping with the influence of Dionysius the Areopagite upon him, was deeply convinced of the incomprehensibility of God. For him, God was the "overtruth," the "overeternity," and the "overwisdom." [6]

Man and the universe did not, however, remain in God. Erigena's second chief interest was the emergence from God, which had as its result the entire world's becoming only an echo and shadow of true being. This emergence took place by way of Adam, whom Erigena regarded not as a historical human person, but as the idea of man. Temporally, man was never in Paradise. In Erigena's view, sin came about at the same time as creation; it did not arise by mere accident. But Erigena found no evil in the nature of things. Wickedness was forgetfulness of the natural virtues; the activity of demons, too, arose out of similar weakness. Finally he uttered the daring doctrine that evil resides merely in the imagination of people who denounce everything that opposes their foolish desires. Underlying this conception of evil, of course, was the Neo-Platonist view of evil as non-being. There is a profound truth contained within this idea. Athanasius, too, considered evil a passing cloud, and Dostoevsky saw it as a transitory thing of no permanence compared with the eternity of Christ.

But Erigena's chief concern was with the return to God. He cannot be accused, as some have done, of misunderstanding Christ. The Irishman accepted the Christology of the Church, but it did not fit smoothly into his conception of the universe. For Erigena conceived redemption not as the reconciliation of God with the world, but rather as universal restitution. Hence the effects of redemption would extend to the angels as well as men, even to animals, trees, the whole of nature. Here was a sweeping cosmic consciousness which had been entirely absent from Christianity since the days of the Gnostics.[7] This manner of embracing

[6] Ibid., Book I, chap. xiv.
[7] Cf. Christlieb: op. cit., p. 391, and J. Huber: *Johannes Scotus Erigena* (1861), p. 375.

the whole of creation in the restitution, such as underlies also Isaiah's vision of the Messianic kingdom, has seldom been examined in any review of Christian thought. Yet it alone really settles the problem adequately. As long as mute creation writhes in torment, it is impossible to speak of a springtide of God. "To put it briefly and plainly, there is no corporeal creature which possesses the motion of life that does not return to the beginning of its motion. For the end of the whole movement is its beginning, and it ends with no other termination than its beginning, from which the motion started and to which it always strives to return." [8]

Erigena's work contains, in magnificent vision, a symbolic interpretation of the world, wherein the Bible too is given a figurative meaning. It represents a new Christian sense of the universe based upon actual experience. To Erigena heaven and hell are states of the human consciousness. *When it is said in the credo: "He will come thence to judge the quick and the dead," we must not consider this in terms of a temporal motion, or of an emergence from the innermost depths of nature into this world, so that he will appear to the physical senses of those he would judge; but rather every good and evil man will see within himself, in his conscience, that arrival, when the books are opened and each man will be the judge of his thoughts and works.*[9]

With such a symbolic conception, the Irish philosopher was a forerunner of the whole of subsequent spiritualism, which likewise has always carried an odor of heresy. There is an amazing boldness about his system, with its many parallels to the thought of Meister Eckhart. His speculative drive led him to systematize everything, to include everything, not excepting the idea of androgynous man. The contradictions in Erigena's work do not lessen its value; contradictions are inherent in every religio-philosophical system because thought can never take in the whole of reality. Erigena was aware of this, and offered himself the comfort that "in this wonderful, divine ignorance evidently the

[8] Erigena: op. cit., Book V, chap. iii.   [9] Ibid., Book V, chap. xxxviii.

highest, inexpressible wisdom smiles graciously upon us." [1] It is folly to pass the patronizing judgment: "The man was better than his system." [2] It would be wiser to speak of this precursor of idealistic philosophy in the terms used by Huber, who has commented that his system manifests a "surprising grandeur of conception, an unexampled boldness of thought, and a wealth of speculative intelligence unique for his time." [3]

Erigena's thinking was so utterly out of key with that of his contemporaries that he could never establish any proper connection with them. When he did occasionally try to do so, complete incomprehension was the result. This emerged in the course of his conflict with Gottschalk. When Gottschalk stirred up the dispute over predestination, the king called upon Erigena to assist in clarifying the question. Erigena responded with an essay which approached the subject from so novel an aspect that both the friends and foes of Gottschalk rejected it with equal vehemence. For Erigena came out strongly against the notion of dual predestination, which struck him as "gruesome madness." He acknowledged only one kind of predestination: that of salvation. He was in fact on his way to the doctrine of the restitution of all things which Origen had espoused. But since this doctrine was universally interdicted, Erigena could not openly voice it; he ventured only to hint at it several times. To Gottschalk's particularism, Erigena opposed the absolute universalism of grace. The redemption brought by Christ had benefited all men without exception, he argued. Apocatastasis alone can content the religious heart; but just as it had been rejected by the primitive Church, it was likewise branded heresy in the early Middle Ages.

Erigena incurred the same suspicion of heresy when he participated in the second big theological dispute of his age, that dealing with transubstantiation, which had been initiated by Radbertus Paschasius. In an essay which has been lost Erigena once again advocated a view that was unacceptable to either of the parties and was condemned as heretical by both.

[1] Ibid., Book II, chap. xxviii.   [2] Christlieb: op. cit., p. 198.
[3] Huber: op. cit., p. 36.

The rumors of Erigena's heresies reached as far as Rome. Pope Nicholas I addressed a letter to Charles the Bold, asking that the man be sent to Rome. But the king did not obey the order, and Erigena remained in Frankland.

The first actual condemnation of Erigena's doctrines took place at a synod in 855. He himself appears to have made no response, perhaps at the king's request, or perhaps because he considered his opponents incapable of understanding his ideas. In any case, he never recanted. Several centuries after his death, in 1225, Pope Honorius III solemnly condemned his principal work, *On the Division of Nature*. Thereafter little attention was paid to his own writings, whereas his translation of Dionysius Areopagita continued to circulate unhindered and to exert wide influence. It was not until 1681 that *De divisione naturae* was printed, by Thomas Gale. The following year it was again placed on the Index. Erigena's speculative doctrine has remained suspect in the Church down to the present day. The odor of heresy has continued to cling to him.

Erigena's intellectual isolation was if possible even greater than Gottschalk's. And he too suffered the heretic's fate because he was an independent thinker who went his way without concern for the opinion of others. If we were to seek an image to describe this great man, we would have to call him the aurora borealis shining in the night of early medieval Christendom. The skies of those times were cold and void; there was only this solitary northern light pouring its radiance into the darkness. We stand reverent and spellbound, gazing at that vast illumination.

9

Eros and Logos

Peter Abelard

Peter Abelard was the first heretic to write an autobiography. In his famous *Historia calamitatum* he revealed himself as had no heretic before his time. For the first time he expressed what goes on in the soul of a heretic. Like most autobiographies, Abelard suffers from the inevitable flaws of self-reflection. Nevertheless, his confession remains one of the most moving documents ever written. Abelard had the gift of couching his feelings in words, and therefore his autobiography is indispensable to an intimate knowledge of the medieval heretics.

The picture of a human being that emerges from the *His-*

toria calamitatum is fascinating from the first line to the last. Abelard was anything but a dull personality. He had a sense of the dramatic that colored his life as well as his writing. The *magister* of Paris was a man of unusual endowments. His wit and the clarity of his intellect drew students to him. As soon as Abelard began lecturing anywhere, the youth of France and all Europe streamed to hear him and acclaimed him to the skies. He could present the subtlest questions in an entrancing, entertaining, and brilliantly cogent manner. With his talent, he made all intellectual discussions an adventure. The enthusiasm he aroused lasted throughout his career. There have been few teachers so adored as Abelard.

What swelled Abelard's fame during his lifetime, and what has kept his *Historia calamitatum* alive to this day, was the celebrated love affair in which he was involved. The whole world knows the story. The "troubadour among the scholastics" demonstrated in his life the truth of Plato's saying that Eros is a child of wealth *and* poverty. Erotic passion burst into his life, raising it first to such heights and then hurling it to such depths that we shudder to hear of it. When thirty-seven-year-old Abelard met the seventeen-year-old Héloïse, who was both lovely to behold and already one of the most cultivated women in France, he discovered the truth of the Greek conception of Eros as a demon. Understandably, this intellectual girl was impressed by the wooing of so celebrated a teacher, for Abelard was then at the peak of his fame. Under the pretext of wishing to direct her education, Abelard secured admission to the house of her uncle Fulbert, and soon the two were "one heart and one soul." They were on such terms that, as Abelard put it, "no stage of love was omitted by us in our cupidity, and if love could elaborate anything new, that we took in addition." [1] They themselves described their passion as "insatiable."

The fascinating figure in this relationship is Héloïse—if, as Plato observed, the loving woman is more divine than the be-

[1] *The Letters of Abelard and Héloïse,* translated from the Latin by C. K. Scott-Moncrieff (New York: Alfred A. Knopf; 1926), p. 13.

loved man. This girl's intellectual disposition was no less developed than her rare depth of feeling. The result must have been surpassingly charming. The power of Eros filled her to the last fiber of her being. "To madness did my love turn," [2] she confessed. To her lover she could say with utmost honesty: "Nothing have I ever (God wot) required of thee save thyself, desiring thee purely, not what was thine." [3] Here were the real marks of true passion. In Héloïse love reached such intensity that she made the unique avowal: "And if the name of wife appears more sacred and more valid, sweeter to me is ever the word friend, or if thou be not ashamed, concubine or whore." [4] For Héloïse the power of her feeling was itself a sacrament which removed the need for any further legitimation. Long before the Renaissance had dawned, Héloïse had liberated herself from traditional views concerning love and marriage. She sounds every bit a modern woman. What she was doing was highly immoral, but she had discovered that love was sacred, and she surrendered to it with religious fervor. There was only one law for her, the law of Eros, which she exalted above all else. In her sacrificial love she laid all she could offer at the feet of her beloved. She made declarations which for a medieval person are of incredible boldness: "For I (God wot) would without hesitation precede or follow thee to the Vulcanian fires according to thy word." [5] With disarming candor she describes the overwhelming effects of desire: "So sweet to me were those delights of lovers which we enjoyed in common that they cannot either displease me nor hardly pass from my memory. Whithersoever I turn, always they bring themselves before my eyes with the desire for them. Nor even while I am asleep do they spare me their illusions." [6]

Their mutual rapture, like Romeo's and Juliet's, was from the beginning threatened by tragedy. There have seldom been two great lovers whose bliss did not end in suffering. When Héloïse became pregnant, it was necessary to spirit her away from her

---

[2] Ibid., p. 57.
[3] Ibid.
[4] Ibid.

[5] Ibid., p. 60.
[6] Ibid., p. 81.

uncle's house. Abelard brought her to some of his relatives, where in due course of time she bore him a son. But the rage of Héloïse's guardian was beyond measure. To pacify him, Abelard offered to marry Héloïse, although under the rather questionable condition that the marriage be kept secret, in order not to damage his reputation. It was a melancholy wedding day when Abelard and Héloïse were bound in matrimony and immediately separated. Anxious to put to flight the rumors of their alliance, Abelard found shelter for his wife in a convent. The uncle was furious, seeing this as a repudiation of the girl. As Héloïse had feared, he took steps against Abelard. An underling was paid to fall upon his niece's seducer in the night and cruelly mutilate him. Abelard was left a eunuch. From now on the joys of love were closed to the two. On Abelard's urging, Héloïse, at the age of twenty, took the veil, thus renouncing any other love but his. He himself joined the monks of St. Denis.

It was a hard lot for a woman like Héloïse. In the end she found strength to bear her predicament with a courage as moving as her great love. Outwardly, Héloïse became a docile nun, fulfilling her conventual duties with exemplary conscientiousness. She had the faculty for winning all hearts, so that "the Bishops loved her as a daughter, the Abbots as a sister, the laity as a mother." [7] But behind her composure she concealed terrible feelings of grief and woe, which broke out in her letters to Abelard. "I have ever feared to offend thee rather than God, I seek to please thee more than Him. Thy command brought me, not the love of God, to the habit of religion. . . . For a long time thou, like many others, hast been deceived by my simulation, so as to mistake hypocrisy for religion." [8] Her heart cried out in anguish: "O—if it be right to say so—cruel to me in all things God! O inclement clemency! O fortune unfortunate!" [9]

She suffered torments of rebellion and remorse: "I find no penance wherewith I may appease God Whom always for that outrage I charge with the utmost cruelty, and, refractory to his

[7] Ibid., p. 41.
[8] Ibid., p. 82.
[9] Ibid., p. 77.

dispensation, offend Him rather by my indignation than appease Him by my repentence." [1] The one consoling element in the tragedy was the fact that Héloïse never broke faith with her first and only love. Her passion for Abelard never faded and never faltered; her love remained alive in her to her last breath. It was the calvary of a human being dedicated to love.

Abelard's conduct was quite different. Anyone who could win the heart of high-minded Héloïse must certainly have been no lukewarm lover. But to this man of lively temperament and receptive mind love was something other than it was to an innocent girl. Sensuality was a large component of his passion. After his emasculation, his desire naturally grew cold, and with it his whole attitude toward Héloïse changed. Her glorious lover became an embittered man who replied to her outpourings of affection with peevish moralizings. He tried to make a virtue out of the necessity of enforced asceticism. None of the godlike Eros was left alive in him. The miracle of their love became for Abelard only an unpleasant memory, which in the end he regarded as an unclean affair. It was not possible for him, after the disaster, to transform their relationship into a higher union, as Héloïse so burningly desired. He came to feel that his emasculation had been God's punishment because he had once made love to his spouse in the refectory of the abbey and had not checked his lust even during Passion Week. It is unpleasant to observe how Abelard translated his desexed state into a kind of theology, so that he replied to Héloïse's ardent letters with sermons. Yet he himself had fled to the protection of monastic walls more out of shame than out of true love of God. His bout with Eros faded out in a shallow rectitude.

Abelard's experience with the Logos is closely related to his immersion in Eros. Both developments were intertwined, and together they constitute the secret of his life. At any rate, we cannot understand Abelard if we examine each aspect by itself. In his intellectual involvements he behaved exactly as he did in his love

[1] Ibid., p. 80.

affair. The course Abelard took in the second half of his life, which ended in heresy, was like a repetition of his love affair on another plane. In the intellectual realm also he played for high stakes and lost the game, at least at the beginning. The game was no less thrilling than his relationship with Héloïse, and it had not only personal but also far-reaching social consequences.

We cannot grasp the significance of this experience with the Logos without calling to mind the historical situation. The Middle Ages were far from unitary. Examined closely, the intellectual life of the Middle Ages is furrowed by profound contradictions. The various centuries show sharp diversities. One decisive turning point in medieval thought came in the twelfth century—one of the most difficult of all centuries to understand. What dawned in the twelfth century was one day to lead to the opening of a new epoch. And Abelard contributed decisively to this new element.

In his intellectual battles Abelard took a position marked by the same subjectivism he had shown in his love affair. This is apparent everywhere in his works. In his "Conversation between a Christian, a Jew, and a Philosopher," the very title suggests the beginning of an exchange of ideas as yet unknown in the Middle Ages. Discussions between representatives of different religions, on an equal footing and with conclusions left in doubt, were certainly a risky enterprise. That no conclusions are arrived at cannot be adequately explained—although there has been a tendency to do so—by the theory that the final section of the manuscript is missing. Rather, a new spirit was at work here.

Akin to this dialogue is Abelard's principal work, *Sic et Non* (*Yes and No*), where his intention emerges even more clearly. Here it is impossible to overlook his insistence upon rationality. Abelard is the heretic who fought for the application of reason in religious questions. He was firmly convinced of the justification of and necessity for rational thinking. The exclusiveness of his stress upon reason is what we mean by his "experience with the Logos." That experience stirred him to the quick. For it is not only the hot desires of Eros, but also the coolness of the Logos which can kindle a man's passions. In bringing reason to bear upon religious questions Abelard acted with great boldness, and it does not detract from his achievement to say that he did not think his project through to the end. He was, after all, part and parcel of the Middle Ages. But if Abelard cannot be separated from his medieval environment, we are nevertheless struck by those tendencies in his thought which helped to bring forth a new sense of life, one alien to his age. In Abelard a new man was pounding on the doors of the church—although these doors were to remain closed until a much later period. Something fundamentally new began with Abelard. This becomes clear when his position on reason is more closely analyzed.

Abelard's extension of the dialectic method represented a further step along the road to a rational view of religion. He had taken the dialectic method over from classical antiquity, and wielded it with great skill. In his own words, "to the trophies of war he preferred the conflicts of discussion," [2] and he soon won the title of "master of dialectic." Abelard loved intellectual combat and plunged eagerly into disputes with adherents of older views. He may be credited with having introduced dialectic into the medieval schools. The method had previously been the property of lawyers; Abelard was the first to apply it to theology. It has been said of him that he tossed Christian truths into the air "like golden balls," caught them again, and played with them like a juggler. He loved to astonish his hearers by the prestidigitation of dialectic. His audience shuddered with fear and fascination as he demonstrated how perilously close one could come to the brink of eternity and yet keep one's footing. This dialectic daring won him the applause of youthful students; they rightly recognized it as an innovation, and the young are rarely loath to be on the side of novelty.

But Abelard took his dialectic seriously. By it he felt he could achieve a better defense of Christianity, and support the truths of the Church's doctrine against unbelief. "I applied myself to lecturing on the fundamentals of our faith by the analogy

[2] Ibid., p. 3.

of human reason." [3] Since Christians were no longer endowed with the power of working miracles, as they had in the early centuries, there remained, Abelard argued, no other method for proving the truth of their religion than logical proof based on the dialectical method. Whereas it had been the traditional view that faith must precede knowledge, Abelard presumed to reverse this assertion. He pointed out that logic came from the Logos which had become incarnate in Christianity. He was fond of quoting from the sayings of Jesus Sirach: "He who believes quickly is frivolous." [4] What Abelard had to say about the use of religion is, according to Hausrath, so persuasive and illuminating "that the discussion might have been closed in the year 1119; the following seven centuries have basically done no more than repeat the same arguments." [5]

Abelard's mind was above all a critical one, and his true concern was freedom of investigation, freedom to examine tradition. Free investigation is taken for granted nowadays, but in those times it took considerable temerity to call for it. In critical capacity and scientific lack of bias, Abelard actually stood head and shoulders above his contemporaries. Because he wished to open the way for new investigation, he took an unusual attitude toward paganism. Revering Pythagoras and Socrates as he did, he would not admit that these pre-Christian pagans could be excluded from bliss.

The application of dialectic and the championing of freedom of investigation dealt some severe shocks to faith in authority. Abelard was quite aware of this, and attempted to discuss the question. Far from minimizing the threat to authority, he underlined it. The very title of his *Sic et Non* had something provocative about it for the simple, ordinary Christian, for here was Abelard offering "yes, but also no" instead of direct, authoritarian assertions. In this work Abelard cited some 1,800 Biblical and patristic passages, grouped under more than 150 headings, which showed that both Scripture and the venerable Fathers of the

---

[3] Ibid., p. 23.   [4] Jesus Sirach, xix, 4.
[5] A. Hausrath: *Peter Abälard* (1895), p. 59.

Church had contradicted one another over questions of faith. He deliberately pitted authority against authority in order to demonstrate the inadequacy of the purely authoritarian approach, and thus show that men had to make their own rational decisions.

In so doing Abelard did nothing less than create the scholastic method, for this consists in marshaling the authorities on either side, and finally offering the writer's own view. Thus a heretic laid the cornerstone of the great structure of scholasticism!

The tremendous shock to authority caused by Abelard's dialectic method was felt by his contemporaries to be a revolutionary blow. With good reason they regarded his procedure as a serious threat to the existing conceptions of religion. Inevitably, Abelard's numerous opponents scented the heretic in him. He was accused of reviving the error of Pelagius. His doctrine of the Trinity was, it was said, tainted by the heresy of Arius. His concept of Christ's redemption was attacked. There appeared, indeed, to be many chinks in Abelard's armor. But the charges were only partly valid, for in these particular questions Abelard was actually moving along traditional lines. All these minor points were merely raised as pretexts. Abelard's contemporaries obscurely felt but could not clearly express the major objection to his views. For the heretical element consisted less in particular formulations than in Abelard's whole method. He himself recognized this and stated it lucidly in his last letter to Héloïse: "For the sake of logic I am hated in the world." The dialectical approach to theological questions was felt to be an undermining of Christianity.

A goodly number of Abelard's fellow thinkers had the gravest doubts about the application of reason to religious questions, and these foes of Abelard must not be underestimated. They were by no means all fools and obscurantists. Certainly no such thing can be said about Abelard's greatest opponent, Bernard of Clairvaux. It is essential to consider the mind of this redoubtable adversary in order to see Abelard's efforts in their true light.

Even in his lifetime Bernard of Clairvaux was looked upon as a miracle-working saint whose prayers alone sustained the existence of the whole world. Against the secularized Cluniac monasticism of his age he set the new ascetic idea of the Cistercian order. The century which was to be called by his name paid him extraordinary respect. Thus, the Church honored Bernard with the title of "the mellifluous teacher." Thomas Aquinas said that he made the whole world drunk with the wine of his sweetness. Dante venerated him above all other human beings and assigned him, in Paradise, the mission of being the last guide to the highest realms of bliss. For Bernard belonged to the company of blessed mystics; he struck certain chords which his contemporaries felt were entirely new and which have never since entirely died away. Bernard's God-intoxicated spirit strove to achieve perception of Jesus, rest in Jesus, union with Jesus, and bliss with Jesus. His thoughts circled around the passion of Christ. In his transports Bernard conceived Jesus as the bridegroom whom the soul, as bride, must take into its fervent embrace. His immortal sermons on the Song of Songs created the language of Christian ecstasy. This man of powerful feeling who coined the dictum "burning is more than knowing"—and what can better illustrate the gulf between him and Abelard?—likewise invaded the field of ecclesiastical policy with such energy that he became virtually an uncrowned pope.

With the keenness of a saint, Bernard was swift to perceive the dangerous tendency in Abelard's endeavors. He saw where the dialectical method led and felt that it was necessary to issue warnings against it. A mystic like Bernard, who threw the whole of himself into the search for God, could not help but mistrust the vanity of reason in Abelard. His rejection of Abelard was not personal; it was based upon his wariness of science in general. Yet his warning took the form of a personal attack: "Outwardly a monk, inwardly a heretic, he [Abelard] has only the name and habit of monk. He opens up the old cisterns and buried puddles of the heretics so that oxen and asses will fall into them." [6] Bernard felt that the twists and turns of dialectic were essentially im-

[6] Ibid., p. 178.

pious, and he was not going to tolerate them. He felt the keenest antipathy for this rationalist who would believe nothing that had not previously been examined by reason. Had not the prophet said: "If you do not believe, you will not understand"? As Bernard saw it, the sort of thing that Abelard was doing was destructive of all religion: *The faith of simplicity is mocked, the secrets of Christ profaned; questions on the highest things are impertinently asked, the Fathers scorned because they were disposed to conciliate rather than solve such problems. Human reason is snatching everything to itself, leaving nothing for faith. It falls upon things which are beyond it . . . desecrates sacred things more than clarifies them. It does not unlock mysteries and symbols, but tears them asunder; it makes nought of everything to which it cannot gain access and disdains to believe all such things.*[7]

It distressed Bernard to see the eagerness with which young students greeted the writings of Abelard. "A new evangel is being preached to the nations; a new religion is being spread, a different foundation laid. The virtues are discussed immorally, sanctity is debated without belief, the mystery of the divine Trinity is examined crudely; everything is twisted, everything treated contrary to custom and tradition."[8]

Bernard was not the only one to recognize the dangers inherent in the work of Abelard. Other theologians exclaimed that the *magister* of Paris had brought down upon France a horde of disputatious students who resembled the Egyptian plague of croaking frogs.

The battle between Abelard and his opponents was conducted with the passion that characterizes most theological disputations. Poor Abelard was harried by his adversaries like a wild beast encircled by huntsmen. Not for nothing did Abelard call his autobiography the *Story of My Adversities*. So desperate was his situation at times that he thought of "crossing the bounds of Christendom. I was ready to remove among the heathen, and

[7] Ibid., p. 222.　　　　　[8] Ibid., p. 230.

there in quiet, by some arrangement of tribute, to live christianly among the enemies of Christ." [9] Whenever he heard "that any gathering of ecclesiastical persons had assembled, I expected to be brought as a heretic or profane person before [it]." [1] For naturally he was given no chance to defend his position in fair debate. The outcome of such disputations was preordained.

Abelard was first called to an accounting at the synod of Soissons. He presented himself before the council in full confidence of victory, for he knew he was intellectually superior to his opponents. But the mental tourney for which he had prepared and in which he had thought his dialectic method sure to triumph failed to materialize. Debate was not permitted at all. "Without any process of discussion they compelled me to cast my aforesaid book upon the fire," [2] Abelard writes in his *Historia calamitatum*. With terrible sadness he watched the manuscript consumed by flames, while the assemblage sat in icy silence.

As if this humiliation were not enough, the heretic was required to read aloud, like an ignorant pupil, the Athanasian creed. Abelard did so in a voice so choked with tears that it often seemed he would not be able to continue, out of shame. He smarted so from the disgrace of this that he considered himself the most unhappy man in the world. Yet Abelard was not the kind of heretic who would unconditionally resist such an affront. His acceptance of the decree was, moreover, connected with his dialectic method: he did not believe in inflexible antitheses. Still, the humiliation rankled in his soul: "With what grief I boiled, with what blushing I was confounded, with what desperation perturbed, I then could feel, I cannot now express." [3]

In spite of this painful incident, Abelard by no means withdrew from the religio-philosophical discussions of his times. His temperament would not allow him to retire to a peaceful, undisputatious existence. Rather, he again and again plunged into the thick of theological battles in order to compensate for the defeat

[9] *The Letters of Abelard and Héloïse*, p. 38.
[1] Ibid., p. 38.
[2] Ibid., p. 28.   [3] Ibid., p. 29.

he had suffered. Although he might have seen that theological questions were decided within the Church by standards different from those of the lecture hall, he seems not to have learned his lesson. On Bernard's instigation a new trial of Abelard was held at the synod of Sens. If Abelard hoped to cut a better figure at this second council, he was sadly mistaken. The decision was pre-arranged—as has been the case at so many church councils. The abbot of Clairvaux wielded decisive influence over the governing body of the council.

A contemporary, Bérenger, has left a description of the proceedings of the synod which gives a graphic picture of the frivolous manner in which the problem of heresy was sometimes handled in the Middle Ages: *After the meal Abelard's book was brought into the assemblage and a crier instructed to read portions aloud. Full of hatred for Abelard and heated by the fruit of the vine—not of that vine Who said, "I am the true vine," but of that which cast the patriarch Noah naked upon the ground— he cried even more coarsely than was desired. After some time one could observe the bishops growing restless, kicking their feet together, laughing and jesting. It was evident that in this place a sacrifice was being made to Bacchus, not to Christ. Meanwhile the cups were hailed, the glasses praised, the wines lauded, the throats of the bishops wetted. . . . When occasionally the tumult was drowned out by something in Abelard's writings that partook of nobility and divinity, to which the episcopal ears were altogether unaccustomed, they became annoyed and gnashed their teeth against Abelard—blind moles berating the philosopher: "Shall we permit this monster to live?" And shaking their heads like the Jews, they cried: "He is destroying the Temple of God." Thus the blind judged the words of light, drunkards condemned the sober man; thus dogs snap at the saint, and swine munch pearls. . . . The bishops had drunk too much wine without water, and its heat so pressed upon their brains that all fell asleep. Meanwhile the reader continued to bellow, with the audience snoring. One propped himself on his elbow, another on a soft cushion, a third had dropped his head to his knees and slumbered. When the reader came upon a thorny passage in Abelard, he shouted to the bishops' dulled ears: "Do you condemn it?" Aroused by these last words, some replied in sleepy voices and with drooping heads: "Damnamus." Others, only awakened by these replies, called out merely: "Namus" (we swim). Truly you swim, but your swimming is like drowning. What they then did, what conclusions these idolators came to, are set forth in Holy Scripture: "The high priests and pharisees held a council." [4]*

Certainly this account is something of a caricature, and reflects Bérenger's bias against Bernard. But that Abelard was treated in a highly un-Christian fashion at Sens cannot be denied. Seeing that he was faced by a wall of hostility, Abelard gave up hope of defending himself directly and decided to appeal to Rome, thus annulling in practice his own insistence on rational argument rather than authority. The appeal did him not the slightest good, since Bernard had already seen to it that the Pope was primed against Abelard. The vicar of God upon earth took the propositions Abelard had sent him and personally burned them before the gates of St. Peter's. He sentenced Abelard to life imprisonment.

This second condemnation was too much for Abelard. After the synod at Sens he was a broken man. Nevertheless, he set out for Rome, hoping to have the judgment revised. But he was too weak to continue the journey and sought refuge en route in the monastery of Cluny, where he was graciously received by the abbot Peter the Venerable. The latter succeeded in bringing about at least a formal reconciliation between Abelard and Bernard. Only six months later Abelard, inwardly spent, died of a painful skin disease. Abbot Peter informed Héloïse of his death in a polished letter which does equal honor to sender and addressee. We catch one more glimpse of the noble Héloïse asking out of her love that the body of Abelard be sent to her. This was done, and he was given his last resting place within the walls of

[4] Hausrath: op. cit., p. 249.

her convent. Twenty years later she was laid in the same grave, so that the two lovers were united again in death.

If we seek to clarify the meaning of this life lived between the flames of Eros and the cold fires of the Logos, we are prone either to decide for Abelard and against Bernard, as did the nineteenth century, or for Bernard and against Abelard, as did his contemporaries. But these alternatives are too simple and scarcely do justice to the complexity of the situation. Abelard is a far from unambiguous figure. It is impossible to say Yes *or* No to him; we would do better to take the cue from the title of his own major work: Sic *et* Non.

Our "yes" applies to Abelard's daring in really making use of his reason. His advocacy of reason was indispensable to the progress of humanity. Without it, the human race would never have been able to free itself from superstition. Those first flutterings of reason's wings had all the freshness and exultation of youth about them. How magnificent reason thought itself, and how new it found itself! Before Abelard, Christianity had not experienced so soaring and triumphant a sense of life. Awakening consciousness of reason represented a historically necessary process. The movement from mythos to logos could no longer be checked; henceforth humanity could not entirely abdicate rationality. Abelard must be counted among the pioneers who founded scientific thinking. What the other theologians of the Occident had hitherto done unconsciously, this heretic raised to the dignity of conscious principle.

Our "no" must be directed at his amalgamation of the use of reason with dialectics. The dialectic method was never meant to be applied to religion because the elements of Christianity can be comprehended rationally only in a highly imperfect manner. They have to be grasped emotionally. Dialectic is useful for disputation, but its technique of statement and counterstatement is inappropriate for religion. Always inherent in dialectic is the danger that intellectual subtlety can twist and turn ideas its own way until the desired result is produced. The dialectic method lacks a sense of reverence. Abelard never asked himself whether it was permissible to talk about God in such a fashion. Indeed, he remained unaware that the principle of dialectic was essentially hostile to faith, for he never saw with complete clarity where his method of argument was leading. Abelard's reasoning stopped short at a certain point, and he therefore clung to the belief that he had found an essential prop for Christianity in which he could justly take pride. He did not realize that the same dialectical method with which he wanted to prove the truth of church dogma could also be used to refute it. As the history of Christianity wore on, dialectic did ultimately lead to unbelief. However little its founders wished it, dialectic terminated in religious nihilism.

The fate of Abelard's ideas has been in keeping with this "yes" and "no." One of the most curious aspects of his turbulent life was this, that his doctrines had to be defeated before they were accepted.

The repeated defeats that Abelard suffered during his lifetime were due primarily to the unscrupulous methods employed by his opponents. Certainly there is much to deplore in Bernard's treatment of Abelard. The abbot of Clairvaux was too disposed to accomplish his ends by ecclesiastical diplomacy, rather than by waging open combat on the philosophical plane. The manner in which Bernard brought about Abelard's condemnation was unworthy of the cause for which he fought; although we may largely agree with him, we cannot endorse his methods. The great mystic was not great in fighting heresy; he showed a rather low cunning and resorted to petty tricks to defeat an exceptional opponent. In reviewing the whole matter, Schiller became so indignant at the fate of Abelard that he termed Bernard a "clerical scoundrel" who suppressed all mental development and promoted "the densest monkish stupidity" because he himself had nothing to fall back on "but prudence and hypocrisy." All this, of course, overlooks the religious power of the man, his heaven-storming mysticism. Nevertheless, in his contest with Abelard, Bernard did stoop to base methods, and Abelard was defeated not by the superiority of Bernard's viewpoint, but by his greater "pull" in the world of ecclesiastical politics.

At the same time, Abelard's own character contributed a good deal to his downfall. The applause of his disciples stimulated his vanity, so that he became an excessively conceited person. He often acted out of arrogance. Since his brilliance as a lecturer attracted the youth away from other teachers, he despised his rivals and spoke condescendingly of them. "I esteemed myself as reigning alone in the world as a philosopher." [5]

The natural reaction to these feelings on his part was a general hostility toward Abelard. His whole life was passed in dispute with his enemies. Wherever he went, frictions at once developed. Whether he lived within walls or outside the cloister, he always turned people into his adversaries—in this the very opposite of Héloïse, whose charm and sweetness brought concord everywhere. Abelard was among the best-hated as well as most-worshipped personalities of his time. He himself always explained the ill will that surrounded him as envy. But his self-assertiveness at least partly evoked this envy. Yes, there was a demon within Abelard that carried him to destruction. In the end only humility conquers, and humility alone is in keeping with Christianity. Abelard succumbed to the diabolic temptation of pride. He had not sufficient character to match his enormous talent, and therein lay his tragedy.

In spite of his defects of character, however, the spirit of the future was on Abelard's side. After his death his books began to be read more widely, although his name was still under a cloud. A hundred years later his way of thinking was universally accepted, for the "summas" of the scholastics were written according to his method. He must be reckoned among the fathers of scholasticism, for the scholastics all followed in his footsteps. The historian of the scholastic method devotes ample space to the work of Abelard,[6] and according to Wolfram von den Steinen he was "for

[5] *The Letters of Abelard and Héloïse,* p. 10.
[6] Cf. M. Grabmann: *Die Geschichte der scholastischen Methode* (1911), II, 168 f.

Catholic science the most important thinker between Augustine and Thomas." [7]

Viewed in terms of the present, the essence of Christianity was actually involved in the struggle between Abelard and Bernard. The former believed in rational, the latter in symbolic thinking. These two modes of thought are neither mutually inclusive nor mutually exclusive. Rather, each must be assigned its proper rank. Reason cannot be excluded from religion; to attempt to stamp out reason is to surrender Christianity to obscurantism. If the dignity of man consists in his ability to think, the Christian is certainly obligated to make diligent use of this noble gift of God. We can never have too much of thinking. On the other hand, in purely religious realms rational thinking is destined to perform only crude drayman's labor. It does best to stay outside in the courtyard, as it were.

Once this rough work of reason is done, the religious man must pass on to the kind of symbolic thinking that, as in Bernard's case, embraces mysticism and must be considered superior to purely critical thought. Such illumined thinking leads to the sources of religious truth, for religious truth is always a synthesis of cognition and faith. Such symbolic thinking, with its supra-logic, unlocks the great figurative content of Christianity in its true profundity; by it the religious man may attain creative activity.

Only that Christian who understands the differing functions of lower and higher reason, and who knows how to use both forms of thinking, has been illuminated by the Logos, which kindles in him that heavenly Eros through which he beholds the divine again. . . .

[7] Wolfram von den Steinen: *Vom Heiligen Geist des Mittelalters* (1926), p. 262.

+   +

10

Underground Currents in Christianity

+   +

The Cathars

For many years historians viewed Manicheanism through the eyes of St. Augustine alone. They know better nowadays. It is true that the African Father of the Church had felt at home in that religion for nine years, and his writings serve as a mine of information on it. But he later developed into a fierce opponent of Manicheanism, so that his polemical writings are by no means unbiased. Only the writings of Mani himself afford a conception of the immensely dramatic cosmological views of this religion, whose consistent dualism held an element of truth of inescapable value to the Christian Church.

According to the meager information we have, the father of Mani turned away from the official Persian religion and joined a sect of "Baptists." Evidently this conversion aroused his son's religious interests, but nothing more is known about young Mani's spiritual evolution. Around A.D. 225 Mani began his annunciation of the new religion at the court of the Persian king, Sapor I. He went on great journeys to disseminate his doctrines, traveling as far as India. Once more in Persia, he won adherents at court, thereby incurring the hatred of the orthodox priests of the Persian religion. Finally he was cast into prison, flayed alive, and crucified. He left behind numerous writings containing speculations on the contradictions between spirit and matter.

The relationship of Manicheanism to Christianity was a curious one. Mani held that Jesus had been in possession of the truth, but the truth had unfortunately been lost again because Jesus himself did not set it forth in writing. The official Christian Church was degenerate, for it had remained static at a low stage of development and had not raised itself to true perfection. Instead, it had remained caught up in pagan sensualism. Like Marcion, the Manicheans considered that those portions of the New Testament which did not accord with their doctrine were the work of a forger. Reason alone, inspired by the Paraclete (the Comforter; see John xiv, 16), could bring about the necessary purification of Christianity from all pagan and Jewish elements.

Nevertheless, Mani had not arrived at his system by way of Christianity. Rather he—or his followers—approached Christianity by way of his system. Mani regarded Jesus as a prophet descended from the world of light, not the historical Jesus but a contemporaneous phantom Jesus who had neither suffered nor died: *Jesus impatibilis.* The Manicheans likewise recognized a *Jesus patibilis,* who, however, was captive in the whole of nature. "The *Jesus patibilis* is born daily in every plant that sprouts from the dark womb of earth; he suffers insofar as the striving soul is always held, in every single plant, within the narrow bonds of matter; he is attached to the material form, and he dies when the plant itself withers and disintegrates." [1] This Manichean idea is a dramatic and moving conception of the everlasting sufferings of God in the world.

One of the most remarkable characteristics of Manicheanism was its talent for mimicry. It could adapt itself so skillfully to other religions that at first glance the unpracticed eye could discern no difference. The Gnostic form of Christianity lent itself especially well to such imitation, and Manicheanism may in fact be regarded as a last offshoot of Gnosticism. Ultimately, Manicheanism became a reservoir into which poured all the streams of Christian heresy, a mightily fermenting basin of curious ideas.

Manicheanism swelled to a great movement which became one of the most dangerous rivals of the Christian Church. For a time during the fourth century it actually challenged the dominion of the official Church. After it had penetrated into the Roman Empire it spread like wildfire, drawing adherents from remnants of the Gnostic sects and from those Christians who were dissatisfied with the way the Christian Church was shaping up. The elevation of Christianity to the rank of a state religion, however, decided the contest in favor of the Church. Manicheanism was overpowered by the might of the state.

Once the Church had state power at its disposal, it began systematically to suppress Manicheanism. All Manichean writings that could be found were destroyed. But the process of extermination was not completely successful; Manicheanism lived on as one of the underground currents of Christianity. For since free expression of opinion was not permitted, such movements were compelled to go underground. In hiding, however, these movements underwent profound evolution. In the course of time Manicheanism became modified into the system known as Neo-Manicheanism, and rose to the surface once again in the Middle Ages, under the name of Catharism, to make considerable trouble for the Church.

The intermediary link between the Manicheans of the early

[1] F. C. Baur: *Das manichäische Religionssystem* (1928), p. 74.

days of Christianity and the Gnostics of the Middle Ages were
the Paulicians. Like the Manicheans, the Paulicians were concerned with the contradiction between good and evil. The good
God was the creator of a higher, invisible world which had nothing in common with this wicked earth, since earth had been created by an evil god. The human body was one of the creations of
the evil god, and is therefore to be regarded as wholly evil. Held
within the prison of the body is a soul made of entirely different
stuff, which constantly yearns for escape from the body. The
tradition does not make clear how this soul came into being,
whether as a creation of the good God or as an emanation from
him. Christ descended from the world of the good God, his ethereal body passing through the womb of Mary, using it as a chan-
nel. In keeping with this Docetist view, the Paulicians did not acknowledge that Christ had really suffered. They apparently as-
sented to the Trinity—but no specific details of their ideas about
the Trinity have come down to us. They took the Apostle Paul for
their teacher; Peter was rejected for having denied Jesus. They
refused to accept the sacraments, since water, oil, bread, and
wine could not possibly be the instruments of supernatural grace,
belonging as they did to the realm of Satan. The Paulicians
dubbed themselves Christians and referred contemptuously to
adherents of the official Church as "Romans."

The Bogomiles, a twelfth-century heretical sect founded by a
monk named Basil, also owed something to Manicheanism. They
went back to a primitive Christian sect who called themselves
Messalians or Euchites. According to Messalian teaching, there
dwells in every man, along with the soul carried down from
Adam, a demon who must be driven out by prayers in order to
allow the entrance of a higher spirit.[2] This doctrine was linked
with a form of quietism: man must strive for a state of utter absence of feeling, for only then could union with the Deity take
place. In Bulgaria, the Messalian-Euchite sect survived into the
second post-Christian millennium and then gave rise to the Bogo-

[2] J. von Döllinger: *Beiträge zur Sektengeschichte des Mittelalters* (1890),
I, 34.

miles, whose name is usually translated as "lovers of God." The Bogomilian heretics spread widely in the Eastern Church and maintained themselves in Russia for many centuries. According to their creed, the divinity is shaped like man, although God's body is not made of crude matter, but of some much finer substance. The Deity had not been trinitarian from eternity; rather, Son and Holy Spirit had come forth from the Father, as emanations from his eyes, in the year 5500 after the creation of the world, and returned to him after the passage of thirty-three years. Satanael, the elder son of the Deity, fell and thereupon created this earth. But he was incapable of animating man, so that God had to intervene and breathe life into man. This genesis explains the dual nature of man, whose body is a work of evil, but whose soul is the creation of the good God. The religion of Moses was condemned as a work of Satanael, its purpose being solely to mislead man. True revelation was brought by Christ. He descended from the upper heavens, passed through the right ear of the Virgin Mary into her body, and then assumed an apparent human body. In reality, however, he brought with him a subtler, more spiritual body, such as was alone worthy of the Deity. In the same fashion he passed out of Mary again. The Virgin, however, noticed neither his entrance nor his exit, but suddenly found him in the manger wrapped in swaddling clothes. Christ broke the dominion of the demons, so that these had to take flight from every Bogomile, and did not dare come closer than the range of a bowshot. The Bogomiles regarded the churches as the abode of the evil spirit; they rejected veneration of images as simple-minded idolatry. Ethically, the Bogomiles were highly ascetic. They condemned marriage as an unclean relationship, forbade the eating of meat, and observed a three-day fast each week. They did not accept the Old Testament at all, and interpreted the New Testament allegorically.

All these branches of repressed Manicheanism, and others such as the Melchisedekians and the Apostolics, ultimately came together again in Catharism. The first traces of the Cathars can be observed shortly after the year 1000. Their sudden emergence "out of the underground" caused great alarm in the Christian world. The Catharist movement was so alien to the whole temper of the Church that there could be no understanding or reconciliation with it. The Church could only counter by slandering the whole movement for its "senseless doctrines" and "frightful deeds." So effective were these libels that to this day reverberations of them can be heard. As usual, almost all the writings of the Cathars—or Albigensians, as they were also called, after the town of Albi in Languedoc—have been destroyed, and most traditions concerning them stem from their opponents. The secrecy with which their faith was surrounded and their practice of hidden worship made it easier to discredit them.

Catharism was particularly widespread in southern France. In the twelfth century sunny Provence experienced a cultural renascence, one aspect of which was the troubadour movement. The greatest troubadours of southern France put into song a new feeling for life, a new conception of spiritual joy. According to the troubadour Montanhagol: "Lovers should be pure of heart and think only of love, for love is no sin but a virtue which makes the wicked good and the good better. Love makes chaste." [3] True love was extolled as something as pure as prayer; it had nothing in common with sexual lust. A Platonic Eros stirred the hearts of the troubadours. Their new, sweet songs were sung to married women whose high morality was considered by the singer to be inviolable. No fleshly cravings must come between the troubadour and the lady of his heart, for he saw in her the embodiment of the divine principle. A new conception of women arose, one that was to be of epoch-making significance for the whole of the West.

There was a connection—one which still calls for study—between the "gay science" of the troubadours and the religious movement of the Cathars. *To be a heretic and to understand the troubadours were by no means mutually exclusive. In fact, most troubadours were heretics, all the Cathars were troubadours, and almost all the ladies of "Romania" became heretics when*

[3] Otto Rahn: *Kreuzzug gegen den Gral* (1933), p. 16.

*the first traces of age scored their faces. The Cathars transferred
the* leys d'amors *to the spiritual realm. In place of women's favor
they sought redemption in God. In place of love they sought the
Comforter. . . . The prayers of the Cathars and troubadours
were only a part of the hymn to the deity of light whom they
heard and saw every day in the tones and colors of their native
landscape. For they were poets.*[4]

The Cathars were a strange-looking lot. In contrast to the old
Manicheans, who wore white clothing to symbolize purity, those
Cathars who had received the "consolation" (see page 188)
dressed in long black gowns by way of mourning for the soul's
imprisonment in matter. Their faces were beardless and their hair
fell to their shoulders. Because of their long fasts, most of them
looked pale and gaunt. The purity of their mode of life made a
great impression upon medieval men; the Cathars seemed like
beings from another world. The Cathar ministers, called "per-
fecti," showed a strength of will so remarkable that it may be likened to a kind of genius. The Cathars thought entirely in terms
of the hereafter; they were resolved to take the kingdom of
heaven by force, and saw no value in this world. These men had
really sold all to win a precious pearl.

According to the usual view, the nucleus of the Catharist
doctrine was a pervasive dualism. This is supposed to be the
.strongest indication of their descent from the old Manicheans,
although they did not slavishly take over the latter's doctrines, but
gave their own rendering of these doctrines. This matter of the
dualism of Catharism is also stressed in any account of the Albigensians. But such terminology does not tell us very much. The
truth is that these heretics felt themselves forced into a situation
which we must understand in existential terms.

To use the language of Herman Melville, a latter-day Cathar,
the Albigensians had seen the white whale, that mysterious creature of which only very few can speak out of direct experience.
Figuratively, Moby Dick had appeared out of the sea and stirred
them to the depths of their souls. The white whale is simply the

[4] Ibid., p. 68.

183

symbol for inscrutable evil, whose overwhelming power and dreadfulness the Cathars met face to face. In the whole history of Western thought few groups have felt the presence of evil with such intensity as did the Albigensians. They were aware of the unbounded savagery and utter mysteriousness of evil as a real power, not merely as a negation. Evil was no intellectual question for them, but a dark menace to the life of man, an everlasting peril to his soul's salvation. Unfathomable absolute evil was engaged in a perpetual attack upon mankind. This evil the Cathars termed the god of darkness, who had created the temporal world and flung ever new terrors at men. The earthly world belonged to the evil god who had called it into existence. Surely this world was the prey of the evil one, for had not Paul regarded it as no better than filth, and had not Christ spoken of plants which had not been planted by his heavenly Father?

But the Cathars did not capitulate before the white whale. For them, the choice was either to destroy evil or be destroyed by it. Only the good could prove a match for the terrible monster. But they regarded the good not merely as a higher principle opposed to evil. To them good was a power, personified in the good God of light, the author of the invisible higher world order. The good God was pure spirit whom no wickedness could touch and whose essence was love. The Cathars had seen the good in all its scope and radiance.

The thoughts of the Cathars were always circling around the eternal contradiction between good and evil, spirit and matter. In keeping with their conception of the unmitigated clash between the two, they divided all men into two classes, the descendants of Abel and the descendants of Cain.

To the Cathars, good and evil were not moral categories but gigantic powers, basic to the existence of the cosmos, as they are in the writings of Melville. Good and evil were metaphysical truths to them, and therein lay the grandeur of their message. Good and evil were realities, supernatural forces, and knowledge of this placed human life on an entirely different footing. Since the contradiction between good and evil was not a theoretical problem accessible to human reason, the Cathars did not attempt an intellectual solution. What is commonly called Catharist ethics was an audacious assault against evil, which they were ready to pursue through all the abysses of hell. The Cathars hunted like Melville's whalers. Their mode of life was nothing but the attempt to slay the white whale. Only in these terms can we understand the intense asceticism by means of which the Cathars hoped to attack the realm of darkness. Tröltsch has declared that their pure and exemplary manner of life sprang from a "principle of abstention from the world." [5] They fought sensuality. Since the procreation of the human race was a result of the fall, sexual union between man and woman obviously bore the taint of Satan. Christ had praised eunuchs as blessed and had declared that merely to look upon a woman with desire—which, after all, every husband does—was sinful. Death could be overcome only by avoiding the reproduction of the human race. But when we consider this fierce asceticism, we must remember that the denial of sensual love was done for the sake of heavenly *caritas*. Behind the rejection stood a positive ideal. A life of perfection, the Cathars held, was possible only in conjunction with the virtue of chastity. He who indulged in sexual pleasure would not be granted a vision of the Deity—a point of view commonly held by mystics of all persuasions. This belief of the Cathars stood in no contradiction to the troubadours' Platonic conception of love. We have only to think of Wolfram von Eschenbach, whose *Parsifal* sprang from this atmosphere:

> The holy standard of the Grail he bears
> Who love of woman utterly forswears.

It is clear that such radical rejection of marriage ran counter to the teaching of the Church. The Church, too, subscribed to a belief in the conflict between God and Satan. But although it, too, occasionally spoke of the flesh as ungodly, it did so without the Cathars' passionate intensity.

For reasons such as these, the Albigensians held, the Church

[5] Ernst Tröltsch: *Die Soziallehren der christlichen Kirchen und Gruppen* (1919), p. 363.

was divided between good and evil. It straddled the fence and could not get up the strength to make a thorough break with evil. The true church, these purists held, must suffer persecution in this world; it must be anvil and not hammer; it must be despised by the world. The Roman Church, on the other hand, enjoyed universal honor and basked in the favor of the world. Some went even farther, asserting that the official Church was so corrupt that it represented the Whore of Babylon foretold in the Revelation of St. John. They held the Pope to be the Antichrist. The services held by the official Church were antipathetic to the spirit of Christ. Even the building of churches was wrong, for the Apostles had had none. Henry of Toulouse, who may be regarded as a forerunner of the Cathars, publicly preached: "Do not believe those deceivers, the clergy . . . who allege that they consecrate the Body of Christ and give it to you for your soul's salvation. They lie. Only once, at the Last Supper, was the body of the Lord given to the disciples; since then it has never happened again, and what takes place at the altars of the churches is an empty, vapid spectacle." [6] The mass, they contended, was unknown to the Apostles, and its very name betrayed its non-Biblical origin.

The Cathars considered the veneration that the Church accorded to images to be plain and simple idolatry. Peter of Bruys made a practice of chopping down all the crosses that lined highways and burning them in a heap. He believed that to worship before the cross was a blasphemy upon the divine nature of Christ, and declared war on the false symbol: "The holy crosses must be broken and burned, because the instrument by which Christ was so fearfully tortured, so cruelly killed, is unworthy of worship and veneration." [7]

The Cathars likewise would have no part of secular authority. Since the secular arm supported the Church, it shared in its evil. The Albigensians held that Christians had no right to take oaths.

[6] Döllinger: op. cit., p. 85.
[7] Christoph Ulrich Hahn: *Geschichte der Ketzer im Mittelalter* (1845), I, 417.

Law-enforcing institutions were unnecessary among true believers, they argued, and were in fact an invention of the evil god. Members of the sect were under no obligation of obedience to secular princes and judges. As they rejected death sentences, so they also condemned all warfare. To answer force with force was not permitted—in this they held views similar to those later adopted by Leo Tolstoy, whose philosophy contained many Catharist elements.

In their campaign against evil the Cathars forbade any taking of life, even of such creatures as gnats. Like Buddha, who had commanded his monks to lay down the staffs with which they were accustomed to strike, the Cathars had a feeling of kinship with all living creatures. This reverence for life had nothing to do with sentimentality; it sprang from religious principles of the highest order, although to implement such principles is a task of almost insoluble difficulty. In line with this, the Cathars were vegetarians. However, and in this way they were unlike the old Manicheans, they permitted the drinking of wine. They had curious eating habits, each individual cooking his food himself and owning his own plates, from which no one else was permitted to eat.

To strengthen the side of good in the struggle against evil, the Cathars created a number of extraordinary institutions. They had their own ecclesiastical organization; bishops and councils were not unknown among them. They practiced their rites largely in forests, for fear of persecution. The caves the Albigensians used for their worship—moving testimony to the hardships of their religious life—may still be seen in southern France. Once again Christians were taking to the catacombs. But the Cathars took pride in their persecution—was not true Christianity always persecuted in this world? "We lead a hard and harried life. We flee from city to city like sheep among wolves, suffer persecution like the Apostles and martyrs, though our only desire is to live piously, austerely and abstinently, only praying and working. Yet such tribulation does not trouble us, for we are no longer of this world." [8] The greatest sin was submission to the world. "The world's money is the corruption of the soul," they declared.[9]

The prime religious act for achieving eternal salvation was the Catharist *consolamentum,* or consolation, as they called the baptism of the Holy Spirit. This was indispensable for salvation and was more than a mere symbolic act. If a man died without having received it, his soul was either doomed to damnation or had to return to earth in another body. For a married man to receive the baptism of the Spirit, the wife had to give her consent, attesting her readiness to loose the nuptial bonds and consign her husband to God. Those who had received the baptism called themselves the "consoled ones" or the "perfect ones" because they had taken this great step. Once baptized, a man was expected to lead a holier mode of life, to pray constantly, to refrain from all unkindness toward his fellow men, and never to harm deliberately any living creature. So rigorous was the life expected of them that in practice most Cathars received the consolation only on their deathbeds. But those who were to be Catharist ministers would receive it when their superiors thought them ready. The vow that such dedicated souls took ran as follows: *I pledge to dedicate myself to God and his evangel, never to lie, never to swear, never to touch a woman, to kill no animals, to eat no meat and to live only on fruit. I pledge furthermore never to travel, never to live or to dine without one of the brethren, and if I should fall into the hands of our enemies or be separated from my brother, to refrain from all food for three days. And then I pledge never to betray my faith, no matter with what death I may be threatened.*[1] The Cathars did not recognize penitence because all sins were regarded as flowing inevitably from the first sin committed in Paradise, and were entirely wiped out once and for all by the consolation.

In all the Inquisition documents that have come down to us concerning this movement, there is not a single allusion to im-

[8] Rahn: op. cit., p. 128.
[9] Arno Borst: *Die Kather* (1953), p. 139.
[1] In Rahn: op. cit., p. 124.

moral conduct. The Cathars observed a strict code from which they did not deviate. Although Bernard of Clairvaux was anything but a friend of the Cathars, he once remarked that there were no people more Christian than these heretics; he could find nothing to reproach in their conversation, and their acts accorded with their words. The Cathars, he continued, cheated and oppressed no one; their cheeks were pale from fasting and they earned their livelihood by honest work.

Yet it did not take long for the Church to recognize the grave menace of the rising tide of Catharism. At first it hoped to lead these heretics back to the Church. Churchmen preached against the Albigensians, but were not averse to conducting many discussions with them. But attempts to convince the Cathars by words were of no avail. The Church's efforts at conversion rebounded ineffectually, for the prideful manner of the representatives of the Church contrasted too unfavorably with the Christlike humility practiced by the Cathars. The austere mode of life of the Albigensians threw a sharp light upon the corrupt clergy of the time, whose evil ways—as the Pope himself acknowledged—were principally responsible for the defection of so many people from the Church. How could the Church win back these heretics when the clergy continued to wallow in self-indulgence? A few sterling exceptions, like St. Anthony of Padua, only served to make the conduct of the other clerics more conspicuous. Observing this, St. Dominic, when he took part in these debates, made a point of dressing as a poor monk, to rob the Cathars of at least this one argument.

When the spiritual sword proved too blunt, the representatives of the Church went on to stronger methods. But the harshest application of force was even more unsuccessful in accomplishing its purpose. The heretics offered an inflexible resistance, and their steadfastness gave further impetus to their cause. Tender maidens became heroic martyrs. As even their enemies attested, the Cathars were not afraid of suffering. "There is no more beautiful death than that of fire," the Cathars taught their followers.[2] Thus

[2] In Borst: op. cit., p. 134.

they would give each other the Christian kiss of peace, and with the words "God is love" would go to the stake, showing no sign of fear of death. These Albigensians were Christians who had learned how to die. Never bewailing their harsh fates, they acted in accordance with the words of Jesus: "Blessed are those who are persecuted for the sake of righteousness, for theirs is the kingdom of heaven." God justified them in their sufferings, they felt, and the blood they spilled proved to be the best seed for their doctrine.

When individual punishment did not lead to the desired result, the Church called upon the rulers of Christendom for aid, and there began those decades of wars—from 1208 to 1244—which have come to be known historically as the Albigensian Wars. These campaigns were only in part motivated by religion; political factors also operated. They might in a way be called civil wars between northern and southern France. The state was as guilty as the Church. The French king was only too glad for the chance to extend his political sovereignty at the expense of the Provençal nobility. The counts of Toulouse were bidden to expel the heretics from the country. They demurred. These people have grown up among us, the counts objected; kinsmen of ours are among the Cathars, and their honorable way of life merits no punishment. But these considerations were ignored and war was launched against the counts.

The Albigensian Wars took on a terrible cast when Pope Innocent III proclaimed a "crusade" against the Cathars. This was a thing which had never happened before in the course of Christianity. For the first time in the history of the Church, a crusade was directed against heretical Christians. To spur enlistment in the operation, crusaders were promised the same indulgence that had been offered for the crusade against the Saracens. However much a sinner a man had been, he could escape hell by taking arms against the heretics. For to the eyes of the churchmen, the Cathar heretics seemed "worse than the Saracens." The crusaders were promised the property of the Albigensians as booty. Representatives of the Church led the war against the heretics with a cruelty that made mockery of all Christianity. The cities of southern France were pillaged, and bloodbaths ensued which have scarcely a parallel in the history of the West. From the infant in its cradle to the feeble old man, no one was spared; the crusaders slaughtered all the inhabitants without distinction. No mercy was shown to prisoners; they were killed at once. The blasphemous watchword of the crusaders was: "Kill them all, God will know his own." The papal legate reported happily to Rome: "God's wrath has raged in wondrous wise against the city [Béziers]." The word mercy had no place in the vocabulary of the crusaders. Whatever the clergy may have thought—and not all were as harsh as Arnaud Amaury, the leader of the crusade—the blood-thirsty warriors had decided that their mission was to annihilate the heretics, not convert them.

Hundreds of thousands perished in the murderous crusade. As the wars raged on, the high civilization of Provence was transformed into a smoking heap of ruins. The glorious troubadour songs were silenced; everything was trampled under the boots of the brutal soldiery. The victors scorched the earth so thoroughly that it seemed as if no blade of grass would ever grow there. To this day one cannot read of the horrible atrocities of the Albigensian Crusade without anguish. One stands aghast before the spectacle of such incomprehensible savagery. It seems incredible that Christians could rage so against fellow Christians. In the end one is forced to think that all the militants of the spirit who set out to annihilate evil were in the end swallowed by evil—as Ahab was by the white whale.

+   +

11

Catalogus Testium Veritatis

+   +

The Waldensians

In the midst of the noise and bustle of a fair at Lyons, flanked by
an animal trainer putting his beasts through their paces and a
troupe of acrobats, a storyteller was trying to catch the interest of
the crowd. The year was about 1170. The storyteller's stock-in-
trade consisted in thrilling and edifying tales. And so he told the
early Christian legend of Alexius who "in the secret stillness of his
wedding night" made a pact with his bride to live in "virgin purity," and the following day stole away from the house. After some
time Alexius returned in disguise to the house of his parents. In
memory of the absent son, of whom no word had been heard, the

pilgrim who knocked at the gates was taken in and given refuge. He was allowed to sleep in a corner of the shed. The servants of the house ridiculed him and played jokes on him, emptying slops upon his head. Alexius patiently and humbly endured all abuse. He sought all types of mortification. For seventeen years he lived as an unknown in his father's house, and only as he was dying did he write his name on a sheet of paper which was found clutched in his hand.

Among the people listening to the itinerant *jongleur,* who accompanied his story with vivid gesticulations, was one Petrus Waldus. While the others found it only an interesting story, its effect upon Waldus was extraordinary and proved once more the secret power of Christian legends. A strange tumult filled his soul; he was so deeply shaken that he took the storyteller home with him and talked with him far into the night.

Waldus was a businessman who had arrived at his present prosperity by means that would not bear examination. For he lent money at interest, thus flouting the rule against usury which the Church had tried to enforce for centuries. The story of Alexius struck like a bolt of lightning into the midst of his life of avarice.

The very next day Waldus betook himself to a pair of priests and told them of the storm within his soul. They diagnosed his trouble as a form of melancholia, but agreed, at his request, to acquaint him with the contents of the Bible. Waldus drew up a contract with the two priests, agreeing to pay them well if they would translate several of the books of the Bible into the common language of the people. Thus the businessman of Lyons began his study of the Bible, thereby only intensifying the deep discontent that had begun when he heard the legend of Alexius.

The more he read the Gospels, the more keenly Waldus felt his spiritual crisis. His sore spot was his dealings in money, and the harsh words of Jesus concerning God and Mammon touched him to the quick. His thoughts returned again and again to Jesus' advice to the rich youth. The longer he read the Bible, the more he felt that Christianity and luxury were irreconcilably opposed. At first he tried to appease his conscience by generous works of charity; during a bad famine he distributed free food to the needy three times every week.[1] But such measures did not assuage the disquiet in his soul. Charity alone, he recognized, was not sufficient for the true early-Christian life; far more than that was demanded of a man.

Waldus did some deep thinking about the way that Mammon dried up the human soul. He did not want to be cast into the eternal flames, as the rich man in Christ's parable had been. If only he could free himself from the fetters of property. After a long struggle he resolved to obey the words of the Gospel to the letter. He transferred all his land to his wife, and set aside suitable dowries for his two unmarried daughters. This done, he followed the example of the publican Zachaeus who directed that his fortune be given back to those from whom he had acquired his wealth. He went out into the streets and threw all his gold down into the dust of the road, announcing: "Friends, fellow townsmen, I am not out of my mind, as you may think. Rather I am avenging myself upon these enemies of my life who have enslaved me, so that I cared more for gold pieces than for God and served the creature more than the Creator." Man, Waldus proclaimed in the words of Jesus, could not serve two masters.

This extraordinary act, which naturally created a tumult in the streets of Lyons, was only the prelude to Waldus' tryst with Lady Poverty. The ideal of voluntary poverty had struck the merchant of Lyons with all its radiance and grandeur; from now on he was determined to beg his bread for the love of God, as Alexius had done. Not that this ideal was his own conception, for it is written in inexpungeable letters in the Gospel story itself. It is there in unmistakable language for every Christian who reads the Bible. In the twelfth century, when a new wave of asceticism was sweeping the Occident, this ideal exerted a strong attraction upon the minds of a great many men. Norbert of Xanten, for instance, was attempting to realize the ideal of poverty when he founded his Premonstratensian Order. But Waldus—and this was new—did not think of the life of poverty in monastic terms. He

[1] Cf. K. Müller: *Die Waldenser und ihre einzelnen Gruppen* (1886), p. 5.

considered it to be the commandment for all Christians, not to be practiced only in a cloister but to be applied in practical life.

In thus espousing poverty Waldus had set foot upon an invisible track that led him on inexorably from stage to stage. He next felt called upon to emulate the apostolic life as it is described in the Gospels. The pattern set by the Apostles had wholly vanished from Christianity, Waldus lamented; God, he felt, had called upon him to restore it. With feverish excitement he read the instructions Jesus had given the disciples as they set forth upon their mission. As if scales had fallen from his eyes, he recognized the binding character of this portion of the Gospel. Waldus took the words literally. Henceforth he would follow nakedly a naked Jesus, would be forever a pilgrim, calling no place on earth his home. His wife attempted to deter him. She even went to the archbishop to complain that her husband preferred to beg his bread from strangers rather than receive it from her. But Waldus would not be swayed from his resolve.

Inherent in the apostolic mode of life is the duty of preaching. Owing to the general debasement of the clergy, preaching was more or less a forgotten thing in Waldus' times. Now, taking his inspiration from the missionary words of Jesus, Waldus conceived it to be all-important to proclaim the Word. Though an unlearned layman, he went out on the streets and began to preach. His preaching was free of rhetorical flourishes. In Biblical phrases he condemned his own sins and those of others. And because of its directness and sincerity, what he said had a startling effect. The poorer classes of the population in particular, who were not caught in the same toils as the wealthy, responded with enthusiasm. The things that Waldus quoted from the Scriptures were largely unknown at the time and their effect was striking. There was, in addition, his own example—a telling argument. Waldus had himself done what he was asking of his listeners, and therefore his tidings kindled their hearts. Men and women came forward to take up the same manner of life as his.

The unlettered thronged to him—so much so that it has been said that his converts consisted entirely of the disinherited who had nothing to lose by following Waldus' call. But although the new movement was largely recruited from the lower classes of the populace, it was in no way motivated by resentment against the propertied class. Waldus told his followers to go about the country preaching the Gospel by twos, with no money in their pockets —but he did so on purely religious grounds. Jesus had expressly commanded itinerant preaching, and Waldus was only repeating that command. His followers were independent preachers proclaiming the Gospel without regard for the hierarchical order of the Church, which drew so sharp a line between clergy and laymen. These Waldensian preachers felt that they were qualified for their role by their apostolic mode of life; they did not need to be ordained by representatives of the Church. A new class of laymen was asserting the same privileges as the clergy. This was, within the framework of the Church, a monstrous innovation.

Like all new movements of this sort, the Waldensians soon came up against fierce opposition. Waldus himself was astonished to find that his main opposition came from the Church herself. For although he had been concerned about the gap which the Church had left in the religious life of the people, he did not regard himself as in any way antagonistic to the Church. Did they not both have salvation of souls as their aim? Everything he did was intended to aid, not compete with, the Church. But the Archbishop of Lyons regarded these self-appointed assistants with highly suspicious eyes. These preachers had arrogated to themselves the office of the Apostles and were poaching upon the preserve of the clergy.

Although Waldus protested that he was merely obeying the biddings of Jesus to preach the Gospel far and wide, Archbishop John gave such notions short shrift. The preaching was banned. At first the matter remained a local issue, though one which boded ill for Waldus. After all, many men had clashed with their bishops without this affecting the greater destinies of the Church. The Church as a whole had not condemned Waldus. All he did, therefore, was to leave the district covered by the ban, without having the slightest thought as yet of a parting of ways with the Church.

In February 1179, when the great Lateran Council under Alexander III was held, a number of followers of Waldus went to Rome. They presented the Pope with samples of their translation of Scripture and petitioned him for permission to preach. One chronicle relates that Waldus himself was in Rome and that at his final audience the Pope embraced him. Whether this is true or not cannot be ascertained; the story is contradicted by another source. At any rate a commission was appointed to examine the matter. It was headed by Walter Map, the author of the *Quest of the Holy Grail* and the friend of Henry II of England and Thomas à Becket. Map, a learned, proud man, and considered one of the greatest of English writers (although he wrote in French and Latin), despised the simple followers of Waldus as blockheads. He made a travesty of the discussions, entangling the Waldensians in the snares of scholastic theology and exposing their ignorance of dogma, until the pilgrims from the Rhone valley fled from the session, humiliated and downcast.

The fact was that these lay preachers were in affront to Map's pride in being one of the priesthood. He disdainfully compared them to birds who would flutter about everywhere, defiling the most sacred things. As he saw it, to proclaim the Word of God should be a monopoly of the priests. "Shall the Church give pearls to the swine, leave the Word to idiots whom we know to be incapable of receiving it? . . . Water ought to be drawn from the well and not from puddles in the street." [2] Map seemed to regard the whole affair only in terms of rivalry. "They now begin with extraordinary humility because they have not yet found a firm footing," he warned. "But if we let them in, they will throw us out." [3]

The Pope, Alexander III, however, looked indulgently upon the Waldensians, for he was at least aware of the ardent piety of these people. In his eyes, they were fools, but not heretics. He

[2] In Hausrath: *Die Arnoldisten* (1895), p. 39.
[3] Ibid., p. 39.

therefore commended their profession of poverty, but bade them cease their missionary activities until they were asked to preach.

Waldus at first abided by this ruling. However, it soon deeply troubled his conscience. He had not begun his preaching of his own accord. Of course he had never claimed to have received direct divine guidance; his appeal was always to the Scriptures. But the clear words of the Bible had indisputable authority for him. Through the words of Scripture the Lord had commanded him to go out into the world and preach the Gospel. And now the Church was blocking his way and instructing him to disobey the Biblical command. One command was set against another, and Waldus was involved in the gravest imaginable conflict a medieval Christian could experience. Was it permissible for him to keep silent? If he obeyed the Church, would he not be disobeying God? Must the principles of early Christianity truly retreat before the principle of hierarchy?

Whatever choice he made, it seemed to him he would be wrong. In this spiritual conflict which threatened to tear Waldus' soul apart, he finally came to the conclusion that the two commands did not stand upon the same plane. One was the Word of God, and hence possessed absolute validity. The Church's interdiction, on the other hand, was only the word of human beings; it might be well meant, but its validity was relative. Waldus resolved the terrible dichotomy in the only way open to a man devoted to the Bible, with the words of the Bible itself: "We must obey God rather than men." [4] This has been the watchword of all religious rebels. Probably there is no sentence in the whole Bible so consonant with the heretical spirit as this bold statement straight out of the New Testament. This slogan of the primitive Christians showed Waldus the direction he must proceed in his dealings with the Roman hierarchy.

To the Church, however, the resumption of preaching by Waldus' followers was brazen disobedience of the papal injunction. If this sort of thing were tolerated, the whole order of the Church, its entire structure, was threatened. The Pope had no

[4] Acts v, 29.

198

choice; he had to respond by excommunication. Five years after the ban on missionary activity, the new Pope, Lucius III, pronounced eternal anathema upon Waldus and his followers. They had defied papal authority and thus revealed themselves as heretics. We must appreciate the weight of this charge in order to have some understanding of the further conduct of the Church toward the Waldensians.

The excommunication frightened Waldus at first, but not to the point of making him forswear what he regarded as his duty. Courageously, he went on preaching, defying the papal ban and appealing from the ecclesiastical tribunal which had condemned him to the Judgment Seat of God. This appeal to divine judgment as a higher court, above that of the Church, is the typical act of the heretic. Against the Church under its papal leadership Waldus pitted the individual's insight into Christ and Scripture—a fundamental revolution in the medieval world-order. He persisted in this attitude until his death.

Whenever we attempt to define Waldus' personality, we are inevitably forced to compare him with St. Francis of Assisi, to Waldus' detriment. No charming legends have sprung up around the life of the Lyons merchant. St. Francis was characterized by an infectious happiness, a charismatic radiation, which Waldus seems to lack. Yet Waldus had one great merit on his side: that of priority. A whole generation before the seraphic Franciscus was wedded in mystic union to Lady Poverty, Waldus anticipated his entire program. The Lyons preacher came first in reinvigorating the magnificent ideal of an apostolic way of life, and this not only within the framework of a monastic foundation. For it was one thing to let this idea be confined to still another monastic order and another to present it as a living necessity for all Christians. The difference is a crucial one. What is more, Waldus remained unshakably faithful to his *imitatio Christi,* despite all ecclesiastical pressure.

There is no need to idealize Waldus; certainly he had his faults. There was, for instance, his rather despotic obstinacy, his determination to carry out his plans without regard for his fellow men. He would refuse to yield even a single small disputed point. As some critics have seen it, his fantastic contempt for the world took the form of sheer tyranny. But others have said that his whole bent was to sow dissension. This, however, is manifestly unfair. According to Albert Hauck, it was purely a matter of chance that "Waldus became a heretic rather than a saint." [5] For all his efforts pointed in the direction taken by the saints. When we think of his career, an insight comes to us that brings a chill: this deeply pious man became a heretic from the very earnestness of his belief. For Waldus desired nothing but to live by the words of the Gospel. He was forced into heresy because he would not allow the hierarchy to prevent him from doing so. He was cast out of the Church for being true to primitive Christianity.

The Waldensian movement followed the example of its founder in clinging unshakably to the Holy Scriptures. The Waldensians read the Scriptures zealously, and discarded the traditional allegorical exegeses in favor of a literal interpretation. "In Waldensian circles laymen for the first time in the Middle Ages were face to face with the greatest religious instrument the Church possesses: the Bible." [6] The Waldensians conceived of Scripture as primarily the Law of Christ. In giving it this legalistic cast, they somewhat subtracted from the emotional impact of the "glad tidings." They meant that the words of Jesus were to be taken as commandments, not mere proverbs and themes for disputation. No, the Waldensians felt that the Bible set a standard by which they could act. The blinding light of Jesus had dawned upon them anew.

In their rapture over the treasure they had discovered, the Waldensians often learned whole Gospels by heart, and there were many among them who could recite the entire New Testament word for word. The Old Testament took a secondary place in their thinking, although they by no means rejected it.

These Poor Men of Lyons should be credited with having

[5] A. Hauck: *Kirchengeschichte Deutschlands* (1903), IV, 862.
[6] Ibid., IV, 869.

been the first missionaries to disseminate a considerable knowledge of the Bible among the people. Laymen that they were, they rescued the Scriptures from the "theological preserve" in which the divine Word had been incarcerated. Once the Waldensians had re-established direct contact with the Law of Christ, the Bible proved to be once more that live volcano whose repeated eruptions forever shake Christianity.

The Waldensian missionaries set forth in pairs, wearing the simplest clothes: woolen robes girded around the waist, and sandals. They were easily recognized by their garments, and when the Inquisition began to persecute them they abandoned this costume and went about disguised, making themselves known to fellow believers by secret codes. In later times they often traveled by night, when it was safer. Stay-at-home Waldensians called these itinerant preachers simply "brethren." In keeping with Jesus' instructions, these missionaries refused to earn their livelihoods by their own labor; their followers provided for their needs.[7]

The missionaries fused in their persons the ascetic life of monks and the functions of priests. They were empowered by the Waldensian creed to hear confessions, since they maintained that the Lord had imposed upon them the office of binding and loosing, which in olden days had likewise been granted to laymen within the church. Every righteous man was a priest, the Waldensians held. Hence the official clergy were superfluous. For spiritual functions to be carried out effectively, the preacher had to have Christ in himself and reflect the life of Christ in his own conduct. This principle, that one had to imitate the apostolic life in order to truly exercise the evangelical power of the keys, was one of the fundamentals of the Waldensian heresy.

The message these Waldensian missionaries proclaimed was exceedingly simple. Their humble conception of the Law of Christ removed the necessity for learned explanations. "They never had any particular dogmas or theological doctrines; we can

[7] Cf. I Cor. ix, 7 and II Tim. ii, 4.

speak of Waldensian 'dogma' only if we mean this word in the most general sense. The points in which they differed from the Church were likewise solely of a practical nature." [8]

The Waldensians demanded a strict adherence to the behests of the Sermon on the Mount. Swearing was strictly and under all circumstances forbidden. They also insisted on an unconditional clinging to the truth. Lies were abhorred, and the slightest deviation from the truth was considered a mortal sin. (To obey such a principle in times of persecution was not easy. It is possible that, faced with the Inquisition, Waldensians occasionally resorted to evasions and equivocal statements.) With equal strictness they forbade killing. They regarded killing in warfare and enforcement of the death penalty by civil authorities as equally impermissible. So strict was the Waldensian manner of life that even their opponents could find nothing to say against it. Here were people who worked hard, kept away from taverns, and withdrew from all public activities. In their fidelity to the Law of Christ, the Waldensians exemplified that folly which puts to shame the wisdom of the world.

The Waldensians, once excommunicated, began to take issue with the Church on many counts. They rejected appeals to the saints, reverence for the host, and the worship of images. Their sharpest criticism was directed against the doctrine of purgatory, which granted people the opportunity to purify themselves after death, thus alleviating the strict alternatives of heaven or hell. Nothing was said in the Bible about this intermediary state, the Waldensians found. The doctrine of purgatory, they held, detracted from the seriousness of this life, since men were led to assume that they could straighten out their affairs in the hereafter. The Waldensians waged a sharp battle against this concession to human frivolity. The Christian, they maintained, is faced with his great decision in this life alone. In so firmly repudiating the doctrine of purgatory, the Waldensians gave impressive proof of their religious earnestness. However, they were robbing men of one of their major solaces in connec-

[8] Müller: op. cit., p. 98.

tion with death, for they failed to understand the deeper religio-philosophical reasons out of which that doctrine had grown.

Along with the Cathars, with whom they are often confused although the two groups were quite separate, the Waldensians formed one of the great heretical movements of the Middle Ages. At first the sect multiplied with great rapidity. The fire they had kindled sent leaping flames in all directions. When the Waldensians were expelled from Lyons, they took refuge in Picardy, and later moved on to Germany. Other Waldensians crossed the Pyrenees and the Alps. In northern Italy the movement found extremely fruitful soil among the cities of Lombardy; brotherhoods of the Lombard Poor Men sprang up. Fairly soon, there were negotiations between the French and Italian Waldensians, though the two branches did not always succeed in reconciling their differences. The characteristic obstinacy of these people stood in the way of this; suave diplomacy was utterly alien to their nature. The Lombards, for instance, were not of a mind to affirm the blessedness of Petrus Waldus, and they also had their own ideas concerning the position of the consecrating priest at communion. Dissensions sharpened because from the start the Italians took a more antagonistic attitude toward the Church. The Lombards were the more radical branch; the French followed in their track with many a qualm. In time, however, all Waldensians arrived at agreement on their tenet that the rites of the Church depended for their sacramental value upon the moral purity of the priests—as the old Donatists had maintained.

The strength of the Waldensians lay not so much in their position on theological questions as in their appeal to the common people. Their missionaries wandered across Germany as far as Bohemia. The songs of itinerant Waldensian minstrels went straight to the hearts of their listeners. They did not go in for learned discussions that were over the heads of ordinary people. Their simple lay devoutness could be understood by everyone. After many centuries the glad tidings of the Gospel were once more reaching the lower classes of the populace and once more proving its vital power.

As Waldensianism spread, the Church was forced to take measures. It began, as usual, by tirades against the heretics.[9] The first indictment was simple: since the movement initiated by Petrus Waldus was of recent date, it could not be the true church of God which had been founded by Christ. When polemic proved of no avail, the authorities had recourse to more militant forms. They began exterminating the heretics, as far as this was possible. The Waldensians endured frightful persecutions. Here was a fulfillment of the words of the Gospel: "The hour is coming when whoever kills you will think he is offering service to God."[1] The result was inevitable: "The merciless persecution which struck at the Waldensians in an unremitting series of blows soon evoked violent outbursts of savage hatred against the Roman clergy."[2] The Waldensians comforted themselves during these terrible days with the words that had become their motto: "The light shines in the darkness." The bloody persecutions inflicted upon these Christians by other Christians makes their story a drama of Christian heroism, a stirring tale of cruelest martyrdom.[3]

However, the Church did not succeed in annihilating the Waldensians. Despite the harshest measures, they survived throughout the Middle Ages. When the Reformation began, they entered into friendly relations with the Protestants—an embassy of theirs went to Wittenberg to obtain the writings of Luther. They likewise withstood the Counter-Reformation with its renewed persecutions. At that time Oliver Cromwell extended his protection to the Waldensians. Switzerland, too, served them as a refuge for a time. The Waldensians, indeed, are the only medieval heretical movement which has lasted down to the present day. A small group of them still live in Italy and maintain a theological faculty in Rome. Spiritually, they have not passed through any major evolution, nor developed a religious culture of their own. One reason for this may be their contempt for languages, for which Luther once reproached them.[4]

[9] Cf. Hahn: op. cit., II, 299 f.
[1] John xvi, 2.   [2] Müller: op. cit., p. 129.
[3] F. Bender: Geschichte der Waldenser (1850).
[4] Luther: Erlangen Ausgabe, XXII, 188.

The Waldensians belong to that tiny flock to whom, according to the words of Jesus, the kingdom of God is given. Their apparent lack of success speaks in their favor rather than against them. The Waldensians are among that "cloud of witnesses" who, according to the Epistle to the Hebrews, have testified to the truth without having received what was promised.[5]

In fact there is no epithet more apt for these warriors for the Law of Christ than that of "witnesses to the truth." The witness to the truth is one of the most extraordinary characters to have arisen from Christianity. He is not merely a marginal figure; in his defenselessness, the witness to the truth is *the* representative of the Gospel in a world of violence. He is *the* embodiment of Christianity, and plays an essential part in the history of Christian thought. The witness to the truth is one who has received an indestructible impression of the power of Christian truth, so much so that he is ready to sacrifice everything to it. He feels truth to be the supreme obligation imposed upon a Christian in this life. He not only stands intrepidly for it in words; he is also willing to lay down his life for it. In times of persecution the witness to the truth invariably becomes a martyr, and we can only pay the ultimate reverence to his courage. He stands firm even when the majority revile him as a heretic. This harsh label has been clapped upon more than one such witness, and on the Waldensians as a body. Hence it is that they deserve an honorable place in the story of heresy—a story that, to use the phrase of Matthias Flacius, may be called a "catalogue of witnesses to the truth."

---

[5] Hebr. xii, 1.

12

The Guilt of Christianity

The Inquisition

No painting better expresses the essence of the Inquisition than El Greco's "Grand Inquisitor." Here is a portrait which not only immortalizes its subject, but grasps the whole nature of the institution for which he stood. Like a spider lying in wait for its victim, Fernando Neno de Guevara sits in his chair. What gives the portrait its sinister cast? The penetrating eyes behind the horn-rimmed spectacles, which seem literally to hypnotize heretics? Or the hand clasping the arm of the chair with a grip which, we feel, will never release any unfortunate it has caught? The icy marble features of this Spanish countenance contain harshness and cruelty behind a sphinxlike inscrutability.

It is understandable that many Christians are reluctant to discuss the Inquisition. They do not like to be reminded of it, and prefer to pass over it in silence. When we tell the story of heresy, however, we cannot omit this chapter of church history—quite aside from the obvious point that the more Christians attempt to evade such facts, the more atheists will make of them. There are Christians who would like to minimize the importance of the Inquisition, to assert that it could not have been quite so bad as it has been painted. To these we must reply: Yes, it was bad, it was so bad that it could not have been worse. To attempt to ignore evil is the response of a guilty conscience and affords no true atonement.

Equally inadequate is the attitude of flaming indignation. Moral outrage at this medieval Gestapo is modern man's most natural reaction. He feels called upon to protest loudly, to cry so all may hear that he is revolted by such a distortion of the Christian religion. Yet such a position, irreproachably moral as it is, too easily exculpates the accuser. Let us remember the words of St. Paul: "Therefore you have no excuse, O man, whoever you are, when you judge another; for in passing judgment upon him you condemn yourself, because you, the judge, are doing the very same things."[1] In the enlightened twentieth century modern man has witnessed, in the concentration camps, a return of the terrible methods of the Inquisition, and found he could do nothing to prevent it. It becomes somewhat tasteless to utter outcries of moral indignation against the darkness of the Middle Ages.

Instead of hushing up the matter or taking refuge in a simple-minded type of accusation, we might more honestly admit the guilt that the Inquisition brought upon all of Christianity. For, if we view the problem in a religious light, that is what emerges. All of Christendom was to blame for the treatment meted out to the heretics. By its fatalistic acceptance of the concentration camps, modern Christendom has similarly incurred a heavy guilt.

[1] Rom. ii, 1.

Here above all is the place for that sentence of Dostoevsky: "All are guilty of everything, and I most of all." When we consider the terrible crimes which were committed against heretics we feel that sense of boundless misery which almost precludes our ever feeling happy again. Faced with the doings of the Inquisition, Christians should fall upon their knees and cry out with the Lamentations of Jeremiah: "Let tears stream down like a torrent." They should be filled with a keen repentance, with the necessity to atone endlessly for the great sin they themselves have committed. All Christians should bow down to the ground and remember to offer prayers for the murdered and the murderers. All branches of Christendom must purify themselves of this guilt by an ever-active repentance, an ever-readiness for atonement. No blessing can fall upon Christendom until at long last and out of deepest conviction it honestly confesses the sin of the Inquisition and sincerely, without reservation, forswears all similar acts of violence in the realm of religion.

How, then, did Christendom come to wreak such fearful vengeance on the dissenters in its midst? For it was not always so. In the course of the centuries Christians had found different answers to the problem posed by heresy. But we can trace a consistent line of mounting harshness, which ended in outright savagery.

Let us consider the first stage, that of primitive Christianity. In the enthusiasm of those early days of faith, heresy simply could not arise. The imminence of the Eternal was too powerful. When Jesus spoke of the "brother who sins against you," he recommended friendly reproof.[2] To Peter he gave the famous reply that a brother should be forgiven seventy times seven.[3] Paul, too, who spoke of the inescapability of heresy,[4] wrote: "Brethren, if a man is overtaken in any trespass, you who are spiritual should restore him in a spirit of gentleness. Look to yourself, lest you too be tempted." [5] Elsewhere, he said: "Do not

2 Matt. xviii, 15–17.　　4 I Cor. xi, 19.
3 Matt. xviii, 22.　　　　5 Gal. vi, 1.

look on him as an enemy, but warn him as a brother." [6] Here we
have the essentially Christian attitude: the man who errs is to be
treated with especial love—as the parable of the prodigal son
makes clear.

It was only when the fire of primitive Christianity began
slowly to fade that this attitude of mercy and mildness changed.
This first took place in the struggle against the Gnostic movement. In certain books of the New Testament, whose authenticity
is not quite assured, the warning was issued to "have no more to
do with" the heretic [7] and not even to greet him.[8] Injunctions of
this sort, which mark the transition of primitive Christianity to
the period of the Early Church, are to be found in the pastoral
letters whose genuineness has been challenged by historical
criticism.

In the second stage we still find traces of the primitive
Christian doctrine of love even for the misguided. The Fathers
urged toleration of those who took different views on Christian
questions. Tertullian forcefully defended the view that no one
must ever be coerced into participating in a religious function,
for that would be inconsistent with the nature of faith and "no
one would wish to be honored by someone who does not do it
gladly." [9] According to Cyprian, "the Lord alone is master of the
iron rod and he alone is permitted to shatter earthly vessels." No
Christian, he said, might "arrogate to himself the handling of the
winnow in order to cleanse and purify the threshing-floor." [1]
Origen, too, held that Christians could not possibly "slay their
enemies and condemn to death or stoning the violators of the
law." [2]

Such insistence on tolerance did not arise out of weakness.
Of course the earlier Fathers were in a position of self-defense;
nevertheless, the ideal of toleration was inherent in their Christian principles. The noble Chrysostomus unequivocally con-

---

[6] II Thess. iii, 15.
[7] Tit. iii, 10.
[8] II John x.

[9] Tertullian: *Apologia,* chap. xxiv.
[1] Cyprian: *Letter to Maximus,* chap. iii.
[2] Origen: op. cit., VII, xxvi.

demned violence against heretics as an inexpiable crime, and warned prophetically: "Therefore, too, it is not permissible to kill heretics, for to do so would bring down upon the world an irreconcilable war." [3]

In keeping with this attitude, the strongest measure Christian communities leveled against heretics was excommunication. In distinct contrast to the Old Covenant, Cyprian declared: "When circumcision of the flesh was still practiced, such sinners were killed by the sword; but now, because spiritual circumcision alone is practiced among the true servants of God, the proud and the intransigent are given their death-blow with the sword of the spirit, being expelled from the Church." [4]

But tolerance was doomed when the commandment of love began to be disregarded and invective was accepted as a legitimate weapon in the struggle against heresy. Ruthless defamation appeared early in the history of the Church. The heresiologists were masters of an abundant vocabulary of vituperation which they poured out upon the heretics. The most baleful expressions were hurled at them—and Christians never seemed to consider the incompatibility of such conduct with the warning of Jesus: "Whoever insults his brother shall be liable to the council, and whoever says, 'You fool!' shall be liable to hell." [5] Such reviling bred an attitude of hatred and contempt, which in the course of time was to lead to terrible things.

The ambivalence of the Christian attitude, wavering as it did between tolerance and denunciation, continued until the hour of decision. This came when the tempter approached Christendom, not in the form of the devil in all his fiendish guise, but cloaked in the garb of imperial majesty. The Church, once persecuted, was now upheld by the power of the state—and failed to acquit itself with honor. No sooner had the Church accepted the privileges offered by the state, when it succumbed to a subtle temptation. This became evident in the prompt change of attitude toward

[3] Chrysostomus: *Commentary on Matthew,* Homily 46.
[4] Cyprian: *Fourth Letter to Pomponius,* chap. iv.
[5] Matt. v, 22.

heretics. The representatives of the Church were not spiritually developed enough to cope with their rapid ascent. They lacked the qualities of soul to meet their new and fortunate situation. Few, indeed, are the men who are not spiritually harmed by the exercise of power. The dramatic upswing that took place under Constantine impaired the spiritual structure of the Church to such an extent that it has never since entirely recovered.

The dominant Church soon forgot the tolerance it had hitherto advocated, and proceeded to persecute those who disagreed with it. Now its spokesmen talked in entirely different terms. Jerome expressed his astonishment that the bishop had not taken steps to impose physical punishment on Vigilantius, who had opposed the veneration of relics, since then the heretic's soul might have been saved! Ruthless stringency toward heretics was true mercy, Jerome argued. Augustine, too, after his frustrating dispute with the Donatists, favored the use of force against heretics. Moreover, the heretics themselves began to follow the same principle, wherever they were in the majority. They too had no scruples about declaring that might was right, as soon as it was to their advantage to do so. The Arians' persecution of adherents of the orthodox Church was upon occasion extremely cruel. In this respect, the Church and the heretics have more in common than either is willing to admit. The Emperor Julian declared after his apostasy that no wild beast behaved so cruelly toward men as Christians toward other Christians.

Once Christianity was launched upon the fateful course, atrocity was inevitable; before the end of the fourth century the first execution of a heretic took place. In A.D. 385, in the city of Trier, the Spanish Christian Priscillian advanced a number of Gnostic ideas, denied the Trinity and Resurrection, denounced marriage and the eating of meat, and cited various apocryphal writings. For these crimes of doctrine, he was put to death together with a number of his followers. Although heretics in the past had been threatened with death as being sons of the devil, this was the first time that the step from theory to practice had been taken. A tremor like an earthquake ran through all of

Christendom. After this first murder of a Christian brother it was as if God's voice once more cried from heaven: "What have you done? The voice of your brother's blood is crying to me from the ground." [6] In fact, this first killing of Christians by other Christians because of a difference in religious views created a tremendous stir. A cry of indignation rang through the Christian world, for in those days the consciences of Christians were not yet hardened. Bishop Ambrose in Milan thundered his horror of this criminal act, and Martin of Tours announced that he would have no fraternal communion with the bishops who had inflicted such a sentence. Feeling ran so high that the authorities who had been responsible for the crime were forced to give up their offices. The case of Priscillian remained an isolated instance for centuries to come and was not repeated elsewhere. But the fact remained and nothing could wipe it out: Christians had been cold-bloodedly slaughtered by Christians because of their religious convictions.

The ruthless extermination of heretics was resumed at the end of the twelfth century. After the year 1200 the campaigns of annihilation against heretics assumed forms that mock all attempts at description. And where the first execution of heretics in the Early Church had awakened unanimous protest, in the later Middle Ages butchery became an institution with the express blessing of the Church.

A number of historical factors prepared the way for this development. At the beginning of the High Middle Ages the number of heretics swelled enormously. Whereas previously they had appeared only sporadically, a veritable tide of heresy began to sweep into all parts of the West. In some regions the heretics outnumbered the orthodox believers.

This tremendous increase of heresy was a direct outcome of the ugly conditions prevailing within the Church. The unending struggles between emperors and Popes for the domination of the world repelled religious spirits. More and more people turned

[6] Genesis iv, 10.

away from a church whose primary interest was the naked battle for power. The un-Christian conduct of the Church directly stimulated the growth of heresy, which in turn made the Church feel that its very existence was threatened. At the same time the Church discovered by sad experience that heretics could not be vanquished by mere words. In fact it became necessary to forbid disputations with heretics, in order not to risk defeats. In self-defense, the Church sought another approach: the application of violence. Ideologically, the Church justified its conduct by claiming that the new heresies, unlike those of the primitive Church, were not the product of any human founder but a direct manifestation of the devil. No consideration, obviously, need be shown toward the devil, and therefore the cruelest measures were permissible.

The Church was strengthened in its intentions by the actions of the Hohenstaufen emperor Frederick II, who boldly led the way in the violent assault against heresy. Frederick was one of the most brilliant emperors in medieval history. But there were shady as well as bright sides to his character. The Hohenstaufen prince was a cynic who could comment coarsely on the most sacred conceptions; in his infinite contempt for the human race he played with the lives of his fellow men as if they were pieces in a chess game. He and his oriental household in Sicily were altogether remote from the spirit of Christianity.

This autocratic emperor opened one of the darkest chapters in the story of heresy. In his own life anything but devout, involved in permanent feuds with the Church, Frederick proceeded against heretics with fire and sword for purely political reasons. He who had been accused of heresy himself by representatives of the Church, and in whom the Franciscans were even prepared to see the Antichrist, beheld the heretics as nothing but enemies of the state whose aim was to sow dissension in the Empire. "His 'Decree on Heretics' was scarcely a gesture of polite reverence to the Pope, as has been thought; rather it was almost exactly the opposite: Frederick intended to show the

Church that it could not exist without the solicitous care of the state." [7]

This freethinking ruler who turned heretics over to the executioner manifested no trace of tolerance. In his savage slaughter of the heretics he exposed himself as a man who felt no responsibility toward God. But the Church was so impressed by his policy that it imitated him, and made his legislation against heretics its own.

It is true that this course met with serious objections. Even in the High Middle Ages there were Christians who were sharply conscious of the incompatibility of the Gospel with a policy of fighting heresy by violence. When the campaign of annihilation of heretics was in full swing, Francis of Assisi was asked by a Dominican doctor of theology in Siena what interpretation he gave to the words of Ezekiel: "If you speak not to warn the wicked, his blood I will require at your hand." [8] At first Francis, in his humility, replied that he would prefer to be taught rather than to give answers concerning a passage in the Bible. After more pressing, however, the saint responded: "If the words are to be understood in a wholly general way, then I take them to mean this: The servant of God must, by his saintly life, become such a flame that the light of his good example and the language spoken by his way of life will strike the consciences of all wicked men." [9]

From the point of view of the Gospel, there can be no attitude toward heresy more proper than this response of Francis. But such Christian voices were crying in a wilderness. The theologians were always able to twist sacred texts to suit their ends. Thus it was a fairly simple matter to take the Old Testament passages in which the most severe punishments were pronounced upon violators of the law and simply transfer these to the heretics. The words of the Pentateuch were particularly pointed: "He who blasphemes the name of the Lord shall be put to death; all the congregation shall stone him; the sojourner as

[7] E. Kantorowicz: *Kaiser Friedrich der Zweite* (1928), p. 241.
[8] Cf. Ezekiel, iii, 18.
[9] Celano: *Das Leben des heiligen Franziskus von Assisi,* ed. Schmitt (1919), p. 178.

well as the native, when he blasphemes the Name, shall be put to death." [1] These words were considered to be a direct call to take merciless action against heresy. The Bible, it was felt, condoned the greatest brutalities, for heresy was so grave a sin that it could only be atoned for by death.

Factors such as these, together with an inner decay of the faith, led ultimately to the establishment of the Inquisition. Its founding was not the work of a single Pope; rather, a number of papal measures contributed to its genesis. It emerged from a complicated historical process whose details can no longer be entirely sorted out. For the Inquisition was not an institution that appeared at once in its ultimate form. It evolved step by step, employing the methods which were readiest to hand and promised to lead most effectively to its goal. It took its cue from the antiheretical laws of Frederick II, and made use of his experiences. But it was an ecclesiastical, not a state, institution. Its beginnings are to be found in papal orders to the bishops to take more energetic measures against heresy in their own dioceses. For some time the matter rested there. But when the Popes were forced to realize that episcopal zeal was not sufficient, and that the ranks of the heretics continued to multiply, they transferred the task to the Dominican order. This was done in 1230 or 1231. Thus the Dominicans became the official Inquisitional order, although even Franciscan monks were often active as Inquisitors. It is difficult to see how the preaching orders, in whose midst ecstatic mysticism was cultivated, could have taken over such tasks.

For centuries nothing was permitted to be written about the Inquisition and its trials. As a result of this ban, an almost impenetrable veil was stretched over its activities. This gave rise to countless rumors and dreads. No biography, for example, can be written of one of the greatest of the Inquisitors, Torquemada. We do not even know exactly where he was born and where he received his education. And yet Torquemada was well-nigh the most powerful man of his time in Spain. He held Queen Isabella

[1] Lev. xxiv, 16.

in the palm of his hand, and imposed his will upon the entire
country.

We do know that this fifteenth-century Inquisitor was an
ascetic who abstained from eating meat and was accustomed to
scourge himself. This gaunt figure of a man in Dominican habit
gave proof of his humility by declining to become Archbishop
of Seville. Inflexible of will, never losing sight of his goal, making
concessions to no one, not even to the most highly placed nobles,
Torquemada looked upon pity as a temptation which it was the
Christian's duty to overcome. Obviously this man was made of
other stuff from ordinary mortals. He felt that he alone was responsible for the purity of the Church. This obsession drove him
from one act of inhumanity to the next.[2] To this idea he was
willing to sacrifice everything: love, truth, religion. The unity of
the faith was all-important; the corpses that strewed the path of
victory did not matter.

The aim of the Inquisition was the stamping out of heresy; its
task, to inquire into the souls of men in order to bring their beliefs to light. Heresy was equated with high treason and lese
majesty, and all the punishments prescribed for these crimes were
simply transferred to it.

The Inquisition proceeded by a judicial method all its own.
This could not be called arbitrary, since the duties and powers of
the Inquisitor were regulated down to the smallest detail. The religious auspices were not for a moment forgotten. "During the
consultation of the court a prayer was pronounced, all kneeling;
the inspiration of the Holy Spirit was besought, and all said
Amen."[3] The presiding Inquisitor was prosecutor and judge in
one. At the same time the Inquisitor was also the confessor of the
defendant. The defendant was sheared of all powers of resistance
by being forced to take an oath to obey all the commandments of
the Church, to answer all questions truthfully, to reveal all heretics,
and to accept willingly all penances meted out to him.

[2] Cf. E. Lucka: *Torquemada und die spanische Inquisition* (1926), pp. 55 f.
[3] C. Henner: *Beiträge zur Organisation und Kompetenz der päpstlichen Ketzergerichte* (1890), p. 163.

On the other hand, an almost impossible task was imposed upon the Inquisitor. He was bound to protect the faith and to avenge God for the injustice done to God by heresy. He was supposed to guess the defendant's secret thoughts. Since it was believed that heretics had the support of the devil, who could blind the eyes of the judges and befog the memory of witnesses, throughout the investigation the judge had to make decisions which constantly reached into metaphysical terrain. The Inquisitor was engaged in a constant struggle with the powers of evil, while at the same time he was obliged to save the defendant's soul. A more grotesque situation can scarcely be imagined: a judge literally combating the devil. Theoretically, the institution derived its justification from the example of God. For had not God been the first Inquisitor when, after the Fall, he tried and condemned Adam and Eve in a secret trial, without hearing any witnesses? Here was a significant parallel indeed, but the Inquisitors seem not to have remembered who had spoken the words of temptation: "You shall be as God!"

The trial began with the arrest of the heretic, who was then cut off completely from the outside world. At the same time his property was sequestered. The defendant was cast into prison where he was kept in chains throughout the proceedings and the sacraments were withheld from him.

Although the defendant was regarded as guilty from the start, the Inquisitor needed proofs in order to convict him. If possible, a confession must be obtained from him. If he did not voluntarily admit his guilt, witnesses were called. Their testimony, even if it was mere hearsay and the most idle gossip, was taken as convincing evidence. Anonymous letters were similarly credited, and the populace was directly invited to make denunciations. The defendant's only chance to overturn the witnesses' evidence was to prove that a deadly enmity had existed between himself and them. All other grounds were rejected. No one was exempted from the duty to give evidence, not even the closest relations. Mothers were expected to denounce their daughters, sons their fathers, husbands and wives each other. If they failed to do so, they were held to be likewise guilty of heresy. The testimony of minors and servants was also accepted if it was incriminating, whereas favorable evidence by such persons was considered worthless. Defense was not allowed. Consequently, no lawyers participated in Inquisitional trials. A legal defense would have needlessly hampered the work of the Inquisitor, and the defense lawyer himself would have run the risk of being charged with heresy. No one dared expose himself to such suspicions. Thus the defendant was thrown upon his own resources, even if he was uneducated and had no knowledge whatsoever of legal procedures.

If the testimony of the witnesses did not lead to the desired confession, torture was applied. The Church had long resisted the application of torture; as late as the twelfth century it had been one of the principles of canon law that confessions must not be extracted under duress. In the thirteenth century, however, torture was introduced into Italy. This step must, as a matter of fact, be regarded as "progress" in legal procedure, since instead of the traditional trial by ordeal it at least required confession by the defendant. Torture was first applied by the Inquisition under Pope Innocent IV, who likewise established canonical rules regarding its use. It saved the effort and the expense of a long imprisonment, for it was an effective method of obtaining any desired confession in the quickest way. The heretic was dragged to the torture chamber, and all the instruments of torture were vividly demonstrated to him. If the sight of these horrible tools did not move him to confess, the torture was begun, slowly and by stages. Theoretically, a heretic could be put to torture only once. But repeated application of torture was simply called a continuation of the one torture. Three- and four-hour sessions of torture were nothing unusual. During the procedure the instruments were frequently sprinkled with holy water.

Of the numerous ghastly implements available, the thumbscrew was usually the first to be applied: the fingers were placed in clamps and the screws turned until the blood spurted out and the bones were crushed. The defendant might also be placed on the iron torture chair, the seat of which consisted of sharpened iron nails that could be heated red-hot from below. There were the so-called "boots" which were employed to crush the shinbones. Another favorite torture was dislocation of the limbs on the rack, or the wheel on which the heretic, bound hand and foot, was drawn up and down while the body was weighted with stones. So that the torturers would not be disturbed by the shrieking of the victim, his mouth was stuffed with cloth. By such means a heretic would be tortured for hours, until his body was a flayed, crushed, broken, and bloody pulp. From time to time the victim would be asked again whether he was ready to confess. Most heretics, half mad with pain, would then be ready to supply any information the Inquisitors wanted to hear, solely in order to escape the torture. We need only read the minutes of one such torture, as reproduced in H. C. Lea's history of the Spanish Inquisition, to see what value could be attributed to the statements produced out of terror and pain in such circumstances.[4]

After the confession had been secured, sentence was pronounced. Its nature depended on the gravity of the heresy, and whether or not there had been a relapse. Theoretically, the Inquisitor had no power to impose penalties. His task supposedly consisted only in saving the heretic's soul from the clutches of the devil. In practice heresy was regarded as so terrible a crime that no amount of repentance could atone for it; therefore sincere penitence could save the heretic's soul from hell but not his body from temporal penalties, of which there were a great variety. One of the most common was scourging. Stripped of his clothing as far as was possible without violating modesty, the penitent had to appear before the priest every Sunday during divine services, stick in hand. The priest would then administer the blows in the presence of the congregation. Pilgrimages were also ordered, to be undertaken by the repentant heretic on foot, often as far as the Holy Land. A further and highly unpleasant penalty was that of wearing the cross. The penitent was required to sew two crosses on his dress as a sign of his estate. This social humiliation

[4] Cf. H. C. Lea: *Geschichte der spanischen Inquisition* (1912), II, 173–6.

made it almost impossible for a man to earn his living, for he carried about with him the mark of a former heretic. Such odium attached to the name of heretic in the Middle Ages that people would draw away in horror from such a man.

In addition, a mark was also affixed to the house of a heretic. Fines were also imposed. In most cases the entire property of heretics was confiscated, without regard for the rights of their innocent children. The children were not only disinherited but also declared without honor for three generations. This meant that they were disqualified for any public office. The confiscated property was divided equally between the Inquisitional tribunal and the secular authorities. On many occasions, however, all of it flowed into the pockets of the Inquisitors, whose livelihood came from such funds and who therefore had a distinct interest in continual confiscations. In case of imprisonment, a distinction was made between the mild and the severe form. In the former case occasional visits from close relatives were permitted. The severer form was called the living grave. All such penalties, it must be remembered, were provided only for repentant heretics who had shown themselves worthy of mercy.

For obstinate and lapsed heretics there was only one punishment: death at the stake. The origin of this ghastly form of execution cannot be precisely determined; probably it goes back to pre-Christian times. At the beginning of the thirteenth century Peter II of Aragon, on the advice of theologians, first gave legal status to the penalty of burning. Frederick II of Hohenstaufen followed his example, and from the middle of the thirteenth century on, the doges of Venice had to vow solemnly in their oath of office to have heretics burned. This form of punishment for heretics gradually became established throughout the Christian world. The papal statutes of 1231 demanded that death by fire be used universally.[5] The same penalty was even applied to the dead, with the bones of heretics being exhumed and consigned to the flames. This was in order to prevent the resurrection of the heretic on the Day of Judgment. The burning of heretics was

[5] Cf. Julius Ficker: *Die gesetzliche Einführung der Todesstrafe für Ketzerei.*

justified by the passage in the Gospel of John: "If a man does not abide in me, he is cast forth as a branch and withers; and the branches are gathered, thrown into the fire and burned." [6]

It is true that the Church itself burned no heretics. It merely cut the heretic off from the vine of the Church and delivered him over to the secular authorities for the execution of the sentence. This delivery was accompanied by a plea that the victim be treated with leniency. But the request was not meant to be taken literally, for the secular authorities were told exactly how they were to understand the word "leniency." The Church itself, however, did not want to be tainted by the office of executioner and therefore forbade its servants to take any part in carrying out death sentences. The priests were even forbidden to write any letters involving such sentences, nor was it allowed for them to be present at tortures. Supposedly this regulation shifted the responsibility for the execution to the secular arm. However, if the secular authorities refused to carry out a command to burn a heretic, they themselves were punished with excommunication. Certainly these sophistries do not exculpate the Church. The blood of the heretics must be upon its head for all time.

The Church organized the act of burning at stake as a grand public performance. The execution was generally set upon a holiday, so that the crowd would be the larger and the warning of the heretic's example the more effective. Special mounted messengers were sent out to announce the event and invite the populace to attend.

The auto-da-fé consisted of two parts: the sermon, held outside the church, and the execution, during which the priests withdrew. Frequently the heretic was tormented with red-hot tongs on the way to the stake, or his right hand was cut off before the execution. He was dressed in a penitent's shirt, and sometimes wore a paper cap on which diabolic marks were painted. In some few exceptional cases the victim was mercifully strangled beforehand. Usually he was bound living to a stake that was raised high enough above the heap of fuel, so that the

[6] John xv, 6.

crowds of the faithful could see every detail of the cruel spectacle. Bundles of twigs mixed with straw were heaped to a height of three feet around the victim. The condemned man was gagged, lest in speaking forth he arouse sympathy among the people and perhaps cause a riot.

After the heretic had been exhorted for the last time to recant, the signal was given for igniting the pyre. Soon the flames leaped upward, and it depended upon the direction of the wind whether the smoke was carried into the victim's face, so that he suffocated quickly, or whether it was blown away from him, so that he had to suffer all the torments of slow burning. Many heretics had the physical and spiritual strength to bear their agony without a sound, with heroic steadfastness, to the last heartbeat. Others, whose nerves had already been shattered by torture, broke out into bestial roars. Usually the crowds of believers surrounding the pyre burst into song—the hymn: "Great God, we praise thee!" When the fires died down, the ashes were gathered and scattered to the four winds, so that not the slightest relic of the heretic would remain.

As for everything else in this world, apologies can be made even for the Inquisition. Its defenders have pointed out that the men of the Inquisition regarded heresy as a horrible plague from which they were obliged to shield the rest of Christendom. The Norwegian writer Sigrid Undset has pointed out that in practicing such cruelties the Church was doing only what it was at all times ready to suffer from its opponents.[7] This is a diabolic apology no Christian should indulge in. It does no honor to Christianity to attempt, with the cunning of serpents, to justify such an institution, or to speak of the "blessed flames of the pyres"—as irresponsible defenders of the Inquisition have actually done in modern times! As for the theological arguments for the Inquisition, these make us think of a comment of Franz Overbeck, who called theology the "Satan of religion." [8] There can be no serious Christian defense of the annihilation of heretics, especially since Christianity teaches that all killing of human beings is

[7] Sigrid Undset: *Begegnungen und Trennungen* (1931), p. 89.
[8] Overbeck: *Christentum und Kultur* (1919), p. 13.

a crime. The activities of the Inquisition can only be described as a "total eclipse" of all Christian feeling. The beast of the abyss rose up and threatened to overwhelm all of Christendom. The Inquisition was the most thoroughgoing effort to keep the Occident by force under the sway of the Church. It was an experiment doomed to failure.

Why did medieval Christianity produce the Inquisition? Did it have something to do with the fact that Christianity had developed from an original community of love into a mere community of ideas, and that all ideas developed without self-discipline lead to diabolic results? Or, as Leo Shestow once suggested, did the famous proofs of the scholastic *Summas* fail to accomplish what had been hoped for? Was the stake necessary to reinforce these arguments?

It must surely be said that anything which requires the collusion of executioners cannot be divine truth. The Inquisition abandoned faith in the spirit for resort to violence, and this was a betrayal of the faith. Its activities amounted to nothing less than a second crucifixion of Christ, undertaken by Christendom itself. It is hard to believe that these ghastly excesses emerged out of the same Church that simultaneously produced glorious saints. Nor is it Catholicism alone which is compromised by the Inquisition. Protestantism too is disgraced by the burnings of heretics. The execution of heretics, supposedly for the greater glory of God, remains an eternal blot upon the history of Christianity. In the face of this Fall of the Church, it is more than questionable whether the Church may go on claiming to be the representative of God on earth. For the Inquisition was in truth the antagonist of Christ, and its dread deeds a mockery of his work.

The Inquisition did incalculable harm to religion. If we ask why and when Western man ceased to believe, there rises out of the past the gruesome history of the Inquisition. The manner in which heretics were treated shook the foundations of belief; a gnawing doubt settled into the hearts of men as to whether Christianity was really the truth revealed by God. The Inquisition drove countless people out of the Church. It destroyed irrevocably confidence in Christian man, in his ability to reflect the love of God. Because of the Inquisition, the faith of Christians wavered and faded, and with the death of that faith, came the birth of European nihilism. The Inquisition was one of the most powerful causes for the emergence and spread of atheism in the West. Paradoxically, too, the Inquisition brought about an increase in heresy. If the blood of martyrs is the seed of the Church, then by creating heretic martyrs the Inquisition contributed immensely to disseminating the heretical seed. It is curious that the Inquisitors themselves never realized this.

The effect of the Inquisition was like that of a disease. It was a cancer on the body of the Church which grew with such vigor that the operation to remove it almost failed. The toxins of this tumor poisoned the entire body. A spirit of cruelty and harshness entered Christendom which no unctuous sermons could gloss over. Since pleasure in the agonies of fellow men was one of its mainsprings, the Inquisition led to a spread of sadism which ultimately gripped whole populations. The autos-da-fé met the basest instincts more than halfway, and satisfied the craving for sensational spectacles, so that often high prices were paid for a place at windows overlooking the scene. The worst part of this malady was that it has infected the thinking of Christians right down to the present. There are still men like Theodor Häcker who claim, perhaps out of a journalistic desire to shock, to see the burnings of heretics as a "fiery act of love." [9]

The terrible burden of the Inquisition upon the conscience of Christianity becomes fully visible when we examine the metaphysical problem inherent in it. For in the phenomenon of the Inquisition, the question of justifying the ways of God to man reaches its peak. This point has been made most succinctly by Bielinsky: *If I were able to reach the highest stage of evolution, even there I would ask you to give me an account of all the victims of the conditions of life and history, of all the victims of accident, of superstition, of the Inquisition of Philip II, etc. Otherwise I would cast myself head foremost from the highest step on the ladder. I do not wish happiness even gratis, so long as I am not reassured concerning every one of my brothers in the*

[9] In K. Guggisberg: *Die römisch-katholische Kirche* (1946), p. 336.

blood. It is said that disharmony is a condition of harmony; perhaps that is highly advantageous and gratifying to some, but not at all to those whose destiny it is to embody the idea of disharmony.[1]

Bielinsky's feelings on the question are those of modern man. In the light of this metaphysical question, we see how the pyres of the Inquisition were incompatible with the love of God. Why did God permit the church to proceed on such a path of error? Why was this senseless cruelty necessary? Can harmony in eternity outweigh the sufferings of even a single heretic? Will these victims ever be atoned for, and can all these men who were tortured and reduced to ashes ever forgive their executioners after the Resurrection? Will the final end of the world be able to undo these things, to drain away this ocean of blood and tears? What explanation can ever account for these atrocities? In the face of such organized cruelty, the problem of theodicy becomes a mountain crushing man beneath its weight. These questions loom before us with a terrible contemporaneity, and who is able to give a satisfactory answer to them? Anyone who has felt them even for a moment cannot help but fall silent. All comment on the Inquisition is inevitably tinged by the shadow of these metaphysical doubts.

The only resolution for this agonizing metaphysical problem has been proposed by Dostoevsky at the end of his "The Grand Inquisitor." He says it all in one little detail. I feel we should be sparing and circumspect in our quotations from this magnificent chapter, lest like so much else it be reduced to platitude. But here it is of key importance. His Christ figure, who has listened to all of the Inquisitor's statements without saying a word, at the end "suddenly approached the old man in silence and kissed him softly on his bloodless, aged lips." [2] That kiss contains the evangelical reply to the terrible guilt of Christianity—a reply which only the Son of Man could pronounce.

[1] In Leo Shestov: *Tolstoj und Nietzsche* (1923), p. iii.
[2] Fëdor Dostoevsky: *The Brothers Karamazov* (New York: Modern Library; no date), p. 322.

13

The Spirit of Mysticism

The Brethren of the Free Spirit

Most accounts of the medieval Brethren of the Free Spirit must be regarded as pure slanders. The bold views of this group were misunderstood as crude pantheism. They were charged with denying the existence of a supernatural God. Supposedly they were moral reprobates who contended that "God does not dwell down to the waist only," but below it.[1] It was alleged that, according to their infernal morality, what men did in practice did not count. They were said to extol freedom of the flesh and to regard whoredom as no sin; like the ancient Gnostics, to oppose

---

[1] W. Preger: *Geschichte der deutschen Mystik im Mittelalter* (1874), I, 211.

226

the moral law and use all the apparatus of philosophy to construct a doctrinal system based on immorality;[2] to pose such insidious questions as: "How is it possible that God should have forbidden sensual appetites, since he created them?" Even historians not bound by ties to the Church have accepted and presented such caricatures of the Brethren of the Free Spirit. Thus Fritz Mauthner in his seemingly unbiassed *Geschichte des Atheismus* ("History of Atheism") represents them as "undisciplined gangs" who lived "not so much by begging as by extortion, which they considered their right, for they were communists and saw nothing improper in robbery."[3] Since each historian has copied these lies from his predecessors, the Brethren of the Free Spirit have remained one of the most libeled movements in the whole of ecclesiastical history.

If ever a thorough revision of judgments were needed, here is the place. One of the primary tasks of a history of heresy is to correct such misconceptions. And in the case of the Brethren of the Free Spirit the distortions are legion. Out of a curious misunderstanding of the questions that the Brethren were really asking, the most nonsensical rumors arose. Possibly some members of the movement did not themselves grasp the secret of their own doctrine, or misused it as a cloak for their carnal appetites. But displays of license were no more characteristic of the movement as a whole than occasional lapses on the part of nuns or monks are typical of cloisters or in any way depict the religious standards and the ethical discipline of monasticism.

The father of the new movement was the inspired Joachim of Floris (1145–1202), one of the great revivers of medieval faith, whose work was to be of lasting value. The repute of this Calabrian abbot has undergone strange vicissitudes. Highly respected in his lifetime, so much so that three Popes urged him to write down his thoughts and mystical experiences, he was afterward regarded as a heresiarch whose doctrines were damned,

[2] Cf. E. J. Nitzsch: *"Die Gesamterscheinung des Antinomismus"* in *Theologische Studien und Kritiken* (1846), pp. 7 f.
[3] F. Mauthner: *Der Atheismus und seine Geschichte im Abendland* (1924), I, 302.

only still later to be taken up again by the Bollandists (the collaborators and successors of Jean de Bolland, first editor of the Jesuit *Acta Sanctorum*) and ranked among the "beatified" of the Church. Joachim has remained to the present one of those Janus figures presenting one heretical and one saintly countenance to the world. And both are genuine.

Joachim's writings present a conception of history as seen by the visionary spirit. He boldly recast the Church's doctrine of the Trinity in terms of three ages. The age of the Father corresponded to the Old Testament era. This was succeeded by the age of the Son, which according to his own curious calculations would last until the year 1260. Then the dominion of the Son would pass into the age of the Holy Spirit. In that age ceremonies would be laid aside and men would be tutored directly by God. In Joachim's writings we find one of the loftiest historical visions ever conceived by the human mind. He literally saw the angels of the Apocalypse flying at the zenith, proclaiming the eternal evangel—by which Joachim meant not a written book like the New Testament, but a spiritual gospel which would come to take the place of that Testament. What wonder that the Church considered this to be heretical!

Joachim's vision of the three ages removed the complex, difficult doctrine of the Trinity from the realm of dogma, and transferred it to living history. This prophecy of the coming of a "spiritual church" [4] kindled the minds of men. Although written in a dry, exegetical style, Joachim's historical vision proved to be one of the most revolutionary documents of its age. It contained a message which could not leave Christians indifferent, for it excited extraordinary hopes. His predictions of the coming age of the Spirit quickly won wide currency; there is evidence that his doctrine had spread as far as Germany before 1240.

The second father of the Brethren of the Spirit movement was Amalric or Amaury of Bena, a little town near Chartres, who was a *magister* in Paris around the year 1200. He was an excellent and effective teacher, being both highly learned and a keen

[4] E. Benz: *Ecclesia spiritualis* (1934), pp. 12 f.

dialectician.[5] Aristocratic by temperament, he was accused by his opponents of a morbid appetite for independent and original ideas. He was called to Rome to defend his doctrines, and Innocent III decided against him. Amalric was forced to recant, although his convictions had not changed. The torments of conscience affected his health, and he died young, about 1206. He received a Christian burial, but several years after his death was excommunicated, his body exhumed, and reburied in unconsecrated ground. The Lateran Council of 1215 condemned Amalric's doctrine once more, although without specifying the heretical items in his works.

Because his writings have been destroyed, it is no longer possible to determine which of Amalric's ideas were his alone and which were derived from his predecessors.[6] We know, however, that Amalric resurrected the work of John the Scot. Evidently he instinctively sensed a kindred soul in Erigena. His propositions may seem at first like riddles. Thus Amalric said: "All is one and what is, is God." Similar formulations, however, occur in the New Testament.[7] Amalric emphasized the identity of creator and creature. God, he said, is the unitary essence of all creatures. Ideas create and are created. All things that are divided into parts and are transitory ultimately return to God, to rest unchangeably in God and become one single individual in him. Abraham and Isaac are not different, but of the same nature; all things are one and that one is God. In saying this Amalric approached mystical pantheism. The connection between his doctrine and Erigena's is obvious; at the same time that the Church began to fight the spread of Amalric's ideas it condemned the writings of Erigena as the source of all such errors.

Another of Amalric's fundamental ideas is expressed in the sentence: "Every Christian must believe that he is a member of Christ, nor can he be saved unless he believes in that as firmly as in the birth and death of the Savior or in other important arti-

[5] Cf. J. H. Krönlein: *"Amalrich von Bena und David von Dinat"* in *Theologische Studien und Kritiken* (1847), pp. 271 f.
[6] Cf. Hahn: op. cit. (1850), III, 176 f.
[7] Cf. Rom. xi, 36 and I Cor. xv, 28.

cles of the creed."[8] For this essentially mystical statement Amalric could again refer to the New Testament.[9] He carried it even farther, insisting that the Christian must believe that as a member of the body of Christ he had suffered jointly with the Redeemer on the cross. This, however, had a dangerous corollary, for it followed that the value of the sacraments was limited. In fact, Amalric also held that the Holy Spirit works inwardly, without external props. The body of Christ is in the host even before the transubstantiation, just as God dwells permanently in every soul. God, he held, had spoken through Ovid just as much as he had through Augustine, and Christ had been God in exactly the same way as every other man. Heaven and hell, according to Amalric, were to be understood symbolically. Those who had the proper knowledge of God carried heaven within themselves, but those who had committed a mortal sin were already in hell. Equally bold was Amalric's ethical system, whose drift is apparent from this statement of his: "No sin is attributed to those in the state of love." That is to say, what ordinarily is called sin is not to be so considered if done by virtue of love. In keeping with this view, he regarded the workings of the will as stirrings of the divine will. God does everything in man, both the willing and the execution of the will's desires. There is no difference between good and evil; qualms of conscience are unnecessary.

We may conjecture that the Brethren of the Free Spirit emerged from the circle of Amalric's followers. These followers linked the views of Amalric with the message of Joachim of Floris, of which they had heard, although it is not possible to say how the Calabrian abbot's ideas were communicated to them. The goldsmith William, one of the few personalities visible from out of the mists surrounding the Brethren, declared: *The Father worked under certain forms, for example, in the sacraments of the altar, baptism, and others. Just as the forms of the Law disappeared with the appearance of Christ, so the forms in which the Son worked will likewise vanish now and the sacraments will fall away, since henceforth the Holy Spirit will reveal himself*

[8] In Krönlein: op. cit., p. 293.   [9] Eph. v, 30.

distinctly to those in whom he incarnates himself. By preference he will speak through seven men.[1]

Statements of this sort clearly stem from Joachim's historical philosophy. They represent a further development of Joachim's ideas, for they assume that the third age which he predicted has already arrived. All external efforts at mediation between God and man were now to fall away and man's relationship to God was to become a purely inward and direct one. Just as the Father was incarnate in Abraham and the Son in Mary, so "henceforth unto the end of time the Holy Spirit will be incarnate in every man and will effect all in all. The incarnation of the Deity means nothing else but its appearance in visible forms."[2]

Amalric's followers had formed a small group in Paris which existed for some time before they were denounced and in 1209 tried for heresy. A number of them were condemned to the stake and the rest were punished with life imprisonment. In spite of such repressive measures, the ideas of the Brethren of the Free Spirit continued to spread. Unfortunately we possess no definite information on the composition of this brotherhood. Apparently they had no fixed organization, but felt themselves to be united by the ties of common convictions. They were joined by a thousand invisible threads which held them more firmly than any legal organization ever can. Moreover, there were not very many of them. They would appear sporadically, and suddenly drop out of sight again. First traces of them date from the time of Albertus Magnus (d. 1280), who heard of them at Cologne. Later Swabia, long a country for religious ferment, became one of the chief centers of the Brethren of the Free Spirit. They were also to be encountered in other parts of Europe.

The Brethren of the Free Spirit lived in the faith that the prophecy of Joachim was about to be gloriously fulfilled, that the longed-for age of the Spirit had in fact begun with them. This was no small claim. Still, they did not feel that they would be the only ones to be so blessed. In a very short time, they felt, the coming of the Spirit would sweep through the whole world. Their

[1] In Krönlein: op. cit., p. 278.   [2] Ibid., p. 299.

enthusiasm was unbounded; they felt themselves transported beyond themselves, filled with the flux of the Spirit. As participants in the age of the Spirit, they called their meetings for worship "paradise." A key aspect of this movement was that the Brethren drew practical conclusions from Joachim's wondrous vision and translated his historical philosophy into everyday life.

When the outward signs of the dawning of the third age did not appear as expected, the Brethren of the Free Spirit shifted their emphasis to a type of mysticism of their own creation. Amalric's ideas were a great help to them in making this shift. Historical enthusiasm and mysticism are by no means mutually exclusive; they lend themselves to curious fusions, as is evident in the eschatological mysticism of the Apostle Paul. In the mystic creed developed by the Brethren the Christian must seek to become God; if he does, he will ultimately become like God. If man turns from external to inward things, lets God be God, then he will resemble God, will be God, and will no longer need God. He will have ascended even beyond love and reached the state in which God accomplishes everything within him. Thus the religious ideal of the Brethren of the Free Spirit became a "complete dissolution and absorption in the divine Being. They regarded quiet, physical well-being, and freedom from the disturbance of unpleasant and distracting impressions as a precondition for the descent of the Holy Spirit." [3] Once he had reached his apogee, a Christian would have exceeded the merits of the saints and the Virgin Mary and would surpass even Christ. Man's task therefore is to free himself, in God, from all legal ties, to abstain from the world's work, not to strain the body, thus paving the way for the influence of the Spirit and making it possible to follow its biddings.

Central to the religious speculations of the Brethren of the Free Spirit was the question of perfectionism. They were concerned not with the striving toward perfection, but the attainment of it. They laid great stress upon the remark of Paul which

[3] H. Haupt: "*Beiträge zur Geschichte der Sekte vom freien Geiste und des Beghardenordens,*" in *Zeitschrift für Kirchengeschichte* (1885), p. 534.

had already fascinated Joachim of Floris: "But when the perfect comes, the imperfect will pass away."[4] Now, with their arrival, perfection had dawned, for this was the third age in which ceremonies and sacraments would cease to be necessary. Should it not be possible for the Christian himself to become perfect and not have to pass through the purgatory fires? Perfect on this earth, in his present condition! What was so new, surprising, and, in the eyes of the Church, so heretical, was that the Brethren of the Free Spirit answered yes to this daring question, and asserted that the ultimate religious goal could be attained in this present life. For they would have it that man in the third age of the Spirit had actually reached the height of moral perfection, so that he was exempt from even the possibility of sinning and did not need the aid of grace.

Here was a promise that transcended anything offered by the Church. The Brethren rejected the institutions of the Church and sought a "transcatholic" ideal. Perfectionism has knocked repeatedly on the gates of Christendom, in various guises, but has never been granted admission. This heretical doctrine touched on a Christian insight which to this day has not found proper expression. A number of great Christians have made similar professions, such as: "To the truly religious man, nothing is sin."[5]

On the basis of this belief, the Brethren of the Free Spirit were pervaded by an unusual joyousness quite in keeping with the central message of the Gospel. An inexpressible gladness filled these brothers; their mood was that described in the Gospel of John in the words: "that your joy may be full."[6] In their spiritual intoxication they could say: "A man who knows that God is in him can never be downcast, but must always be joyous."[7] In this statement is contained the essence of the movement. The Brethren did not try to reach God by penances, tears, and pain. To them joy was a holy thing, purifying, transforming, and elevating man. The Brethren of the Free Spirit radiated a euphoric

[4] I Cor. xiii, 10.   [5] Novalis: *Fragmente*, 2875.
[6] John xv, 11 and xvi, 24.
[7] In H. Grundmann: *Religiöse Bewegungen im Mittelalter* (1935), p. 373.

ecstasy of the kind that is inspired when in Beethoven's Ninth Symphony the chorus begins to sing, *"Freude, schöner Götterfunken!"* In the gloom-ridden, ascetic Middle Ages this was an extremely rare note.

The doctrines of perfection led the Brethren to the conviction that they had achieved a new freedom. The Christian, they believed, had at last laid aside the earlier stages of servitude and childhood; in the third and concluding era he was ready to enjoy mature freedom.

As happened so often, this new libertarianism was misinterpreted as libertinage, and storms of indignation were directed at the Brethren of the Free Spirit. But anyone who studies the sect carefully must conclude, as does Grundmann, that "so bold and enthusiastic a philosophical revaluation of Christian morality cannot by any means be thought to spring from the same sources as the widespread moral corruption among the clergy of the time. Rather, it was one more attempt to close the great gap between Christian doctrine and the way of life practiced by most members of the Church." [8] The Brethren did not imagine that their new freedom could be attained easily. They insisted on a long, austere probationary period "because human nature, which is in itself unfruitful, must be broken and in all things made subject to the divine will in order to attain perfection and win full freedom"; only then can man enter "into the state of spiritual freedom" in which "everything is permitted him." [9] Clearly, the Brethren insisted on effort—an attitude fundamentally different from that of the libertine.

According to a medieval chronicler, the Brethren of the Free Spirit spoke only of divine goodness but not of divine judgment. To the man united with God everything was sacred, so that he could no longer sin. In support of this view, they cited the first epistle of John: "No one born of God commits sin; for God's nature abides in him, and he cannot sin because he is born of

[8] Ibid., p. 372.
[9] H. Wattenbach: *"Über die Sekte der Brüder vom freien Geist,"* in *Sitzungsberichte der königlichen preussischen Akademie der Wissenschaften zu Berlin* (1887), pp. 527, 528.

God." [1] Hence the perfect man is permitted to do what he likes, for no matter what he does, he cannot sin. And if sin does not exist, no one can be punished for it by God. The corollary follows: virtue is no more praiseworthy than sin is reprehensible.

These statements must be regarded as a first attempt to establish pansacramentalism—the belief that everything is sacred and every act sacramental—within Christianity. The Brethren were striving to achieve a sanctification of the world of a sort otherwise unknown to the Middle Ages. Since they viewed all things as the work of God, they were eager to understand redemption as a fulfillment which freed Christians from the necessity to renounce the world, but rather allowed them to possess the world and enjoy it in good conscience. It is true that this novel sanctification of the world, with its interesting solution of the problem of dualism, was rudely suppressed in *status nascendi*. Had fate permitted it to prevail, the Western world would in fact have witnessed the dawn of Joachim's third age—the age of the Holy Spirit.

In the light of this novel ethical system we can better understand the attitude of the Brethren toward Eros. This has been gravely misconstrued. They by no means championed a libertinistic nihilism. They have been charged with promiscuity and wantonness, but the charge has never been proved. There are no indications that the movement practiced ritual orgies. Their religious doctrine of love consisted in a synthesis of Platonic Eros and Christian *agape* into what might be called an Adamic eroticism, in keeping with their idea that in the era of the Spirit the state of innocence which had reigned in Paradise would be renewed upon earth. The new unison of the sexes was also referred to as "angelic love"; the epithet was intended to suggest a sensuality above sensuality. Since this conception was closely guarded as an element of secret knowledge, it gave rise to all sorts of calumnious rumors. But in fact the Brethren of the Free Spirit tried to combine chastity and sinless sexual love. Women were treated as the equals of men, and angelic love was to rescue the

[1] I John iii, 9.

union of man and woman from the corrupt morass of sin into which it had fallen as the result of Christianity. The manner in which the whole matter of human procreation had been linked with the doctrine of original sin had poisoned erotic life. Christians suffered from guilty conscience in their marital relations. For Christians of fine temperament, this was a constant source of torment.[2] The Brethren of the Free Spirit sought to return to the original order of creation in which sexual relations had been sanctified. Thus they were led to declare, as we know from the records of an Inquisitional trial, "that the natural sexual act can take place in such a manner that it is equal in value to a prayer in the presence of God"—a statement springing directly from pansacramentalism.[3]

The body was no longer regarded as an enemy to be crushed by ascetic practices. It was expressly included in the sanctification of the world. We must go far into the Middle Ages to find a similar noble attempt to raise nuptial relations from the level of mere gratification of animal rut to a divine plane. Only the Cabala (in the book called *Sohar*) casts the same divine light upon pure Eros and attempts to prove the worshipful nature of amorous pleasure: "In a place where no male and female are to be found united, the All-Holy does not set up his dwelling . . . because the joy of connubial union is a joy of duty. . . . For when he does not remember his wife, he sins, because he thus diminishes the honor of celestial union which his wife has made possible for him."[4]

The Brethren of the Free Spirit undertook a dangerous journey along the ridges of the highest mountains. Abysses yawned on either side, and probably more than one among them slipped and fell. Their fellowmen must have been profoundly shocked by these daring, too daring conceptions of complete sinlessness. The Brethren seem to have forgotten that only God, not men, can be beyond good and evil. Certainly, too, they formulated some of

[2] Cf. W. Schubart: *Religion und Eros* (1941), pp. 196 f.
[3] In W. Fränger: *Hieronymus Bosch, das Tausendjährige Reich* (1947), p. 31.
[4] *Der Sohar*, ed. E. Müller (1932), pp. 121–3.

their doctrines in far too paradoxical language, and thus gave rise to fatal misunderstandings. But this tendency to rhapsodic language is something they shared with many mystics. How falsely even St. Augustine's maxims could be interpreted: Love and do as you like! The words of mystics must not be taken at their face value. Rather, they must be studied, carefully, subtly, with an ear to all their overtones and undertones.

The Brethren of the Free Spirit had become aware of the disparity between the Gospel and morality, and had recognized those aspects of the message of the New Testament which are beyond morality. In so doing they apprehended an essential side of Jesus, whose proclamation of the forgiveness of sin is also beyond morality. In refusing to suppress the instinctual force of Eros in man, in seeking rather to give Eros a religious form, they raised erotic love to a pinnacle which was only glimpsed again six centuries later by Novalis in that "Hymn" whose multiple meanings can never be fully unraveled:

> *Who has guessed the earthly*
> *Body's lofty meaning?*
> *Who can declare*
> *That he understands the blood?*
> *Once all body was*
> *One body.*
> *The blessed pair*
> *Swims in heavenly blood.*

Meister Eckhart

A good priest, member of the brotherhood of mystics known as the Friends of God, once came to Eckhart to recommend that he not squander his noble words like pearls before swine. True Friends of God, he said, already knew within themselves what he wished to say, and the others had no profit from it. Eckhart was not in the least offended by this reprimand; he embraced the venerable priest, gave him the kiss of peace, and said: "Dear

Father, know that for many years I have not heard any speech so gladly as this of yours, God be eternally praised." But there the matter rested, and Eckhart continued his preaching as before.

This incident is one of the relatively few personal anecdotes that has come down to us concerning Eckhart, the great Dominican mystic (c. 1260–c. 1328). The priest's advice was well intentioned, and had a valid basis. Simple minds could easily be confused by Eckhart's words. Eckhart was aware of this, and aware of the concern the good man felt—hence his cordial response and embrace. What was more, Eckhart would have been spared a good deal of personal upheaval and anguish if he had followed the advice. But how much would have been lost to posterity if he had kept his counsel. One of the most glorious conceptions of Christianity would have remained forever unknown.

Fortunately Eckhart did not and could not obey the recommendation. It would have meant gainsaying himself, for like Jeremiah he acted under divine compulsion. He was forced to proclaim his redeeming message, whether or not men understood him. "He who has understood this sermon, I wish him well. If there had been no one here, I would have had to preach to this poor-box." [5] Such words reflect a sense of prophetic mission. Eckhart was one of the greatest preachers of all times; his extraordinary sermons seem to be woven out of the stuff of eternity. Those who have once listened to these sermons with their inner ear will henceforth be hard to please; the ordinary language of the clergy will seem inadequate.

To fully understand Eckhart's sublime language, we must consider it in terms of the age of scholasticism, to which he belonged. Our knowledge of scholasticism is too often confined to its last phase, when it had already entered upon its decadence and lost itself in formalistic subtleties. At its beginnings, scholasticism represented a grand undertaking. As the cathedrals rose up from the tangle of small houses in medieval cities, so the scholastic *Summas* loomed up from the flatlands of life, confronting men

[5] *Meister Eckharts Schriften und Predigten*, ed. Büttner (1917), I, 148.

with the ultimate questions of being. Eckhart, too, had a share in these scholastic efforts. In the nineteenth century Denifle pointed out that Eckhart stood "on scholastic ground," for which reason more attention must be given his writings in Latin.[6] Certainly Eckhart's philosophic and theological system cannot be understood apart from these Latin writings. But granting his participation in scholasticism, it is clear that he so reshaped Thomistic ideas that in the end they acquired a new content. Eckhart was strongly influenced by the Arabic and Jewish religious philosophy of the Middle Ages. Whereas Thomas Aquinas vigorously fought the resurgence of Neo-Platonism, Eckhart was extremely receptive to it. The telling factor here was Eckhart's mysticism.

In recent years there has been much discussion of the kinship of scholasticism and mysticism. It is true that in medieval intellectual life there were mystics with scholastic interests and scholastics with a mystical vein. But that circumstance should not mislead us; scholasticism and mysticism were fundamentally opposed. Scholasticism is intensely rational and uses the language of abstract ideas, whereas mysticism with its immediacy speaks from the heart. For a true picture of Eckhart we must concentrate upon his writings in German, which threatened for a time to be overshadowed by his newly discovered Latin works. The German writings represent his attempt to break out of scholastic intellectualism. Only a scholastic could turn against scholasticism in this manner, because he had himself come to know the pitfalls of Aristotelian rationalism.

In the course of time theology had nearly succeeded in enclosing living religious feeling within the armor of a system. But in the case of Eckhart this deplorable process was reversed; the fresh wind of his mysticism swept away scholastic pedantry like chaff. Eckhart's passionate mysticism overcame scholastic rationalism, and therein lies his eternal validity. Those who do not understand this struggle will regard him as a "morbid muddle-

[6] H. Denifle: *Meister Eckharts lateinische Schriften und die Grundanschauung seiner Lehre,* in *Archiv für Literatur– und Kirchengeschichte des Mittelalters* (1886), p. 421.

head," as one Neo-Thomist once called him. There was a grandeur in scholasticism, but Eckhart overthrew it for the sake of something greater, the mystical relationship with God. He sought to move from learned discussions of God back to God, for whom he hungered and thirsted. He was no second-rate scholastic [7] but a man whose religious intensity was matched, in the Middle Ages, only by Francis of Assisi.

In spite of the mighty questions with which it deals, Eckhart's mysticism is of an inspiring simplicity—and this again makes it a monumental achievement. He himself has stated the gist of his message: *Whenever I preach, I am in the habit of speaking of detachment, exhorting man to strip himself of himself and of all things. Secondly, that one should again become incorporated into the simple good which is God. Thirdly, that one ought to consider the great nobility which God has placed in the soul so that man, through it, can enter into the wonderful life of God. Fourthly, of the purity of the divine nature—what the clarity of the divine nature is, is inexpressible.* [8]

These points also sum up Eckhart's spiritual biography, and hence are especially interesting to us here. For the outward course of his life still remains obscure. Probably that life was not particularly eventful, for all Eckhart's power to experience was concentrated upon the inner life. The significant events took place in the soul of this man.

"Whenever I preach, I am in the habit of speaking of detachment, exhorting man to strip himself of himself and of all things." This call for detachment reveals that what Eckhart was teaching was not so much a metaphysic as a religious road to salvation. His theme is how the Christian may reach God, and to his mind the obstacles in the path are not the world or the devil. Man himself is his own worst stumbling block. "It is you yourself who hinder yourself in things, for you have the wrong relationship to things. Therefore begin with yourself: Let yourself

[7] Cf. Erich Seeberg: *Meister Eckhart* (1934).
[8] In J. Bernhart: *Die philosophische Mystik des Mittelalters* (1922), p. 181.

be." [9] By detachment Eckhart meant the effort to empty oneself completely, to cast all images out of the soul until one had arrived at nothingness. Ultimately, even the "nothingness" must be overcome, for as long as some of that nothingness clings to a man, he has not yet achieved completely the indispensable estrangement. Prayer, too, must cease. "Detachment and purity cannot pray at all. . . . Therefore the devout heart is empty of all prayer, and its prayer consists only of the desire to be uniform with God." [1] Only when man has left all creatures and images behind him does he arrive at that ultimate detachment which is the only door to the inner kingdom.

As a prior of the Dominican Order, Eckhart was addressing himself to monks and nuns who were already leading an intense religious life. His mysticism was not meant for those who were only casually interested in religion. At the same time he did not equate this "desert" of the Godhead with withdrawal into the cloister. "A man cannot learn this by fleeing from things and turning to solitude apart from all externality; he must learn an inner solitude, wherever or with whomever he may be." [2] Great courage is needed to set out on such a course. Detachment penetrates to that boundary where this whole world vanishes from the sight of the mystic. But this was not Eckhart's final goal. For much as he speaks of detachment, he considered it as only a negative factor—although an indispensable one. His passionate, far from detached concern was with the unfathomable mysteries which were revealed in the depths of this detachment.

Through detachment man arrives at this deepest substance, what Eckhart terms the "ground of the soul." The soul, Eckhart held, is much more closely united with God than with the body. "If you ask how great the soul is, you must know that heaven and earth could not fill its greatness, but only God himself." [3] Man's soul is inexpressible, as God is inexpressible. The ground of the

---

[9] *Meister Eckhart,* ed. Walter Lehmann (1919), p. 52.
[1] *Eckhart,* ed. Büttner, I, 19.   [2] *Eckhart,* ed. Lehmann, p. 57.
[3] *Meister Eckhart,* ed. Otto Karrer (1926), p. 136.

soul is by nature divine. "All the goodness that all saints possessed, and Mary, Mother of God, and Christ by his manhood—all that is by virtue of my nature already my own." [4] Men call Christ their Lord "because he was a messenger from God to us, and brought to us our blessedness, but the blessedness that he brought to us was our own." [5]

The conception of the uncreated ground of the soul, which is as eternal as the essence of God, is a heretical deviation from the doctrine of the Church. We can understand why the good priest was troubled at hearing this doctrine proclaimed from the pulpit. For such statements about the soul "no reason can grasp and no church approve." [6]

If the Christian becomes conscious of this ground of the soul, he will once more be incorporated into the eternal good and will experience "the birth of God in the soul." God is born in the pure soul by "revealing himself in a new way which is unlike all ways, in an illumination which is no longer illumination, but the divine light itself." [7] God created the world in order that this birth of God in the soul should take place. "If I am asked: why do we pray, why do we fast, why do we all do good works, why are we baptized, why did God become man?—I answer: So that God may be born in the soul, and the soul again in God." [8] According to Eckhart, it is *this* birth Christianity celebrates at Christmas. The event in the stable at Bethlehem is only an image of that birth which God brings forth incessantly in eternity: "But if it does not happen within me, of what help is it to me? The chief thing is that it take place within me." [9] And the soul must undergo this birth not only once, but again and again: "The soul in which the birth takes place is formed after God—it is surpassingly formed by God in God—and the more often this birth occurs, the more the soul is incorporated into God and into the Father's heart." [1] For God alone, and not man, accomplishes this birth, by which the image of God perfects the inner self of man

[4] *Eckhart*, ed. Lehmann, p. 185.   [5] Ibid., p. 186.
[6] W. Muschg: *Die Mystik in der Schweiz* (1935), p. 171.
[7] *Eckhart*, ed. Karrer, p. 136.   [9] *Eckhart*, ed. Lehmann, p. 136.
[8] *Eckhart*, ed. Büttner, I, 1.   [1] *Eckhart*, ed. Karrer, p. 117.

in a new way. "As long as you still suffer sorrow for anything, even for sin, your child is not yet born; you lie in labor, the birth is still impending. But once the birth is completed and man no longer feels sorrow in his heart for anything, he has regained his being and his nature and his substance." [2] The birth of God is the great mystery in the life of the Christian, and one which surpasses all rational understanding.

When this birth has taken place, when "God glows brightly in the soul's beauty," man has become *homo nobilis,* deified and like unto God. This part of Eckhart's message is based upon the eighty-second Psalm, which he expressly cites: "You are gods." Eckhart's ethic arises out of this conception of the *homo nobilis.*[3] Since the deified man no longer beholds himself as a poor sinner, he must take a new attitude toward the world. Eckhart never reviles the world as a vale of tears, in contrast to the bliss of heaven. He endorses neither flight from the world, born of fear of it, nor stoic indifference. "Now our good people say one must become so perfect that no sort of love can move us any longer and we will be unaffected by love and suffering. They wrong themselves! I think that no saint was ever so great that he could not be affected." [4] Eckhart was filled with an ecstatic joy in existence and regarded life as a merciful gift of God, for which he was ready to thank the Almighty fervently every day of his life. So deeply did he feel the beauty of the world that he exclaimed: *Therefore I would like to remain till the Day of Judgment. . . . Many people think that in this life they have only a creature being, but in that other life a divine being. However, that cannot be. Many are deceived by thus opposing the one life to the other. I have said that man beholds God in this very life in the same perfection and is blessed in the same manner as after this life.*[5]

According to Eckhart, works do not sanctify man; rather, man must transfigure his works by being filled with God. Eck-

[2] Ibid., p. 109.
[3] Cf. H. Piesch: *Die Ethik Eckharts* (1935).
[4] *Eckhart,* ed. Karrer, p. 161.
[5] In R. Otto: *West-Östliche Mystik* (1926), p. 295.

hart imperiously thrusts aside the whole medieval concept of religious devoutness in favor of an inner ethic. "God does not regard the works themselves, but only the love, the reverence, and
the principles in the works. He does not greatly care about our
works, but about our principles in all our works." [6] Being is an
efflux of the birth of God in the soul and not a result of moral
training. It has nothing to do with striving toward virtue. Virtue,
according to Eckhart, is only an intermediate step between vice
and perfection. It has to be transcended. Man must not abandon
morality, of course—if he did, he would fall into ethical chaos—
but he must also not be obsessed by the ideal of virtue. Perfect
virtue means being free of virtue! The counterpart to these statements on virtue, with their startling resemblance to the teachings
of Lao-tse, are Eckhart's ideas on sin: "To have sinned is no longer
sin as soon as we are sorry. . . . Indeed, he who rightly identified himself with the will of God would not desire that the sin
into which he has fallen had not happened." [7]

It is not that Eckhart failed to see the reality of sin. But he
was more concerned that even in sin man should "never and in no
way feel himself remote from God. . . . For that is a great error,
when man moves away from God. Man moves away or approaches; God never moves away, he remains constantly near." [8]
Whatever shame or bitterness may come to man, everything
comes to him through God and "thence receives its savor and becomes God-colored." [9] The presence of God, for which a merely
metaphysical system never provides, permeates everything in
Eckhart.

True action flows out of roots in God-filled being. It is surprising to find Eckhart, the advocate of detachment, making a
strong plea for activity. He placed the active idea of Martha
above the contemplative ideal of Mary—a highly unusual rank-
ing. This came about because he considered profane work equal
in dignity with religious meditation—although he did not by any
means reduce all things to a similar level. *Certainly it would be*

[6] *Eckhart,* ed. Karrer, p. 157.   [8] Ibid., pp. 73, 74.
[7] *Eckhart,* ed. Lehmann, pp. 67, 68.   [9] Ibid., p. 66.

wrong to regard all occupations or all places or all people as of equal value. Certainly praying is better than spinning and the church a nobler place than the street. But you should preserve and carry with you into the crowd and into the tumult of the world the spirit with which you are in the church or in your cell. The same mood must be in your heart wherever you are, and you must everywhere cling to your God with the same earnestness.[1]

Eckhart held that ordinary life should not be despised and compared unfavorably to monastic life. The supreme commandment remained love of neighbor and readiness to give help. "If someone were in such an ecstasy as came to St. Paul, and knew of a sick man who needed a bowl of soup from him, I would judge it far better that for love he should forget his ecstasy and rather serve the needy one." [2] This single quotation should make it clear that mysticism is never a refined form of egotism whose primary aim is to enjoy exalted emotions. Eckhart did not divide human life into sacred and profane domains. The divine, he held, is revealed in everyday life, and if it is not experienced in the midst of crude reality, it is not present in any real fashion. *For truly, you who imagine that in absorption, reverence, ecstatic feelings, and suchlike clinging you have more of God than at the hearth fire or in the stable, you are doing nothing else than if you took God and wrapped a cloak around his head and thrust him under a bench! For he who seeks God in particular forms no doubt grasps the form, but God, who is hidden in it, escapes him. Only he who seeks God in no form at all grasps him as he is in himself.*[3]

The fourth point that Eckhart expounded dealt with "the purity of the divine nature—what the clarity of the divine nature is, is inexpressible." Man cannot know at all what God is. The eternal secret is nameless; one can neither make any statement about it nor understand it. Whatever anyone says of God is not worthy of God and at best is adapted only to the human understanding. Man can really only say what God is not. Every predication we

---

[1] *Eckhart,* ed. Karrer, p. 182.   [2] *Eckhart,* ed. Lehmann, p. 63.
[3] *Eckhart,* ed. Büttner, I, 100.

make concerning God makes God into an idol, because it is inadequate. Anyone who "has a God" does not yet have the highest, and only stands on the brink of eternity, not within it. Even he who speaks of God in figurative language speaks impurely of him. All speech about God is only unintelligible mumbling. But Eckhart feels pressed by the omnipresence of the Eternal, and cannot leave off his stammering attempts. His yearning for God is characteristic of the Gothic age, marked as it was by that "climbing spirit" which rose into the infinite like the pillars of a medieval cathedral, a never-resting ascent, an everlasting aspiration. *Man's spirit does likewise. It is not simply content with the earthly light; it presses forever forward, through the firmament, presses through the heavens until it has reached that spirit which animates the circuit of the heavens, where through the heavens' circuit everything that is on earth sprouts and blossoms. Nevertheless this spirit still does not rest content, but presses on and on into the vertex and primal source from which it has taken its origin.*[4] There is a dynamism in these words which comes from a direct experiencing of God. Such language has nothing in common with the learned disputations of the theologians of the time. In Eckhart's hands the often sophistical intellectual problems of the medieval theologians and philosophers become bolts of lightning. As one historian of mysticism remarks: "What a strange drama of God he builds up out of scholastic concepts! How fantastically, magically, Gothically, wonderfully do these dead embers of scholasticism glow when he touches them with his magic wand! Did any scholastic before him, however similar his terms, ever compose such a novel of God?"[5]

At the chapter meeting of the Dominican order held in Venice in 1325 a complaint was lodged that certain brothers in the German provincial order had been preaching in the vulgar tongue to the laity and proclaiming certain things which could easily lead their listeners into heresy. The accusation was directed at none other than Eckhart. Shortly thereafter Heinrich von Virne-

[4] Ibid., I, 139.   [5] Otto: *West-Östliche Mystik*, p. 239.

berg, the Archbishop of Cologne, already noted as a persecutor of the Brethren of the Free Spirit, launched an attack against Eckhart, who, to his mind, espoused the same heresy as the Brethren. A first trial of Eckhart's writings was held; two censors found in them a number of sentences which they deemed heretical. The sentences were wrenched completely out of context. On September 26, 1326, Eckhart made a public reply: "In consideration of the freedom and the privileges of our order I am not required to appear before you." [6] He added: "If I enjoyed a smaller reputation among the people and displayed less zeal for justice, in truth I am convinced that those who envy me would never have attempted to raise such charges against me. However, it is incumbent upon me to bear this patiently." [7]

In his defense Eckhart expressed his astonishment "that more objections have not been raised against the contents of my various books; for there is no doubt that I have written a hundred and more things which these people in their ignorance do not understand." [8] Eckhart was quite willing to admit that he might have been in error, but maintained that he could not have fallen into heresy. For the seat of error lay in the intellect, he declared; of heresy, in the will. He did not hesitate to ascribe to his adversaries "ample malice or crude ignorance"; their coarse understanding was incapable of grasping anything divine.[9] He implied that his censors were acting out of subjective spite as well as objective incomprehension. Along with this display of sovereign superiority, however, Eckhart went to the trouble of refuting every single passage of the charge. His comment on the hostile inquisitors was: "The error of my opponents consists in their dubbing wrong everything they do not understand, and furthermore considering what is wrong to be heresy—whereas only obstinate clinging to error makes heresy and the heretic, as canon law and the preceptors say." [1]

By way of apology for the censors it may be said that Eckhart

[6] Karrer-Piesch: *Meister Eckharts Rechtfertigungsschrift*, p. 77.
[7] Ibid., p. 77.
[8] Ibid., p. 78.
[9] Ibid., p. 88.
[1] Ibid., p. 99.

did not make things easy for the ordinary reader of his writings, and that it is only human nature to take amiss whatever lies beyond the scope of one's understanding. To understand Eckhart it is necessary to love him; those who do not, even today, will only find him engaged upon a dubious intellectual game.

Eckhart emerged victorious from this initial skirmish. The papal nuncio, Nicholas of Strasbourg, who had been entrusted with the investigation, was a member of the mystical group among the Dominicans. Eckhart was cleared of the charge of heresy and was only asked to refrain for the time being from treating speculative questions in the pulpit.

The archbishop was by no means pleased with the outcome of the proceedings, for it meant a loss of prestige to him. Secretly, he assembled new evidence against Eckhart. Given Eckhart's paradoxical mode of expression, this was not difficult to find. Moreover, there existed copies of his sermons which, Eckhart avowed, contained many things he had never said, taken down by sleepy students. After six months had passed, the archbishop formally reinstituted the charges against Eckhart, and a second trial was held. Ugly passions played a considerable part in the renewed attack upon the mystic of Cologne, and intrigues among rival orders added to his difficulties. The Franciscans leaped at the chance to discomfit the Dominicans, and the latter, as the Inquisitional order, felt that its honor was at stake.

Eckhart himself protested against these new proceedings by the Inquisition, and finally appealed to the Pope, before whom, he declared, he was ready to appear at any time. In his own defense he read aloud from the pulpit in February 1327 the following statement: *I, Master Eckhart, doctor of holy theology, declare before all things, calling God to witness, that I have always abhorred all error in the faith and all excess in conduct, as far as it has been possible for me to do, since such errors would be contrary to my status as doctor and member of the order. If anything erroneous should be found that I have written, spoken, or preached, publicly or not publicly, wherever and whenever, di-*

*rectly or indirectly, out of wrong understanding or reprehensible
intention, I hereby do recant publicly and in the presence of all
and sundry who are here assembled, because I desire that henceforth any such error will be regarded as not having been said or
written. I have been so ill understood that it is claimed I preached
that my little finger created all things. Yet I neither meant nor
said that, but I did say by the fingers of that small boy Jesus.
And then, that there is a something in the soul of such nature
that if the entire soul were of the same kind, it would have to be
called uncreated; and that opinion I held and along with my
colleagues, the teachers, still hold in the sense that it would be
uncreated if it were reason's essence. Also I never said, so far
as I know, nor meant, that there is something in the soul which
is a part of the soul and yet uncreated and uncreatable because
then the soul would be constituted partly of created and partly
of uncreated stuff. Rather, I wrote and taught the contrary of
this; unless it be that one would say that uncreated or not created
means the equivalent of not created in and for itself, but rather
additionally created. Saving all that, I correct and recant, as I
have said, and will continue to correct and recant in general and
in detail as often as is necessary everything which should prove
to be of unsound meaning.[2]*

We may well wonder how to take this explanation. There is
not the slightest trace of remorse in Eckhart's statement, nor
could there very well be any, since the pastor continued to uphold the orthodoxy of his doctrines. All he does is to promise to
recant if it should be demonstrated that he had harbored any
heresies. Wilhelm Preger comments: *What Eckhart would have
done if he had lived to receive the papal decision is not for us
to conjecture. Death spared him the difficult reply. The evening
of his life was stormy and gloomy; but as far as our eyes can
follow him, we see him standing firm and upright, convinced of
the truth of his teachings and adhering to them. The spiritual
strength which shines forth from his statement seems to have*

[2] Preger: op. cit., I, 360.

remained with him until his death.[3] It was a mercy of providence that Eckhart died that same year, before the negative outcome of his second trial.

Two years after his death the papal bull containing the condemnation was published. It read: *With sorrow we are compelled to pronounce that one of our brethren in Germany, Eckhart by name . . . not limiting himself simply and modestly to the measure set by religion, claimed to know more than others, turning his hearing away from the truth and giving ear to fictions. Seduced by the Father of Lies . . . this man, contrary to the crystal-clear truth of the faith, sowed thorns and thistles upon the field of the Church and with great diligence made poison and weeds grow amid the corn. He taught much which could not but obscure right faith in the hearts of the multitude, openly presenting it to the simple folk in his sermons and also setting it forth in writings . . .*[4]

John XXII condemned seventeen sentences of Eckhart as heretical, and eleven as verging upon heresy. Thus the great oak in the forest of German mysticism was felled to the ground. We stand aghast at the wantonness of the act. Certainly it was one of the most fateful condemnations in the whole history of the Church, and no fine reasoning can explain it away. The stigma of heresy has remained attached to Eckhart to the present day. Present-day Catholic scholars, have, it is true, endeavored to bring about a rehabilitation of the condemned mystic within the Church. So far they have failed, since the line they have taken has been to represent Eckhart's condemnation as a misunderstanding on the part of the Church of his time. The objectionable expressions, they argued, are insignificant arabesques within the great master's system. The Church gave undue emphasis to them. But in thus attempting to represent Eckhart as a "fundamentally Catholic" mystic [5] they water down his doctrine. The same mis-

[3] Preger: *"Meister Eckhart und die Inquisition,"* in *Abhandlungen der historischen Klasse der bayrischen Akademie der Wissenschaften* (1872), pp. 28, 29.
[4] Mirbt: *Quellen des Papsttums* (1924), p. 220.
[5] A. Dempf: *Meister Eckhart* (1934), p. 88.

take in reverse is made by others who try to classify him with Luther.

The publication of the condemnation created great excitement at the time. It struck like lightning out of a clear sky. The best sons and daughters of the Church were stunned, and the glorious landscape of mysticism was devastated like the countryside after a hailstorm. To be sure, this condemnation did not suppress mysticism, which continued to survive in the Church because it was God-given, and represented the best strain in Christianity. But the Church's repudiation of mysticism's leading spirit was felt as a shattering blow. Heinrich Suso, who wrote devotedly of "holy Meister Eckhart," was overwhelmed with grief. He recovered his equilibrium only after the condemned man appeared to him in a vision and let him know that he was now "in a superabundant glory in which his soul was purely deified in God." He bade Suso to be troubled no further by the verdict of "wolfish men"—an apt name for these hunters-down of heresy.[6]

The unfortunate effect upon medieval intellectual history, however, was that Eckhart's mystical writings were more and more ignored. Only Cardinal Nicholas of Cusa, who had a distinct spiritual kinship with Eckhart, continued to collect the latter's precious writings. But there followed a long period of obscurity for Eckhart. The greatest of Western mystics was almost completely forgotten throughout Christendom. To this day Eckhart does not occupy the central position he deserves. To many Christians—and this is quite incomprehensible—not even his name is known.

As a son of the Dominican order, Eckhart naturally did not oppose ecclesiastical Christianity. Nevertheless, he was not always in accord with traditional doctrines. This is not to say that he was or was not a pantheist. Rather, he distributed his emphases differently from traditional teachers, moving certain aspects of Christianity into the foreground and pushing others into the background. This deliberate shift of accent, and the place he gave historical revelation, constitute the potentially heretical

[6] *Heinrich Seuses deutsche Schriften,* ed. W. Lehmann (1922), I, 20, 53.

sides of his thought. He was not led astray solely by his love for
excessive phraseology. Rather, his command to seek God without
intermediaries pointed toward new regions of religious thought
and feeling.

In thus boldly reinterpreting Christian dogma Eckhart became one of the greatest figures in the history of heresy. He maintained, for example, that when a man had achieved true "inward-
ness," he could dispense with all vows, even those from which
neither bishops nor Pope could release him. The birth of God in
the soul made all such pledges superfluous. On genuflections,
bowings of the head, and similar practices, he remarked: "You
adore what you do not know."

In sum, Eckhart's religious approach dispensed with the
whole ceremonial apparatus of the Church. His mysticism was
imbued with an extra-ecclesiastical spirit. Although he needed
Christ for his message, in order to have some image of God, the
concept of the intermediary Redeemer was by no means central
to his system. Traditional Christology was replaced by a new conception: "The deified Christian, intimately united with Christ,
virtually became Christ himself through grace." [7]

Eckhart's imperishable significance lies in his rediscovery of
the immediacy of God. He broke through all intermediary authorities and reached God himself, who stands behind every one
of his words. Eckhart knew very well that he was saying strange
and new things, which had not hitherto been heard. Again and
again in his writings he reveals his proud sense of being a bold
innovator. Nor did he attempt to palliate in the slightest degree
the alarming strangeness of what he had to say. One might meta-
phorically designate his mysticism as "the church of John"—a
Johannine church alongside the Petrine and Pauline concepts of
Christianity.

[7] *Eckhart,* ed. Karrer, p. 123.

+   +

14

Rebellion Against the Power of
the Priests

+   +

"For the lips of a priest should guard knowledge, and men should
seek the law from his mouth, for he is the messenger of the Lord
of hosts." [1] These words of the Old Testament touch upon the
mystery of the priesthood. The priest is surrounded by the atmosphere of the Eternal; he has become involved with the supernatural world, is touched by divine powers. He proclaims to his fellow
men the will of the Godhead, and likewise brings human distress,
in an intercessory sense, before the throne of the All-highest. The
way of the priest is mysterious, and must result in a tremendous
[1] Malachi ii, 7.

straining and heightening of the sense of life. That was clear to Nietzsche, for example—his hatred for priests had nothing in common with the usual laymen's prejudice against hypocritical parsons. Rather, he obviously had a sense of their uncanny grandeur when he makes his Zarathustra say: "Here are priests, and although they are my enemies, for my sake pass them by quietly, and with sword at rest! There are heroes even among them; many of them have suffered too much, and so they wish to make others suffer. . . . But my blood is akin to theirs." [2]

A class which, according to the words of Malachi, stands on a par with the angels, is exposed to far greater perils than ordinary men. Falling prey to temptations of the flesh is the least of these. Far graver is the craving for wealth which can enter their souls. But the subtlest lure to the priesthood as a class is that of power. This temptation is implicit in the power of the keys, the function of binding and loosing. This, the *potestas clavium*, is the Achilles heel of the priesthood. The primal impulse to sin lurks within it. The question may well be raised: Can these be a Christian power at all, since Jesus, when the disciples were disputing over rank, spoke to them of the authority which the great men of this earth wield, and expressly commanded: "It shall not be so among you" [3]? Unless there is a clear recognition of the danger inherent in all exercise of rule, the priesthood can be overwhelmed by the demoniac forces of power. A sense of power is a sweet poison, and the priesthood can become addicted to it as to a narcotic. In the history of the Church the craving for power has often proved insatiable. The tremendous struggle between the Church and the Holy Roman Empire was only the visible expression of the obsession for power which had gripped the priesthood. In its drive to rule the world the Christian priesthood gave way to the third temptation which Christ had rejected upon the mountain: "All these I will give you if you will fall down and worship me." [4]

[2] Friedrich Nietzsche: *Werke*, VI, 131.
[3] Matt. xx, 26. [4] Matt. iv, 9.

The priesthood paid dearly, however, for its thirst for power. Its gaze was beclouded. It grew forgetful of its true mission. The result was a paralysis of Christianity. That the clergy bore the principal guilt for the corruption of the people was clearly expressed by no less a personage than Pope Innocent III: *The watchers are all blind, mute dogs which cannot bark; they bury the talent entrusted to them by the Lord like the unfaithful servant; for they were meant to speak God's word. All of them, from the highest to the lowest, do as it is said in the prophets: they are enthralled to avarice, love presents and seek rewards; for the sake of bribes, they pronounce the godless righteous and deny the righteous man his rights; they call evil good and good evil, make darkness into light and light into darkness, turn sour sweet and sweet sour; they fear neither God nor man; they twist the teachings of the Gospel by misinterpretation, and make nought of the ordinances of the Church. Therefore the insolence of the heretics has waxed and contempt for the Church is gaining ground.*[5]

Here the wearer of the tiara himself has pointed out one of the principal causes for the rise of medieval heresy. The anti-priestly movements of the Middle Ages were a reaction to the clergy's intoxication with power, which had caused their main interests to shift to non-religious fields. The heretics decried not only the vices of the clergy, as zealous moralists have done in all eras without necessarily falling into heresy, but the priests' exercise of power as such—not merely its abuse. What made these heretics fundamentally different from ordinary preachers of morality was their thesis that power has no place in Christianity. By objecting to the intrusion of Cæsarism into the Church they were attacking one of the basic tenets of the medieval Church, which considered power as part and parcel of its being and believed that without power it could not secure conformity with its doctrines. As the Church concentrated more and more upon power,

[5] In G. Lechler: *John Wycliff und die Vorgeschichte der Reformation* (1873), I, 40.

the rebellion of the heretics became a general conflagration which could no longer be extinguished by local measures of suppression here and there.

Although this uprising against the power of the priests sprang from purely religious motives, its effect was to undermine authority. The order upon which the medieval world was founded received a severe blow. The rebellion of the heretics may be compared to the breaking of a dam, which flooded extensive fields belonging to the Church. But the Church had brought this catastrophe upon itself.

Arnold of Brescia

The rebellion against the power of the priests began at first like a distant rumble of thunder in the first half of the twelfth century. Flashes in the sky came closer and closer, until at last the storm broke. The first signs of discontent came from Arnold of Brescia, concerning whom, however, the traditions are extremely scanty. His writings were destroyed on papal orders, so that not a single document composed by Arnold himself has come down to posterity. Only the outlines of his tempestuous life can be sketched; most of his motives remain obscure. Through the descriptions of his enemies we catch glimpses of a "fighter, half monk, half tribune of the people, a reformer charged with ascetic earnestness and a townsman's craving for freedom, skilled in writing and enamored of classical antiquity, enthusiastic, unclear, and striving toward a better future." [6]

Arnold was abbot of the Augustinian canons, in his native city of Brescia. His rise to that post was rapid, and he seems to have fervently dedicated himself to the ideal of sanctity. Arnold was also highly esteemed for his eloquence as a preacher. He had the faculty of attaching people to him. "Loved by all, admired by all," Walter Map, who was certainly not one of his followers, says of him.[7]

[6] A. Hausrath: *Arnold von Brescia* (1895), p. 5.
[7] Ibid., p. 16.

Arnold was, however, not content with leading a saintly life for himself alone. He felt he had to guide other members of the clergy back to similar conduct. Early in his career he began to inveigh at the corruption of the clergy. He is quoted as saying: *There they sit all day long at their feasts and drinking bouts with ignorant, morally corrupt folk, gossiping nonsense with them and doing obscene things which one dare not even name. They dress themselves in the wool of the Lord's flock, live on its milk; but the sheep die of hunger, lacking the divine word. The holidays pass, the whole year passes, without there falling from their lips a single word that might edify the community entrusted to them, might lead it away from evil and call it back to the good.*[8]

From Arnold's indictment we learn much about the degeneration of the Church. But he was not satisfied merely to reprove the priests for telling indecent jokes and dressing luxuriously. He wanted to get to the bottom of the evil. To his mind the life of Christ had obligated his followers to live in poverty. The call to evangelical poverty had a novel sound at the beginning of the twelfth century. Arnold arrived at it before St. Francis, and was the first in the Middle Ages to proclaim it. To the zealot of Brescia, the secular power of the hierarchy and its wealth in lands and goods was an apostasy from the message of the Gospel. He issued a strong cry for the clergy to renounce power and wealth.

This message met with enthusiastic approval on the part of the laity, and made the clergy his irreconcilable enemies. When Arnold's preaching began creating a ferment of unrest in Brescia, the local clergy accused him of spreading heretical doctrines, and he was sent to Rome to answer the charges. The Pope promptly unfrocked him, imposed perpetual silence upon him, and banished him from the country. This sentence wrenched Arnold from the normal ecclesiastical paths. He was never to find his way back to them.

The banished former abbot made his way to France to join Abelard, whose pupil he had been. It cannot be definitely said to

[8] Ibid., pp. 19, 20.

what extent Arnold shared Abelard's religious and philosophical views. He arrived, however, at the very moment when the second condemnation had come down upon the head of Abelard. Since Arnold impetuously supported his teacher, he was carried down with Abelard in his fall. When Abelard submitted to the Church authorities, Arnold continued the battle alone, thereby incurring the lasting hostility of Bernard of Clairvaux.

The famous abbot of Clairvaux became one of Arnold's fiercest opponents. Here were two ascetics whose goals were almost identical, but who differed radically on the way to achieve them. But differences of this sort make deeper cleavages between men than anything else, for each sees the end endangered by the means. Bernard said that the Italian was outwardly a John, inwardly a Herod, while Arnold accused the Cistercian abbot of vainglory. An ugly personal spite developed out of their disagreements. Bernard gave his opponent no rest from persecution. Since the abbot of Clairvaux had powerful connections throughout the hierarchy, it was a simple matter to have the heretic expelled from France. Not content with that, he dispatched letters beyond the borders of France, warning others against this dangerous man who questioned the power of the clergy. Arnold fled to Zurich, where he found a temporary refuge and was allowed to deliver lectures. Later he was given asylum by Cardinal Guido of Bohemia. Here, too, Bernard tried to turn his protector against Arnold: "Arnold of Brescia, whose way of life is honey, but whose doctrine is venom, who has the head of a dove and the tail of a scorpion, whom Brescia had spewed forth, Rome rejected, and France expelled, whom Germany abhors and Italy will not take back, is now said to be with you." [9]

Finally wearying of this fugitive existence, Arnold returned to his native land. There he complied with the penance imposed by the Pope and was accepted back into the bosom of the Church. Arnold's submission was short-lived, for political troubles broke out in Rome. Arnold's active disposition impelled him to throw himself into the popular movement, and very soon he was heading

[9] Ibid., p. 84.

a political faction. He saw a welcome opportunity to accomplish the religious ideals which he still cherished by using the political movement in an attempt to restore the old Roman republic. With all his powers of oratory he painted the ideal of a restoration of ancient Rome. Political and religious elements merged in his preaching of this utopian dream. And in this conjunction of political and religious efforts we may see the tragedy of Arnold, for he thus introduced an impure component into his campaign.

Yet it was an inevitable development. If the priesthood was to be shorn of all exercise of power, a new political institution would have to be created in Rome which would be able to assume the reins of government. As Arnold saw it, this could only be a secular, republican authority. Once that was established the priests "would not bear the sword and the sacred chalice simultaneously"; they would renounce power, lead a life of poverty, and add force to their sermons by their good example. *Arnold himself was frequently heard on the capital and in public meetings. Now he openly attacked the cardinals, saying that their assembly, because of their pride and avarice, hypocrisy, and manifold wickedness, was not the Church of God, but a house of business and a den of thieves, and that they themselves acted as scribes and pharisees among the Christian people.*[1] Nor was the Pope himself spared tongue lashing. Arnold declared that the vicar of Christ was a man of blood and a torturer of the Church, in whose name arson was committed and who was concerned only with filling his own coffers.

Speeches such as these had a powerful effect upon the inflammable Roman populace. Matters reached such a pitch that the Pope was compelled to leave Rome. He promptly struck back by excommunicating Arnold as a heretic "without citation, without defense and without his presence, not on the evidence of his writings, but because of his preaching." [2] Then he pronounced an interdict upon the Eternal City for the first time in its history.

[1] *The Portable Medieval Reader*, ed. J. B. Ross and M. M. McLaughlin (New York: Viking Press; 1949), p. 340.
[2] Hausrath: op. cit., p. 106.

With this weapon, the Pope gained the upper hand over Arnold. Although the people were deeply attached to their prophet, they could not bear being deprived of all Christian rites. When the bells stopped ringing, the citizenry of Rome abandoned Arnold, and he was forced to flee the city.

There followed negotiations between the Pope and the Holy Roman Emperor, Frederick Barbarossa. One of the Pope's principal demands was that the heretic who was threatening his rule be delivered up to him. The emperor agreed without considering the precious pawn he was surrendering—one he would have later been glad to hold in his hand. Arnold was captured in his hiding place, and Barbarossa yielded him to the Pope. Arnold's enemies were eager to have the heretic killed before he could again escape. According to a contemporary description, before his execution in 1155 he was asked *if he would renounce his false doctrine, and confess his sins; . . . he replied that his own doctrine seemed to him sound, nor would he hesitate to undergo death for his teachings, in which there was nothing absurd or dangerous. And he requested a short delay for time to pray, for he said that he wished to confess his sins to Christ. Then on bended knees, with eyes and hands raised up to heaven, he groaned, sighing from the depths of his breast, and silently communed in spirit with God, commending to Him his soul. And after a short time, prepared to suffer with constancy, he surrendered his body to death. Those who looked on his punishment shed tears; even the executioners were moved by pity for a little time, while he hung from the noose which held him.*[3] His body was burned to ashes "lest perchance something might be left to be honored." In spite of this death on the gallows, the Roman people continued to regard the "agitator" as a prophet.

It is significant that the movement which Arnold headed was a local one. Its center was Rome, the very spot where the power of the Church hierarchy was concentrated. Yet the papacy learned nothing from this episode. For this reason Arnold of Brescia's assault upon priestly power was only the prelude to a

[3] *The Portable Medieval Reader*, p. 343.

more general rebellion of the heretics. It is hardly conceivable that Arnold could have had anything more than temporary success, for his idea of the separation of the priesthood from power ran altogether contrary to the philosophy of the medieval Church. The time was not yet ripe for his ideas to triumph. In the historical context, Arnold's importance was that he sowed seed which would not be harvested for centuries. The radical of Brescia had taught men no longer to regard the clergy with uncritical reverence. The seed Arnold sowed did not fall on barren ground. It sprouted, though slowly, and we find the same idea arising among the Lombards and Waldensians. To what extent these movements were directly connected with Arnold can no longer be demonstrated. But his ideas retained their life, and knocked repeatedly upon the gates of Christendom, until at last they were granted admittance.

John Wycliffe

John Wycliffe is widely regarded as a forerunner of the Reformers, though one who had not yet reached the heights of reformational insight. There are two things wrong with this view. It springs from a Continental superiority complex, and it considers Wycliffe from the viewpoint of subsequent history, not in terms of his time. Wycliffe was in fact no minor forerunner, but one of the greatest of leaders in the rebellion against the power of the priests. He had carefully and systematically thought out the problem involved with that power. Quite deliberately he struck his blow at the root of that problem. He stirred up the revolt against ecclesiastical ideas of rule, supplied the necessary weapons, and initiated a movement which was to continue straight on into the Reformation. England has produced few revolutionaries to match him.

Born around 1324, Wycliffe early exhibited a clear, critical intelligence. In his youth he took a lively interest in natural science, as he relates in one of his sermons: "When I was still a young man and devoted to numerous pursuits I made extensive excerpts from textbooks on optics, on the characteristics of light, and so on . . ." [4] But theology soon predominated over all other studies. With his talent for keen reasoning, Wycliffe established a place of honor for himself in scholastic theology. His physical appearance, too, commanded respect. According to one description he had a "gaunt frame clad in a long cloak, black in color, with a girdle around the waist; his face, adorned with a long, thick beard, had bold, sharp features. His eyes were penetrating and clear, his lips firmly compressed, testifying to his resolution. His whole appearance was that of a man of noble gravity, impressive and strong in character." [5] His manner of life was highly moral, and was an inspiration to others. Thus Lord Cobham declared that, before he had met Wycliffe, he had never been able to conquer his sinful nature, but that after Wycliffe had entered his life he began constantly trying to better himself. Wycliffe started his career as an English patriot, thus beginning where Arnold of Brescia had left off, in nationalism. A sense of national identity was, in the fourteenth century, only slowly beginning to germinate in the West; for this Englishman, however, nascent nationalism was already an extraordinarily powerful force. His patriotism came to the fore in the contest between *sacerdotium* and *imperium*. Pope Urban V had renewed his demand for feudal dues from King Edward III, but English pride rose up against this affront to the country's independence. Wycliffe, along with other patriotic Englishmen, was angered by what he considered a piece of papal presumption. Wycliffe spoke out boldly against payment of the dues. His statements proved him to be both a passionately patriotic young man and a theologian with a gift for striking and subtle argumentation. The crown recognized that here was a bold, highly intelligent and useful advocate, and henceforth Wycliffe enjoyed royal protection.

It was in the king's own interest to support Wycliffe when he was called to account by the Church. Summoned to appear be-

[4] Lechler: op. cit., I, 270.   [5] Ibid., I, 369, 370.

fore the Bishop of London, Wycliffe went to St. Paul's accompanied by the Duke of Lancaster and by Lord Percy, the marshal of England. The crowd was so thick that the party had difficulty making its way through. A fierce quarrel broke out between Wycliffe's secular defenders and the ecclesiastical accusers, and tempers ran still higher when the discussions began. The marshal insisted that Wycliffe be given a seat, so that he could rest while answering the questions that would be directed to him. In effect, Lord Percy was demanding respect for the crown's advocate. The bishop was adamant; he argued that, as the defendant, Wycliffe would have to stand throughout the interrogation. The dispute waged hotter: the representatives of the two sides hurled insults at each other and the whole assembly was in a tumult. It was a shocking scene to take place in a house of worship. In the end, the session was disbanded without Wycliffe's saying a single word. Evidently the ecclesiastical dignitaries were somewhat chary of dealing with a man who directly challenged their excessive claims to power.

Wycliffe, however, refused to be silenced. He wrote prolifically, and his writings had great influence. His indignation had been first aroused by the curia's demand for money, but now it became clear to him that the Church had long been unfaithful to its true mission. Since the days of Constantine secularization of the Church had advanced steadily, he decided, and the clergy itself was to blame for this. Thus, like most medieval heretics, Wycliffe concluded that the Church had long since been decadent. The priesthood should be a *ministerium,* not a *dominium*—this sentence summed up Wycliffe's fundamental view. Since the existing Church had lost sight of this idea, Wycliffe was led to seek a new church. Although he did not find it, he started out to meet it, and that in itself is important. He felt the first intimations of a new era, although he did not live to see it.

In attacking the priesthood's claims to power, Wycliffe struck directly at the head: the papacy. In the course of the struggle, Wycliffe's opinion of the papacy steadily hardened. From a moderate acknowledgment of papal primacy he moved by degrees to outright hostility toward this institution, eventually challenging both its powers and its indispensability for salvation. Ultimately he reached the point of saying that the Church could exist without the Pope because its head is Christ. He grew increasingly disenchanted with the arrogant pride and secular character of the representatives of the Holy See. Power had corrupted these men to the core, he maintained; the Popes no longer understood the exercise of secular rule as a mere feudal donative for which they would some day be required to make an accounting. By right, Wycliffe pointed out, the Church should have only deacons and priests for its officialdom; the hierarchical ladder was an aping of secular arrangements for which there was no justification. The Pope ought to be an imitator of Christ in moral virtues, not a ruler striving for absolutist power.

More and more, as Wycliffe considered the matter, the papacy appeared to him a blasphemous institution. Its power drives, he concluded, had transformed Christ's ideal of humility into its opposite. Yet it must have been a shocking and terrifying moment for Wycliffe when he finally decided that the papacy was the very citadel of Antichristianity. No medieval scholar, however independent was his mind, came easily to such a conclusion. It must have risen up before him like the vision out of a nightmare, for its implications were terrifying. He could only have admitted it to his mind after a long siege of spiritual torment.

Yet Wycliffe could not banish this strange and alarming insight, however it ran counter to all custom and tradition. He found himself forced to apply to the Pope the dreadful phrase "man of sin" that Paul had used in speaking of the Antichrist. To the Pope —the very man whom Christians addressed as Holy Father! Moreover, he did not see the matter, as did the Franciscans, as a question of the personal inadequacy of the man who happened to occupy the throne of St. Peter. No, for Wycliffe the institution itself had become a manifestation of the Antichrist. No more heretical position is conceivable.

Wycliffe did not content himself with attacking the degeneracy of the clergy, while leaving doctrine unassailed. Rather, he asked himself: What is the support of the priesthood? What gives it its unassailable prestige in the eyes of the people, which apparently any amount of corrupt living cannot destroy? In thinking this question through, Wycliffe decided that the strongest prop to the power of the priesthood was the doctrine of transubstantiation. His repudiation of this doctrine was directly connected with his anticlerical struggle. The mass is founded upon the doctrine of transubstantiation. In setting out to shatter that doctrine, Wycliffe struck at the very heart of Catholic worship.

The consecrated host on the altar, he maintained, was not Christ himself, but merely a sign of Christ. He found no evidence for transubstantiation in the Scriptures, and concluded that Bérenger's doctrine of communion was the correct one. Transubstantiation, he decided, was an idea which had been trumped up in order to increase the prestige of the clergy. Sacramentalism gave the priest a supernatural radiance by pretending he was able to transform bread into the body of the Lord.

Wycliffe's violent attack upon the doctrine of transubstantiation was couched in the dry language of scholastic learning, but its effect was like a charge of explosive. His writings contained in essence the whole program of the coming ecclesiastical revolution, which was to usher in a new age.

The mendicant orders, Wycliffe perceived, were the second institution by which the papacy bolstered its claim. In his battle against the power-hungry papacy, Wycliffe did not scruple to attack monasticism as well. True, once upon a time it had made magnificent contributions to Christianity. But by Wycliffe's day monasticism had come a long way from its original aims. The monks were no longer God-seekers who had fled the world. The mendicant orders in particular had become the fighting troops of the papacy and were sent to the front whenever the vicar of Christ wished to press his claims. To Wycliffe they were the essence of reaction, and he was ready to employ his sharpest weapons to break their power. The life of the mendicant friars had in any case become a travesty of the principles of St. Francis, whose heavenly poverty they had degraded to miserable beggary.

Above and beyond that, however, Wycliffe was outraged by
the very idea that special forms of practicing the religious life
were necessary alongside of simple obedience to the word of
Christ. Therefore he furiously fought the whole idea of monasticism—and in so doing set a mine which was bound to lead to an
explosion. His rancor against monks was genuine and unbending.
Thus he was once deathly ill and was visited by four learned
prelates of the mendicant friars, who had come, they explained,
in the hope that he might shrive his soul by penitently recanting
the shameful things he had often said against their order. The
sick man gathered all his strength, sat up in bed, and bellowed at
his visitors: "I will not die, I am going to live and denounce the
evil deeds of the mendicant monks!" [6]

Like all the medieval heretics, Wycliffe had a positive program. In place of the self-seeking and corrupt clergy, Wycliffe
envisioned a type of priest poor in worldly goods and dedicated
to the task of serving his fellow men. For it is significant that
Wycliffe, despite his polemics against the mendicant orders, fully
understood the evangelical idea of poverty as it had been intended by the originators of mendicancy. In all likelihood he hit
upon this idea without any knowledge of the Waldensians—nor
did he develop it to the extent that they had done. Wycliffe put
this ideal into practice by sending forth itinerant preachers, to
whom he gave the name of "evangelical men." *These men walked
barefoot, dressed in long red garments of coarse woolen material,
a staff in their hands to signify that their travels were a kind of
pilgrimage and they themselves pilgrims. The coarse cloth of
their dress was a sign of poverty and humility. Thus they wandered from village to village, from city to city, from one county
to the next, never resting, and preaching, teaching, admonishing
wherever they found willing listeners, sometimes in a church
or chapel, sometimes in the churchyard, sometimes in the
marketplace.*[7]

[6] F. Böhringer: *Die Kirche Christi und ihre Zeugen, Johannes von Wycliff*
(1878), pp. 85, 86.
[7] Lechler: op. cit., I, 421.

The Lollards, as they were mockingly called—the word meant a "mumbler" (of prayers)—were charged with the task of sowing the seed of the divine Word. Their sermons dealt with moral rather than dogmatic matters, and by the simplicity of their style stirred the consciences of the people.

Wycliffe instructed the Lollards to proclaim the law of Christ which, he held, the Church had suppressed. In order to make that law accessible to all, Wycliffe set to work on a translation of the Bible. To what extent the translation of the Holy Scriptures into English was his own work, to what extent he was assisted by others, can no longer be determined. But there is no doubt that Wycliffe personally had a hand in it. He had conceived the bold and splendid idea of making Scripture the common property of all believers—a genuinely reformational project. His aim was to present to the people the entire Bible, not mere excerpts from it. In the preface to the translation of the Bible Wycliffe expressed his intentions with utmost clarity: *But coueitous clerkis of this world replyen and seyen, that lewed men [laymen] mowe soon erre, and therfore they schul not dispute of cristen feith. Alas! alas! what cruelte is this, to reeve [deprive] al bodely mete [food] fro al a rewme [realm], for a fewe folis mowen be glotons, and do harm to hem self and othere men, be this mete take vnmesurabli. . . . What resoun is this, if a child faile in his lessoun at the first day, to suffre neuere children come at lettrure for this defaut? . . . Eche man is bounden to do so, that he be saued, but eche man that schul be saued, is a real prest mad of God, as holy writ and holy doctours witnessen pleynly . . . and eche man is bounden to be suche a verri prest.*[8]

This point, the doctrine of universal priesthood which Wycliffe had extracted from the Bible, was destined to put an end to power-hungry clericalism.

Wycliffe was one of the most radical spirits in the chronicles of heresy, for he dared to question the whole tradition of the

[8] *The Holy Bible Made from the Latin Vulgate by John Wycliffe and His Followers*, ed. Rev. Josiah Forshall and Sir Frederick Madden (London: Oxford University Press; 1850), p. xv.

Church. What was more, the Church could not harm him. He was forced to withdraw from teaching at Oxford, but that was all. He continued to exercise his functions at the rural rectory of Lutterworth. He died of a stroke in 1384, while hearing mass in his own church.

Fifteen years later Church and state in England united to exterminate the Wycliffites. Some Wycliffite preachers had fanned the flames of the Peasants' Revolt of 1381, although Wycliffe himself remained aloof. In 1415 the Council of Constance condemned forty-five articles by Wycliffe and averred that he had remained to his death an obstinate heretic. The Council attempted to carry out on the dead man the punishment it had been unable to inflict on him while alive. It ordered that his bones be exhumed and scattered far from any consecrated burial ground. But this belated vengeance upon the man who had attacked the power of the priests failed to extinguish his memory. Wycliffe survived in the minds of men, as had John the Scot before him, and his resurrection came a century and a half after his death. In freeing the Church of England from the domination of the papacy, Henry VIII was following one of Wycliffe's primary behests. His ideas proved an even more powerful influence upon the leaders of the English Revolution. John Milton spoke of Wycliffe's divine and wonderful spirit which had been denied its proper glory because of the "stubbornness of the prelates." The radical Puritans adapted many of Wycliffe's ideas, for they drew their principles from the same Biblical source. But even more than in England, Wycliffe's words had a lasting effect upon the Continent.

John Hus

Though he was known to have a penchant in his youth for chess and music, John Hus was at the same time extraordinarily devout. He would give up his last four coppers to procure an indulgence from his confessor. He applied himself diligently to his studies, though he felt it necessary to keep an open mind toward what he learned. As he himself put it: "From the very beginning of my studying I made it a rule that whenever, in any matter, I heard a sounder viewpoint, I abandoned the one I had had, since I know well that we know far less than what we do not know."[9] Thanks to his considerable gifts, he rose rapidly in the Church hierarchy. As pastor of the Church of Bethlehem in Prague he soon exerted wide influence upon the intellectual and spiritual life of the capital of Bohemia. His sermons were passionate diatribes against immorality among laity and clergy. "Our present-day bishops and priests," he thundered from the pulpit, "and especially the canons and lazy priests can scarcely contain themselves until the end of the services. They rush out of the church, some to the taverns, others hither and thither, to seek entertainment in a manner unworthy of priests—some even to dance. . . . Thus, those who ought to be first in the imitation of Christ are the greatest foes of our Lord Jesus Christ."[1]

Hus borrowed extensively from Wycliffe, as recent research has clearly demonstrated. Although he never met Wycliffe, he may be called his greatest disciple. He adopted some of the Englishman's ideas word for word, but not uncritically. Thus he agreed with Wycliffe in opposing the dominion of the clerics, but did not go along with Wycliffe in the repudiation of transubstantiation. In the end, although Hus owed much to Wycliffe, the latter's thought formed only one element among others in the Hussite movement.

Hus's sermons, wherein his own moralism was combined with Wycliffe's hostility to the clergy, drew vast audiences. So highly did the people esteem him that they called Hus the "fifth evangelist." But the outspoken preacher made bitter enemies. The clergy of Prague lodged a complaint against Hus, charging him with exposing them to ridicule. The strife was given a keener edge by the nationalistic controversies that sprang up at the University of Prague between German and Czech teachers. Ulti-

[9] M. Vischer: *Jan Hus* (1940), I, 175.
[1] Jan Hus: *Ausgewählte Predigten,* ed. Langsdorff (1894), pp. 1, 2.

mately these led to the departure of the German professors and an intensification of Bohemian patriotism. Hus, too, was filled with the spirit of nationalism, although he was to undergo a crucial disillusionment on this particular score.

Hus's enemies succeeded in persuading the archbishop to excommunicate the bold preacher. But Hus paid no more heed to the ban than Savonarola was to, seventy years later. He continued to mount the pulpit in his church, and his words became ever more daring. The tremendous crowds that filled the church to hear him chanted their approval. Soon Hus had reached the point of directly attacking the actions of the Pope. He declared from the pulpit: "Our Popes and successors of Peter have turned themselves into hangmen and executioners; they call faithful Christians heretics and burn them." [2]

Soon he extended his criticism to the rulers of the state—in this going beyond Wycliffe and proclaiming himself the forerunner of revolution. "The last, that is to say the wretched and despised of this world, shall be first, and those who are now the highest and the first in the world, but who do not serve God in simplicity of heart, shall be last. The merest peasant will precede the emperor and king . . ." [3] But Hus could not indefinitely defy the might of Church and state. On orders from the king he left Prague in 1412 and went into exile. In Constance, where he went to defend his ideas before the council held there from 1414–18, the drama reached its peak.

The council had supposedly been convened to put an end to the incredibly debauched conditions within the Church and to bring about the long-desired reform. But the council itself was far too deeply infected by the decadence of the times to carry out this task. Instead, the whole thing turned into a social event, enlivened by tournaments and swelled by the hosts of loose women who appeared in Constance for the occasion. Any attempt at Church reform was impossible in such an atmosphere. There were serious and famous theologians in Constance at the time, men deeply concerned with moral improvement of the Church.

[2] Ibid., p. 18.   [3] In Vischer: op. cit., I, 303.

But they failed because Church reform could not be achieved by moral means alone. It had become a political affair in which a multitude of wordly factors played a part, and consequently was a lost cause from the outset.

Not one of the distinguished theologians supported Hus. He was a single individual pitted against this great assemblage. Here was the austere reformer directly confronting the high dignitaries luxuriating in their fleshpots. The contrast was too glaring. Hence it was that the college of cardinals ordered Hus arrested. He was thrown into a dark dungeon, directly adjoining a sewer, in the Dominican monastery. After some months he was transferred to the prison of the nearby castle and kept in chains. This treatment, be it noted, was meted out to Hus before his ideas had even been discussed by the council. From the very first he met with savage hatred; there could be no doubt that his case had been decided against him in advance. When he was denied the services of a lawyer, he responded: "Then let Lord Jesus be my defender and advocate, for in a short time he will surely judge all of you." [4]

When at last he was permitted to address the assemblage, he was constantly interrupted and shouted down. In the midst of this hurly-burly Hus remained calm, only remarking when he was at last allowed to speak: "I had thought to find more decency and better manners in this holy assemblage." [5] At a second hearing, Hus professed his deep reverence for Wycliffe, at which the council broke out into scornful laughter. His appeal from the Pope to Christ was likewise received with blatant mockery. Unflinchingly, he told the dignitaries: "All who deliver an innocent man up to the secular arm for death are doing exactly as the high priests, scribes, and pharisees did who surrendered Jesus to Pilate." [6]

The council refused to engage in any discussion with Hus; they demanded a recantation which he refused to make. Hus was a man of conscience; he could not sign a formula which ran

[4] Ibid., II, 90. [5] Ibid., II, 134.
[6] Ibid., II, 149.

counter to his deepest convictions. The unanimity of the great council did not impress him; he would rather be named an obstinate heretic than taint his conscience by recantation. Early in his career the premonition had come to him that he would someday have to suffer death for his preachings, and with melancholy heroism he regarded martyrdom as the highest destiny a Christian could achieve. He had implored God to grant him steadfastness—and in fact he showed not the slightest sign of weakness when the council pronounced its condemnation.

The last hours of John Hus were solemn and consecrated. While yet in his prison cell he forgave his personal enemies and included them in his prayers. A sublime composure had come over him. Before he was deprived of his rank of priest, Hus fell to his knees and quietly prayed for himself, despite the crude mockery of the ecclesiastical assemblage. They then addressed him with the following formula: "Accursed Judas who has left the council of peace and become one with the Jews, we take from you the chalice of salvation." [7] Thereupon his vestments were stripped from him and his tonsure shaved away—a humiliation which Hus accepted quietly, saying: "I suffer this shame for the sake of our Lord Jesus Christ." [8] The assemblage now ruled that he was stripped of all ecclesiastical rights and was to be turned over to the secular arm to be burned as a heretic, since his soul had already been surrendered to the devil. The magistrates of the city were entrusted with execution of the sentence, while the council proceeded with its agenda as though nothing had happened.

Hus, however, went on to the further stations of his Passion. A huge paper hat, on which three devils were pictured, was placed on his head. It bore the inscription: Arch-Heretic. While this was being done, Hus commented calmly: "Christ bore a far heavier crown of thorns; why should I not bear the lighter one?" [9] Then Hus was dragged off to the place of execution, where he knelt once again and prayed fervently: "Lord, I

[7] Ibid., II, 180.   [8] Ibid., II, 181.
[9] Ibid., II, 185.

have placed my hopes in thee. Into thy hands I commend my spirit. My Jesus, I gladly suffer this cruel and shameful death for thee and thy word's sake." [1]

The executioner tied his hands behind his back and fastened his neck by a chain to the stake. Hus's feet stood upon a bundle of faggots, and around him faggots mixed with straw were heaped up to his chin. Once more he was asked to recant; if he did, his life would be spared. He replied: "I call God to witness that I neither taught nor preached what false witnesses have testified against me! I wished to lead men away from their sins. Whatever I said and wrote was always for the truth, for the truth!" [2]

The moment that the pile of wood was ignited, Hus began singing in a high, clear voice. The hymn rose above the crackling of the flames: "Christ, thou Son of the living God, have mercy upon us." When he came to the words: "Thou art born of Mary the Virgin," the flames leaped into his face; the song stopped abruptly, and only his lips continued to move. After a brief torment Hus died. The day of his martyrdom was July 6, 1415. His ashes were thrown into the Rhine.

Though priestly power had once more walked roughshod over Christian conscience, Hus's Passion was by no means in vain. In actuality he won a victory in the only manner that Christianity can win—by capitulating. Out of his defeat there emerged an invincible force which proved to be a grave menace to the corrupt Church. A wild cry of indignation resounded through Bohemia after Hus's death. "The greater part of the populace of Bohemia were fervently attached to Hus as to a prophet, and after his death he was venerated as a saint and martyr." [3] The blood-guilt of Constance was fearfully avenged. The Czech people were aroused, and the rebellion against the power of the priests burst forth with elemental violence. The Hussite movement swelled to a raging torrent that went far beyond anything its founder had intended. To this day, Tomáš Masaryk has said, the cause of Hus is inseparable from the intellectual development of the Czech

---

[1] Ibid., II, 187.   [2] Ibid., II, 188.
[3] J. Losert: *Hus und Wycliff* (1884), p. 156.

people. They have always felt that this martyred heretic represented the very essence of the nation's spirit. Their love and veneration for him is boundless. For the land of Bohemia Hus is, as
Poggius Florentinus once put it, "a star that leads the way surely
to Bethlehem, and a cock's cry in our ear which must waken all
men of truth to repentance for our denial of our Lord, as Peter
was once so wakened." [4]

[4] *Todesgeschichte des Jan Hus und des Hieronymus von Prag, geschildert in
Sendschreiben des Poggius Florentius* (no date), p. 55.

+   +

15

Stepchildren of Christianity

+   +

The Witches

Belief in witches is of pre-Christian origin; its religious and historical roots extend far down into the ancient world.[1] In the Late Middle Ages, however, this old conception was given a peculiar and fateful twist: The power to perform witchcraft came from the devil, as did magic of any kind. It was the devil's gift to apostate Christians. On the basis of this theory, the ecclesiastical mind made an identity between witchcraft and heresy, and the witch trial became a variety of the heresy trial. The crime of the

[1] Cf. A. Mayer: *Erdmutter und Hexe, eine Untersuchung zur Geschichte des Hexenglaubens und zur Vorgeschichte des Hexenprozesses* (1936), p. 9.

witches consisted in their defection from God and their joining the devil's camp. Hence the horror felt during the declining Middle Ages and the incipient modern age toward witches and all that pertained to them.

The conception of witches grew slowly, the popular mind supplying all kinds of embellishments and additions to the original picture. Painters like Baldung and Dürer, with their striking depictions of witches, helped a good deal to form the terrifying images which were current. But the witch hunt really got under way when the churchmen, with all the theological subtlety at their command, began to justify the notions circulating among the people. What was more, these scholastic writings received the direct endorsement of the Church with Innocent VIII's bull of 1484. The papal bull put the stamp of legitimacy upon belief in witches.

Five years later the notorious *Malleus Maleficarum* or "Witches' Hammer," by Heinrich Institutoris and Jakob Sprenger, was published. Its authors were two Dominicans, who had been sent to Germany as Inquisitors, bearing the papal blessing. However, for one reason or another, they were given a cool reception, and even, on occasion, were shown the door by a number of bishops. Both of them were somewhat unsavory characters. It is known that an ecclesiastical warrant had once been issued against Institutoris, who was charged with embezzling fees for indulgences. Both he and Sprenger were later implicated in the forging of notarized documents.[2]

Their *Malleus Maleficarum* was a detailed commentary on the papal bull concerning witches. It was the authors' good fortune that printing had just been invented, for their book was destined to run to some thirty editions. Considered from the modern point of view, the *Malleus Maleficarum* makes a strange impression: "No antediluvian beast, no cuneiform script, no implement of some utterly unknown primitive tribe, today strikes us as so

[2] Cf. Josef Hansen: *Zauberwahn, Inquisition und Hexenprozess im Mittelalter* (1900), pp. 475, 476.

strange, remains so wholly incomprehensible, as this book."[3] A
product of scholasticism's decadence, it is a work of appalling
dryness. Completely arbitrary in its pattern, the "Witches' Hammer" raises a number of questions whose pros and cons are
debated in long-winded dialectic, replete with references to the
authority of the Bible, the Fathers of the Church, and the scholastics. It thus conveyed the illusion of being scientific and scholarly
in its approach, and its influence was enormous and persistent.

The book has been denounced—quite properly—as a
"monstrosity full of intellectual debauchery" proceeding out of a
"stupidity bordering on idiocy." But such descriptions do not do
justice to the uncanny malignancy of this work. What we find
here is a diabolical state of mind into which not a ray of Christian
charity falls, not a trace of the New Testament spirit. Its pages
are haunted by primitive fanaticism, by the triumph of Satanism.

According to the *Malleus Maleficarum*, both men and women
can practice witchcraft, but the female sex is far more inclined to
do so. The two Inquisitors protest that they are not misogynists,
but this treatise of theirs is unmistakably filled with a pathological hatred of women. They give a number of reasons why women
succumb to witchcraft more easily than men: "Because the female sex is more concerned with things of the flesh than men";
because, being formed from a man's rib, they are "only imperfect animals" and "crooked" whereas man belongs to a privileged
sex from whose midst Christ emerged.[4] The chief reason for the
increase of witches, the authors contend, lay in the "vile contention between married and unmarried women." They warn
against the "spitefulness of womankind," from which the whole
world suffers.[5] The reader who thinks in psychoanalytic terms
will find all this most revealing, especially the expatiations on the
ability witches have to hamper men's powers of generation and
in general to baffle sexual relations.

[3] O. Snell: *Hexenprozess und Geistesstörung* (1891), p. 22.
[4] *Der Hexenhammer*, ed. J. W. R. Schmidt (1906), I, 99.
[5] Cf. ibid., I, 127, 131.

Understandably enough, the authors were out to demolish the conception "that witches are nothing real but exist only in the opinions of men." [6] The slightest doubt of the existence of witches was branded by them as a most dangerous heresy. Thus any dissenting voice was smothered in advance. To breathe the slightest doubt of the belief in witches was to lay oneself open to the charge of heresy. The views of the *Malleus Maleficarum* had acquired unassailable authority.

The authors' reasoning ran as follows: it is not within the power of men to work magic of their own accord. The power, therefore, is given to them by Satan. The devil, however, asks something in return. He teaches his black arts only to those who voluntarily enter his service. This view was a far cry from the theory of "possession" found in the Gospels. True, the idea that men could voluntarily ally themselves with the devil cropped up here and there in the Early Church.[7] But in the Middle Ages this notion of a league with the devil appeared more and more frequently. It was based upon the words in Isaiah: "With Sheol [hell] we have an agreement." [8] Man and the devil, it was held, can negotiate with one another as equal partners. The two contracting parties undertake certain obligations toward one another. The witch abjures Christ, to whom she has belonged since baptism, and signs her immortal soul over to Satan, who in return makes all sorts of forbidden things available to her. This act is, of course, betrayal and blasphemy of God. Worship of the devil replaces worship of Christ.

The pact with the devil was followed by concubinage with the devil. The witch recognized the devil as her lord and master and practiced sexual intercourse with him. No one could question the possibility of such intercourse, since there was the passage in the Book of Genesis which described the fleshly commingling of the sons of God with the daughters of men.[9] Augustine's statements in the *City of God* provided additional sub-

[6] Ibid., I, 127.
[7] G. Roskoff: *Geschichte des Teufels* (1869), I, 284, 285.
[8] Isaiah xxviii, 15 and 18.   [9] Genesis vi, 1 f.

stantiation.[1] Whereas in former times devils had misused men against their wills, nowadays, it was held, witches voluntarily sought debauchery with these evil spirits. The devil would assume the form of an incubus and beget gruesome monsters upon witches. The witch then had to kidnap little children to serve as food for these changelings who came into the world with a wolf's head or a fish's tail. If the practitioner of magic were a man, the devil assumed the form of a woman and lived with him as a succubus. The *Malleus Maleficarum* could cite the case of a woman who "received an incubus in her bed for six years, even at the side of her sleeping husband, and no less than three times in the week, on Sunday, Tuesday, and Friday or other even more holy times."[2] As a rule, however, witches left their houses for such assignations. To hoodwink their husbands they would leave a phantom body in their place.

German witches usually made nocturnal jaunts to meet the devil at the Blocksberg, the highest peak of the Harz Mountains. They came to these affairs riding on such animals as bucks, pigs, and three-legged goats or, in the absence of such mounts, made do with broomsticks and fire tongs. Witches could fly, of course; all they had to do was to rub their limbs with a salve made from the limbs of children and pronounce the spell: "Up and away, hoo-ee, up through the chimney, out go we." There was considerable brooding on the subject of the flying witch, called the *striga*. Some held that the witches only imagined that they were flying because the devil had placed an illusion in their heads. Most people, however, were firmly convinced that the nocturnal flights of the witches actually took place, whether visibly or invisibly.[3]

When the *strigae* were all assembled at the Blocksberg, the witches' sabbath began. Between 9,000 and 12,000 witches participated in the rites of this "synagogue of Satan." The meeting opened with a horrific cursing of God and abominable worship of the devil. Every sexual perversion that a filthy imagination could

---

[1] Cf. Augustine: *The City of God*, XV, xxiii.
[2] *Hexenhammer*, II, 40.   [3] Ibid., II, 49, 52.

conceive was supposed to have been practiced at these orgies, which presumably began around nine o'clock and ended after midnight. The meeting had to dispense before cockcrow.

Since the world of evil was regarded as a grotesque reversal of the world of good, everything at the witches' sabbath was reversed. In paying homage to the devil the witches stood on their heads, and Satan turned his back on the assemblage. The black mass was a diabolical caricature of communion; a turnip instead of a host was held up, and fearful blasphemies were intoned. After this ceremony the devil paired with witches, but strangely enough they felt not the slightest pleasure. With the claw of his left hand he impressed a sign upon the witch's body, by which she could be recognized as belonging to the diabolic community. Then a banquet was held in which repulsive foods like toads were eaten. Human infants were slaughtered and consumed as delicacies.

After the banquet came the dance, to the sound of bagpipes, fiddles, and drums. It grew wilder and wilder, until all were whirling madly, the cripples and lame dancing more lightly than those who were sound of limb. At the end the devil gave the witches lessons on how to transform themselves into cats and goats, how to cast the evil eye, how to raise hailstorms, how to make women barren, and how to cause men to be impotent. Finally the devil sent the witches home to resume their mischief against their fellow men.

The period of persecutions for witchcraft is one of the most shocking in the history of Christianity, not because of the hypothetical misdeeds of the witches, but because of the way Christianity responded. The antiwitch hysteria represented a metaphysical darkness that threatened to extinguish the light of the Gospels in the Western world. Few Christians behaved as did Nicholas of Flüe, who told a peasant accusing a neighbor woman of witchcraft: "You have a wicked suspicion of the woman; you are wronging her. Go, therefore, and ask her forgiveness, and your cattle will be safe henceforth. It is *because* you have passed such sinful judgment upon this woman that the Evil One has been given power to attack your cattle."[4] But to most Christians of all confessions the accusation of witchcraft was tantamount to the proof of it. The hatred and cruelty unleashed in Christian communities was terrifying. Like the wicked stepmother of fairy tales, the churches savagely set upon these defenseless creatures.

Pope Gregory IX (1227–1241) was the first Pope to issue orders that witches be indicted along with heretics. The first witch trial under these orders took place in the vicinity of Trier between 1230 and 1240.[5] Once the first step had been taken, the Inquisitional machinery began to move everywhere.

Defendants brought before a judge were asked whether they believed in witchcraft. To say that one did not was the most incriminating answer one could give. If one replied in the affirmative, the Inquisitor began to entwine the defendant in a snare of questions. What had she been doing in the field before the thunderstorm? Why had she quarreled with such-and-such a person? Why had she laid her hand on this or that little boy? Why did her garden thrive better than her neighbors'? For what reason had she entered the neighbor's barn? And so on.

If this cross-examination did not lead to a confession, the defendant was examined for the witch's mark. For this purpose she was stripped naked and the executioner shaved off all her body hair in order to seek in the hidden places of the body the sign which the devil imprinted on his cohorts. Warts, freckles, and birthmarks were considered certain tokens of amorous relations with Satan. This procedure alone, with its brutal violation of all modesty, was an ordeal for women of the least sensitivity. But if the examination did not bring to light the witch's mark, the suspect was handed over to the torturers. The *Malleus Maleficarum* provided legalistic justification for torture on the grounds that witchcraft was an exceptional crime. "Without torture the witch trials would never have become the force they did in the history of the human race," writes Soldan-Heppe.[6] One purpose

[4] R. Durrer: *Die ältesten Quellen über den seligen Niklaus von Flüe* (1917–21), II, 999.
[5] Cf. Otto Henne am Rhyn: *Der Teufels– und Hexenglaube* (1892), p. 79.
[6] Soldan-Heppe: *Geschichte der Hexenprozesse* (1911), I, 340.

of the torture was to see whether the defendant could weep, since witches "according to the tradition of credible men" could not shed tears, although among the characteristics of women were "to weep, to spin, and to deceive." [7] The Inquisitor was bent not only on extracting a confession from the witch, but also on having her implicate all those who had taken part in the nocturnal sabbath with her. Many women, reduced by indescribable agonies to a state in which they were no longer responsible for what they said, denounced their own mothers or daughters as fellow witches, solely in order to be spared further torture. Of course it did not help if next day they withdrew the confessions that had been extorted from them.

Yet there were also heroic souls who suffered all the degrees of torture with clenched teeth, never uttering a single word other than asseverations of their innocence. Such strong-nerved women were considered by the Inquisitors to be exceptionally obstinate witches whom the devil had made impervious to pain. For however these stepchildren of Christianity behaved upon the rack, whether they screamed in unutterable pain and despair or steadfastly kept silent, they were doomed.

The crimes of devil worship confessed under torture could be atoned for only by death. In principle there was no mercy for the witches. They had to be burned. Such was the commandment of Scripture: "You shall not permit a sorceress to live." [8] This one Biblical sentence cost the lives of countless Christians. Anyone who ventured to protest against the burning of witches became himself a moral outcast.

Witch burnings on a large scale first took place in France, but were soon checked there when the trials passed from the hands of the clerics to secular judges. The hysteria then spread to Switzerland and Germany, where it raged in its most virulent form. It passed on to Scandinavia, England, Spain, Italy, Hungary—in short, to all of Europe. Everywhere the pyres flamed. Women and men, idiots and scholars, children of four and grandmothers of eighty—all were burned indiscriminately. Even saints

[7] *Hexenhammer,* III, 90, 91.   [8] Exodus xxii, 18.

like Joan of Arc were sacrificed to the inexorable Moloch. A somewhat too long nose or a malformed body, but also rare beauty or
unusual intelligence, sufficed to arouse suspicion of witchcraft.
As the Middle Ages drew to a close, the persecutions of witches
swelled to a torrent, reaching a crest in the post-Reformation age.
There were villages left with only two women after the witch
trials were over. It seemed as if the flames of the pyres could
never be extinguished as, from the fourteenth to the eighteenth
centuries, countless human beings went to their deaths.

But as the burnings spread, there gradually arose in the
midst of the Christian world some opposition to these horrors.
The greatest stumbling block was the fact that denial of witchcraft was regarded as heresy. Nevertheless, men were found
whose hearts could be moved by the fate of the hapless victims.

Among the first of the defenders was a physician, Johann
Weyer by name, who in the middle of the sixteenth century
wrote a pamphlet on the delusions fostered by demons. He advanced the thesis that the witches were victims rather than willing instruments of the devil. As a physician Weyer was able to
make the observation that the only "teacher" the witches had was
their own imagination. Incubi, he declared, were the products of
their nightmares. These propositions were daring in the extreme, and could not, in the nature of things, be widely accepted. The Church authorities were enough incensed by their
implications to place the pamphlet on the Index. It was then forgotten completely in the tumult of the religious wars.

But Weyer had successors who were, surprisingly, members
of the Jesuit order. The Austrian Jesuit Tanner maintained that
the confessions made by witches under torture were usually only
the products of disordered senses—a statement which exposed
him to dangerous accusations. A second Jesuit, Lagemann, repeatedly called for caution in the treatment of witches. If the
trials went on as they had been going, he warned, whole cities
would be depopulated and no one's life would be secure, not even
the lives of the clergy. Lagemann met with no better reception
than Tanner.

The most forceful personality to fight against witch persecution was Friedrich Spee (1591–1635), an inspired pastor and a poet of some stature. While still a young man, his hair had turned completely gray. This was the consequence, he said, of his accompanying witches to the stake in his capacity of priest. He had learned a good deal from these experiences. "All of them bewailed with heart-rending lamentations the malice or ignorance of the judges and their own wretchedness, and in their last agonies they cried out to God to witness their innocence. This pitiable spectacle, so frequently repeated, moved him so deeply that he turned gray before his time," [9] wrote Leibnitz. Spee himself reported: "God knows how often I sighed from the bottom of my heart as I lay through sleepless nights considering this matter and finding no way to dam the torrent of universal madness." [1]

In defense of hapless victims of the future, Spee wrote his *Cautio criminalis, seu de processibus contra Sagas liber* (1631), which became a milestone in the history of justice. Spee pointed out the irresponsibility of a procedure in which the princes transferred the work of prosecution to officials and these officials in turn silenced whatever qualms of conscience they might feel by referring to the prince's mandate. "No German lord would allow his hunting dog to be thus mangled, and yet a human being may be so mangled again and again? . . . We have no right to play with human blood, and men's heads are not balls to be thrown back and forth." [2] He dared to say that if the dignitaries of the Church, the judges, or he himself were given the same treatment as those unfortunates, they would all be discovered to be sorcerers.

Spee's book blasted a huge breach in the wall of prejudice. It is true that he questioned only the practice, not the principle. He conceded the existence of witches, but called for a complete revision of the judicial procedures. Nevertheless, with the methods of investigation he proposed, there would scarcely have been a single witch burning.

[9] J. Diel: *Friedrich Spee* (1901), p. 21.
[1] Ibid., p. 86.   [2] Ibid., pp. 87, 92.

In the Protestant camp as well there arose some intrepid adversaries of witch burnings. The Protestant clergyman Johannes Greve was the first to write a work condemning the whole principle of torture. A Lutheran theologian Johann Matthias Mayfort had observed "how the witch carts thumped daily through the streets and yet the witches hourly increased, so that the forests of Thuringia would not suffice to burn them all. . . . The day will come," he cried to the Inquisitors, "when you shall have to give an accounting for every order you have given to trap, to scourge and behead and burn; for every mockery you poured upon the poor tormented creatures; for every tear they wept; for every drop they bled!" [3]

The strongest blow from the Protestant side was delivered by the Dutch divine Balthazar Bekker (1634–98) in his book *The World Bewitched*. Bekker was the first to declare war on *belief* in witches. He went directly to the root of the evil: the doctrine of diabolism. Satan, he pointed out, had a very secondary part in the Bible. The true Christian believed primarily in God, not in the devil. The devil, he argued, is only a servant of God and can do nothing against the will of the Almighty.

Bekker was removed from his pastoral office for daring to hold this position. But sooner or later such arguments founded upon Scripture had to take effect, although the process was fantastically slow. In fact, full acceptance of all these ideas did not come until the eighteenth century. The age of Enlightenment is often decried by Christians as an age of belief; but its humanitarian bias put an end to centuries of incomprehensible cruelty. The Enlightenment understood one aspect of the Gospel better than did the Late Middle Ages, the Reformation, and the Counter-Reformation. Yet a prolonged, tenacious struggle was needed to overcome the belief in witches. The turning point came when Frederick the Great prohibited the use of torture in Prussia. All at once, confessions by witches ceased. Gradually in the course of the eighteenth century the pyres went out throughout Europe—the last one in Poland in 1793.

[3] J. von Görres: *Mystik, Magie und Dämonie*, ed. Bernhart (1927), p. 570.

The whole witch mania is often classed as an example of superstitious delusion. Certainly this was the view held by the Enlightenment. But it is time that we moved somewhat beyond this limited interpretation. Certainly the belief in witches was constantly nourished by superstition. But the essence of that superstition existed in classical antiquity and was to a great extent taken over by Christianity. Since ideas of magic did penetrate Christianity and become component elements in the Christian world-view, Christians cannot disclaim responsibility for them. Granted, then, that superstition constituted a significant factor in the genesis and dissemination of the belief in witches. But it was not the sole factor.

It is also an oversimplification to explain the belief in witches as a series of hallucinations. This notion has led modern investigators more and more to consider the persecutions a pathological phenomenon. A study of the documents of witch trials may lead one to conclude that the persons involved were insane, or were individuals of distinctly hysterical character. In periods of transition, mental diseases are apt to appear on the same wide scale as influenza epidemics; a large number of neurological diseases, like St. Vitus's Dance, seem to be outbreaks of this sort. The self-accusations of so many witches who claimed to have participated in the witches' sabbath can be explained as the delusions of melancholic women suffering from paranoia.[4] Moreover, they may have used various drugs and potions to stimulate voluptuous dreams and peculiar sensory states. In his discussion of the physiology of witches' rides Görres has a good deal to say about the salve with which the witches anointed their bodies. He is not always reliable, of course, but he cites cases of women who sat upon a bread trough and after anointing themselves fell into a dreamlike condition in which they began to talk in low, jubilant voices about Lady Venus and to imagine that they were taking long journeys.[5]

It is quite clear that repressed and pathological sexuality played its part in the belief in and persecution of witches. Many

[4] Cf. Snell: op. cit., pp. 124, 125.   [5] Görres: op. cit., pp. 356, 357.

pages of the *Malleus Maleficarum* can be understood in no other terms. The intensive discussion of incubi and succubi leaves no room for doubt. All the sexual perversions which were forbidden to the Christian, and which survived as tempting desires in his subconscious mind, were projected into his picture of witches. These could wallow in sin and revel in imaginary orgies. This element is linked with the breakdown of sexual morality which was so signal an aspect of the declining Middle Ages. The new licentiousness was bound to produce pathological phenomena, since it ran so sharply counter to the ethics of the Church. The obsession with witches must be regarded as a symptom of deepseated sexual tensions. Through it men revealed psychopathic fear of that mysteriously tempting living creature who bore the name of woman, who could not be resisted, and who therefore meant, to men, the loss of their salvation. A direct line leads all the way from the *Malleus Maleficarum* to August Strindberg, who in his madness was haunted by the same concept.

But granting all these components, we must look farther. For the metaphysical explanation is still to be found. Belief in witches extends into such bottomless abysses that all merely psychological interpretations are ultimately inadequate. So long as we see the matter purely in terms of this secular world, it defies understanding. Again and again, as we read accounts of the witch trials, we are stunned by the fantastic subtlety with which theologians and jurists justified these grotesque proceedings.

Let us remember the heresy of which the witches were accused: that they had made a pact with the devil. This obsessional idea is of key importance. In dealing with witch trials and the belief in witches we are dealing with the devil. Although it is extraordinarily difficult to say anything at all about this obscurest of all obscure subjects, and although every word may be one word too much, the problem of the devil's existence cannot be evaded. The fact is that people do exist whom we feel to be connected with demonic powers. Black magic exists; this is beyond doubt.[6] And even though the "enlightened" mind regards the ex-

[6] Cf. W. E. Peuckert: *Pansophia* (1936), pp. 54 f.

istence of the devil as outmoded nonsense, belief in witches bred such frightful consequences that the whole thing can only be understood as a work of Satan. Of course no scientific treatise can be written to explain the outbreak of demonism in the witch persecutions. Yet when we truly consider the gruesome devastation wrought by the witch mania we can only say, awe-struck: "The enemy has done this," as the parable of the weeds in the field puts it. Inexplicable forces came into play, and for several centuries enjoyed a ghastly dominance. The devil had his hand in it, just as he is shown to operate in Dostoevsky's *The Brothers Karamazov* and in Bernanos's *Sous le Soleil du Diable*. But here he was not a symbol but a horrid reality! One can only say, in truth: Behold him, behold him plainly at his work!

We cannot exorcise the devil by merely ridiculing the absurd creature with horns and tail invented by the popular imagination of the Middle Ages. Explanations in the spirit of the Enlightenment may get rid of the image, but not of the content which lies behind it. Satan possesses a titanic power, as Dante and Milton understood. The apocalypse envisions the devil as of cosmic magnitude, and anyone who has been conscious of the noble products of the modern age, from fourteen-hour work days for children to the gas chambers at Auschwitz, must realize that here we have the devil in all his dreadful reality. The horrible visions of evil stand. But they bring us no nearer any understanding of the problem of whether Satan is a personal or an impersonal force, whether he is independent of God or dependent upon him. For all such questions exceed the limitations of the human mind and can at best be circumscribed by a series of paradoxes.

It is certainly not good to speak too much of the devil, as though he had the same stature as God. But it is also ill advised to deny his uncanny reality, for then the danger increases of falling victim to him. We must, indeed, see the diabolical element in the world as even more fearsome and mysterious than the Cathars saw it. We must, as does the Book of Job, behold Satan as a being within and not outside the sphere of divinity. Only then can we sense to the full the metaphysical darkness of the witchcraft persecutions.

Having grasped the matter in this way, even the most stout-hearted Christian will pale and be compelled to murmur in a trembling voice: It is true; the devil was actually involved in this witchcraft affair; he was present in the heart of it, as a cosmic monstrosity. His servants were on the scene, but they were not the legion of the poor terrorized, tortured, and cremated witches. No—what an incredible case of mistaken identities!—his servants had entered into the Inquisitors and judges. They were the bewitched ones. Paul tells us that "even Satan disguises himself as an angel of light." [7] So these officials were his instruments, without their being aware of it. Who but the devil stood behind these ecclesiastical and secular judges who carried out his fiendish intentions? The devil has always stood, an unreal reality, on the side of the persecutors, the torturers, and the Inquisitors. He will go on exercising this function until the end of the world.

[7] II Cor. xi, 14.

16

The Protestant Protest

Martin Luther

On the morning of December 10, 1520, a number of students and professors of Wittenberg University accompanied Martin Luther to the Elster gate of the town, outside of which was the town rubbish pit. Here the students lit a bonfire into which they threw several books, including three editions of the canon law. Then Luther stepped forward and, trembling, approached the fire. Murmuring prayers, he tossed a small pamphlet into the flames, and spoke in an almost inaudible voice: "Because you have corrupted the truth of God, may the Lord today destroy you in this fire." Whereupon those standing closest to him responded:

"Amen." Since he had avoided the slightest appearance of a
theatrical gesture, many of those present did not even observe
that he had consigned to the flames the papal bull excommunicating him. The whole ceremony lasted barely ten minutes. Luther and the professors went back into the town, while the students followed up the "pious spectacle" with all sorts of pranks.

Here was a case where the fearful prayer and the bold gesture of protest are not to be regarded as two separate and contradictory aspects of a man's nature. In Luther, they were intimately connected. Out of circumspection and prayer there
emerged the most daring rebellion. This formula sums up the
mystery of Luther, of a life and character compounded of anxiety and courage.

In spite of the enormous scholarly literature in which Luther
has been embalmed, the true image of the leader of the German
Reformation remains difficult to see. In a good many works Luther is painted as a not very appealing paterfamilias, playing his
lute in the midst of his family—an embodiment of that complacent *Gemütlichkeit* which represented the ideal of the German middle class in the middle of the nineteenth century. Nor is
this overblown caricature improved by doctrinaire efforts to put
his theology in the forefront.

It is true that Luther was much concerned with his doctrines,
which he built up in opposition to late-medieval theology. But in
reality he believed that "no one can become a Christian solely by
ideas and doctrines; he must also be one in his works and attempt
to bear the cross which destroys our flesh." [1] Luther was carrying
out this requirement when he donned the cowl. All interpretations of Luther must start from that fact: that Luther was a monk
and in a certain sense always remained one. Even as a student he
hoped to find peace behind monastic walls. He became a monk
not out of love of God, but out of fear of the flames of hell; this
fear drove him to such extremes of asceticism that he fell into a
swoon in his monk's cell in Erfurt. His spirit was essentially
monastic. "To be a monk means to be hated by the world and to

[1] Luther: *Psalmen-Auslegung,* ed. Eberle (1873), II, 291.

seem foolish to it," [2] he wrote. The monk is after all the *homo religiosus* who devotes himself to the divine with all the strength of his soul, who is ready to sacrifice everything to God.

As a monk Luther had a religious experience which was crucial to his later development. Sequestered in his Augustinian monastery, he felt menaced by the wrath of God. Neither daily confession nor ascetic exercises sufficed to overcome this sense of terror. Luther's religious struggle brought him to the verge of madness. Yet to brand his excessive anxiety as a psychic abnormality would be to ignore the nature of the religious experience. For this is what it was. Luther the monk cried to God out of the depths; he felt crushed under the weight of all that God required of a human soul. And so he suffered infernal terrors; after these crises he felt as if his bones had been burned to ashes. As he himself described it, in such moments of dread he saw not the slightest gleam of light. Sometimes he was filled with a wild hatred of God for making demands which no human being could fulfill; later he would suffer agonies of repentance for these sinful feelings.

For years this struggle with God raged within Luther's soul. Then, suddenly, the turning point came. It took the form of an illumination which came to him when he was in the tower room of the monastery reading the first chapter of the Epistle to the Romans. He suddenly realized that Paul had meant a merciful and not a punitive justice, a justice which is conferred upon men through Christ and which in no way can be separated from the Redeemer. Through Christ, this trembling, guilt-stricken monk felt liberated—although he remained, ever afterward, oriented more toward the Pauline epistles than toward the Gospels. After this revelation, Luther felt like a man for whom the gates of Paradise had been reopened. With the selfsame intensity with which he had previously hated God, he now drank in the sweet, excessively sweet, pledge. It is not man who finds God but

[2] Luther: *Die Vorlesung über den Römerbrief 1515/16*, ed. Ellwein (1927), p. 472.

God who finds man. This was the revolutionary idea which had come to him.

With this new understanding of God, he became a different man. For the rest of his life this once fear-stricken monk was able to cling to the incomparable reassurance God had given him. Henceforth he was never troubled by the slightest doubt of the reality of God. God had entered his life as an incontrovertible fact. After that revelation he regarded any efforts to comprehend God as inadmissible anthropomorphism. He was filled with a mystical certainty of the closeness of God; and this alone gave him the religious strength and inner security to challenge the whole world.

It is no light thing when the gates of Paradise, so long closed against man, swing open, and the angel with the flaming sword steps aside. Luther always considered this an extraordinary grace, and formulated what it meant to him in tremendous paradoxes, which are not easy to assimilate. He felt that the message of the Gospel could not help being paradoxical in this world —"because we are liars, the truth can never come to us except in a form that contradicts our comprehension."[3] From statements such as these, it is evident that the Reformer was at bottom not at all concerned with sanctifying the ambitions of the nobles and the burgher class, as has been so often claimed. There was a radiance of divine idiocy about such precepts as these: "It must be not as your reason requires, but beyond your reason; bury yourself in unreason, and I will give you my reason. Unreason is right reason; not to know whither you are going is to know rightly whither you are going. My reason makes you unreasoning."[4]

These are words that St. Francis might have spoken, conveying as they do a profound opposition to the Humanists. Luther's break with Erasmus was no temperamental flight on his part; it sprang directly from his religious outlook. Perhaps Luther's as-

[3] Ibid., p. 132.
[4] Luther: *Psalmen-Auslegung,* p. 478.

saults upon rationalism went too far, for in his vehemence he forgot that the intellect, too, is a gift of God, and that there is such a thing as reason illumined by the Logos. But Luther could not afford to make these fine distinctions in his struggle with scholastic rationalism. His robust attacks upon the "whore reason" reveal him as the monk in whom the "wisdom of the desert" had come to life again. Luther was not concerned, like the Humanists, with the harmonious development of the human mind. He stood before a Mount Sinai wrapped in fire and smoke, before a mighty mystery which flesh and blood could scarcely stand.

The highly charged faith of Luther's fruitful early period clashed directly with the decadence of the Late Middle Ages. Luther's perception of God, born to him after terrible travail, inevitably took the form of protest against existing Christian religiosity. The protest was intensified by his apocalyptic convictions; he was sure that the "dear Day of Judgment" was imminent. Excommunicated by the Church of his time, he countered by burning the papal bull. No arbitrary spirit or delight in contention prompted him to enter the public forum; his religious conscience left him no alternative. "God is carrying me away," he confessed. He regarded himself as only an instrument in a protest that must go on to all eternity. "I have done nothing; the Word has done all," he said.[5] Only if we consider that Luther acted under the compulsion of a higher power, can we do justice to the Protestant protest which he hurled into the world and for whose sake he became the heretic who founded a new conception of Christianity.

The immediate cause of Luther's break with the Church was Tetzel's sale of indulgences. He was outraged by the un-Christian commercialism that dealt so shamelessly in the salvation of souls. His religious conscience impelled him to post the famous ninety-five theses on the door of the church at Wittenberg in 1517. His anger was directed against this degenerate form of Christianity, in which escape from punishment became the highest goal. The

[5] Luther: *Erlangen Ausgabe*, XXVIII, 260.

priests were asleep—it was up to him to take action. "God will not tolerate this flea market!" he declared.[6]

But the sale of indulgences was only a symptom of a deeper malady within the Church. Even before his public action Luther had analyzed the situation in his lecture on the Epistle to the Romans: "A lamentable judgment of God's wrath has come down upon us in this day. For he must desire it that we pass our lives suffering such chastisements. We are made to look passively upon so dire a desolation of Holy Church, for never has it been worse devastated nor more sore beset when the hand of a foe was laid upon it." [7]

The youthful Luther's holy horror at the evil state of the Church can only be compared with Jeremiah's preaching against the temple. "Here you see why the thunder commonly strikes the churches before all other houses, for that God is more hostile to them than to any others, for in no den of thieves, in no house of iniquitous women are to be found such blasphemers, such sin, such murder of souls and destruction of the Church as in these houses of God." [8]

There could be no amelioration of Christianity, he became convinced, unless the statutes of the Church and scholastic theology were refashioned from the ground up. With concentrated force Luther turned his protest against the doctrines of the Church, and fought them from all sides. He rejected Thomas Aquinas as author of the "now dominant doctrine of Aristotle the destroyer." As for the theologians, he arraigned them for their manner of discussing the highest questions. They talked of these things with unpardonable conceit, like shoemakers talking about their leather.

When he thus began examining the doctrines with a critical eye, he found to his horror that even monasticism ran counter to the principles of the Gospel. He who had been one of the most

---

[6] *Evangelien-Auslegung,* ed. Eberle (1857), p. 196.
[7] Luther: *Römerbrief,* p. 49.
[8] Luther: *Erlangen Ausgabe,* VII, 213.

zealous of monks now began inveighing at monasticism itself. The rule of celibacy more and more appeared to him unnatural and contrary to the divine order of Creation. Christian truthfulness demanded a recognition of man's biological constitution. Ultimately, Luther came to the conclusion that man should "put ideas out of your head and plunge cheerfully in. Your body demands it and has the right; God wills it and compels it." [9] Luther not only preached the relinquishing of celibacy on principle; after considerable inner resistance he, the monk, finally took a wife, who happened to be a former nun. Here was an act which, in the eyes of his contemporaries, was shocking in the extreme. It was one of his most revolutionary steps and cannot be regarded blandly as the "foundation of the Protestant parsonage." Yet this did not mean that Luther simply truckled to the finite; he always looked upon this world only as an inn, and exhorted Christians to deal in earthly affairs only with their left hands, while stretching their right hands toward heaven.

Having come more and more to regard the priests as "the veritable enemies of the cross of Christ," [1] he began to direct his protest against the head of the hierarchy. Of course, to modern Protestants, the vicar of Christ on earth has become a wholly remote figure. It was quite different in Luther's day, and his struggle was far more daring than we can imagine. If we would understand the sacrilege involved, we must put ourselves in the Catholic's place, must feel what the Holy Father means to him. Luther was not concerned about the corruptness of the Curia, or about the concupiscent Popes, of whom there have been a goodly number in the course of history. His quarrel with the papacy centered upon the divine predicates that the Popes had claimed for themselves. This seemed to him robbery of the Almighty. With what horror Luther must have begun to apprehend that the secret of evil was present within the Church itself. With what reluctance he came to the conclusion that the Pope was not only a false leader of the Christian people, but also the very Antichrist prophesied in the Second Epistle to the Thessalonians who "takes his

[9] Ibid., LIII, 288.   [1] Luther: *Römerbrief*, pp. 200, 201.

seat in the temple of God." "The Pope is a disguised devil incarnate, for he is the Antichrist." [2]

When the apocalyptic vision of the Roman See as the most abominable of Babylons had taken possession of Luther, the impact of the idea was so great that his language lost all measure. The night before his death he wrote on the wall with chalk: "In life, Pope, I was a plague to you; in death I shall be death to you." [3]

Of course Luther was unjust to the papacy. But we cannot expect historical objectivity of a man who is engaged in a life-and-death struggle. Unfortunately, Luther lost all self-control and abused the papacy in the filthiest terms. His violence can be explained if not excused only on the grounds of the metaphysical hatred he felt toward the whole institution. Luther's struggle against the Pope had ceased to be fought on a human plane; he saw him as the dragon of the Apocalypse. The immoderate curses the Reformer uttered against the vicar of Christ must be understood as arising out of this eschatological view.

Throughout the centuries, heretics had protested against the secularization of the church. That theme once again was the common rallying cry for the religious opposition of the Middle Ages. Luther, however, was not of this camp, for he wasted few words over the symptoms of decadence within the Church, and rather directed his polemic against elements which most people could only find morally unobjectionable. The majority of Protestants did not understand this aspect of his struggle. The fact was that Luther felt himself more at odds with the so-called pious men of his time than with the licentious clergy. The obedient souls, he declared, who have a good opinion of themselves, and the virtuous folk who engage in honorable works are curiously enough those to whom God has always been most repugnant. They have already rejected Christ, whom God had made his cornerstone. "But mark you, who are those who reject this stone? They are not wicked people, but the best of all, namely the

[2] Luther: *Erlangen Ausgabe*, LX, 180.
[3] In H. Grisar: *Luther* (1912), vol. III, p. 848.

holiest, the most prudent, the most learned, the greatest, the noblest; they are the ones who are offended by the stone." [4] As Luther saw it, the devout man who thinks he is righteous is constantly committing the sin of pride. Those who boast of possessing divine grace are those who most obdurately fend it off.

This idea formed the apex of Luther's paradoxical argument. His protest against the Church triumphant in this world was given still one more dimension by this battle against the self-righteous "little saints." It arose out of the same source as his antipathy toward Humanism. To have any real understanding of the Reformation we must understand Luther's struggle against so-called good men. It is this element in Luther which makes him puzzling—an eternal problem for every Protestant. There is no reason to idolize Luther. He was certainly not the only true Christian since Paul, although certain uncritical glorifiers seem to think so. He committed a number of grave errors; it is impossible to admire him unreservedly. But in his struggle against moral self-righteousness as an obstacle to the way to God he came very close to the spirit of the Gospel, so close that only a few exceptional men in the history of Christian thought have ever equaled him in this.

The effectiveness of Luther's protest undoubtedly was related to the anti-Roman feelings of the German nation, to the awakening consciousness of the towns and cities, and to the fact that Luther had found an answer to the question of his times. But the one thing with which he is always credited did not spring directly from him: namely, Reformation. Luther did not achieve the goal which he, along with all his contemporaries, had in mind during his early tempestuous years: to reform the head and limbs of the Church. He was cast out by the Church before he had the chance to carry through the needed improvements, and to this day the Roman Church has not met Luther's call with the seriousness that it merits.

Instead, the outcome of Luther's efforts was religious revolution. There is no other word for it. His break with the past was

[4] Luther: *Psalmen-Auslegung*, II, 217, 218.

far more radical than anything reform-minded men could possibly desire. He destroyed large segments of tradition, for he scorned to preserve continuity with the medieval Church. And in sweeping away tradition he produced the greatest revolution that Christianity had undergone up to his time. For Luther was destined to win that thoroughgoing triumph which had been denied to almost all the heretics before him. His religious revolution signified the end of one historical epoch and the beginning of another. He dislocated his own age, and with one titanic gesture shattered the whole medieval order. In overthrowing sacramentalism and proclaiming universal priesthood, he delivered the death-blow to clericalism. The net effect of his work was that division in Christianity which could never afterward be repaired.

On the other hand, Luther's bold stroke lifted the ecclesiastical pressure which had weighed so heavily upon men. His greatest achievement, and one which made up for a vast deal of harm, was his rediscovery of the Gospel. Along with Luther genuine Christianity reappeared, after having been for so long smothered under the weight of rituals. For the sake of this one act, everything else must be accepted. The dynamism of the Gospel produced this religious revolution whose consequences have continued to operate down to the present day—a revolution which turned new soil in all the nations of Europe.

Only a heretical person could bring about such a revolution. The conventional Protestant may find it offensive to hear the founder of his religion called a heretic. But can there be any serious question that after the Leipzig disputation in June, 1519, Luther was declared a heretic? Luther's protest on the basis of the Gospels was felt at once by his contemporaries to be heretical—a feeling which Tetzel expressed immediately after the posting of the ninety-five theses: "I want that heretic thrown into the flames within three weeks." [5] Soon afterward the rebellious monk was formally arraigned in Rome on suspicion of heresy—"dishonest, blasphemous, heretical fellow" were the terms used of him. In Leipzig Dr. Eck was bent on demonstrating that Luther

[5] H. Böhmer: *Der junge Luther* (1925), p. 163.

was a heretic, in fact a Hussite, for which reason he kept alluding to the Council of Constance. Luther at first stoutly denied he was any such thing, for at this time he himself regarded the Bohemians as heretics misled by the devil. But after a good deal of hectoring, he replied bravely that among the doctrines of John Hus there were many which were genuinely Christian, which the universal church could not condemn.

Thus, after the disputation in Leipzig, Luther stood exposed as an open heretic, at least to all good Catholics. As such he could not possibly reform Christianity from within. The emperor, Charles V, decided that Luther "like the Wicked Fiend in monkish garb collects old and new heresies." Nor was this impression altogether wrong. Luther had done far more than censure the sale of indulgences; in his struggle against the papacy he had attacked the foundations of the Catholic faith. Anyone who accused the Pope of being Antichrist had parted ways with the Catholic Church. No true son of the Church could speak in such terms. After Luther burned the papal bull, he was an apostate. To pit the individual conscience against the Church was, in Catholic terms, sheerest subjectivism and "the fundamental erroneous attitude underlying all heresy." [6]

This man, whose religious conscience had driven him to these extremes, had some illuminating and contradictory remarks to make on the whole problem of heresy. It must be noted, however, that conceptual thinking was not Luther's strong point. Because of his impulsive nature and his continuous psychological development, we cannot expect to find him giving any unequivocal definition of the idea of a heretic. In fact, he used the word "heretic" in a number of different ways. One definition, "to be a heretic meaneth not to believe the things which are needful and commanded to be believed," accords with the traditional conception of heresy.[7] Later on, too, Luther was apt to speak of heresy in contemptuous terms: "All heresy floweth thence and hath its source therein that reason will master Holy Writ and turn it head

---

[6] J. Lortz: *Reformation in Deutschland* (1941), I, 231, 396.
[7] Luther: *Erlangen Ausgabe,* XXVII, 22.

over heels." [8] He takes some comfort, however, in remembering what Paul had to say concerning the inevitability of heresy: "Summa, there must be heresies, one cannot prevent them, do what one will. So it was in time of the Apostles; we shall not have nor do better than our forefathers! If tyranny and persecution cease, heresies follow." [9] That being so, Luther tried to see a good side in heresy, indirectly: "If heresies and offenses come, Christendom will only profit thereby, for they make Christians to read diligently in Holy Writ and ponder the same with industry. . . . Thus through heretics and offenses we are kept alert and stouthearted and amid wrangles and battles understand God's Word better than before." [1]

This traditional conception was supplanted by another view of heresy which inevitably arose in a man who was forced onto the side of the heretics. There is already a note of this in the sentence: "Not to believe rightly maketh heretics." [2] For of course Luther accused his opponents of not believing rightly and of interpreting the Bible wrongly. When he began examining the past history of Christianity with new eyes, he saw to his astonishment that the former heretics had been martyrs who had demonstrated a true love of the cross, and thus acted in far more Christian fashion than those who merely kissed a silver monstrance as if it were an idol. *All those whom the Pope hath burned and killed as heretics, like John Hus and Jerome of Prague and many others, now and again, they rightly bore the cross; for their concern was held to be wrong and heresy by the whole world, so that they were disgraced and called false leaders of the people, as indeed happened to the Lord Christ himself and to the holy Apostles and all martyrs and as will happen to the very end of the world.*[3]

This startling perception represented a fundamental revaluation of the whole problem. Luther had broken at last with the traditional condemnation of the heretic, had discovered that among

---

[8] Ibid., XLIV, 161.
[9] Ibid., LXI, 81/82.
[1] Ibid., XLIV, 54.

[2] Ibid., XXVII, 99.
[3] Ibid., XV, 335.

the Christians so maligned stood the true bearers of the cross. Suddenly he understood that: "Some are called God's folk and saints and were not at all; some of the small, despised little flock were not called such and yet were such." [4] Thereafter Luther no longer scrupled to call even the Bible a heretics' book,[5] and step by step fought his way to that long overlooked conception which contains one of the greatest truths of all time: There is truth concealed in heresy, too.[6]

In line with this new insight, Luther took issue with the practice of burning heretics, which he now regarded as a violation of the Gospel itself, which had commanded: "Let the weeds grow until the harvest." Bluntly, unequivocally, he declared: "To burn heretics is against the will of the Holy Ghost." [7] In his sermons, too, he preached against the cruel massacre of heretics, arguing that he who trembled for his life one day might be in the right on the next. "What wrathful folk have we been so long a time, we who have sought to compel the Turks by the sword, the heretics by fire, the Jews by slaughter to come to the faith, and have uprooted the tares by violence, just as if we were folk who could reign over hearts and minds. . . . They burn the true saints and are themselves heretics," [8] he concluded. He proposed the Christian slogan that heretics be conquered with the pen and not with fire, for otherwise the executioners must be the most learned doctors on earth.

We cannot depreciate these clear-sighted words on the grounds that Luther was speaking in his own defense. On the contrary, he was proclaiming a principle, not arguing for himself. His conscience, awakened by the Bible, was revolted on religious grounds by the burnings. God did not desire the death of sinners, but their conversion and life.

[4] Luther: *Vom unfreien Willen,* ed. Gogarten (1924), p. 79.
[5] Luther: *Erlangen Ausgabe,* LXI, 72.
[6] Cf. Köhler: *Reformation und Ketzerprozess,* p. 13, and K. Holl: *Luther,* p. 355.
[7] Luther: *Erlangen Ausgabe,* XXIV, 139.
[8] Ibid., XI, 78.

How then should heretics be dealt with? Luther gave an inspired answer: *This should be done by the bishops, for to them such office is commanded and not the princes. For heresy can never be fended with force; a different touch is needed and this is another fray and dispute than that of the sword. God's Word must wage battle here, and if that doth not do it then it will no doubt remain undone by worldly force though it fill the world with blood. Heresy is a thing spiritual, the which no iron can hack, no fire can sear, no water can drown. Only the Word of God is there for it, and that will win men to the truth.*[9] He was prepared to take the consequences: "Let minds break and strike against one another. If some are thereby misled, so be it, that is the way of war: where there is brawling and battle, some must fall and some be wounded; but he who fighteth stoutly will be crowned."[1]

It is a pity that Protestantism was not prepared to learn Luther's "different touch," but continued with the burnings, beheadings, and drownings, thus dishonoring anew the resurrected Gospel. It is also a pity that Luther himself was not capable of sustaining the noble viewpoint which he had attained fairly early in his revolutionary career. A relapse ensued, for he was unfortunately a man who could not cling to all his significant insights. Still, his message enjoining tolerance to heretics resounded through the world, and could no longer be totally silenced. Luther's regrettable change of sides indicates how difficult it is to accomplish Christian non-violence; it is never a matter that can be taken for granted. Luther's change of views is connected with the whole tragic turn his movement took during the second half of his life. His abandonment of the "different touch" in favor of the old policy of suppression and coercion was in fact a worse crime than the Inquisitors', who after all had never possessed that deepened religious insight which had once been vouchsafed to Luther. What he had once said proved only too applicable to himself: "Everyone who hath the Gospel groweth too sure; thereby

[9] Ibid., XXII, 90.　　　　　[1] Ibid., LIII, 265.

the spirit waxeth sluggish, careless, and slothful, and faith is lost, so that one is not stout to root out the other sins." [2]

After the Church had rejected Luther's reformist efforts, he more and more found himself compelled to establish a new church. Certainly the activities in which he engaged after the Diet at Worms must be so construed. Of course his foundation of a church was an inevitable necessity, and led to great things. And yet it was a misfortune, a lamentable misfortune. A heresy which becomes consolidated is no longer a protesting heresy; by its own inner logic it must develop into a new orthodoxy. The tragic and culpable development of Protestantism consisted in this fact: that what started as a heresy became a legitimate church. The process, indeed, is self-contradictory. Therein lies, moreover, the ambiguity of Protestantism, which is a heresy and yet does not want to be one.

Imperceptibly, Luther developed from a rebellious heretic to a churchman; he was forced to do so by the course of events which he could not escape and which proved stronger than his defiant personality. Thus a completely changed situation arose; he could no longer afford to uphold his earlier views. He had to repudiate his one-time revolutionary ideas in favor of a new ecclesiasticism. And so Luther developed, like all churchmen, a distinct distaste for all heresies. Of course the Catholics constantly charged him with being a heretic; but he countered by saying that his followers formed the true church, while his opponents were guilty of apostasy from the Gospel.

Upon discovering that the "free sectarians" could not be overcome by the word of God, Luther's treatment of heretics came more and more to resemble that of the medieval Church in general. He no longer spoke of the "different touch." The new independent church required this changed attitude. Thus, during the second half of his life Luther found it quite in order that rebellious Anabaptists should be killed, and was capable of uttering ferociously un-Christian words on the subject. Whereas earlier he had rejected the death penalty, he now approved a statement of

[2] Luther: *Psalmen-Auslegung*, I, 341.

Wittenberg theologians sanctioning executions. The ancient heretic statutes derived from Roman law re-entered Lutheranism—for which reason the Reformation can hardly be called a renewal of early Christianity.

Attempts have been made to explain this about-face in terms of Luther's highly contradictory character, some of whose traits we alluded to when we spoke of the fear and trembling with which he burned the papal bull. Certainly his was a disposition not easy to comprehend; we need only think of the bewildering variety of verdicts which have been passed upon him. He has been execrated as often as he has been eulogized, nor can this be explained as simple sectarian prejudice. Luther *was* one of the greatest men of all time, and he *did* contain within himself the most contradictory qualities. On the one hand, he was an inexhaustible spring; on the other hand, the richness of his nature made him incapable of finding the golden mean. In his extraordinary character ebullient humor lived side by side with deepest melancholia. When launched on a polemic, he would often resort to that repellent brand of coarseness which only the Teuton descends to, and yet he was a sensitive lover of music and a gifted composer. He fought virtually hand-to-hand combats with the devil, and then again he talked with God like a second Abraham. In short, his personality contains insoluble riddles; in this he was a true son of his nation, which he simultaneously loved and reviled. This mighty revolutionary, who brought the world to the point of explosion, was at the same time a born conservative who drew back in dread from violence and unrest. A tremendous stream of religious spirit poured from him. Yet with his sense of mission he came dangerously close to megalomania; and that was all the more frightening against the apocalyptic background of his thought, for he considered himself the "last trumpet" sounding just before the second coming of Christ. A gigantic, tempestuous figure, a religious colossus and a true man of the spirit, whose work seemed to be sustained by supernatural powers, he was also frightening in his obsessiveness, intolerance, and immaturity. Here was an overwhelming spiritual greatness which could not be reduced to a formula, and therefore could only evoke contradictory results.

To be accurate, we must divide Luther's development into three phases. The first extended from his entrance into the monastery to his nailing the ninety-five theses on the door of the Wittenberg church. The second, his really heretical period, concluded with the start of the Peasants' War in 1525; and the third went on from this until his death. For simplicity's sake, however, we can also differentiate merely between the younger and the elder Luther. Certainly Luther was a changed man after his dispute with the *Schwärmer* (the free sectarians) and his fateful stand against the peasants in 1525. The writings of this second phase begin to abound in ideas incompatible with the principle of evangelical freedom. It is significant that Kierkegaard in his diaries speaks of the later Luther with the greatest contempt. In his last years Luther fell prey to a pessimistic melancholia which is sad to behold. With advancing age his conservative disposition came more and more to the fore; he was increasingly concerned with preserving what had already been attained. Lutheranism itself emerged from the activities of the later Luther, and from the work of Philipp Melanchthon. And certainly Lutheranism was an inspiring force; we need only think of men like Johann Sebastian Bach or Paul Gerhardt. But Lutheranism was more concerned with its own importance than with the original conceptions of its founder. This ecclesiastical Lutheranism also propounded the highly dubious principle that "the earlier Luther must be explained by the later" because the old reformer had "supplemented and corrected" the mistakes he made as a young man.[3] Thus there developed that Lutheranism whose spirit of noble endurance commands our respect, but whose effect was to train its communicants in the most servile kind of obedience—a tendency for which Germany was to pay dearly.

Too little has been made of the true heritage of the young Luther, who was filled with protestant courage and protestant wrath. And yet he personified the future. He embodied the prin-

[3] T. Harnack: *Luthers Theologie* (1927), I, 9, 10.

ciple of eternal protest against the idolatry of a complacent church. The strength of Protestantism lies in this refusal to identify divine truth with any ecclesiastical institution. Such an attitude has nothing whatsoever to do with mere negation; rather, it is a protest that flows out of the substance of the Gospel. To give new life to Protestant criticism is the task of true heirs of the younger Luther, as Hermann Kutter suggests when he writes:

I think that if Luther and Zwingli were to rise again from their graves, they would drive us from the building site and say to us: We know you not, in spite of all the fine sermons you make on Reformation Day. You are not Protestants at all; you do not protest one bit; you only commemorate our protests. . . . Is there nothing else to do but to denounce the Catholic Church and to idolize the words that we used, as one collects old tools and weapons in museums? People look at such antiques, but no longer use them; they use new ones. But where are your new weapons, and where are the battle lines of your modern foes? Do you not see that what we said in our time to a rotten church must be said today—not in the same words but in the same spirit—to a rotten society dedicated to Mammon: Let us have God's justice. . . . Do penance; put off your lukewarm natures, rise out of your shadow existences, protest again, not against ancient ghosts who are of no account, but against the enemy who dominates our age. . . .[4]

---

[4] H. Kutter: *Das Bilderbuch Gottes für gross und klein* (1917), pp. 156, 157.

17

Heretics of the Reformation

"A new world is marching up, the old is dying off." Thus Kaspar Schwenkfeld described his own age.[1] And whenever a new message knocks upon the gates of the world, the world's foundations are shaken. Incipient Lutheranism was not the only religious movement in that fruitful period of ferment, the sixteenth century. Along with it went Humanism, Baptism, Spiritualism, and Calvinism—all these were earnest efforts to formulate the new message. A whole procession of men, each with his own conception of Christianity, stepped upon the stage during that tempestu-

[1] K. Ecke: *Schwenkfeld, Luther und der Gedanke einer apostolischen Reformation* (1911), p. 100.

ous sixteenth century. Erasmus of Rotterdam, Paracelsus of Hohenheim, Andreas Karlstadt, Kaspar Schwenkfeld, Jacobus Acontius, and many others put forth new views of Christianity. It is impossible to discuss them all here. But a few must be mentioned in order to make it clear that Protestantism too had its heretics, and treated them with no more leniency than did the medieval Catholic Church. For here were figures who called to mind early Protestantism, which Protestants would fain forget. In their failure these men make a greater claim upon our affection than does victorious Protestantism, and it is time to consider their efforts in an impartial spirit.

Thomas Müntzer

Like all the men of the first Reformation generation, Thomas Müntzer (1490–1525) was a product of Catholicism. But the emptiness of the Church became all too evident to him. He spoke of "wretchedly dilapidated Christendom," contended that it had become a "bestial mockery," and that never in his life had monk or priest been able to show him "the proper practice of religion." [2] Corruption had begun early, he maintained, and evil had set into Christendom at the start. Immediately "after the death of the disciples of the Apostles the stainless virginal church was made a whore by spiritual adultery, that the scribes might benefit." [3] The Councils had been scandalous childish pranks, and, indeed, what more could be expected from *"Pfaffen und Affen"*—parsons and apes (i.e. fools). Müntzer was animated by a fierce hatred of the Church which led him to such hyperbole as this: "Then came the shameless woman with her red skirt, the spiller of blood, the Roman Church, and broke with all other churches and declared that her ceremonies and gestures, patched together out of paganism, were the best and all others were an abominable atrocity." [4]

And yet Müntzer's great adversary was Luther, whom he felt

[2] *Thomas Müntzer, sein Leben und seine Schriften*, ed. Brandt (1933), p. 59.
[3] Ibid., p. 61.   [4] Ibid., p. 136.

at their first encounter to be made of a different stuff from himself. Müntzer's heretical activities were directed against the Reformation, whose faults he unsparingly exposed. For Protestant authority had crystallized around the person of Luther, and Müntzer, the spirit of protest itself, could not accept this. What he felt toward Luther was far from mere jealousy. Such pettiness was alien to Müntzer's spirit. Rather, it appeared to him that Luther was falsifying Christianity; he charged Luther with complacency and mendacity. "I preach a Christian religion which is not synonymous with that of Luther," he wrote, "but which takes the same form in the hearts of all the elect upon earth." [5] Müntzer had only scorn for Luther's conception of justification by faith without works; this was only a way of reassuring despairing Christians by false consolations. Such a doctrine "made an abomination of all Christian earnestness," Müntzer declared.[6] He pilloried Luther as "Brother Live-gently" and "Father Tread-softly," and as the "white-pope." His angry pamphlet "Against the Spiritless, Gentle-living Flesh of Wittenberg" can be summarized in a single point: Luther was reducing Christianity to bourgeois respectability. Fundamentally speaking, the charge was true; Protestantism was an accommodation of Christianity to bourgeois culture, for soon after it arose, it became firmly established in the urban cultured and propertied class whom Müntzer so bitterly opposed. Rebel in Christ that he was, Müntzer was in principle antipathetic to the bourgeoisie, who on their side cannot abide prophetic religiosity. Christ had come to set a fire upon earth; the turning of his message into a comfortable middle-class religion was bound to strike a heretic like Müntzer as sheer betrayal. Müntzer himself, with his revolutionary impulses, was one of the most unbourgeois figures in the whole history of Christian thought.

Müntzer saw Wittenberg becoming the center for an idolization of Scripture which came dangerously close to making a paper pope out of the Bible. He regarded blind trust in the Bible as baleful and wrong. Christians, he held, should not be taught

[5] Ibid., p. 71.   [6] Ibid., p. 142.

that God had spoken once in the Bible "and then vanished into the air."[7] True salvation consisted in the eternal Word of God; every preacher must have revelations, for otherwise he could not truly announce the good tidings. "Therefore all prophets use the phrase, 'Thus saith the Lord.' They do not say, 'The Lord has said,' as if it were past, but they speak of it in the present tense."[8] The central issue with Müntzer was the living conception of a God who directly addressed man, whereas Luther reasoned that Scripture had been given to man because they could not endure God's speech. "They talk directly with God!" Luther exclaimed with a shudder upon hearing of Müntzer's claim. Müntzer's mockery of Holy Scripture—"Bible, babble"—struck him as scandalous blasphemy.

Direct revelation of God, however, is accorded only to one who has proved by suffering that he is a genuine imitator of Christ. Müntzer's repudiation of Scriptural authority and his proclamation of direct revelation emerged from a mystique of suffering borrowed directly from mystics like Johann Tauler (1300–61), whom Müntzer loved and had studied deeply. But he himself had also experienced the mystical ecstasy of suffering, so that he was able to tell of it in his own words. In his letters he declared that "no one can feel God's mercy unless he has been abandoned," and that "only in poverty of spirit can the regiment of Christ be established."[9] He who had not suffered the night of abandonment did not know the artistry of God. Müntzer would have none of a honey-sweet Christ who would be the worst of poisons in this fleshly world; his was a bitter Christ. Only in suffering could man undergo that strange reshaping which had been the concern of mystics in all ages. According to Müntzer, "the elect must become Christ-shaped and with much suffering and discipline pay homage to God's work."[1]

Müntzer's strongest disagreement with Luther, however, was in regard to social reform. For Müntzer extended his new spirit to

[7] Ibid., p. 61.　　　　　　　　[8] Ibid.
[9] *Thomas Müntzers Briefwechsel*, ed. H. Böhmer and P. Kirn (1931), pp. 40, 44.　　　　　　　[1] *Müntzer*, ed. Brandt, p. 134.

the social realm. Müntzer was conscious of social distress with an intensity such as few Christians before him had felt. Hence he took that further step which Luther was loath to take—as was to become clear during the Peasants' War. Müntzer was convinced to the bottom of his heart that the social movement of the day, with which he had early identified himself, was a matter of divine justice. "The old proposals are no longer of the least avail," he declared with astonishingly keen insight.[2] He concluded that great social upheavals were impending. The time of princes and their intrigues was over: "Their power has an end and in a short time will be given to the common people," he prophesied with understandable impatience.[3] The true Gospel was meant only for the disinherited of society. The poor man should not allow himself to be squeezed and flayed by tyrants. Boldly, he wrote to Albrecht von Mansfeld, one of the foremost supporters of Luther and Protestantism: "Do you think that God does not care more for his people than for you tyrants?"[4]

Müntzer charged the lords themselves with responsibility for the peasant uprising, because they did nothing to eliminate the causes of social distress. He clear-sightedly recognized those causes, unlike those apostles of later Christian socialism whose concern was only to bind up the wounds, not to strike at the source of misery. Müntzer was a sincere friend of the poor, their selfless and eloquent advocate. There is not the slightest reason to question the purity of his motives, even though his revolutionary efforts tended to introduce communism into Christianity. He felt the cruel lot of the common people as his own distress, and denounced it with a holy impetuosity. Once again we must stress that the first person in the Age of Reformation to recognize social questions as divine questions was a heretic. Christendom had taken such a form that, one may almost say, it was necessary to become a heretic in order to feel sympathy for the terrible distress of the peasants, not, like the priest in Jesus' parable, to pass by it indifferently.

Müntzer thought that he could overcome social misery with

[2] Ibid., p. 68.   [3] Ibid., p. 66.   [4] Ibid., p. 77.

chiliastic hopes, which represented the connecting link between his mystical and his revolutionary interests. Chiliasm—the doctrine that in the Last Days Christ and the saints will reign on earth for a thousand years—was the pillar upon which the whole structure of his religion rested; we cannot understand this intense man apart from it. Müntzer was obsessed by the apocalyptic conviction that the battle of the Lord had already begun. "The time is come," he cried rejoicing. "Summer is at the door!" Not for nothing was Müntzer a Joachimite who had read the writings of this Calabrian abbot with utmost excitement. He placed his hopes in a "new Daniel" who was bound to arise. His thoughts circled incessantly around the lofty goal of "how alone through the arrival of faith it shall be vouchsafed and shown to us that we fleshly, earthly men shall become gods through the incarnation of Christ and thus along with him God's disciples, taught and deified by himself; far more indeed, transformed entirely and wholly in him, so that earthly life will soar aloft into heaven." [5] Never has the eternally youthful idea of chiliasm been given more ecstatic expression! "A true preacher must indeed be a prophet, however much the world mocks." [6] It was out of this prophetic intoxication that his social heresies flowed.

Fevered by such apocalyptic feelings and gnawed by his consciousness of social distress, Müntzer was led to take an extreme position. As he himself described it, he was determined "to spare no man on this earth who resists the word of God." [7] The godless, by whom he meant the princes who exploited the peasants, had no right to life. They must be exterminated. In what has been called his "Daniel Sermon" this creed took precedence over everything else, and Müntzer announced himself as a "destroyer of the unbelievers" to whom God had entrusted the "sword of Gideon." [8] This grim decision may, however, be viewed as arising out of Müntzer's realism rather than out of his utopianism. To put the matter paradoxically: Müntzer's peaceful principles

[5] Ibid., p. 170.   [6] Ibid., p. 200.
[7] *Thomas Müntzers Briefwechsel*, p. 48.
[8] *Müntzer*, ed. Brandt, pp. 63, 78.

313

urged him toward a policy of violence. It was a dark hour in
Müntzer's life when his revolutionary impulses led him to come
out for violent annihilation of the godless. No amount of sympathy for this great rebel in Christ, whose intense revolutionary
passion was born from the highest spirituality, should induce us to
justify this regrettable decision. In denying the godless their right
to live, Müntzer took the same position as the Inquisition, a position involving infidelity to the Gospel.[9]

One episode in Müntzer's life sums up the matter perfectly.
It is as it were symbolic of the disastrous import of this creed of
violence. Müntzer had become the spokesman for the rebellious
peasantry of Thuringia during the Peasants' War. On May 15,
1525, a well-equipped army of knights under Landgrave Philip of
Hesse and Duke George of Saxony confronted a peasant army of
some 8,000 men, led by Müntzer. At the sight of their enemy, the
ill-armed peasants suddenly lost courage. Müntzer tried to rally
them by eloquent words, but this time he could not succeed. It
was a day when brief showers alternated with spells of sunshine.
Suddenly a radiant rainbow appeared in the sky. Joyfully, Müntzer turned to the peasants, crying: *You see, God is on our side,
for he has given us a sign. Do you not see the rainbow in the
sky? It means that God will help us, who bear the rainbow on
our banners, and that he threatens the wicked princes with
judgment and punishment. Therefore be unafraid, comfort yourselves that you will have divine aid, and defend yourselves. God
does not wish you to make peace with the godless princes!* [1]

Once more the demoralized peasants took heart; they began
singing their religious songs, convinced that victory was in their
grasp—did they not have a sign from God himself? But scarcely
had hope returned to their hearts when the first balls from the enemy cannon began striking into their midst, sowing such terror in
the ranks of the peasant army that they fled wildly without a

---

[9] Cf. M. M. Smirin: *Die Volksreformation des Thomas Müntzer und der
grosse Bauernkrieg* (1952), pp. 49 f.
[1] *Müntzer,* ed. Brandt, p. 45.

fight. The fleeing peasants were mercilessly cut down by the knights. Thus Müntzer's apocalyptic beliefs and faith in violence led him to self-delusion and to deluding others.

After this military debacle, Müntzer fell into the hands of the princes, who avenged themselves in terrible fashion. He was stretched on the wheel until he screamed with pain, while the fat duke who watched him grinned scornfully and asked: "Thomas, does that hurt?"[2] There is no proof that he weakened under torture—nor would such weakening mean anything. But, according to Luther, he died an obstinate heretic, refusing to recant in spite of the most fearful tortures. Concerning his last hours, we have only the accounts of his enemies, and these are contradictory. Certainly there is something terribly moving about his appeal to the princes from the scaffold "that they be not harsh to the poor people." Even on the threshold of death this young man of thirty-five gave thought to the fate of the suffering common folk.[3]

Opinions of Müntzer have always ranged from one extreme to another. To Luther it was a settled matter that "whoever hath seen Müntzer can say that he hath seen the devil incarnate in his fiercest fury."[4] For centuries Protestantism accepted the thesis that Müntzer was a diabolic personality. Theologians and historians expressed satisfaction that the rebel had been caught and given his due. This attitude on the part of the representatives of official Protestantism is somewhat understandable, for Müntzer's revolutionary conflagration had threatened their very existence. He had desired the impossible, and that is always a sin in the eyes of rational people.

More than 300 years had to go by before the vilification of Müntzer ceased. In the nineteenth century Heinrich Heine came forth with the blunt statement that "Luther was wrong and Müntzer right." In the twentieth century this view found more and more advocates; the tendency was to raise the revolutionary on a pedestal, while Luther was systematically denigrated, the

[2] Ibid., p. 49.   [3] Ibid., p. 50.
[4] Luther: *Erlangen Ausgabe,* LIII, 306.

more so because little credit was given to the religious force of the Wittenberg Reformer.[5] The time has really come to stop playing one off against the other and to arrive at a more balanced judgment of both men. This does not mean to achieve a synthesis by lazy compromise, but to accord each man his due. The more scholars have delved into the life of Müntzer, the more impressive a figure he appears. This Protestant heretic must be fitted into the scheme of things. Luther and Müntzer no longer appear to be mutually exclusive. Müntzer must be understood as a corrective of Luther. For Müntzer stood for another and highly important aspect of Protestantism: he carried the Protestant protest into the social area. Müntzer recognized that the Reformation could not remain confined to religion alone, for that robbed it of its future. Social reform was an essential component of its message. What is more, Müntzer perceived this truth with magnificent clarity, because his faith still comprehended the Whole. "Müntzer is dead, but his spirit has not yet been exterminated," Luther had said. And, we add, it must never be exterminated. The active spirit of rebellion which insists upon reforming conditions in the name of God's justice must take its place beside the spirit of patient endurance which for centuries dominated Lutheranism. For this new synthesis we must draw upon Müntzer's conception as the needed corrective to Luther. The resulting ideology might be called the perfection of Protestantism.

Hans Denck

Hans Denck was in a bleak mood as he tramped along the road from Strasbourg to the Palatinate on December 24 in the year 1526. While rich and poor, high and low, prepared to celebrate Christmas next morning, and carol singers roamed the streets singing of the joy which had that day befallen all people, Denck was tasting the forlornness of the homeless. In the Christ-

---

[5] Cf. H. Ball: *Die Folgen der Reformation* (1924), pp. 24–35, and Hans Mühlestein: *Russland und die Psychomachie Europas* (1925), pp. 76 f.

mas story this is summed up in the words: "There was no room at the inn." And, indeed, for Denck there was no room at the inn. He had not set out on that wintry night of his own free will. The previous day he had been ordered by the city magistrate to leave Strasbourg immediately. That was why Denck, expelled by his fellow Christians, was traveling northward, lost in thought, hoping that somewhere he might find a new roof over his head.

Only two years before, the Town Council of Nuremberg, where Denck had been a rector at the municipal school, had banished the young man from its precincts. His wife and children had to be left behind. He had been forbidden to come within forty-five miles of the territory of Nuremberg. In St. Gallen, too, he had suffered the same fate, for there too he had spoken of his favorite idea, the ultimate "sanctification of all the godless." Nowhere had Denck succeeded in finding a safe refuge, let alone a permanent home. He was harried from town to town. Since there was no room for him in Christian inns, he was condemned to the life of a perpetual fugitive. This time it was not only the cold that beset the poor wayfarer. The germ of a disease was wasting his body and slowly undermining his spiritual resistance as well. In his despair he sent an appeal to Johannes Oecolampadius, the Reformer of Basel, under whom he had once studied. Oecolampadius remembered that he himself had once been an exile and opened the gates of the city to Denck. Nor did Denck have time to wear out his welcome, for he died shortly after his arrival, probably of the plague.

What sort of man was this, whom no city would take in? A dangerous agitator, forever preaching sedition? If our picture of the heretic is of a militant fighter for his ideas, Denck does not fit the bill at all. He was a markedly quiet and reticent person. As his contemporaries describe him, he was a youth of tall stature, friendly manners, and unusually earnest conduct. Denck was an aristocratic personality, in spite of the refugee life imposed upon him. Nor did he show the slightest bitterness at his lot, for he was convinced that this was the price he had to pay for his beliefs. "When I began to love God, I fell into the disfavor of many men, and from day to day it grows apace." [6] He did, it was true, wear an expression of faint melancholy, but this, in conjunction with his learning and brilliant intellect, made him all the more appealing. He wielded considerable influence upon people. He deliberately avoided ill-natured argument, remarking: "God did not command us to break bread with one another like quarreling dogs." [7] It cost him much grief to be obliged to live at odds with other Christians because of his views. Far from being a rabble rouser, Denck was soft-spoken and inclined to avoid controversy: "I open my mouth against my will and reluctantly speak of God before the world; but the world so presses upon me that I dare not keep silent, and in his name alone I would speak cheerfully, hard as that always is for me." [8]

Here, then, was one of the most engaging personalities in the whole age of Reformation. But because he held religious views which differed from those of the official party, he was driven from pillar to post and could find nowhere to lay his head.

To be sure, Denck did not have the stature of the Wittenberg Reformer. Luther's gigantic personality overshadowed all other men of the sixteenth century. It was inevitable that an antagonist like Denck should have been crushed by the greater man. "There are some brothers who think they have penetrated the Gospel to its ultimate depths, and whoever does not agree in all points with what they say must be a heretic of heretics," Denck lamented. [9]

Denck had met Thomas Müntzer in Nuremberg, and had learned from him to see a good many questions in a light different from Luther's. The first controversial point was the question of infant baptism, which, Denck pointed out, was never stipulated in the Bible. He himself had been baptized by Balthasar Hubmaier, and he in turn baptized Hans Hut, an important figure in the history of chiliasm. Denck moved gradually toward the

[6] *Hans Denck, Ein Vorkämpfer undogmatischen Christentums,* ed. Schwindt (no date), p. 56.
[7] L. Keller: *Ein Apostel der Wiedertäufer* (1882), p. 91.
[8] *Hans Denck,* p. 31.   [9] Ibid., p. 33.

Anabaptist position. He defined baptism as the "covenant of good conscience with God." But it was not of central importance to his religious ideas, as has been alleged. In fact, Denck considered ceremonies in general as superficial and secondary. The imitation of Jesus was what counted; ceremonies were justified only if they furthered love. Anyone who thought to achieve salvation merely by practicing certain forms was steeped in superstition. Inner baptism was far more important than outer baptism. Toward the end of his life Denck went so far as to declare: "Therefore I would not baptize at all." [1] These are not the words of a narrow-minded "sectarian," but of a man on the road to a spiritualistic conception of Christianity. Although the question of new religious rites is becoming increasingly important in modern times, the danger of ritualism must never be overlooked; all ceremonies tend to degenerate into sterility, as the prophets of the Old Testament warned. The question of baptism simply led Denck to survey other aspects of Protestant doctrine with a critical mind.

Far more vital to Denck was the question of a Christian conduct of life. The followers of Luther were particularly touchy on this matter, for here was the weak point in their doctrine. Schwenkfeld had already laid his finger on it, and Luther must privately have known that his own answer was inadequate. But faced with the religious lukewarmness of the Protestant masses, Luther had retreated into a plaintive pessimism. Denck was unwilling to accept such a point of view, which to him was tantamount to capitulation. Christ had "paved the way that no man can find of his own accord in order that we walk upon it." [2] The mode of life is what counts, for "Christ cannot truly recognize anyone who does not imitate him in this life." [3] This position scarcely leads back to a justification by works alone. Moreover, any serious effort to walk in the way of the Apostles generates such a force that even unbelievers feel its impact.

Since Denck put this stress upon the evangelical life, he like-

---

[1] Ibid., p. 61.   [2] Ibid., p. 29.
[3] In W. Wiswedel: *Bilder und Führergestalten aus dem Täufertum* (1928), I, 148.

wise assigned far greater importance than Luther to love as a supplement to faith. Denck did not belittle faith; he regarded it as obedience to God. But in the style of the primitive Christians he upheld love as the supreme attitude for the Christian, superior alike to faith and to hope. Denck thought of love as a spiritual force; the more the Christian loved love, the closer he was to salvation. "Therefore a man should not eat a morsel of bread without considering how God loves him and how he should love God." [4] There was a spark of love in every man, Denck believed; but in those troubled times, he lamented, it had been extinguished in almost all men. Yet no matter how minute this spark might be, it came from the perfect love which was God himself. In this concern with *caritas* Denck sounded a chord which was seldom enough heard in the age of the Reformation.

Denck also began to think differently about revelation. Protestantism in general considered Scripture the sole source of revelation. Denck, too, esteemed the Bible "above all human treasures," but he did not equate it with God's Word. He was careful not to make an idol out of Holy Scripture. It was, to be sure, the light shining in the darkness, but it could not remove the darkness since it too had been written by human hands. Only "when the day, the infinite light dawns, when Christ rises in our hearts—only then will the darkness of unbelief be overcome. That has not yet happened in me," Denck added, with his characteristic modesty.[5] A man illumined by God could achieve salvation even without Holy Scripture. It depended upon the heart; Denck attributed revelatory powers to the spark in the soul, as the medieval mystics had done. The inner light, he said, "speaks clearly in everyone, in the deaf, dumb, and blind, even in unreasoning beasts, even in leaves and grass, stone and wood, heaven and earth, and all that is in them, that they may hear and do his will. In man alone, who does not want to be nothing and yet is even more nothing, is there resistance to it." [6]

It followed from Denck's conception of inner revelation that

---

[4] *Hans Denck*, p. 31. [5] Ibid., p. 24.
[6] Ibid., p. 36.

God and man are not wholly separate. The inner voice is a spark of the divine spirit, and shows man the way. This view did not lead Denck into the byway of pantheism. He explicitly ruled out pantheism in such words as: "Bliss is in us just as God is in all creatures, but not therefore of them, rather they are of him."[7] In his discussions of the inner spark, Denck anticipated a first principle of that deeply religious movement to be known as Quakerism. We may well meditate upon Denck's fundamental insight: "It is not enough for God to be in you; you must also be in God."[8]

Denck's independence as a religious thinker also appears in his appreciation of paradox. The perception of truths which can only be communicated to the human mind in the form of contradictions was very much the fashion of that age. Luther had a good deal to say on this question, and Sebastian Franck devoted a whole book to the subject. Denck, too, was much concerned with the paradoxical formulation of Christianity, and in various *Gegenschriften* (this was the term he coined for paradox) placed side by side such quotations as these:

"*I will not be angry for ever.*"[9]

"*And they will go away into eternal punishment.*"[1]

He sensed, however, that couching questions in paradoxical terms did little to solve the innate problem. In the age of Reformation, when everyone sought to prove his position by citing from the Bible, Denck reminded the contending parties that there was truth not only in their Biblical passages but also in those of their opponents.[2] Finally, Denck attempted to resolve the contradiction of paradoxes with a profound idea: "Two paradoxes must both be true, but one is included within the other as the lesser in the greater, as time in eternity. He who allows paradoxes to stand and cannot unite them lacks the ground of truth."[3] In these sketchy suggestions we may see flashes of the idea of synthesis, still totally unknown to the age of Reformation.

[7] Ibid., p. 34.   [8] Keller: op. cit., p. 130.
[9] Jer. iii, 12.   [1] Matt. xxv, 46.
[2] Cf. Heberle: "*Hans Denck und sein Büchlein vom Gesetz,*" in *Theologische Studien und Kritiken* (1851), p. 149.
[3] Keller: op. cit., p. 70.

All these ideas of Denck culminated in his ideal of freedom. He believed that "in matters of faith all must proceed freely, willingly, and unforced." He had not too long to live when he voiced the touching plaint: "It seems to me an unjust law that it should not be permissible for one man to think differently from another." [4] What a frail voice was raised here; like a violin string drawn too taut, it sounded only a thin note and snapped all too easily. How many religious persecutions in the past, how many political persecutions in the present, have arisen because it was not "permissible for one man to think differently from another"? Men set up freedom of conscience as an ideal, but for the most part they do not have the strength to put it into practice. The men of the Reformation, too, called for freedom of conscience, but in their turn trampled dissent underfoot. It is to Denck's eternal credit that in his darkest hours he maintained his belief in freedom of thought. He made every effort not to hate his religious adversaries, and he insisted that although he had been barred from the community of believers, he had not allowed his heart to be turned away from them. A true religious spirit, not any weakness, underlay his admonition: "But you, if you hear your brothers say something that is strange to you, do not at once contradict, but hear whether it be right, whether you may accept it. If you do not like to hear it, still, do not condemn him, and if it appears to you that he is mistaken, consider whether you may not be more mistaken." [5]

It is revealing of the tragedy of the Reformation age that there was no place within Protestantism for such a man, who was purity itself. There was no room for him in the inn and he was forced to take refuge in the stable, thus enacting the symbol of eternal Christendom.

Protestantism did the same thing to the entire Anabaptist movement, of which Denck was certainly one of the leading figures.[6] The Anabaptists refused to take oaths, rejected secular authority, and resorted to rioting and rebellion. Official Protestant-

[4] Ibid., p. 223.　　　　　　　　　　[5] *Hans Denck*, pp. 28, 29.
[6] Cf. Heberle: *"Hans Denck und die Ausbreitung seiner Lehre,"* in *Theologische Studien und Kritiken* (1855), pp. 847, 872.

ism felt obliged to use the strongest measures to suppress them. Thousands of them suffered martyrdom for their religious convictions. Even when they themselves renounced violence, the determination to annihilate them persisted. To this day their Christian motivations, their determination to live in accordance with the Gospel, remain widely misunderstood.

Michael Servetus

Michael Servetus was a gaunt man of medium height with lively, melancholy eyes. He came from a prosperous Spanish family. In temperament he was the typical Spaniard, proud and passionate, restless and enterprising, a "fiery spirit, like a salamander, living always in the presence of flames."[7] Even though Servetus left his native land early in life, and was never to return there for fear of the Inquisition, he nonetheless retained his Spanish character, and can only be properly understood in terms of it. He belonged to the country which, in that same century, produced Teresa of Avila, Ignatius of Loyola, and John of the Cross, and which for centuries had fought for its Christian faith against Mohammedanism. Servetus himself was no saint, but a highly emotional man, of uncommonly rich endowments, possessed of more than a touch of genius, equipped with sparkling wit, indomitable energy, and an extraordinary imagination. It was said he had something of the Don Quixote about him. Certainly there was a fantastical side to his character; he was convinced, for instance, that by virtue of his first name he was called to be one of the greatest fellow warriors of the archangel Michael. Armed with this apocalyptic belief he dashed headforemost against all realities with as much zeal as the knight of the woeful countenance. He became the greatest heretic of Spain. This strictly Catholic country has, however, exulted in its radiant saints far more than in Servetus the heretic, who remains unhonored and unsung in his own country to this very day.

[7] Tollin: *Das Lehrsystem Michael Servets* (1876), II, 2.

After leaving Spain, Servetus studied jurisprudence in Toulouse and then turned to medicine. In science he proved to have keen gifts of observation. He considered all study of nature a branch of divine philosophy. Long before Harvey he discovered the circulation of the blood, though his discovery had no consequences for medical science. His treatise on digestion, however, based on his own experience as a physician, attracted considerable attention. In his younger years he had published a new edition of Ptolemy; this, however, was soon outmoded by the great discovery of Copernicus.

Alongside his scientific work, Servetus was deeply concerned with religious matters. His natural piety was intensified by the multitude of religious problems that were in the air during the sixteenth century. As a youth he had been a zealous Catholic. But he began studying the Bible and the writings of the Reformers, and this reading transformed him into an opponent of the papacy, which he came to regard as an anti-Christian institution. His thoughts began to circle incessantly around the figure of Christ, whom he hailed as his sole master. In the end he had constructed a whole theory around Jesus. Jesus was the heart of the world, Servetus said. He enjoined Christians to forget the Christ of dogma and return to the Christ of the Bible.

By temperament Servetus was not one to belong to any guild; his doctrines, too, show the stamp of his strong individuality. Thus, he became a passionate antagonist of the doctrine of the Trinity, which he sought to replace by a system "whose novelty, originality, and boldness cannot be denied." [8] The dogma of the three eternal hypostases in the Deity, which had been established at the Council of Nicaea, was incompatible with the unity of the divine Being, Servetus argued. The doctrine of the Trinity necessarily led to polytheism and was therefore a diabolic delusion.

He traced more and more of the evils of Christendom to the doctrine of the Trinity, and was soon referring to it as "a three-headed Cerberus." In penalty for its conception of the Trinity,

[8] Kampschulte: *Johann Calvin, seine Kirche und sein Staat* (1869), II, 170.

Servetus declared, the Church had been saddled with the papacy, and thus had lost Christ.[9] He became convinced that his mission was to overthrow this insidious doctrine and set Christianity back upon the right path. This was the purpose of his *Christianismi restitutio* (1553), "The Restoration of Christianity." The title itself reveals his reformist intentions—and in the case of Servetus what he intended is more important than what he accomplished. Christianity, he believed, had to retrace its way back to the primitive church. This was the only hope for preserving the unity of the church. The structure of the church must be built anew, from the foundation. This task of restoration was the great battle of the angels which he foresaw, wherein he would stand at the side of St. Michael. He was completely serious about this; it was no idle notion. He believed that God himself had appointed him for this mission, and that he would risk God's wrath to neglect it. He gave up his whole life to this high calling—and did so with premonitions of his early, violent death.

Protestantism, Servetus held, had committed the serious error of accepting dogmas that had formed during the first three centuries of Christianity, for it was these very dogmas which had governed the whole later evolution of the religion. There was a good deal of validity to this argument. Granting that Servetus was somewhat partial to the pre-Nicaean Church Fathers Tertullian and Irenaeus, he was generally opposed to applying philosophical notions to religion. For religious philosophy he wanted to substitute the Bible which, as he pointed out, contains no statements on the Trinity. Yet, with Servetus also, the religious concern became a theological one, and a good many of his subtle arguments are understandable only to the professional theologian. His Christology, too, is a highly obscure affair, and is hardly intelligible on a simple basis.

The sixteenth century considered Servetus' "restoration of Christianity" not as a theoretical exercise, but as a direct attack upon a sanctified tradition. For the Catholics, of course, his whole approach was unacceptable. They would not even enter into dis-

[9] Ibid., I, 154.

cussions with him. He was aware of this, and was careful not to publish his works under his own name. But his authorship came out; indirectly denounced by Calvin, he was arrested by the Catholic Inquisition in Vienne, where he had been serving as personal physician to the archbishop of that city. At the interrogation he denied that his name was Servetus, and subsequently managed to escape his jailers. In the course of his flight he came to Geneva. He thought to remain here only briefly, and had already rented a boat for continuing his journey, when he made the mistake of attending a sermon by Calvin. In church he was recognized, and there were officers ready to arrest him immediately after the services. What was more, he was made to stand trial, for Calvin's Protestantism laid as much store on the question of the Trinity as did Rome. The Geneva Reformer considered Servetus' arguments sheer "madness" which could only have sprung from an "arrogant spirit." As an "obstinate heretic" he had all his property confiscated without more ado. He was badly treated in prison. It is understandable, therefore, that Servetus was rude and insulting at his confrontation with Calvin. Unfortunately for him, at this time Calvin was fighting to maintain his weakening power in Geneva. Calvin's opponents used Servetus as a pretext for attacking the Geneva Reformer's theocratic government. It became a matter of prestige—always the sore point for any dictatorial regime—for Calvin to assert his power in this respect. He was forced to push the condemnation of Servetus with all the means at his command.

Not only a struggle for power was involved. The theological problem was of no less importance. Other eminent Protestants besides Calvin were honestly horrified by Servetus' theses, which struck them as arrant blasphemy. Martin Bucer, the eminent German Reformer, stated from the pulpit that this man should have his intestines ripped from his body. When the Geneva Council solicited the opinion of other Swiss churches, all unanimously condemned Servetus and branded his views as error contrary to Scripture. With that, Servetus' fate was sealed. The Geneva Council pronounced the death sentence upon the forty-two-year-old heretic.

On the morning of October 27, 1553 a silent procession led Servetus to the stake. Guillaume Farel, the great orator of the Reformation and the man who first converted Geneva, was called specially from Neuchâtel so that he might, if possible, convert the unfortunate before his death. Farel walked beside the condemned man, and kept up a constant barrage of words, in complete insensitivity to what Servetus might be feeling. All he had in mind was to extort from the prisoner an acknowledgement of his theological error—a shocking example of the soulless cure of souls. After some minutes of this, Servetus ceased making any reply and prayed quietly to himself. When they arrived at the place of execution, Farel announced to the watching crowd: "Here you see what power Satan possesses when he has a man in his power. This man is a scholar of distinction, and he perhaps believed he was acting rightly. But now Satan possesses him completely, as he might possess you, should you fall into his traps."

When the executioner began his work, Servetus whispered with trembling voice: "Oh God, Oh God!" The thwarted Farel snapped at him: "Have you nothing else to say?" This time Servetus replied to him: "What else might I do, but speak of God!" Thereupon he was lifted onto the pyre and chained to the stake. A wreath strewn with sulfur was placed on his head. When the faggots were ignited, a piercing cry of horror broke from him. "Mercy, mercy!" he cried. For more than half an hour the horrible agony continued, for the pyre had been made of half-green wood, which burned slowly. "Jesus, Son of the eternal God, have mercy on me," the tormented man cried from the midst of the flames, testifying to the last moment of his life that his faith in his creed had not wavered.

Servetus, then, died as a martyr to his religious convictions. Whatever dross there may have been in his character, it was burned away by the flames. He belongs in that long line of sacrificed ones whose song, "God is love," runs along as the thorough bass under all the soprano voices, to use Kierkegaard's image.

But what of Calvin, who waylaid Servetus and saw him burned? The Spaniard had once approached Calvin, thinking to meet with a sympathetic reception, but had been severely rebuffed. For Calvin in his early days had had some doubts about the Nicene Creed himself, and for this reason was all the more intent upon proving himself free of heresy in this respect. Moreover, Calvin had difficulty understanding the opinions of others. He did not have the faculty for entering into another person's ideas. Rather, he tended to decide arbitrarily that such ideas were diabolically inspired. Seven years before Servetus passed through Geneva, Calvin had written to Farel: "If he comes here I will not let him depart alive, if I have any say in the affair." [1] Similarly, without the slightest awareness of the un-Christian nature of such feelings, Calvin wrote to his friend during the trial: "I hope that the verdict will call for the death penalty." [2] These authenticated statements of Calvin show how the highest and the lowest impulses may be inextricably mingled within a single human soul. Yet no amount of human or historical broad-mindedness can bring us to excuse Calvin's action. "Servetus' ashes will cry out against him as long as the names of these two men are known in the world." [3]

As for Calvin's coreligionists, they all, almost without exception, approved of the burning of Servetus. The guilt, then, must be borne by all of Protestantism. Ironically enough, the execution of Servetus did not really bolster the strength of the Geneva Reformation. On the contrary, as Fritz Barth has indicated, it "gravely compromised Calvinism and put into the hands of the Catholics, to whom Calvin wanted to demonstrate his Christian orthodoxy, the very best weapon for the persecution of the Huguenots, who were nothing but heretics in their eyes." [4] The procedure against Servetus served as a model of a Protestant

---

[1] *J. Calvins Lebenswerk in seinen Briefen* (1909), I, 237.
[2] Ibid., p. 484.
[3] J. L. Mosheim: *Anderweitiger Versuch einer vollständigen und unpartheyischen Ketzergeschichte* (1748), p. 239.
[4] Fritz Barth: *Calvin und Servet* (1909), p. 22.

heretic trial. And—how we wish we did not have to say this—it differed in no respect from the methods of the medieval Inquisition. Thus every line written to condone the burning of Servetus was likewise an apology for Torquemada. The victorious Reformation, too, was unable to resist the temptations of power. The manner in which Protestantism dealt with its heretics is far from edifying. In taking the course they did, the Protestants lost any right to protest against Catholic persecutions of heresy. As for the monument to Servetus which was erected half a century ago by the "grateful sons of Calvin," that is a belated but gratifying testimony to Protestant repentance and atonement.

Protestantism in its turn was forced to discover that pyres could not refute ideas. The burning proved altogether useless, for Servetus' ideas lived on. They were taken up by Lelio and Fausto Sozzini and carried further. The Sozzinis, uncle and nephew, did not have the Spaniard's speculative fervor. They were more sober and above all far more rationalistic. But through their activities, Antitrinitarianism became, along with Anabaptism, the second great heretical movement of the age of Reformation. It has entered history under the name of Socianism. The Socianists criticized the theory of satisfaction (the doctrine that the sufferings and death of Christ satisfied the requirements of God's justice and thus prepared the way for the forgiveness of sins) as well as the doctrine of the Trinity. Socianism put more emphasis on "rationalism" than Catholicism or Protestantism, though it was still a far cry from the radical rationalism of modern man. Like all the offshoots of Protestantism, this movement had to endure severe persecutions. Nevertheless, the Socianists have persisted down to the present day under the name of Unitarians.

Sebastianus Castellio

We know what was in the minds of the burners of heretics. They thought to preserve Christianity from a plague, and they felt that heretics had no right to exist. From scattered utterances we can also reconstruct the state of mind of those Christians who endured the terrible martyrdom. But what were the emotions of those who stood in the mob at an auto-da-fé? Out of those anonymous throngs Sebastianus Castellio emerges and affords us some insight into the souls of those gaping onlookers.

In January 1540 when he was a young man of twenty-five, Castellio attended an execution at Lyons. He had stood fascinated, unable to turn his eyes away from the terrible spectacle. It was no hunger for sensation that compelled him to see the horrible process through to the end. Rather, some deeper compulsion held him rooted to the spot; he stared fixedly at the stake, stunned by the intrepid bearing of the victim and horrified by the cruelty of the execution. That experience marked Castellio for life. What he had seen haunted him day and night. He could not shake off that vision of unspeakable torment. To him it was impossible to understand how Christians could do this to a human being.

The immediate effect of this experience was Castellio's defection from Catholicism. He could no longer accept a religion which employed such means to remain in power. And so he fled from France to throw in his lot with the Reformation. In Geneva he worked with Calvin for some time, and conducted himself with exceptional bravery when pestilence broke out in the city. But, by and by, he became involved in differences with the Reformer, and resigned his teaching post in Geneva. Rather than compromise his principles, he preferred to make a pinched livelihood for himself and his family by working as a proofreader for a printer, and later as a reader at the University of Basel. Here was a man of staunch and independent spirit.

This independence brought upon Castellio the suspicion of heresy. In the strict sense of the word he was certainly no heretic. Nevertheless, he made a great and honorable contribution to the tradition of dissent. When the Protestants began to imitate the Catholics and Servetus' pyre blazed up in Geneva, Castellio's memories at Lyons came to life once more. This was one thing he had never expected from the opposite camp. He was shocked to the core. His conscience demanded that he protest—and for that protest Castellio's name deserves to be mentioned with reverence in the history of Christian thought.

What he had to say must appear all too obvious nowadays. But in his time his protest was anything but commonplace; had it been so, his contemporaries would not have resisted it so fiercely. Castellio was not the first to protest against the fearful practice of burning heretics. Other people had come to realize that killing heretics was incompatible with Christianity. But their objections had remained isolated statements that carried no great weight. Castellio collected all these statements and combined them into a principled assault upon persecution of heretics, an attack of such density that it was extremely difficult to refute. Nor did he rest his case upon the mere quoting of authorities. Rather, he supported his objection with a structure of religious argument which made it all the more impressive.

His first argument revolved upon the problem: What is a heretic? Everyone talks about heretics, feels abhorrence for them, and crosses himself as if they were the personification of evil. But what actually is a heretic? What must a man have done to merit such an appellation? The Bible offers no definition; the Old Testament speaks mostly of blasphemers. Castellio's answer was: "After diligent investigation of what a heretic may be, I come to no other conclusion than that we are wont to charge with heresy all those who are not of our opinion." [5] What an astonishing formulation—astonishing in its simplicity! There can be no specific content to the idea of "a heretic" because the nature of heresy has been constantly changing through the centuries. It is a relative, not an absolute concept, assuming a different form in every age and every religion. But mostly it is a convenient term of abuse, and Christians have made more than liberal use of it for that purpose. Castellio's definition of a heretic exposed the intellectual fraud that men had been committing for centuries.

The next point for Castellio to tackle was the question: Is it permissible to persecute heretics? Under the pseudonym of Mar-

[5] In Peter Hemmi: *Sebastian Castellio* (no date), p. 51.

tinus Bellius, he published a significant treatise, *De non puniendis gladio hereticis* (1554), in which it was maintained that the sword of secular power must not be employed to punish heretics. How many centuries had gone by before a Christian clearly and specifically examined the moral basis of persecution? Here was Castellio's reply to the burning of Servetus. To strengthen his protest, he assembled a considerable number of pronouncements by Erasmus, Luther, Augustine, and others, all directed against the idea of persecution. To persecute men for the sake of religion is irreligious, Castellio held, since God desired the salvation of all men and had created none for damnation. (This was, on Castellio's part, a pointed attack upon Calvin's doctrine of predestination.) Nothing but evil could come out of the widespread mania for condemnation among Christians. *Let us not condemn one another, but rather, if we are more learned, let us also be better and more merciful. For it is certain that the better a man knows the truth, the less is he inclined to condemn others, as the example of Christ and his Apostles shows. . . . When I examine myself, I see that my sins are so great and so many that I would be unable to believe I should receive forgiveness from God if I were to condemn others.*[6]

Then again, Castellio asked: "Is it not absurd to employ earthly weapons in a spiritual struggle?" He pointed out, as others had done before him, that it was counter to Scripture to pull up the supposed weeds which the Lord had expressly commanded should be let stand until the harvest.

Nor were these arguments presented as dry formalistic matters. Castellio's strong feelings can be felt in every line of his writing. "To kill a man does not mean to 'defend a doctrine,' but to kill a man. When the Genevans burned Servetus, they did not defend a doctrine, but killed a man."[7]

For his third and final argument Castellio posed the question: What would Christ do if he were here now? There is a touching simplicity about this question. But woe to the Christian

[6] In J. Maehly: *Sebastian Castellio* (1862), pp. 40, 41.
[7] Hemmi: op. cit., p. 58.

who thinks to dismiss it as a piece of absurd naïveté. What Christ would do is actually a guiding principle for Christians; it is a question they should always be silently asking themselves. Certainly no one can say that Christ would have called for men to be tortured for their beliefs. As Castellio put it: *Christ demanded of us that we don the white dress of a pure and holy life. But what instead occupies our thoughts? We do not dispute concerning the way to Christ, but on his relationship to God the Father, on the Trinity, predestination, freedom of the will, the nature of God, the angels, the state of the soul after death—on a multitude of things which are not essential to salvation; things which, in truth, we can never know unless our hearts are pure, for these things must be comprehended spiritually.*[8]

Not only are Christians preoccupied with questions which divert them from what should be their true effort, but they also obstruct others from making that effort. "When one man endeavors to obtain the white dress for himself, that is, to live in a holy and just way, all unanimously rise against him, especially if he is not wholly of their own opinion in some small point."[9]

It was especially horrifying that Christians should spread the mantle of Christ over their crimes. Castellio cried out: *O Christ, Creator and King of the world, do you see these things? Can it be that you have become so altogether different from what you once were, so cruel and self-contradictory? When you were still on earth, none was milder, gentler, more forbearing; like a sheep before its shearer you uttered no sound though you were beaten and spat upon. Have you now wholly changed? I implore you, by the holy name of your Father, to ask whether you really ordain such punishments for those who disagree with our masters in interpretation of your commandments and instructions; whether you would truly have them plunged under water, the flesh flayed from their bones with clubs, their wounds strewn with salt, pricked by swords, roasted over feeble fires, and with all possible agonies tormented as long as possible? O Christ, do you*

[8] Sebastianus Castellio: *Traité des Hérétiques*, ed. Choisy (1913), p. 13.
[9] Hemmi: op. cit., p. 48.

333

command and do you approve these things? Are those who tor-
ture these victims really your representatives in this butcher's
work? [1]

This treatise of Castellio's was one of the first manifestoes for
freedom of conscience. The Christian's obligation to tolerance,
Castellio explained, derives from the commandment of love.
Everyone who bears the name of Christian must be prepared to
exercise gentleness and leniency. It is impossible to love one's
neighbor as oneself if one hates him for differing religious views.
Castellio roundly denounced the theologians' passion for "sound
doctrine." "Oh their sound doctrine! How Christ will despise them
on the Day of Judgment for this sound doctrine!" he wrote.[2] Instead of such zeal, Christian love, the willingness to bear another's
burden, must be practiced. By love he meant not the emotional
experience but the religious attitude whose genuineness emerges
precisely in a man's bearing toward those who think differently in
religious matters. Castellio's greatest contribution was his emphasis on love as the key element in Christianity. He may have
been no towering genius in the kingdom of the mind, yet we feel
ourselves more closely drawn to this simple Christian than to all
those intellectual giants who had forgotten the supreme commandment of Christianity, the one which God had equated with
himself.

If ever a century needed to hear this message, it was Castellio's. Yet his cry for tolerance was drowned out by the theological
noise of his time. His basic tenets met with sheer incomprehension. Théodore de Bèze called the demand for tolerance a "diabolical doctrine," and everything was done to bury such pernicious thoughts. But though his writings had but small effect, Castellio had pronounced the decisive verdict on persecution and the
treatment of heretics. His is the view that, in the light of the
Gospel and of eternity, emerges as the only just one.

---

[1] Castellio: op. cit., pp. 31, 32.   [2] Hemmi: op. cit., p. 61.

+   +

18

The Heretic's View of Himself

+   +

Sebastian Franck

To understand a man, we must first determine his position. Sebastian Franck coined two pungent maxims to describe his own: "Blessed is the man who lies hidden in darkness. No one who lies under the bench is envied." [1]

These words give us the key to Franck's personality. They also sum up the situation of the heretic. Under the bench is where he belongs. He regards life from this unenviable position. The heretics were true Christians in that they did not sit at the festive board of life, did not occupy honored and leading positions in the

[1] In W. Peuckert: *Sebastian Franck* (1943), p. 479.

world. It was their fate to be relegated to a corner, to crouch under the bench. And such a man, Franck could assert, is blessed.

Born around 1500 in poor circumstances, he was enabled by kind patrons to study for the priesthood. When not yet twenty, he met Luther in Heidelberg and was won over to the Reformation. But his adherence to the Protestant Church was brief. To his intense disillusionment he discovered that the doctrine of justification did little to induce inward change in a man. "How does it help us if we know that the Pope is a scoundrel, if we do not wish to change for the better ourselves?" Franck asked with that Christian earnestness which springs from self-reform. The ineffectuality of Protestant preaching, its lack of influence over the populace, convinced him that "just as there is a commandment to preach, there is likewise one to keep silent and go away." [2] Franck was one of the few men who reflected upon the consequences of the Reformation deeply and intelligently. He courageously drew his own conclusions and voluntarily laid down his Protestant ministry. It was preferable, he felt, to earn his livelihood as a soap maker than to continue preaching to deaf ears.

We must imagine this gifted intellectual standing over the boiling caldrons of soap, the hot vapors rising around him, if we would understand the import of this decision. Like a second St. Sebastian, he exposed himself to the arrows that came flying at him from all directions. In breaking first with Catholics and then with Protestants, in refusing to fit into any of the existing religious groups, he made himself an outlaw. As a result he was harried from place to place, for no city would take him in. His worst experiences took place in Ulm, where he was involved in a trial for heresy such as "had not been staged in Germany since the trial of Meister Eckhart in Cologne." [3] The documents of this trial have survived, and we can follow its course down to the most minute particulars.[4] When we examine these documents, we can only

[2] Sebastian Franck: *Paradoxa*, ed. Ziegler (1909), p. vii.
[3] A. Grolman: *Wesen und Wort am Oberrhein* (1935), p. 77.
[4] Cf. A. Hegler: *Beiträge zur Geschichte der Mystik in der Reformationszeit* (1906), pp. 113–216.

agree with what Will-Erich Peuckert says in his excellent biography of Sebastian Franck: "After reading the testimony of this preacher Martin Frecht, one has an urgent need to wash one's hands for five minutes. Even after this, one has the feeling that some of the slime of this detestable personality still clings. This was no open battle; the very air was poisoned with arrant lies." [5]

Franck was banished from the city of Ulm. Nor was this all. He had to contend with the malice not only of the Lutheran clergy, but also of such men as Erasmus. Harried on all sides, he ultimately found refuge in Switzerland but did not long enjoy his peace. Exhausted by all his difficulties, he passed away at the age of forty-three.

Franck was a double heretic, anathema alike to Catholics and Protestants. He proclaimed his independence of all the creeds of his time in a famous song:

> *Popish I can and will not be,*
> *Lutheran I can and will not be,*
> *Zwinglian I can and will not be,*
> *Nor Anabaptist will I be.*

People saw these words as an outright defiance to all existing religion. But Franck was neither a nay-sayer nor defiant. Rather, he insisted on the necessity for re-evaluation. "We must unlearn all that we have learned in early life from our Papists, and must change everything we have received from the Popes, Luther, and Zwingli—must change all that we have absorbed and thought to be true." [6] Again and again, he declared, man must cast all his old views into the melting caldron and pour them out in new shapes. Only thus does he remain inwardly alive. This heretical soap maker was a man who "penetrated more deeply than a hundred churchmen and theologians into the nature of Christ and the great truth." [7]

It was not enough for Franck to reject the existing confessions. He was also evolving a positive ideal which he de-

---

[5] Peuckert: op. cit., p. 375.
[6] In Hegler: *Geist und Schrift bei Sebastian Franck* (1892), p. 58.
[7] Peuckert: *Die grosse Wende* (1948), p. 365.

scribed in these words: *In our times three principal faiths which have a great following have arisen, these being Lutheran, Zwinglian, and Baptist. But the fourth is arising, and it shall sweep aside as needless all outward preaching, ceremony, sacrament, ban, and vocation and move toward an invisible spiritual church in union of spirit and faith assembled among all peoples and governed solely by the eternal invisible word of God without any outward mediations.*[8]

It was no new church which Franck awaited. Rather, he had something of that certain hope that Christ expresses in the Gospel of John when he speaks of worshipping God neither on this mountain nor in Jerusalem, but in the spirit and in truth. Very likely Franck underestimated the problem of form. He gave too little consideration to the fact that every religion must create a vessel into which it can pour its content. This is in the nature of things; we must understand the organizational activities of churches as arising out of such an imperative. A man like Franck, who did think in historical terms, should have realized this. Nevertheless, we must agree with him that the formalization of religion also involves externalization, and thus a tendency to falsify the truth of the religion. As Franck put it: *As soon as people attempt to frame Christianity within rules and fit it into a prescribed law and order, it stops being Christianity. There is a general failure to understand that Christians are handed over to the Holy Ghost. The New Testament is not a book, doctrine, or law, but the Holy Ghost. Where God's Spirit is, there freedom must be; there Moses must keep silent, all laws withdraw, and let no one be so bold as to prescribe law, rules, order, goals, and measures to the Holy Ghost, nor attempt to reach, govern, and lead those who belong to him.*[9]

In Franck's symbolic conception of the Bible, Scripture itself became "eternal allegory." Christ's Passion, death, and Resurrection must be repeated daily in the soul of each Christian. In this "Christian philosophy" of his, Franck transmitted the ideas of me-

[8] Franck: op. cit., p. xiv.
[9] In Peuckert: *Sebastian Franck*, p. 233.

dieval mysticism—with which he was well acquainted—to modern spiritualism.

The book Franck published under the title of *Paradoxa* may be considered the manifesto of the "fourth religion." His purpose was not to startle the reader by setting contradictory statements side by side. Rather, he was concerned with truths which lie upon a higher plane than can be discerned by common sense. What Franck did was to work out the antinomies of life's duality with an uncanny, almost frightening acuteness. "Everything in the world must be reversed, must be in opposition to God, and all things must be different from what they seem. Thus seeming and being will eternally remain opposed and God's word will remain an eternal paradox." [1] As in the New Testament the wisdom of the world is called folly in God, so all things, Franck held, are in truth different from what they outwardly appear to be. "Stand against and you stand with God, for if God is even, the world is odd." [2]

Franck's prescription that the true Christian must lie "under the bench" and be envied by none is a direct corollary to this magnificent revaluation of values. The Christian cannot triumph in this life because "victory is with the defeated." [3] This insight into the victory of the defeated led Franck to a new view of history. He refused to restrict the Kingdom of God to Christians, and cheerfully counted "Plato, Plotinus, Hermes, and other illustrious philosophers" [4] among the blessed. For Franck had stumbled upon the perception that men were not the guardians of the Kingdom; that it had to be understood as an aspect of God's universality, whose vastness men could not even conceive. But Franck's contemporaries in the sixteenth century were not able to grasp this universalist vision. It was as incomprehensible to them as his fourth religion, and they expelled Franck from their midst. Yet he, as had few of his contemporaries, had experienced the *theologia crucis* and had kept himself free from all *theologia gloriae*.

Franck's insights arose out of the combination of his religio-

[1] Franck: op. cit., p. 93.   [2] Ibid., p. 41.
[3] Ibid., p. 32.   [4] Ibid., p. xxxvii.

philosophical views and his personal destiny. He who has never lain under the bench will always see the heretic from outside. Franck, having himself suffered the heretic's fate, was equipped to understand heresy from inside. He had lost all fear of the dread name of heretic, had liberated himself inwardly from this foolish terror. Among heretics, he emphasized, he had found "many dear, godly folk who have more spirit in one finger than the Antichrist in all his sects." [5]

As a non-partisan, Franck was excellently suited to achieve his new comprehension of heresy. There is a noble statement of his describing his free point of view: *Belonging to no party and having no bias I can, God be praised, read all, and am captive of no sect or man on earth. All the devout please my heart, though in many trivial things they may be mistaken, and I am sworn to no man's word, but to Christ, my God and Mediator, to whose obedience I alone acknowledge my reason captive. I cast out no heretic, for that would be to pour out the child with the bath water, and hurl the truth away with the lies. Rather I separate the gold from the filth. For there is scarce a pagan, philosopher, or heretic who did not happen on some good thing, which I would not therefore cast away, but revere as fine gold and find something of my God in heathens and heretics. . . . Therefore a truth to me is a truth and God grant I may love it, whosoever says it; even heretics, and for their other errors I ask God that he forgive them or else uncover them, that they may know them and refrain. And I am accustomed to error and misdoing in all men and hate no man on earth for that, but bewail, know and see myself, my own wretchedness and condition, in them.* [6]

This touching statement sprang from a deep love of truth and a humble heart. The soap maker had arrived at that kind of insight which makes no distinctions of persons; like the Apostle Peter after his experience with Cornelius, he was led to recognize among all people some who are pleasing to God. He was not too

[5] In Carl Alfred Hase: *Sebastian Franck von Wört* (1869), p. 39.
[6] In Hegler: op. cit., p. 247.

fine to learn from every one, having seen that all heretics stand for truth along with their errors. Only such spiritual openness can serve as a basis for true understanding of the phenomenon of heresy.

At the same time Franck was quite aware of the negative aspects of heresy. He knew that heretics were prone to fall into the same error as the church, claiming truth for themselves alone. "In all times there have been sects and bands; Arius would not admit anyone a Christian unless he were Arian; likewise Ebion, Kerinth, Nestor, Pelagius, Manichaeus, etc.—all claimed our Lord for their own. . . . So today the folly persists, each sect seizing and claiming God for itself alone."[7] Franck himself escaped this trap only because he clung to his independence and would join no party. Here was one heretic who was not a sectarian, who did not share the delusion of having unique claims upon God. He had the courage to treasure spiritual independence. He was perpetually enjoining men not to tread the common road nor to follow the crowd. "Every man," he declared, "must always suffer, die, go to heaven in the Body of Christ himself, and none can suffer, die, believe, or be a Christian for any other."[8]

It is a great pity that Franck's literary account of the history of heresy is not all that one might have hoped for and expected. To his immensely popular universal history, *Chronika, Zeitbuch, und Geschichtsbibel,* he appended a "Chronicle of the Roman Heretics" in which he listed a large number of heretics in alphabetical order. This chronicle is no longer of importance to the contemporary reader for its historical material—in fact, Franck borrowed heavily from a Dominican source. Its importance lies in the statement of principle with which Franck prefaced his account: *I would not have you think that I regard as heretics all those whom I have here included in the catalogue of heretics. The verdict upon their faith is not mine, but that of the Pope, of the Councils and of their adherents, whom I here cite as judges. For if the judgment were mine, I might turn everything*

[7] In Peuckert: *Sebastian Franck,* p. 402.
[8] Franck: op. cit., p. 149.

around and canonize many of these, making saints of those who are here denounced as heretics and consigned to the devil.[9]

It is plain from these words that Franck had no respect for the old stories of heretics with their stereotyped accusations. The bold notion had occurred to him that he might transform the book of heretics into a roll of honor. No medieval man before him would have hit upon so revolutionary an idea. It is as though the blinkers which had for centuries covered the eyes of Christians were being removed with one swift pull. Suddenly men were being shown the truth: that heresy was not deviltry, nor spiritual outlawry. The heretic was no criminal; rather, he was fulfilling a mission imposed upon him by God, one which brought him disgrace, woe, and even death. Franck saw quite clearly that "true Christians have always been heretics to the world," [1] and that on this earth truth is always decried as heresy.

Since Franck only intimated his new understanding of heresy in a few scattered lines, his ideas remained unclear to many. His opponents found it an easy matter to defame and discredit Franck, thereby nipping a dangerous doctrine in the bud. It was Luther's unkind condemnation in particular which dealt the death blow to that fourth religion, which Franck had felt was already on the way.

---

[9] Franck: Preface to *Chronika der römischen Ketzer* (1536), no pagination.
[1] Ibid.

19

Heretic Philosophy

✛ ✛

Giordano Bruno

Giordano Bruno came into the world in the little town of Nola, situated between Vesuvius and the sea. Fanciful writers have concluded from this fact that there was something volcanic about Bruno from birth. He scarcely looked it, for he was a small man, of frail build, with a pallid face, a pair of glowing, deep-set eyes, and chin framed in a dark beard. Yet spiritually Bruno was indeed a volcanic personality. His genius spewed out a fiery hail of inspirations. In his life as well as his work he was an arch-heretic.

Like so many of the heretics, Bruno was a product of monasticism. About 1563, at the age of fourteen, he entered the Dominican Order. His was the same South Italian monastery to which Thomas Aquinas had once belonged—but Bruno had nothing in common intellectually with that orderly, categorizing mind.

It is hard to say what motivated Bruno to enter a monastery. Perhaps he was obeying an inner vocation; perhaps this was the only way for him to obtain the education he longed for. In any case, Bruno wore the Dominican habit for many years. He was steeped in the writings of the scholastics. Of these, he was particularly fond of Raymond Lully (1235–1315), the much-misunderstood Spanish thinker. Bruno regarded Lully's "great art" not as a curiosity, but as a device which could and should be made to yield intellectual fruit once more. Monasticism and Lully, both significant and expressive aspects of the Middle Ages, were the two great influences upon Bruno's thought.

But Bruno did not remain a monk forever. He was ill fitted for the cloister and the life of contemplation. By the time he was eighteen he was already doubting the Trinity. In conversation with fellow monks he was so incautious as to speak warmly about certain heretics. He threw away his images of the saints and advised one of the brethren to read a more sensible book than the *Lives of the Holy Fathers.* The Inquisition began to take an interest in Bruno. In order to avoid interrogation, he broke his monastic vows and took to his heels.

With his departure from the monastery, a radically new phase of Bruno's life began. After remaining for a time in Italy, he went to Geneva. Here, however, he found that he was even less in sympathy with Calvinistic spirituality than he had been with the Catholicism he had just forsaken. Calvinistic austerity was repellent to his southern temperament; his natural gaiety revolted against its mood of gloom. He began to feel a veritable hatred for puritanical Calvinism and took up arms against it in all his writings.

After the brief sojourn in Geneva he went on to Toulouse, where he began to deliver lectures. He did the same in England for some time, then moved to Germany. Here, too, he stirred up a hornet's nest by his attacks upon the academics, whom he despised for making a trade out of philosophy. Soon he was again making his restless pilgrimage through the countries of Europe, vainly seeking to settle down somewhere, and nowhere finding what he hoped for. His own restlessness drove him on from place to place. Each refuge was abandoned for a new sphere of activity. Wherever he went he manifested a joyous and combative courage, never shrinking from the perils of life, driven by an insatiable hunger to meet new people and become acquainted with new views.

Bruno's life of restless wandering came to a sudden end when, seduced by longing for his native land, he went to Venice. He had long been thinking of coming to a reconciliation with the Catholic Church, if it would not require him to return to the Dominican Order. Bruno's relationship to Catholicism had undergone a good many vacillations; at times he would lash out against it in his writings, at times confess that the Catholic Church was "after all dearest" to him. In Venice he was handed over to the Inquisition by a piece of shameful treachery, and thrown into prison to await his trial.

The documents of these proceedings have been published. Bruno at first failed to recognize his peril. He thought he could go scot free by readily co-operating with the Inquisition. Therefore he watered down his statements, contending that certain remarks had been carelessly uttered and were not to be taken too seriously. He had not really meant it when he called monasticism the quintessence of superstition, avarice, and hypocrisy, nor when he denounced the papal Curia for being a vicious tyranny. And he went to some trouble to testify to the greatest respect for Thomas Aquinas. With expressions of deepest sorrow and intense indignation he rejected all charges that he was anti-Christian. By means of these concessions he hoped to propitiate the Inquisition. Many heretics had tried the same tack before him, and had likewise been cruelly disappointed. In all ages executioners have never rewarded compliance.

After it became evident that the Inquisitors were listening to his statements with scarcely the same deference as his students had listened to his lectures, Bruno's confidence ebbed away. He was now forced to plead for his life by recanting all his heresies and promising amelioration.

The trial in Venice ended without a verdict. Nevertheless, Bruno's freedom was not restored to him. The Inquisition in Rome had taken a keen interest in his person, and demanded that Venice surrender the captive heretic. The independent-minded doges at first refused this request, but eventually backed down and consented.

Unfortunately we do not have much information about the proceedings of the Inquisition at Rome in Bruno's case. No one knows exactly what he went through during the long years of imprisonment in the Eternal City. No word of his fate reached the public, nor could any sign of fellowship penetrate the gloom of his prison. Abandoned by all men, Bruno languished in his cell. The Inquisition had hoped to break his spirit in this way. But as Bruno had formerly miscalculated the nature of the Inquisition, the Inquisition found that it had miscalculated the nature of its prisoner. The longer Bruno was held captive in his dark dungeon, the more he found himself. Through suffering he learned firmness. At his last interrogation he declared bluntly that he had nothing to repent of and nothing to recant. Instead of a broken man, the Inquisitional tribunal found a wonderfully composed heroic soul. Now he steadfastly refused to make any concessions, saying only that the Inquisition had misunderstood his doctrines. Finally the verdict was pronounced; he was declared an impenitent apostate. The last phase of the Roman trial has been described by an eyewitness. When the death sentence was announced, Bruno replied proudly to the judges: "Perhaps you proclaim your verdict against me with greater fear than I receive it." [1] Those were his last recorded words. After he had been degraded and excommunicated, he mounted the pile of faggots on February 17, 1600. Not a single cry of pain passed his lips, and when a crucifix was held before his dying eyes, he turned away with an expression of unspeakable contempt, as if to say that he would have nothing more to do with

[1] Giordano Bruno: *Gesammelte Werke*, ed. Kuhlenbeck (1909), VI, 232.

a religion that condemned its opponents to so bestial a death. According to the account of a Roman newspaper that was published two days afterward, Bruno had considered himself a martyr and had declared that he would die gladly because "his soul will rise out of the flames to Paradise."[2]

If we are to understand Bruno, we must think of him primarily as a poet-philosopher. He himself felt that a wondrous spiritual affinity existed among true poets, musicians, painters, and philosophers. Philosophy was poetry, and poetry divine truth. For Bruno, thinking was a matter of sketching the images born to his fiery imagination, and for that reason we must not expect precise concepts and definitions in his works. "He aims at intuitive thinking, at conceptual images of things, at illustration of ideals."[3] Indeed, he clad a large part of his philosophy in verse, in each case adding a commentary in dialogue form—a technique rather similar to that employed by his contemporary, St. John of the Cross, for expounding mysticism. Bruno's ideas were scarcely furthered by their appearance in verse, for they became less rather than more accessible to the intellect. He himself, it would seem, thought of himself as poet rather than philosopher. "A poet I am, and am so by God's grace," he announced proudly. "My own heart crowns my brow with laurel wreaths."[4]

What had drawn Bruno to the northern countries was not only their atmosphere of greater freedom, but also the fact that the north had nurtured a man who had exerted the most powerful attraction upon him. This man was Copernicus. Bruno's philosophical views sprang first and foremost from his reading of Copernicus' works. Copernicus had dedicated his *Of the Revolutions of Heavenly Bodies* to the Pope, only to incur the displeasure of the Church in spite of this. Luther was equally adamant toward the astronomer; the Copernican views, he said, were refuted by a single verse in the Book of Joshua. The novelty of the Copernican system frightened away a great many serious thinkers, but

[2] Ibid., p. 228.
[3] Moritz Carrière: *Die philosophische Weltanschauung der Reformationszeit* (1847), p. 373.
[4] Bruno: op. cit., V, 30, 31.

Bruno was captivated by it. He early became acquainted with Copernican astronomy, and it proved to be the great influence upon his life.

But Bruno was not a scientist and he did not apprehend Copernicus' arguments as a man of science. He grasped them more with his imagination than his intellect. In his studies of the Copernican system Bruno was struck by the concept of infinity. More than that, he was overwhelmed by the idea of myriads of stars set in inconceivable expanses of space. Consciousness of infinity, which comes to men through the study of astronomy, is one of the most powerful of human experiences. The idea of infinity is a metaphysical concept extremely difficult for the mind to grasp. But Bruno was one of those men who, like Kant, are rather inspired to religious reverence by the sublime spectacle of the starry firmament. The conception of an infinite number of worlds made Bruno literally ecstatic, sent him into transports of joy. It stirred him to a "cosmic consciousness"—a sense of being that men had forgotten since the days of the Gnostics. Bruno wrote: *It is neither natural nor proper to demand that the infinite be understood or proved to be finite. Rather, it appears to me natural and proper to strive infinitely for the infinite, since by its nature it is infinite. This striving is not a physical but a metaphysical movement which does not proceed from the imperfect directly to the perfect, but moves in a circular orbit through all the degrees of perfection, gradually approaching the infinite center which neither has been given form nor gives form.*[5] Shadow, too, leads to light, and although it is not the whole truth, it comes from the truth and has truth as its goal.

For all his intoxication with infinity, however, Bruno remembered that this vision was not for all men, but only for those who had wings. Even these could not "look upon the sun itself, see the universal Apollo and the absolute light in its highest and most sublime form; but at least its shadow, its Diana, the world, the universe, the nature which is in things, the light that is reflected in the darkness of matter, the light that shineth in the darkness."[6]

[5] Ibid., p. 75.   [6] Ibid., p. 184.

Herein lay Bruno's real heresy. It was this affirmation of infinity which the Church felt to be the stupendous threat to its system. For sweep away all boundaries and what was left of high and low? How could they go on speaking of the abode of the blessed, and of a heaven to which Christ had ascended? The Church had already indicted Copernicus' theory because it saw it as ruinous to its philosophical structure. This was even more true of Bruno's doctrine of infinity, which threatened to dissolve into nothingness the comfort offered by Christianity. The arching firmament of heaven, to which the Christian had looked up beseechingly, would be lost to him, and with it, his last safety. Instead of feeling that he enjoyed God's protection, he would be face to face with a yawning void. The dread inspired by such a view emerges in the outcry of Pascal: "The eternal silence of those infinite spaces makes me tremble." [7] It is not hard to understand why the Church so vehemently objected to Bruno's doctrine.

Bruno, however, saw nothing dreadful in the displacement of man and his earth from the center of the universe. He did not feel that he had lost his religious home thereby, although he was inspired to seek a new understanding of Christianity, to conceive of heaven as an inner reality. The concept of infinity seemed to him a proof of the incomprehensibility of God. He had the feeling that he had moved on from the God of the Church to a greater God who could not be confined within dogmatic definitions. This was not the Church's personal God, but a distinctly pantheistic God— a conception poets have always been partial to. As Bruno explained: *I consider the universe the infinite creation of an infinite divine omnipotence because I would think it unworthy of divine goodness and omnipotence to have created a finite world when it would be possible for another or countless other such worlds to be created alongside this one. For this reason I have declared that there are countless worlds similar to this earth which I, with Pythagoras, regard as a heavenly body similar to the moon and the other planets and countless other stars. I regard all these heavenly bodies as worlds, and their number as limitless. To-*

[7] Pascal: *Pensées* (Paris: Nelson; 1932), Fragment 206.

gether they contitute an infinite whole nature in infinite space, and this is the infinite All in which are innumerable worlds of the same kind, so that there is a dual infinite both of the size of the universe and the number of worlds. Indirectly, it must be granted, this conception challenges one of the doctrines of religion. However, I place in this universe a universal Providence by virtue of which every being lives, preserves its life and moves, existing in its perfection, and I take this always in a twofold sense. In the first place this Providence is omnipresent as the soul, present wholly throughout the whole body and wholly in each of its parts, and as such I call it nature, the shadow and trace of the divinity. But in the second place it is present in an inexpressible manner as the omnipresence of God according to his nature and as an omnipotence in all things and above all things, not as a part, not as soul, but in an inexplicable fashion.[8]

All things, according to Bruno, had some degree of soul, for soul was present in all matter. He thought of God as that urge permeating all nature, which manifested itself in a flowering meadow, in the singing of a thrush and the glory of a sunset. The Church was outraged by this animation of all nature, just as it was outraged by his assertion of an infinite number of worlds. It condemned both ideas as wicked heresy. Bruno, undeterred, went on exulting in the beauty of the universal Whole. He endeavored to resolve the dualism of spirit and matter. Like the pantheists who consider nature to be God in things, Bruno identified himself with those "profound theologians who say that we honor God more by silence than by words and see more when we close our eyes than when we open them, for which reason the negative theology of Pythagoras and Dionysius is far more famous than the *demonstratio* of Aristotle and the scholastics."[9]

If we look for the spiritual fathers of this pantheistic Renaissance philosophy, we come across a number of ancestors whose ideas served as raw material out of which Bruno forged his views. The foremost of these was Paracelsus of Hohenheim, whom Bruno

[8] Bruno: op. cit., VI, 174.   [9] Ibid., V, 217.

revered, and Nicholas of Cusa, whom he called "one of the most original geniuses" who ever lived.[1] With his keen scent for hidden and misunderstood currents, Bruno also discovered the Cabala and was much impressed by its doctrines.[2] Finally, we should mention Plotinus. But though he took from all of these, he made something original of his borrowings. Wherever he came across a useful building block, he utilized it for the new structure which he was proudly determined to erect. His philosophy was only intended for cultivated men, he explained; for the masses, faith was indispensable. But the thinking mind demanded rational proofs—although on the other hand he made the observation: "The sound human intellect does not always hit the mark of truth." [3]

Bruno's heretical philosophy can, like all pantheisms, be criticized on a variety of grounds. It operated with extremely imprecise concepts and could easily slip into atheism. Bruno glided far too rapidly over the religious inadequacy of pantheism, which in its intoxication with life tends to ignore the evil of the world. Moreover, he frequently wrote to suit the taste of Italian Late Renaissance society; his style is often excessively sensual and pompous—to say nothing of its arrogant and mocking tone. Bruno's writings do not send forth those glorious radiations of divinity that we find in the works of Jakob Böhme, who, a few years later, was to be persecuted as a heretic by the Protestants.

Despite these necessary reservations, Bruno's was an ardent, a sparkling spirit. His metaphysics have an untrammeled, altogether unconventional quality. Along with this went a passionate affirmation of life that overthrew the spirit of asceticism. In this sense Bruno burst the bonds of the Middle Ages and spoke, in philosophy, the word that the times craved to hear. He helped to open the door to the modern age, despite the fact that the modern mind scarcely finds him a kindred soul. There is no doubt that he exerted a lasting and fruitful influence upon many who followed him. Probably Spinoza read him. We know that Goethe was ex-

---

[1] Ibid., III, 93. [2] Ibid., V, 73, 157.
[3] Ibid., III, p. 45 and IV, 56.

tremely fond of him. Schelling, too, gave Bruno's name to the title
of one of his dialogues. Bruno's powerful affirmation of the world,
coming as it did after the medieval terror of nature, had the effect
of a revelation. In modified form it became one of the prime
tenets of modern man.

Baruch Spinoza

After the judgment of the Angels, and with that of the Saints, we
excommunicate, expel and curse and damn Baruch de Espinoza
with the consent of God, Blessed be He, and with the consent of
all the Holy Congregation, in front of the holy Scrolls with the
six-hundred-and-thirteen precepts which are written therein,
with the excommunication with which Joshua banned Jericho,
with the curse with which Elisha cursed the boys, and with all
the curses which are written in the Law. Cursed be he by day
and cursed be he by night; cursed be he when he lies down, and
cursed be he when he rises up; cursed be he when he goes out,
and cursed be he when he comes in. The Lord will not pardon
him; the anger and wrath of the Lord will rage against this man,
and bring upon him all the curses which are written in the Book
of the Law, and the Lord will destroy his name from under the
Heavens, and the Lord will separate him to his injury from all
the tribes of Israel with all the curses of the firmament, which
are written in the Book of the Law. But you who cleave unto the
Lord God are all alive this day. We order that nobody should
communicate with him orally or in writing, or show him any
favor, or stay with him under the same roof, or within four ells
of him, or read anything composed or written by him.[4]

After these words had been read out on July 27, 1656, all the
candles in the synagogue in Amsterdam were extinguished, and
Baruch de Spinoza, aged twenty-four years, was solemnly cast out
of the Jewish community. Henceforth Spinoza was to live the rest
of his life under this ban of excommunication. Excommunication

[4] *The Oldest Biography of Spinoza,* ed. A. Wolf (London; 1927), pp. 146–7.

was the central fact of his existence; everything he thought was colored by it. We must keep this in mind if we are to understand the atmosphere in which Spinoza's life was lived.

Possibly under the influence of the dramas of Uriel da Costa, performances of which he had seen in his youth, Spinoza early had begun to doubt the traditional tenets of Judaism. He was candid enough to express these qualms to the rabbi of his community, who attempted unsuccessfully to set them to rest. Other members of the synagogue alternately threatened him and pleaded with him, but neither their abuse nor their attempts at cajolery had any effect upon the recalcitrant young thinker. Expulsion from the Jewish community became inescapable. The pronouncement of the curse upon Spinoza was not done hastily, but it was done, and Israel, for its self-protection, lost one of its most vital sons. For Spinoza was one of the best minds produced by Judaism. Still, his thought led beyond Israel, and therefore could not be accepted. How far Spinoza had moved away from Judaism is evident in his *Treatise on Theology and Politics* (1670), which represented his reply to the excommunication—although with characteristic dignity he purged it of all traces of personal motivation and made his work of general interest by keeping it to a lofty, objective plane.

At one stroke the *Treatise on Theology and Politics* made Spinoza's name famous far beyond the borders of Holland—though hardly in a favorable sense. Few of its readers recognized the work as the act of liberation its author had intended. They were shocked by its boldness and stunned by its blasphemies. As might have been predicted, a ban was quickly issued against it. From the point of view of the times, this measure of repression was quite understandable. A number of the doctrines Spinoza advocated were as horrendous to Christian as to Jewish ears. Moreover, he sounded a new note in the history of heresy, for he refused to conceive of the Bible as the Law of Christ or the Word of God. Here was a departure more daring than that of the most deep-dyed heretics of previous times. Nor was Spinoza himself greatly surprised, for he had written in his foredoomed text that people "consider everyone a heretic who holds a different opinion."

The *Treatise* ushered in the first historical criticism of the Bible. It is true that a few scholars before Spinoza, such as Maimonides, had expressed doubts of the authorship of particular books of the Old and New Testaments. But such occasional and offhand remarks had attracted little attention. Spinoza, however, attacked the problem systematically; he called for a critical method of Scriptural exegesis and laid down the guiding principles of Biblical criticism. He had ceased to regard Scripture as a kind of letter from heaven sent by God to man. With full awareness of what this would mean, he abandoned the traditional notion of revelation. Spinoza openly declared "the Word of God faulty, mutilated, falsified, and contradictory" and forcefully asserted "that we possess only fragments of it and that the original version of the Covenant which God made with the Jews has been lost."

Spinoza not only made this hair-raising assertion, but went to considerable lengths to prove it. Incisively, he demonstrated that the sacred books "were not composed by one man and not for the people of a single age, but by several men of different types of mind and different ages." Repeatedly he stressed the human origin of Scripture; it was, he pointed out, adapted wholly to the mental capacities of the "fickle and inconstant Jewish people." The five books of Moses, Spinoza proved on grounds of form and content, could not have been written by Moses himself. He also took issue with Israel's central doctrine of being a chosen people. Mercilessly, he shattered the whole idea of miracles. So brilliantly did he go about his task that he forged the entire science of Biblical criticism singlehandedly. All who have followed him in this field have necessarily stood upon his shoulders.

It is little wonder that such Biblical criticism was branded by Spinoza's outraged contemporaries as "the sin against the Holy Ghost." Since the days of Marcion critical examination of the Bible has been heretics' work, and will remain so always. Biblical criticism is not a harmless, purely philological affair, for it deprives Scripture of its timelessness and threatens its essential sanctity. It necessarily calls into question the authority of the Bible. People cannot be asked to obey unreservedly Scripture that has been declared "faulty, mutilated, falsified, and contradictory." If the Word is subject to error, it has forfeited its divine radiance.

The ultimate tendency of Spinoza's Biblical criticism was to undermine the Old Testament Law. To Spinoza, Israel's law no longer appeared as an effort to introduce order into life and to sanctify all the actions of men. He had lost all feeling for the living relationship between God and the Law; the Torah had become an unbearable yoke to him. Surely we can see how a man punished by "all the curses which are written in the Law" should have come to this view. He could scarcely feel this Law as a benefaction of God and the course of joy. He felt the Law as a crushing, repressive force, and called it "a scourge of God and a torment of life."

Spinoza had to shatter the Law of the Old Covenant in order to clear the way for the greater law that had been revealed to his wonder-struck eyes. The Old Testament Torah had been designed for a single nation; but Spinoza believed he had come upon the law of the cosmos, and that he must awaken men to an understanding of it. In several places in his *Treatise* there are distinct suggestions of this greater law; but it was to be revealed in all its brilliance in his posthumous work, the *Ethics*.

The *Ethics*, with its mathematical arrangement, scarcely endears itself at first sight. The geometrical method that Spinoza employed to set forth his heretical philosophy has, in fact, been termed lifeless. But beneath the rigid armor of the method, there is a fiery intuition. The use of geometrical techniques was not Spinoza's original contribution; it was merely an expression of his age. Like his contemporaries he believed that the book of nature was written in numbers and mathematical symbols. Nevertheless, the technique played into his hands, for he was able to replace the teleological point of view by that causal approach which in the seventeenth century was regarded as the supreme achievement of philosophy. Moreover, the geometrical method possessed a clarity and stringency which excluded vagueness. And after our initial drawing back, we are likely to feel the curious enchantment that the method exercises, as all mathematics does, even though the proofs are not in every case stringent. Method and content are intimately connected in Spinoza's work.

The greater law, Spinoza believed, was made manifest in reason. However, Spinoza's concept of reason has nothing whatsoever to do with crude rationalism. For him "reason" had religious overtones; it was a faculty illuminated by the Logos. He called it "the most precious gift, divine light," and argued that it must no longer be subordinated to the letter of the Bible. "What altar can a man build who offends against the majesty of reason?" Spinoza asks. Of course men can build other altars, he continues, but if these are built upon the grave of reason they can have no permanency.

The law of the cosmos is further expressed in freedom. Spinoza did not conceive of freedom merely in ideal terms; for him it extended into practical life. It is strangely stirring to find him maintaining that democracy is less subject to injustice and corruption than any other form of political organization, and that it affords the greatest freedom to man. Like so many heretics, Spinoza was one of the great forerunners of freedom of conscience. He held that the purpose of the state is to guarantee men freedom. *Can a greater misfortune for a state be conceived than that respected men, merely because they hold deviant opinions and are incapable of hypocrisy, should be banished from the country like criminals? What, I say, can be more corrupt than that men should be declared enemies and led to their deaths not for some crime or atrocity, but solely because they have free minds; that the scaffold, the terror of the wicked, should become a glorious theater offering the most sublime examples of self-denial and virtue?*

On behalf of freedom of thought Spinoza called for a separation between philosophy and religion. "Theology may not serve reason, nor reason theology; rather, each must dominate its own realm." Genuine religion, he said, allows "to each man full freedom to philosophize, so that men may think as they please about everything without its being counted a crime." If certain people should be condemned as heretics and schismatics, let it be those who incited to hatred and wrath.

His belief in the higher law, which he summed up in the words *Deus sive natura,* persuaded Spinoza of the unalterable necessity of all events. This belief filled him with a peculiar composure; he assumed that attitude toward the Eternal for which he coined the famous phrase *"amor Dei intellectualis."* On this subject Spinoza wrote wonderful passages whose élan breaks through the dry mathematical terminology. It becomes apparent that this destroyer of the Torah was one of the most religious men who ever lived. Indeed, his thoughts circled incessantly around the theme of love of God; only the great saints of Christendom have exhibited a similar burning fervor. Spinoza's mysticism has been called sober and cool, but as Margarete Susman cogently puts it, it has the "coolness of water," which is bound to be refreshing.

Spinoza's *amor Dei intellectualis* was not a contradiction to his rationalism, but its sustaining foundation. All rationalism is surrounded by a far wider belt of irrationalism; this was the case with Spinoza also. But both rationalism and irrationalism are inept hieroglyphs for his ineffable mysticism. People have taken issue with his formula of *amor Dei intellectualis* on the ground that love and intellect are mutually exclusive. But that is interpreting the expression in too intellectualistic a manner. Just as, in the time-honored idiom "Adam knew his wife Eve," what is meant is both sexual knowledge and love, so it is in Spinoza; he was speaking of a higher function which cannot be communicated by ordinary terms. Inexpressible bliss, this heretic philosopher was saying, consists in the love of God, and such love necessarily proceeds from knowledge of God. Out of purest love of God, without a trace of egoism, he could state in the *Ethics:* "He who loves God cannot strive to have God love him in return."

Spinoza's perhaps ill-chosen phrase, *Deus sive natura,* has led to the widespread and erroneous notion that his mysticism is a sort of pantheism. This misconception has remained linked with his name. A comparison of Spinoza's philosophy with that of Giordano Bruno, however, clearly shows how far Spinoza was from real pantheism. It is true that Spinoza did not separate God from nature, as theology does—all the more so since he considered it impermissible to use theological terms when speaking as a philosopher. But in his letters he unequivocally denied that he identified God with nature. *I conceive God as the immanent and not as the external cause of all things. I assert, in fact, that everything lives and moves in God, just as did Paul, and perhaps also all ancient philosophers, though in different fashion; and I may also say, as did all ancient Hebrews, as far as it is possible to draw conclusions from various frequently falsified traditions. But if there are people who think that my* Treatise on Theology and Politics *starts from the assumption that God and nature are one and the same, they are entirely mistaken.*

Nature, then, must not be equated with God. But there must be a connection between God and nature, and this was the higher law which had been revealed to Spinoza. The reason he so strongly emphasized the superpersonality of God was his desire to avoid all anthropomorphism in speaking of God. Certainly this was a legitimate effort. For its sake he moved into the vicinity of pantheism. But there can be no objection to this pantheistic element in religion—it is present in the Bible, too, after all—so long as it remains a subordinate component.

Misunderstood from the start, this system of Spinoza's aroused a storm of indignation among his contemporaries. He was denounced from all sides as a "heretic and godless man" intent on destroying the law of the Old Covenant. As Spinoza himself wrote in a letter, "the theologians everywhere harried me," and did their best to have his works banned. These works were reviled as unspeakably corrupting, "worthy to be cast back into the darkness of hell whence they had emerged into the light to the harm and disgrace of the human race." [5] He was the target of endless slanders, but no refutations. Not a single opponent confronted him honestly.

[5] E. Altkirch: *Maledictus und Benedictus, Spinoza im Urteil des Volkes und der Geistigen* (1924), p. 51.

Then, after a hundred years, a great reversal began; unbounded admiration took the place of the former odium. As if scales had fallen from men's eyes, they saw to their horror and astonishment that he who had been treated as someone accursed was in truth a blessed spirit. Gotthold Ephraim Lessing, the German philosopher-writer, asserted categorically: "There is no philosophy other than Spinoza's. . . . Few have tasted such peace of the spirit, such a heaven of the intellect, as this bright, pure mind created." [6] Goethe called him "*christianissimus.*" In the late eighteenth century the *Ethics* was read as if it were a second Bible. The leading minds of German idealism spoke, with Novalis, of this "God-intoxicated man." It may be that these Spinozists read too much into their hero, but there can be no doubt that Spinoza enormously enriched Christian thought by his creative synthesis of the Occidental and the Jewish spirit.

In order to strike a balance between outright rejection and supine devotion, we must consider the true essence of Spinoza's heresy. It is to be found in his conception of God. Leo Shestov, in a penetrating essay on "The Historical Fate of Spinoza," has pointed out that this son of Israel killed God by withdrawing God's personality! Yet, Shestov says, paradoxically enough, only a man "who had come to love the Almighty beyond all the treasures of the world" could possibly have been capable of this. It is true that Spinoza no longer recognized the existence of a dialogue between God and man, and he considered prayer useless. Yet the incomprehensible dialogue which petty man conducts with the Eternal is the very core of a true relationship with God. It does not matter that such conversations seldom come about, and that the prayers of most Christians are mere monologues. The possibility of addressing God is a mystery in the life of the religious man; to abolish that possibility is to take a far more extreme step than to abolish the Law. In this respect Spinoza was actually a heretic. He was aware of this, so much so that in his sketchbook he drew caricatures of himself looking like a wild-eyed revolutionary.

[6] Ibid., p. 102.

Yet Spinoza also conveyed the impression of an unusual goodness, with his freedom from all base emotions, his greathearted generosity despite his extreme poverty, and above all his ardent love of God. Goethe spoke of him as "our saint." Heine commented that Spinoza "suffered like Christ for his doctrine and wore the crown of thorns." His mode of life was simple and austere. After the expulsion from the synagogue, and his banishment from Amsterdam, he moved to a small village called Rijnsburg and henceforth lived in great solitude. His only association was with the Collegiants, a sect whose doctrines resembled those of the Quakers, and this connection was a loose one. Yet Spinoza was by no means a misanthrope, or an eccentric, or one of those self-styled individualists who proclaim themselves so by an untidy appearance. He used to say that "such affectation of negligence is the mark of an inferior mind, in which wisdom is not to be found at all." [7] He never showed the slightest pride or haughtiness, and the innate nobility of his nature shone through his smallest actions. He was fond of chatting about trivial daily affairs with his landlord, and attentively followed the political events of his times. But whatever contact he had with the intellectual and political life of his age only emphasized his mysterious quality of alienation from life in the seventeenth century. His livelihood was secured by a small pension given him by an illustrious patron; his work of grinding lenses was more an avocation than a source of income. But it furthered his hereditary tuberculosis. However, he simply ignored his ailment, as saints are wont to do.

His life of thought in his self-imposed solitude was so dear to him that he declined an invitation to become professor of philosophy at the University of Heidelberg. A genuine philosopher in the Socratic sense, he felt no urge to pontificate from the lecture-hall rostrum. He preferred the quiet of his little room and his diet of groats and milk to the concomitants of prestige and worldly position. Such utter freedom from ambition and the craving for status is very rare in men. With Spinoza the impulse was undoubtedly genuine. There was a seamless unity between his

[7] *The Oldest Biography of Spinoza*, p. 64.

life and work such as characterizes men who are in harmony with the greater law. His insight into human emotions was very great, as is evident from the *Ethics,* and he led the existence of a man guided by reason who had overcome all the vacillations of feeling. Spinoza ultimately arrived at the stage of neither condemning nor laughing at the actions of men, but of really understanding them. In contrast to Plato, who held that true philosophy taught men how to die, Spinoza held that the wisdom of free man consisted "not in meditation on death but in meditation on life." And this he himself did to the last moment of his life.

Which, then, of the two impressions is right? Was Spinoza an accursed heretic or an exemplary saint? These alternatives point to an almost insoluble riddle. Only by not insisting upon a single angle of vision, by regarding the truth as the sum of phenomena, can we arrive at a synthesis of these apparent opposites, and call Spinoza a saintly heretic! Spinoza actually conceived of himself as a heretical saint who had created one of the most religious heretical philosophies of all ages. It was out of this exalted feeling that he declared in a letter: "I do not claim to have found the best philosophy, but I know that I have understood the true philosophy."

20

The Drama of Conscience

✝   ✝

Blaise Pascal

During the night of November 23, 1654, Blaise Pascal had an experience that was to be of significance for the whole of his life to come. He stood before the burning bush that had once made Moses tremble. For more than two hours Pascal confronted the fire of God. No other metaphor than that of "fire" occurred to Pascal himself to describe the incomprehensible event. What he set down in his famous *Memorial* was no mere emotional upheaval, but an inner illumination which made him conscious of God as a reality. In his ecstasy Pascal felt the presence of God, and cried out in overflowing bliss: "Certainty, certainty, joy, joy!"

362

Three times in succession he used the word "joy"; he wrote of the "tears of joy" that he shed. He had broken through to an unshakable certainty that God was *his* God.

Pascal never said a word to anyone about this vision. Throughout his life he did not break his silence. Posterity learned of the matter only by chance, through a servant's finding after his death the sheet of parchment on which he had recorded the event. He had always kept this parchment on his person, sewed into the lining of his vest.

Since Pascal himself preferred not to speak of it, taste dictates that the historian refrain from prolix commentary on his vision of the burning bush. Yet the *Memorial* represents the key to Pascal's life. This midnight experience with God determined his future course of thought and action; his relationship with Christ also was decided by this mysterious event. It must have been this that led him to the conclusion: "It is one of the great principles of Christianity that everything that happened to Jesus Christ must be experienced again in the soul and the body of every man."

Before this midnight vision Pascal had lived what may be called the worldly phase of his life. He was addicted to the writings of Montaigne, whose skeptical views exerted great influence upon him. For he himself was a polished and elegant young man, distinguished in manner and appearance, a brilliant conversationalist who charmed everyone. This is not to say that he led the life of a pleasure-seeking libertine; rather, he tried to be an *honnête homme,* that ideal of France's classical period. He devoted himself to mathematical and scientific studies for which he showed such a singular gift. He invented the calculating machine and, moreover, promptly secured the rights to its industrial exploitation. He was intrigued by experimental physics and succeeded in proving conclusively Torricelli's theory of atmospheric pressure. With equal authority he took part in the mathematical discussions of his time. A Pascal without this concern with scientific problems would not have been Pascal. It was an inseparable component of his personality. He never entirely shook off these scientific interests, even when, in the second half of his life, he turned his mind to such different matters. Many years later, while suffering from violent toothache, he distracted himself from it by working out a mathematical basis for the game of roulette. Even his practical talents never left him. Thus, only a few months before his death, he founded the first omnibus company in Paris.

However, after his great visionary experience all of Pascal's scientific interests receded into the background. As he himself put it in a letter: "The first thing that God instills into the soul whom he has condescended to truly touch is a new insight, an altogether extraordinary perception of things and of one's own soul, as though one were seeing them for the first time." In line with this new insight, Pascal abandoned the life he had been leading, and withdrew to the abbey of Port Royal, living there as a guest. Pascal's attitude toward Port Royal was a subtle one, a close connection but not an identification. The pious men of Port Royal always felt somewhat uncomfortable with this impassioned thinker, although they gladly drew upon his brilliant intellectual resources.

While Pascal was thus devoting himself, in the seclusion of Port Royal, to the salvation of his soul, a violent conflict flared up in France between the Jansenists and the Jesuits over the Augustinian doctrine of grace.[1] Pascal, with his newly awakened religious interests, became absorbed in the dispute. Finally the Jansenists asked their illustrious sympathizer for assistance. Thus Pascal became involved in one of the greatest dramas in the history of thought.

[1] The Jansenists were a prominent group within the Roman Catholic Church in the seventeenth and eighteenth centuries who revived the ancient dispute between Augustine and Pelagius over the relationship between human freedom and divine grace. They took their name from Cornelis Jansen (1585–1638), a Dutch theologian whose book on Augustine was published posthumously in 1640. The Jansenists argued that the Church had in the course of history drifted into a position of Semi-Pelagianism (see pages 139 ff.), and called for a revival of the Augustinian doctrine of predestination. The Jesuits accused them of Calvinism, and succeeded in having the Jansenist position condemned by the Pope as heretical. The Cistercian abbey of Port Royal became the center of the Jansenist movement. There were actually two Port Royals: the mother house of Port Royal des Champs, situated about eight miles south of Versailles, and Port Royal de Paris, in the Paris suburb of St. Jacques.

Pascal chose for his vehicle the highly readable epistolary form. Such was the origin of the famous *Lettres provinciales,* which were published during the period from January 1656 to March 1657. He wrote under the pseudonym Montalte; the royal censors searched high and low, but entirely in vain, to discover the author and the printer. No one guessed that the author of the audacious letters was Pascal; he succeeded in keeping his secret although he lived directly opposite a Jesuit monastery. So excellent was the writing and so sprightly was the reasoning of these epistles that they were read everywhere. Yet it was no little thing to take issue with the Jesuits. They were, after all, the leaders of the Counter-Reformation, cofounders of baroque culture, the most faithful sons of the Church, and the most powerful and influential of the Catholic orders. But Pascal felt impelled by his conscience to join in the struggle against them. He believed that his age was one in which "God is abandoned . . . and the service one does him is highly welcome."

The Provincial Letters were concerned with revealing the diplomatic tricks of the Jesuits and their manner of twisting things. In the course of this unmasking Pascal drew all the stops, from mockery: "There is nothing superior to the Jesuits. . . ." to utmost gravity: "The spirit of Christian discipline does not prevail in the Society of Jesus."[2] The crux of his argument was that the Jesuits were chiefly concerned with exercising their power and preserving their dominion. To achieve this secular goal they had necessarily to deviate in many respects from the teachings of Christ and make concessions to the desires of the people. He quoted a Jesuit father as saying: "Men today are so corrupt that we must go to them since they do not come to us." This was a dubious watchword for a religious order, for in following it the Jesuits were lenient to a fault, offering remission to all and sundry, even to a venal judge, an avaricious usurer, or an unregenerate procurer. All such persons who lacked genuine penitence and a readiness to change their ways should be refused confession; in-

[2] Pascal: *Pensées* and *The Provincial Letters* (New York: Modern Library; 1941).

stead, the Jesuit fathers readily "conceded to human weakness and sapped the strictness of the religion." To this end they had invented "light devotional exercises" and wrote books on "effortless piety."

To Pascal's mind, this sale of Christianity at reduced prices could only drive true piety out of the market. He cried out in indignation against the tendency. Describing all the tricks of the overclever Jesuit fathers, he asked hotly: "Are these monks and priests who speak thus? Are they Christians? Are they Turks? Are they human beings? Are they devils?" The man who had written the *Comparaison des chrétiens des premier temps avec ceux d'aujourd'hui* could not but be outraged to the depths of his soul by the irresponsible frivolousness with which the Jesuits of his time strove to make Christianity palatable to the most shallowminded.

The Provincial Letters not only attacked the Jesuits, but defended the Jansenists against the Jesuit charges of heresy. "In your language," Pascal asked, addressing the Jesuits, "is it one and the same thing to attack your society and to be heretical?" For Pascal, too, had stumbled into that situation in which the Christian who takes his religion seriously must endure the charge of being a heretic—a fate shared by so many before and after him.

With the keenness and clarity characteristic of him, Pascal summed up the essential theme of his *Provincial Letters* in the phrase: Force against truth. The twelfth of the letters ends with an interesting analysis of this dichotomy: *You believe that you have power and impunity on your side; but I believe that I have truth and innocence on mine. A long and strange struggle arises when force seeks to repress truth. But all the endeavors of force are not capable of blotting out truth; they only intensify its radiance. Force cannot daunt the light of truth; it can only show its wrath against it. When power stands against power, the stronger destroys the weaker; when one word combats another, the one which is truthful and convincing prevails against the one which is nothing but vanity and mendacity; but force and truth have no power against one another. One must beware, however, of concluding therefrom that they are equal in value. There is this fundamental difference between them: that force practiced against God's commandments . . . has only a limited course, whereas the truth lasts forever and ultimately wins victory over all its enemies because like God himself it is eternal and omnipotent.*

It must be said that Pascal was not altogether just to the Jesuit order. Not that he distorted any of his opponents' words—aside from a few insignificant oversights. But *The Provincial Letters* concentrated entirely on the weaknesses and more dubious aspects of the Jesuits, and ignored their great achievements. The result was a one-sided picture of the Jesuit Order. Above all, Pascal overlooked the fact that the impulse to make Christianity easy by changing the strict ethical demands of the New Testament into a comfortable commonplace morality was not peculiar to the Jesuits. Long before the Jesuits ever appeared on the scene, this approach had reigned in certain quarters of the Church. The Jesuits were only a symbol for this adaptable Christianity. Pascal did not consider the painful fact that Jesuitism, regarded as "Christianity become worldly wise," is—as Overbeck says—"the consequence of every Christian theology" and that "only a heroic Christianity always ready to oppose the currents of its times can escape this fate of Jesuitization." [3]

But these objections do not greatly detract from the value of *The Provincial Letters*. The true importance of these letters has been too little emphasized. They have been read for their entertainment value, for the excellence of their style and the brilliance of their wit. They are regarded as a literary monument to a movement somewhat quaint and faraway. Yet to enjoy *The Provincial Letters* only for their audacity—as the greater part of Pascal's contemporaries undoubtedly did—is to miss their real intention. Modern Catholicism has not produced many works imbued with a more powerful passion for truth and a purer Christianity than these letters. The man who composed them had stood before the burning bush, had known that God who is a consuming fire. This

[3] Overbeck: *Christentum und Kultur,* pp. 124–6.

alone accounts for the fervor, strength, and courage which over-whelm one again and again as one reads through the letters. After reading them we literally feel that the air has been purified. Pascal's everlasting contribution was to warn the Christian world against the two-edged Jesuitical morality with its dubious casuistries and its doctrine of mental reservations, and to declare that the essence of Christianity is the love of God as a supernatural, all-penetrating force—without which love all virtuousness is shallow.

The Provincial Letters must be conceived as an uprising of Christian conscience against the falsification of the Gospel. The Jesuits were simply the historical opponent produced by the conditions of the seventeenth century. For Pascal's campaign against them was only a new instance of a timeless process, renewed in every century, which may be called the battle against pseudo-Christianity. If *The Provincial Letters* are regarded in this light, we will understand why it is that they have taken second place in the supposed Pascal renaissance of the present day; why, in fact, they are so often passed over in silence—with the result that we are presented with a false picture of this great militant. Any religious interpretation of Pascal must start with them, for in *The Provincial Letters* the very heartbeat of that mighty spirit may be felt. "One cannot claim the *Pensées* for one's cause without accepting the *Provinciales*." [4]

But the ecclesiastical world of the seventeenth century could make no such acknowledgment without severe damage to its pretensions. To this day prominent Catholic writers call these letters "demagoguery" and insist that "measured by the ultimate standard, they are bad." [5] Among Pascal's contemporaries, even the men of Port Royal were not altogether delighted with the *Letters*. The Jesuits, of course, seethed with rage. No one had ever gone so far in attacks upon them. They, who had explicitly dedicated themselves to the greater glory of God, were being accused of betraying Christianity.

The Jesuits brought their dispute with Port Royal before the

[4] Landsbaerg: *Pascal's Berufung* (1929), p. 25.
[5] Guardini: *Christliches Bewusstsein,* pp. 271 ff.

Pope, who ruled that the Jansenists must make what amounted to a recantation. As for the scurrilous *Lettres Provinciales,* the Pope condemned them and placed them on the Index. The condemnation was repeated by the Sorbonne, the Spanish Inquisition, and the French king, who had a copy of the work publicly burned by the executioner.

For the believing Catholic it was well-nigh unendurable to conceive of the Pope as an enemy of truth. The Jansenists themselves shrank from the consequences of Pascal's logic, and in the hour of need broke with their most able propagandist, and espoused a compromise theology which led them toward Jesuitism.

Pascal, however, remained unalterably convinced of the validity of his position. In the *Letters* themselves he had already noted: "I stand alone." Now this loneliness was intensified. In this terrible solitude he noted: "Am I alone against thirty thousand? Not at all. Take care—you have the court, you have the fraud; I have the truth and it is my strength; if I were to lose it, I would be lost." [6] Thus he upheld the sovereignty of conscience above the creed of the Church, and inevitably—though unwillingly—found himself on the road to heresy.

So clear a thinker as Pascal could not be unaware of this. Nevertheless, his conscience would not allow him to submit. "Never did the saints hold their peace," he wrote in his notebook, and added boldly: "After Rome has condemned the truth, it is necessary to cry out even more loudly that she has condemned it unjustly." [7] An enemy of authoritarianism in thought, Pascal spoke out against the spiritual collectivism the Church had stood for since the Council of Nicaea. He would adhere to the truth as it had been revealed to him. And in a sudden outburst of passion he exclaimed: "If my *Letters* are condemned in Rome, what I condemn in them is condemned in heaven: O Lord Jesus, I appeal to your tribunal." [8]

That last exclamation was the significant one. Here we behold the kind of independence Pascal claimed. We can see why

[6] Pascal: *Pensées,* Fragment 921.
[7] Ibid., Fragment 920.   [8] Ibid.

the pious fathers of Port Royal, when they published the *Pensées* after Pascal's death, concealed this bold appeal from the churchly to the divine tribunal. They simply dropped the sentence from the text. For in appealing to Christ after a papal condemnation, Pascal was indubitably using the language of a heretic. Thus Petrus Waldus had spoken when he was excommunicated; thus Hus had answered the council which condemned him. All the condemned heretics appealed from the authority of the church to the higher tribunal of God—and it was precisely this form of appeal which the church could never recognize. Precisely this form of appeal was what marked the "obdurate heretic." The Jesuits had not been altogether wrong when they scented heresy in Pascal's *Provincial Letters*. Only the naïve can suggest, however, that Pascal would have been spared this problem if he had belonged to the Protestant Church.

It was only a little while, however, that Pascal balanced on the edge of this abyss. Then in a letter he pronounced the anguish-laden words: "I shall never depart from the communion of the Church." He collapsed—literally—for in the midst of a passionate discussion of these questions he was stricken by a fainting fit. He came to terms with the Church by a curious train of thought. The Church had suffered for him for 1600 years, he said. "Now it is time to suffer from the Church; we must all suffer for her and give her our all."

Catholics had been aghast at his appeal from the authority of the Church to the verdict of God. Now with this saintly statement, Pascal astonished all the Protestants who had been rejoicing in his rebellion. They could not understand what lay behind this capitulation. We today are also hard put to it to understand Pascal's profoundly religious readiness to martyr his own conscience for the sake of the Church. But to make this observation is to say nothing against Pascal's road to sanctity; it is only to comment on our own limits. There have been many sincerely mistaken heretics in the history of Western thought, but very few who fell into silence out of Christian humility. Hence Pascal occupies a unique place in the chronicle of heresy. He was one of those unusual

Christians who in every situation act differently from what was expected of them.

In taking this attitude Pascal was by no means being untrue to himself, although his spiritual state was so complex that all mere psychological explanations are inadequate. For it was only outwardly that Pascal yielded; inwardly he never abandoned the ideas in his *Provincial Letters,* and could not have done so without abandoning himself. Only a year before his death he stated bluntly: "I am asked whether I do not regret having written *The Provincial Letters.* I reply that I am far from regretting them; if I were to write them today, I would write them in an even stronger tone." [9] Jesuit critics, too, recognized this—with a good deal of bitterness, of course. "There was never any question of a recantation of his admitted slander of the Jesuits, or of a reconciliation with the Pope." [1]

While thus imposing outward silence on himself, Pascal inwardly attempted to lead the life of a saint. He sold his rugs, his silver, and his fine table appointments. He began eating with a wooden spoon out of an earthen dish, lived in a room whose walls were bare of paper, devoted much of his time to the poor, visited churches, donned a spiked belt, and so on—as his sister Gilberte has described in her biography. It was this furiously ascetic mode of life on Pascal's part that caused Goethe to say that nothing had done so much harm to religion as the morbid state of mind of this man of Port Royal. Nietzsche, too, was indignant at the picture of a Pascal grown humble; Christianity could never be forgiven for having crushed a man of Pascal's caliber, he declared. Similar outrage, if unspoken, pervades most of the literature on Pascal. Almost all who have written about him regret this extinguishing of a brilliant scientific mind, and find his gloomy penitent's life hard to fathom.

Attempts have been made to explain Pascal's course by his illness—so grave that he once confessed he had spent not a day

[9] In Buchholz: *Pascal* (1939), p. 183.
[1] Pascal: "Lettres à Mademoiselle de Roanne," Lettre VI, in *Pensées* (Paris; 1869), p. 436.

without pain since his eighteenth year. Sickness, he added, was
the normal state of the Christian—a statement difficult to assimilate. But to deplore the asceticism of Pascal's last years is to ignore
the religious core of his personality. It is true that Pascal was often
deeply melancholy, that he seemed unable to achieve spiritual
equanimity. But at the heart of his gloom there always remained
his religious joy. His letters ordinarily conceal more than they reveal the secret of his life, but in one of these he wrote of that private rapture which can be compared only to the soaring of a lark:
"We would never leave the joys of the world and embrace the
cross of Jesus Christ if we did not find more sweetness in ad-
versity, in poverty, in destitution, and in the rebuffs of men than
in the delights of sin. . . . We leave behind some pleasures for
others far greater. . . . People in the world do not know this joy."
There is an inexpressible mystery in such religious joy. This
alone accounts for the otherwise inexplicable riddle of Pascal's
outward silence and inner fealty to his beliefs.

The same strange impression of a man who stands with one
foot in the Church and one outside it emanates from Pascal's other
great legacy, the *Pensées*. Compiled from the hundreds upon
hundreds of little notes found in Pascal's night table after his
death, this work above all has established his immortal fame. We
cannot speak of Pascal without considering his *Pensées*, which are
of decisive importance for an understanding of his religious attitudes—along with and in connection with *The Provincial Letters*,
of course. The underlying theme of these notes was the defense
of Christianity against unbelievers. Because of his illness, Pascal
was never able to carry out his project, and the work remained
unfinished. Nevertheless, even in its fragmentary form it eclipses
all more comprehensive works in this field. Whatever objections
may be raised against such works of apologia, and in spite of the
deficiencies of the aphoristic form, the *Pensées* remain a magnificent achievement. It is impossible to say a word in praise of Pascal's *Pensées* which has not already been said somewhere long
ago. It remains one of the imperishable works of world literature,
of inexhaustible import. One can read it ten times, and the elev-

enth time still discover in it things that had been previously over-looked. It contains cruel truths such as are found in few other books, but loses nothing of its magic thereby. Who can forget what Pascal has said concerning the grandeur and misery of man? How true what he has to say of man's mediate position: "To leave the middle is to leave humanity; the greatness of the human soul consists in knowing how to stay in the middle path. It is far from a great thing to stray from that path; rather, greatness lies in not straying at all.[2] Who has matched the melancholy sweetness of his meditation on "the mystery of Jesus": "Jesus is alone on earth; not only does no one feel or share his suffering, but no one even knows of it; he and heaven are alone in the knowledge of it. . . . Jesus will be in agony until the end of the world; until that time comes we must not sleep." [3]

According to Pascal, Gethsemane is perpetual. The book abounds in such original Christian truths, many of which are of the highest importance to the Church. And yet the Church cannot hail it without reservation. For in this mighty quarry are yawning abysses into which Pascal stared steadily, gorges which most men do not wish to see, for fear of vertigo. The *Pensées*, too, were written by a man who stood for more than two hours in the fire of God, and incomprehensibly came away unscathed. It would be imprudent indeed for any churchman to ally himself with such a person, even in defense of the Christian religion. Attentive readers who have thoroughly studied the *Pensées* can only subscribe to Overbeck's opinion: "He knocks down passions and doubts as vigorously as he arouses and stimulates them again. Pascal's plausibility is astonishing, but that is also his troubling weakness. He overwhelms his reader, who nevertheless departs shaking his head." [4]

In his *Pensées* Pascal speaks of skeptics. But how does he speak of skepticism? Certainly not in the usual way. He does not simply "dispose of" it with sham reasons which will not hold water, in the manner of other apologists. Pascal displays a great un-

[2] Pascal: *Pensées*, Fragment 378.   [3] Ibid., Fragment 553.
[4] Overbeck: *Christentum und Kultur*, p. 128.

373

derstanding of skepticism, so great that he has been suspected of partaking of it. This suspicion is false. Pascal is no skeptic. But he does see a partial truth in skepticism. "Here on earth every single thing is in part true, in part false. . . . Nothing is pure truth, and therefore nothing is true that we consider to be pure truth. . . . We possess both truth and goodness only in part, and mixed with evil and falsehood." [5] This is not the language of the Church. The Church maintains that it possesses pure, absolute truth, and therefore cannot entirely welcome Pascal's conduct of her defense. Pascal's observations on skepticism ring a strange note, which is one of the reasons why outsiders are far more enthusiastic over the *Pensées* than pious Christians. Those outside the Church feel that he understands them; they find in the *Pensées* a mind in touch with the modern sense of life, one that knows we are not able to prove dogma irrefutably. Church Christians, however, will sigh over Pascal's lack of "contact with the traditional intellectual content of theology." [6]

The philosophy contained in the *Pensées* likewise does not follow any of the ecclesiastical patterns as developed by Thomas Aquinas. Its effect is to drive men farther and farther, until they have reached the outermost pole. Here is one example (many could be cited) of Pascal's philosophic tone: "The two opposing reasons. We must begin with that; otherwise we do not understand, and everything is heretical; and even at the end of every truth we must add that we recall the opposite truth." [7] Here he was obviously bent on avoiding heresy. In reality, however, he was voicing one of the basic maxims of the heretics. For the conception that "all principles are true, those of the skeptics, those of the stoics, those of the atheists, etc., but their conclusions are false because the opposing principles are equally true," [8] is a view that the Church would never admit and from her standpoint could never admit. Contradiction forms the basis of Pascal's thinking— and this, the Church would say, is highly perilous. To propound the idea that at the end of every truth we must remember the op-

[5] Pascal: *Pensées*, Fragment 385.
[6] Cf. H. Platz: *Pascal* (1937), pp. 17, 44.
[7] Pascal: *Pensées*, Fragment 567.   [8] Ibid., Fragment 394.

posite truth is to imply that heresy is a proper supplement to the view of the Church! For in Pascal we will find the strongest arguments for the eternal validity of the heretics' concerns. Such things could be said only by a man who was deeply convinced that earth is not the home of truth—again something the Church cannot admit, since she proclaims herself the guardian of truth. For Pascal, however, truth is to be found in a never-attained synthesis which will ultimately unite the contradictions.

Pascal's heretical aspect likewise emerges in his discussion of the problem of God. He ventures so far as to say: "It is incomprehensible that God is, and equally incomprehensible if he were not." [9] Such a statement, too, is not in accord with the Roman catechism. It expresses the modern torment with the problem of God, as we find it, for example, in the works of Dostoevsky. To Pascal, however, the central problem was the way man must take if he wishes to reach God. Naturally, he offers us the traditional answer, that God will be known "only through Jesus Christ." But what is astonishing, what compels our attention, is his reiterated assertion that the heart is the true path to God. This insight is all the more extraordinary because it is the product of a mathematical mind. Yet Pascal had early endeavored to anchor faith in feeling. His key perception came in answer to long groping: "It is the heart that feels God, and not the reason. That is the faith: God felt in the heart, not in the reason." [1] Few of Pascal's aphorisms have found such enthusiastic agreement in modern times as his: "*Le coeur a son ordre.*" [2]

And yet the problem is not so simple. When Pascal speaks of the heart, he is not speaking in terms of sentimentality or feeling; rather, he means the deeply shaken heart. One must descend into the depths to understand it. But if it is this mystical heart that feels God, what becomes of the authority of the Church or of the Bible, which alone are supposed to point the way to God? This question rears its ugly head, and the only possible reply is that these authorities have quietly vanished. In place of authority Pascal has installed what theology technically calls inner evidence. Now the churches of every confession have never liked

[9] Ibid., Fragment 230.   [1] Ibid., Fragment 278.   [2] Ibid., Fragment 283.

inner evidence because it opens the door to subjectivism. In fact, inner evidence has always been the hallmark of the heretic. The heart which feels God cannot make a church the basis of its doctrine; here is the heretic's religious spirit in its purest form. In his statements on the logic of the heart Pascal approached closely to that new language of which he once spoke in private letters. Yet to forge such a new language is one of the most important tasks confronting the modern Christian, if he wishes to speak of the Deity with the majesty and force the subject requires.

The *Pensées* are not the apology of the Church; rather, they are the personal apology of Pascal. Those who have proposed Pascal for canonization, as has Maurice Barrès, have little prospect of ever seeing their nomination seriously taken up. The Jesuits have never forgotten *The Provincial Letters*, and other Catholics evince a timid fear of the author of the dangerous *Pensées*. Young seminarians are warned against occupying themselves with those ambiguous doctrines. Pascal's tie with Jansenism alone would make him suspect, since many Catholics still regard Jansenism as "adulterated Calvinism." Unamuno, in his study, *Pascal's Faith*, comes to the conclusion: "Pascal is constantly and on principle in the opposition. He is an orthodox heretic!"

Any unbiased student of Pascal must ultimately come to this conclusion. Pascal had eaten of the fruit of the tree of knowledge, and he betrays again and again how sweet it tasted to him. He wanted to be Catholic, and could not be wholly. His spiritual situation resembled that of Meister Eckhart; like the medieval mystic, Pascal was at bottom a heretic and hated the thought of being one. As a result of this dichotomy he became the mediator who to this day connects church and heretics; this is what attracts the modern Christian to him as strongly as it alarms or repels faithful Catholics. Nevertheless, we must never forget that Pascal was the man who stood before the burning bush. One who has undergone such a destiny cannot be fitted neatly into any category. Pascal became a marked man; in the opinion of the majority he was a heretic, and yet he was taken directly into God's heart.

21

The Heretic in the Eastern Church

Leo Tolstoy

The Eastern Church has a radiance all its own. One senses its Oriental tone at once upon seeing those curious churches from the outside, with the slanting rays of the setting sun glittering upon their dark blue, bright green, or gilded onion domes. We are even more struck by the mysterious beauty of the Russian Church when we come to know something of its inner life. The icons themselves, for example, express a remarkable religious spirit when one becomes lovingly absorbed in them. The Eastern Church cultivates a mysticism which is one of the most valuable elements in any religion. Moreover, it knows how to communicate this mysticism to its believers; its liturgical services are steeped in a mystical atmosphere.

All the many endearing qualities of the Russian character are connected with Eastern Christianity, for the Orthodox Church has had a tremendous formative influence upon the Russian people. It taught the muzhik that humility and forgiveness are virtues. The Eastern Church retained an element of Johannine Christianity, of disinclination to strive for worldly power. In the past, it brought forth wonderful saints. Unfortunately, we have too few written accounts of their spiritual experiences. Remarkable, too, has been the Orthodox Church's capacity for suffering. Her believers truly knew how to die. For many years the West haughtily ignored the Christian beauty of the Greek Orthodox Church, but that attitude is now giving way to an unmistakable attraction.

The bright side of this picture is, however, offset by deep shadows. The Eastern Church entered into extremely close ties with Tsarism, and gave its blessing to all the measures of an absolutist state. This lack of reservation toward the state had fateful effects, and was terribly avenged after the October Revolution. One consequence of this unfortunate involvement with Tsarism was the lack of any confrontation with the modern situation. The Russian Church was oriented so entirely toward the hereafter that it concerned itself very little with the earthly life of its faithful. Its education was purely ecclesiastical. It was totally indifferent to the social distress of the common people. The result was a system of fearful rigidity.

As the bureaucratic character of the Eastern Church hardened, numerous movements rose up within the Church to oppose it. The State Church brusquely excommunicated such movements as heretical sects. Yet the well-known Russian critic Belinsky declared as early as the middle of the nineteenth century: "Genuine religiosity is to be found among us only among the sectarians and heretics." [1] With the dawn of modern times, the

[1] Vissarion Belinsky in *"Brief an Gogol," Gogols sämtliche Werke,* ed. Buek, V, 488 f.

antiheretical activities of the Church steadily increased, even as the Raskolniki, as dissenters were called, multiplied. One should read the remarkable autobiography of the "protopope" Avvakum to obtain a deep insight into the religious culture of Old Russia. One cannot read this seventeenth-century heretic without being struck by the Christian force of his spirit: "With fire and knout and gallows, they want to fortify their church. What apostles have taught them to do so? I know them not. For my Christ never commanded our Apostles to use fire and knout and the gallows in order to lead me to the faith." [2] A strange fervor possessed the heretical movement of the Skoptsy, for this was the sect that practiced self-mutilation. The extraordinary forms taken by Eastern heresy may be explained partly by the wild vigor of the Russian people, partly by sheer religious intoxication. All these groups cultivated such intoxication; all called for a "departure from sin," by which they meant the world.

Out of the long procession of Russian heretics, we can cite here only a single one. He is, however, one who may be most readily understood by Western men.

The place Leo Tolstoy occupies in the consciousness of modern man is primarily that of a writer. He is one of the principal representatives of that great Russian literature which belongs among the mightiest creations of the nineteenth century. He himself said of his own novel, *War and Peace:* "Without false modesty, it is like the Iliad." And it is true: in his epic power he seems a second Homer. The works of Tolstoy are full of masterly descriptions of people and nature. But more than that, in these works human life itself, in all its heat and tragedy, speaks out. Tolstoy can make a landscape flower, he can show the awakening of love in a human heart, with a faithfulness to reality that is virtually unsurpassable. In these novels the reader is confronted point-blank with life; he looks directly into its face. The works of this artist are not only psychologically and realistically true, but they are also sustained by an unmistakable ethical content which

[2] *Das Leben des Protopopen Awwakum,* translated by R. Jagoditsch (1930), p. 149.

gives them lasting value. Tolstoy's art is great, but his personality is almost greater; the standards by which it can be judged are not yet available.

Among Tolstoy's posthumous works was found a tale entitled "Memoirs of a Madman." It describes a landowner who begins his story with the words: *Today I was taken to the Provincial Government Board to be certified. Opinions differed. They disputed and finally decided that I was not insane—but they arrived at this decision only because during the examination I did my utmost to restrain myself and not give myself away. I did not speak out, because I am afraid of the madhouse where they would prevent me from doing my mad work. So they came to the conclusion that I am subject to hallucinations and something else, but am of sound mind. They came to that conclusion, but I myself know that I am mad.*[3]

As a child the landowner had once looked on while a small boy was punished for being naughty, had seen the grimaces of pain on the boy's face as he endured the blows, and had observed how in spite of the child's howling promises to be good, more blows had been rained down upon him. "And then it came upon me! I began to sob, and went on so that they could not quiet me for a long time. That sobbing and despair were the first attacks of my present madness."[4]

His second bout of madness occurred when he was told how Christ had been tormented, and no one could tell him why. "And again I was overcome by it. I sobbed and sobbed, and began knocking my head against the wall."[5] The "Memoirs of a Madman" are written in the first person and constitute a veiled autobiography. Tolstoy himself was the madman in the story, which is one of the subtlest and most significant of his tales. According to Leo Shestov "the 'Memoirs of a Madman' may in one sense be considered the key to Tolstoy's creative work."[6]

---

[3] Leo Tolstoy: "Memoirs of a Madman," in *Ivan Ilých and Hadji Murád* (London: Oxford University Press; 1935), p. 210.
[4] Ibid., p. 211.   [5] Ibid., p. 212.
[6] Leo Shestov: *Auf Hiobs Waage* (1929), p. 152.

To achieve a deeper understanding of Tolstoy, we must assess the meaning of Tolstoy's describing himself as a madman. This is a significant detail. Certainly little is gained by regarding him as the Tolstoyans do. Their tedious studies present the picture of a crotchety eccentric who need not be taken seriously. Equally misguided is the picture of him as a person closely related to the West, a great and enlightened mind who spoke of Christ when he meant Marx. (This interpretation stems, surprisingly enough, not from some Soviet critic, but from Oswald Spengler.[7]) Although Tolstoy does show a good many Western influences, his work is permeated throughout by the latent presence of a great deal of Eastern Christianity. In his whole nature the author of *War and Peace* was a distinctly Russian figure. Rilke, after his visit to Tolstoy at Yasnaya Polyana, called him "the eternal Russian"; the man had grown beyond such categories as liking or dislike, he said. But above all Rilke felt Tolstoy to be "very alien."[8] This characterization seems to hit off the essential Tolstoy, whose alien note is connected with his Eastern spirit, and also with the atmosphere of the Russian sectarian movements. He was far more strongly influenced by the Raskolniki and Dukhobors than is generally assumed. Tolstoy sprang from the same Russian soil as these heretical movements— which, by the way, should not be equated with Western sects. This Eastern side of his nature explains the strange forms of asceticism to which Tolstoy was increasingly prone, a trend which reached its climax in *The Kreutzer Sonata*. Western sensibilities will always be repelled by the grating sound with which, in this story, the knife penetrates through the woman's corset. But to the self-multilators of Russia, such a detail did not seem extreme.

Under the thin European outer layer there lay another, an uncanny Tolstoy—the Russian bear touched by madness. Tolstoy was at the peak of his literary fame when this madness came alarmingly into the open. Here was the strange spectacle of a man

[7] Oswald Spengler: *Der Untergang des Abendlandes* (1922), II, 234–7.
[8] Rainer Maria Rilke: *Briefe aus den Jahren 1892 bis 1904* (1939), p. 66, and C. Osam: *Rainer Maria Rilke* (1941), p. 82.

so powerfully rooted in nature, so bursting with vitality, enjoying all the riches of a brilliant life, suddenly plunged into a grave spiritual crisis. He has described it in detail in *My Confession*—a document indispensable for a religious interpretation of Tolstoy. He traces his spiritual history back to his youth, when he fell away from the Orthodox religion and lived wildly. Whether he really committed all the misdeeds which he ascribes to himself need not be discussed. Certainly as a young man Tolstoy did live the superficial and irresponsible life of a Russian nobleman who gave free rein to his animal instincts.

The sight of an execution in Paris produced an initial shock whose effects, however, wore off quickly. A few years later he began to be assailed by questions that literally brought him to a standstill. It was a form of mental illness which took the guise of his no longer knowing how he ought to live. At first he tried to drive away these paralyzing doubts, this questioning of the meaning of life. But neither distraction nor stupefaction helped him. The meaninglessness of life grimaced at him from every side. He tried to explain his state by attributing it to nervous exhaustion. But though he took a rest cure in the Caucasus and drank health-giving mares' milk among the Bashkirs, the trouble was not alleviated. It had emerged from strange depths, and must be related to the madness of which he speaks in his posthumously published story.

Overbrimming with life, Tolstoy found himself suddenly confronted by a wall which stopped him in his tracks. That wall was death. Horror at the vanishing of life, at life's inexorable movement toward death, drew its veil over everything, and put Tolstoy into that state of mind which he describes in the "Memoirs of a Madman": "Always the same horror: red, white, and square. Something tearing within that yet could not be torn apart." [9] Death as the great reality overshadowing all else had entered his field of vision, and could no longer be banished from it. The problem of death became the dark companion of his whole life. Tolstoy's very animal vigor attracted its opposite pole: death

[9] Tolstoy: "Memoirs of a Madman," p. 217.

that makes mock of the insatiable thirst for life. Tolstoy thought incessantly about death; his diaries are filled with discussions of this subject. "If I am still alive," he would add, and observe: "I write this and think that it is possible that tomorrow I shall no longer be living. Every day I try to make this thought more familiar to me, and I am growing more and more accustomed to it." He was overcome by that terrible feeling which he described in his great short novel, *The Death of Ivan Ilych*: *"It's not a question of appendix or kidney, but of life and . . . death. Yes, life was there and now it is going, going and I cannot stop it. Yes. Why deceive myself? Isn't it obvious to everyone but me that I'm dying and that it's only a question of weeks, days . . . it may happen this moment. There was light and now there is darkness. I was here and now I'm going there! Where?"* A chill *came over him, his breathing ceased, and he felt only the throbbing of his heart. "When I am not, what will there be? There will be nothing. Then where shall I be when I am no more? Can this be dying? No, I don't want to!"* [1] Only a Russian could have written such a tale of death, because Eastern Christianity has always been preoccupied with men's dying. Arseniev has objected to Tolstoy's painful concern with death on the grounds that "the depth of his questions on the meaninglessness of death is not balanced by a corresponding depth in the solution" which he found.[2] But this is unjust. No one can solve the problem of death, and anyone who thinks he has done so is harboring an illusion. The greatness of Tolstoy consists precisely in the consistency with which he remained caught up in the distress of death. Only the doggedness with which he faced to the end the insolubility of the riddle made it possible for him to utter that astonishing phrase, "blessed death"—to come, that is, to an attitude analogous to Ivan Ilych's, who experienced a strange transformation as he drew his last breath: " 'And death . . . where is it?' He sought his former accustomed fear of death and

---

[1] Tolstoy: "The Death of Ivan Ilych," in *The Short Novels of Tolstoy* (New York: Dial Press; 1946), pp. 443 f.
[2] N. Arseniev: *Die russische Literatur* (1929), p. 68.

did not find it. 'Where is it? What death?' There was no fear because there was no death. In place of death there was light." [3]

In his own spiritual crisis, Tolstoy anticipated the crisis of
modern man: the crisis which in those days was still concealed by
the hurly-burly of a general faith in progress but which, after the
foundering of Western civilization in two successive world wars,
was to affect more and more people. In his personal destiny the
destinies of humanity were foreshadowed. The "spiritual standstill" of which he speaks is a common ailment of modern man
who, bereft of the old metaphysical framework, is only too prone
to become acutely sensitive to the meaninglessness of life.

Tolstoy first sought a cure for this mental agony in science.
But science was not able to answer his questions. Here his experience once again went further than the nineteenth century with
its wholly uncritical scientific positivism. The fruitlessness of his
quest added to his inner confusion.

In the midst of this inner turmoil, Tolstoy turned his attention
to the working folk of Russia, toward whom he had always felt a
kind of physical love. He did not idealize the peasants, for he
knew all their faults from precise observation. But he became and
remained for the rest of his life deeply moved by their social
condition. He felt to the full the contrast between the opulent
life-style of the privileged classes and the want and misery in the
peasants' huts. The peasants starved and the rich played Beethoven! After a walk through a wretched village he noted in his
journal: "How they live is good; how we live is a disgrace."
Tolstoy overcame his pride of class and descended to the common
people, not to teach them, but to learn from them. The life of the
Russian peasants occupied his thoughts more and more; when he
was on his deathbed he sighed: "But the peasants—you know how
they die." He entered so deeply into the life of the peasants that
he at times virtually became one himself; dressed in caftan and
hip boots, he took pleasure in guiding a plow with his own hands.
When we see a picture of Tolstoy in his old age, with his flowing

[3] Tolstoy: "The Death of Ivan Ilych," p. 455.

beard, furrowed face, and small, keen eyes, we must acknowledge that this is the very image of a Russian peasant. Here was a great writer who had nothing of the literary-salon intellectual about him; he belonged to an altogether different breed.

Shaken as he was by his spiritual crisis, Tolstoy could not help observing the enormous capacity for suffering which enabled the peasants to endure their often unspeakably harsh existence. The muzhik became a metaphysical guide for him. For what sustained the muzhik through his life of incessant toil and hardship was his religion. As a youth Tolstoy had haughtily thrown overboard the Christian religion—like most of the enlightened men of the middle of the nineteenth century. But he later came to the conclusion that only the "answer of faith" gives man the sense of the infinite in his finite existence.

The faith by which the Russian people lived was the faith it had received from the Orthodox Church. The choice was, Tolstoy saw, to perish in the desert of nullity or to turn back to that Church. Faced with the alternative, Tolstoy did not hesitate. He returned to the Church as a penitent son. He started reading the legends of the saints. These soon became his favorite reading matter—and to his agonized mind, ridden by the fear of death, these tales seemed to reveal the meaning of life. He thought that he had found his way home, and for a considerable time the Church played a vital part in his thinking. He was by no means unreceptive to its mysticism.

But Tolstoy's history also demonstrates with painful clarity what difficulty modern man has in returning to the Church. With his complicated psyche modern man can no longer become the simple church Christian of earlier times. Tolstoy's cordial relationship with the Orthodox Church did not last long. Nor could it have lasted, if Tolstoy were not to become untrue to himself. The rift, when it inevitably came, was no longer due to indifference, but to his highly alert religious conscience. A profound disillusionment overwhelmed him; he had been imagining that he had come to God, and instead found that he had fallen into a filthy morass.

He became aware of the symptoms of degeneracy which many of those who praised the Orthodox Church were unwilling to see because they themselves shared the same faults.

What first aroused Tolstoy's doubts were certain ethical questions. He was troubled by the Church's attitude toward dissenters, by its condoning of the death penalty. Even more, he was horrified that the priests should give their blessing to war. He became repelled by the frozen ritualism of the Church. He found himself unable to accept the doctrine of transubstantiation and the dogma of the Trinity. It was more and more borne upon him that in Orthodox Christianity truth and error were indissolubly joined. Since the third century, it seemed to him, the Church had cherished lies and cruelty. Theology had completely obscured Christian truth.

His conscience forced him to protest, and the result was a break with the Church which soon became irreparable. Once he had rebelled against the Church, he launched upon a comprehensive criticism of it. With characteristic Russian radicalism, he attempted to wipe the slate clean. Thus Tolstoy became a heretic and the greatest religious rebel that the Eastern Church has produced in modern times. His heresy was a thoroughly conscious matter, conditioned by his personal development; Tolstoy meant every word of it, and unless we understand it we cannot understand the true depths of his nature. Long sections in his theoretical works are comprehensible only if we constantly keep in mind that they were written by a deliberate heretic who was irreconcilably at war with the Christianity of the churches.

The violent dispute with the Church which followed this second break with Orthodox Christianity occupied a considerable portion of his life. He did not shrink from a direct assault on the principles of the Eastern Church, and to this end composed his *Critique of Dogmatic Theology*. In this work Tolstoy examined the Orthodox catechism under a magnifying glass, and unsparingly tore it to pieces. With anger and contempt, he called Orthodox doctrine a lie, and said that he was duty-bound to expose it. Not only was it an outrageous insult to the intelligence, but also a blasphemy of the Holy Spirit: "I had once read the so-called Godless works of Voltaire and Hume, but never have I had so firm a conviction of the utter untrustworthiness of a human being as that which overcame me in regard to the authors of the catechism and the theologies." He left not one stone of the Orthodox doctrinal structure unturned. Ruthlessly, he bared all the logical flaws and contradictions of which the ecclesiastical authors had been guilty. With fierce intelligence Tolstoy denounced the greed and ignorance of the priests, whom he likened to "a stupid boy just dismissed from the seminary who can scarcely read, or a besotted old man whose only concern is to obtain as many eggs or kopeks as possible." With Russian intemperance Tolstoy blasted the whole Orthodox doctrine; in this respect he effectively paved the way for the subsequent Bolshevist destruction of the Church. In his book, *My Religion*, he stressed that Church Christianity as a whole had outlived its day: *All these churches—Catholic, Orthodox, Protestant—are like so many sentinels still keeping careful watch before the prison doors, although the prisoners have long been at liberty before their eyes, and even threaten their existence. . . . In these times the life of the world is entirely independent of the doctrine of the Church. The Church is left so far behind, that men no longer hear the voices of those who preach its doctrines. This is understandable enough, since the Church still clings to an organization of the world's life which has been forsaken, and is rapidly falling to destruction.*[4]

Despite this stinging criticism of the Church, Tolstoy did not take the position that religion in general was a mistaken course. The religious side of his nature had been awakened, and could no longer be repressed. Although he parted ways with the Orthodox Church, the question of God was more vital to him than ever. Those who knew him closely could see that the idea of God dominated his thoughts. His mode of life was rather like that of

[4] Tolstoy: *My Religion* (New York; 1885), pp. 224–5.

the typical Oriental pilgrim "who all their life long, stick in hand, walk the earth." [5] His madness overcame him again and again, and according to the "Memoirs of a Madman" these spells of madness brought him wonderful illuminations: "And it suddenly became clear to me that this ought not to be, and not only ought not to be but in reality was not. And if this was not, then neither was there either death or fear, and there was no longer the former tearing asunder within me and I no longer feared anything. Then the light fully illumined me and I became what I now am." [6] The insights emerging from such mystic illumination represented a far more dangerous threat to the Orthodox Church than his *Critique of Dogmatic Theology*. The latter, in spite of its logic, was a blunt instrument, since rational argumentation does not attack the core of religious convictions. The "illuminations," on the other hand, were waves of that Christian spirit which the New Testament designates as folly in Christ. They led Tolstoy to raise questions which no church could answer. Orthodox Christianity had every reason to be alarmed at the light that was beginning to glow in him and out of him, for it made visible once more the Christianity from which orthodoxy had sprung, so long ago, and which in the course of centuries had been obscured by ritualistic forms. Tolstoy not only condemned the Church for diverting attention from the ethics of Christianity. He also made himself a powerful spokesman for that other conception of Christianity which had manifested itself repeatedly in the Russian sectarian movements.

By this act Tolstoy became a creative heretic, proclaiming imperishable truths; he moved from sheer negation to a positive stand of far greater worth than his criticism. Here is where the inner spiritual face of Tolstoy emerges. His message is of such timeless truth and beauty that we cannot, as literary critics are always doing, rank his religious writings as unfortunate subsidiary productions. He may have failed to see all sides of the problem, in these treatises, but the cause with which they deal is of infinite

[5] Maxim Gorky: *Reminiscences of Tolstoy, Chekhov and Andreev* (London: Hogarth Press; 1934), p. 17.
[6] Tolstoy: *Ivan Ilých and Hadji Murád*, p. 225.

grandeur. Reading them, we understand quite well why Tolstoy could no longer go on writing novels. Such darkness and such light had been revealed to him, such an overpowering religious reality, that it was his merely literary art which became secondary.

Tolstoy's conception of Christianity differed both from that of the Orthodox Church and that of the West. It was supremely Russian, however, and drew inspiration from Eastern heresies. He focused his full attention upon the Gospels, which he read again and again, his enthusiasm growing with each rereading. This fact alone was of key significance. For although Orthodox ritual utilized the Bible insofar as it was held out to the faithful, who were supposed to kiss the cover of the venerable book, it was seldom opened. Tolstoy let the content of Scripture work upon him and bear fruit, not only for himself, but also for the vast number of people whom he influenced. While his ethics took on strongly Catharist features, his penchant for Bible reading brought him close to the Waldensian heretics. Through constant reading of the Gospels he grew ever more confirmed in his love of Christ. His friend and cousin A. A. Tolstoy reports that at the mere mention of Christ's name "his voice quivered and his eyes gleamed moistly. This memory consoles me to this day; without admitting it to himself he loved the Redeemer with deepest love and felt him to be more than an ordinary man." [7]

After intensive study, Tolstoy decided that the most important part of the Gospels were the sections concerning the Sermon on the Mount. The familiar words had an entirely new sound to him. He felt that no one had ever read them before. This attitude must not be dismissed as a subjective illusion. Tolstoy was indeed the great discoverer of the Sermon on the Mount in our day and age. Once again it was a heretic who after many centuries sought to hammer that sermon home to the conscience of Christendom. Tolstoy beheld the Sermon on the Mount as the incomparable Magna Carta of Christianity—and all that has been written in recent decades about this greatest of Christian documents consciously or unconsciously follows this thesis of his. If Tolstoy had

[7] Countess A. A. Tolstoy: *Erinnerungen an Leo N. Tolstoj* (no date), p. 38.

done nothing else but rescue the Sermon on the Mount, so long buried under the dry formulas of catechisms, and restore it to its original sublime radiance, he would have earned his own immortal glory.

But the most extraordinary aspect of his rediscovery of the Sermon on the Mount was his uncovering of its fundamental base. By a stroke of genius Tolstoy selected and underlined Christ's words: "You have heard that it was said, 'An eye for an eye and a tooth for a tooth.' But I say to you, do not resist evil." [8] These words of Jesus were, in Tolstoy's view, the "key to the whole," and express the core of Christianity. Tolstoy was the first Christian in modern times to see that the nucleus of the entire Sermon on the Mount lies in those words: "Do not resist evil." These words, which had been, as it were, tossed into a corner as worthless, began to sparkle for him like the most precious gems, and by their light he perceived the innermost mystery of Christianity.

But is it not sheer madness to make non-resistance to evil the heart of the Gospel? Yes, we must say that it would occur only to a madman to regard this phrase from the Sermon on the Mount as the beacon which is to illuminate the darkness of modern man. The watchword "Resist not evil" is an expression of true and traditional Russian Christianity, and the nineteenth century could scarcely come to terms with it. Nietzsche alone grasped the significance of the phrase, at least in theoretical fashion, when he wrote in his *Antichrist* the words: "Resist not evil, that profoundest saying of the Gospels, in a certain sense the key to them." [9] Conscious renunciation of all violence is indeed one of the deepest of Christian motifs, and has strong affinities to Lao-tse's *Tao Tê Ching*, a work which also strongly appealed to Tolstoy. There is an enigmatic passivity here. The West is inclined to give it short shrift, dismissing it with the epithet "Oriental." And yet it can accomplish more in the long run than

---

[8] Matt. V, 38–39. The Revised Standard Version of the Bible, otherwise cited throughout this book, here diverges too far from the traditional versions used by Tolstoy. RSV has: "Do not resist one who is evil." The King James Version gives: "Resist not evil," which is in keeping with Tolstoy's interpretation.—*Translators' note.*   [9] Nietzsche: *Werke*, VIII, 242.

Western man's morbid activism, as has been shown by the example of Gandhi, Tolstoy's greatest disciple. No sharper antithesis can be conceived than that between Tolstoy's emphasis upon non-resistance to evil and the ordinary man's faith in power.

We must not equate Tolstoyan passivity with the kind of lethargy that Goncharov represented in his lovable Oblomov. "Oblomovism" was a spiritual illness which Tolstoy did not in the least share. Non-resistance to evil has nothing to do with tacit acceptance of the phenomena of evil. Tolstoy was never averse to fighting evil by every moral instrument at his command, and hurling his massive protests into the world. This Christian, uncorrupted by patriotism, thundered against war, against pogroms, against death sentences, against harsh social conditions. He was keenly conscious of the agonizing poverty of the lower classes and clearly recognized the incompatibility between the Gospel and the feudal social order that still persisted in Russia—a recognition the Eastern Church refused to make. The pain of social inequality burned incessantly in his soul. He wrote in his diary: "I have not slept all night. My heart pains me constantly. . . . Yesterday I saw eighty-year-old Akim plowing, met Yaremich's wife, who has no fur coat and only a single skirt, and Maria, whose husband froze to death; she has no one to get in the grain for her, and her child is dying." Prophetically he sensed the approaching catastrophe: "It will finally lead to the downfall of our civilization as a whole, similar to the fate of the Egyptian, Babylonian, Greek and Roman civilizations." [1] For Tolstoy, too, had something of the apocalyptic strain of the great heretics, although this has not often been remarked on.

His stirring outcry against the anti-Christianity of the world's terrible conditions could not eliminate those conditions. But he did succeed in making the world look up and listen. It was no small thing that there was one man who said unfalteringly what was right and what wrong before God. The Tolstoy residence of Yasnaya Polyana became a place of pilgrimage for people from every corner of the globe.

[1] Fülöp-Miller: *Der unbekannte Tolstoj* (1927), p. 256.

It would be a shallow critic who would suggest that there was a contradiction between Tolstoy's "resist not evil" and his fiery protests. In fact, the linking of these apparently contradictory elements signifies that Tolstoy really penetrated to the heart of the Gospel. He issued no call to the barricades; nevertheless, his words created upheavals in the world. Such revolutionary effects are always a sure sign of whether truly religious forces are at work. Tolstoy's preaching of non-violence and his stirring protests shook governments to their foundations. *But to every serious and sincere man of our time the incompatibility of true Christianity (the doctrine of humility, forgiveness, and love) with the State and its pomp, violence, executions, and wars, is quite obvious. The profession of true Christianity not only excludes the possibility of recognizing the State, but even destroys its foundations.*[2]

The Tsarist state feared the seditious force of Tolstoy's conception of Christianity. The police often descended upon the house of the great writer and subjected it to a thorough search. His pamphlets were banned by the censorship. But in defiance of suppression, Tolstoy's Christian revolution spread. There were many parallels between it and early Christianity, which had likewise been defenseless before the might of Roman civilization and which also had represented a grave menace to the rule of the state. What Tolstoy was after amounted to a "total overturning and annihilation of the whole existing order." Uncompromising in his principles, Tolstoy denounced the whole system of justice, militarism, landowning.

Both his criticism of the Orthodox Church and his interpretation of the Sermon on the Mount were rejected by his contemporaries. Even Dostoevsky, when shown a summary of Tolstoy's arguments, "clapped his hand to his head and cried out in despair: Not that! Anything but that!"[3] Similarly, Soloviëv decided that Tolstoy was an example of secret anti-Christian spirit at work.

[2] Tolstoy: *The Kingdom of God and Peace Essays* (London: Oxford University Press; 1936), p. 282.
[3] Countess A. A. Tolstoy: op. cit., p. 29.

Florensky characterized Tolstoy's religion as "a calloused, evil, hard tumor of the heart which blocks his way to God."[4] Others spoke of a "mania for simplification"[5] and condemned the Tolstoyan creed as "positivistic mysticism which remains unsatisfactory in every aspect."[6] But what does such slashing criticism signify if not guilty conscience? For Tolstoy pricked the consciences of all these men. Tolstoy confronted every reader with that inescapable alternative which the great Christian writer Leskov, who sided with Tolstoy, formulated concisely: *Like a lightning flash severing the night sky, the words of Tolstoy struck directly at the doctrine which had secretly taken the place of Christ's teachings, shattering and annihilating it. Only one of two reactions is possible: either to shake the author's hand, or to go to one of the old altars and, sobbing, implore Him to protect Himself and mankind from this destroyer whose strength and resolution are beyond compare.*[7]

The sharpest reply to Tolstoy came, as indeed was only logical, from the Orthodox Church. For a long time the Church had suffered Tolstoy's attacks in silence, and made no reprisals, probably because of Tolstoy's noble rank and his great fame as a writer. Only occasionally had it expressed its anger. A number of his books had been banned by the clerical censorship and the author denounced from the pulpits as an enemy to Christian society. But when it became convinced that his attitude was unalterable, the Church pronounced excommunication upon the seventy-year-old writer. *In our days, under God's sufferance, a new false teacher has arisen, Count Leo Tolstoy. A writer known to the world, Russian by birth, Orthodox by baptism and training, Count Tolstoy, seduced by his proud intellect, has arrogantly defied our Lord and His Christ and His holy legacy; he has openly renounced the mother who nourished and trained him, the Orthodox Church, and has dedicated his God-given literary talent to spreading among the masses teachings contrary to those*

---

[4] *Östliches Christentum*, ed. H. Bubnoff and H. Ehrenberg (1925), II, 44.
[5] Arseniev: op. cit., p. 68.
[6] *Religion in Geschichte und Gegenwart*, 2nd ed., Vol. V, col. 1225.
[7] Nikolay Leskov: *Gesammelte Werke* (no date), IX, 319.

of Christ and the Church, and to uprooting in the minds and hearts of people their fathers' faith, the Orthodox faith, which has been accepted as universal, by which our ancestors lived and were saved, by virtue of which our Holy Russia until this day has been maintained and kept strong. Therefore the Church no longer counts him among her members and can no longer count him among them until he repents.[8]

Thus the Russian Church expelled the madman from its midst. Tolstoy was not upset by this excommunication. It in no way altered his life. He had long ceased to attend church, and had made known his desire to be buried without the intervention of priests (which in fact was done). To the decree of excommunication, which only increased his prestige, he gave a dignified reply: *Whether or not my views on religion offend anyone, cause anyone sorrow or are a stumbling block to anyone, I can no more change them than I can change my body. I must live my own life, and I myself must meet death—and that very soon—and therefore I, who am preparing to go to that God from whom I came, cannot hold any other beliefs than those I do hold. I do not think that my belief is valid for all times; but I see no other that answers all the questions of my intellect and my heart more simply, more clearly or better. If I were to find any such, I would accept it at once, for God demands nothing but the truth. But I can no longer return to that religion which I left with such suffering, any more than a bird can return to the egg-shell it has left behind.*[9]

To appraise Tolstoy's religious attitude from a Western point of view is not easy. Obviously, it is a mingling of great truths with patent exaggerations. But if Tolstoy, as he grew older, was increasingly unable to be just to the Church, we must also take due account of the valid elements in his criticism of the Church. Not all his charges against the Orthodox Church were mistaken,

[8] Alexandra Tolstoy: *A Life of My Father* (New York: Harper & Bros.; 1953), p. 406.
[9] Leon: *Leo N. Tolstoj, Leben und Werk* (1946), p. 380.

though he may have failed to perceive certain depths in the creed of that Church. Above all, his basic premise can hardly be contested: that a religion which lends itself to the defense of existing wrongs sacrifices much of its truthfulness.

One frequent objection to Tolstoy is that he understood Christianity as a new law, not as an evangel—that is, that he reduced Christianity to mere moralism and often made use of it merely to preach boring sermons at his fellow men. He himself contributed to this false picture by his own pedagogic passion. He often slipped into moralizing and seemed to use the Gospel to sell a particular social program. This cannot be denied. But it is scarcely fair to label Tolstoy's Christianity as pure ethics, as has been done so often. His moral fervor was of another order from a dreary preaching of virtue. The Tolstoy whom Gorky found to be a figure "terribly homeless and alien to all men and things," who at times sat in a corner in his own house looking "as though the dust of another earth were on him, and gazing attentively at everything with the look of a foreigner or a mute" [1]—this Tolstoy was not a tiresome do-gooder.

Merely his emphasis on asceticism is a token of the intensity of his Christianity. He was, of course, extremely serious about the ethical message of the Gospel and this could be misconstrued as a confounding of Christianity with a narrow scheme of morality. But he was only laying utmost stress upon those actions which are essential to a Christian. For Tolstoy's message was this, that the important thing is not the saying, Lord, Lord, but doing the will of God. That was what this heretic never tired of repeating, in consonance with Jesus. The maximalism of Christian ethics emerged again in Tolstoy, even as it did in the great saints of Christendom. He pursued the imperishable ideal of incessant self-perfecting. To challenge this striving on dogmatic grounds is to rob Christianity of most of its meaning. In the face of this effort, it is altogether improper to say that Tolstoy did not take the person of Jesus Christ seriously enough. The charge is grotesque,

[1] Maxim Gorky: op. cit., pp. 17, 42.

in view of the fact that Tolstoy made Christ's doctrine the center
of his world.

As we have already said, Tolstoy went directly to the Sermon
on the Mount and derived his whole system from it. He rebelled
against the idea that the Sermon on the Mount propounded
beautiful but impractical rules of conduct. On the contrary, he
insisted, the Christian is obligated to follow the Sermon on the
Mount. For Tolstoy personally, the struggle to introduce its
principles into practical life was all-important. In his last great
novel, *Resurrection,* he attempted to show the consequences for
men's personal lives of the effort to put the Sermon into practice.
As a work of art *Resurrection* has certain flaws. But it remains one
of the greatest of penitent novels. In it Tolstoy not only painted
the unsatisfactoriness of the life of sin, as so many Christian
novelists are fond of doing, but attempted to describe the new
way in positive and concrete terms. It is true, he concedes, that
the task is of infinite difficulty, but the significant thing is the
effort.

Not only his fictional characters seek redemption by living
according to the principles of the Sermon on the Mount. Tolstoy
seriously attempted to apply these principles to his own life. Of
course it is easy to poke fun at Tolstoy's cobbling or carrying
firewood and so on, and call these childish follies. And of course
the prejudices of the propertied class clung to him; very few
people succeed in throwing these off entirely. But he never took
the habits of the higher class as a matter of course. By fiercest
exertion he strove to break through into Christian reality. His
biography shows how frightfully difficult it is for a rich man to
lead a Christian life in earnest. The struggle he waged is a moving
illustration of Jesus' saying that a camel will sooner pass through
the eye of a needle than a rich man enter the kingdom of heaven.
In his drama, *The Light Shines in the Darkness,* he has his hero
sum up his own experience in realizing Christianity: "Thou
wishest me to be humiliated, so that every one may point his
finger at me and say, 'He preaches, but he does not perform.'

Well, let them! Thou knowest best what Thou requirest: submission, humility! Ah, if I could but rise to that height!" [2]

Tolstoy has also been criticized for falling into rationalism. There are some grounds for this criticism. To a certain extent his assault on the Orthodox Church was based on rationalistic elements. Such rationalism was new to Russia, but not to the rest of the Occidental world. Other thinkers such as D. F. Strauss had anticipated all Tolstoy's arguments. In fact, the validity of Tolstoy's criticism of the Church is almost obscured by the harshness of his rationalism. He subjected the orthodox doctrines to the same test as a set of mathematics problems. Everything was examined by reason; everywhere he operated with strict logic— a strange procedure for the otherwise non-logical Tolstoy, and one which led him to completely overlook the sacramental aspect of the Faith, which is of such great importance in the Eastern Church.

And yet, in spite of this rationalistic vein in Tolstoy—which was no doubt connected with his enormous gift for keen realistic observation—Tolstoy was not a rationalist. He did not have the kind of limited scientific intellect which never ascends above the empirical realm. How otherwise could he have written so truly: "To consider religions from a historical point of view means to destroy them." [3] Rather, in this he resembles Buddha, who could also argue keenly in an entirely rational manner when he wished to lead his listeners to insight, and who yet strove for a suprarational goal. Here, in the cases of both Buddha and Tolstoy, we see that reason can be applied to the realm of religion without its necessarily leading to an emptying of religious content, as has almost always been true in the West. As a creative artist Tolstoy could not be a thoroughgoing rationalist, although he sometimes pretended to be one with all his strength. His rationalism was his misunderstanding of himself; it was also merely a front that he

[2] Tolstoy: *The Light Shines in the Darkness*, in *Plays by Leo Tolstoy* (London: Oxford University Press; 1933), p. 394.
[3] Leon: op. cit., p. 239.

presented to the world. It is not even accurate to say that in his head Tolstoy was a rationalistic "enlightener" and in his heart a profound irrationalist. He was not even rationalistic to this degree. It is noteworthy that in his later writings he eliminated the term "rational consciousness," quietly substituting "Christian consciousness."

Tolstoy's wonderful folk tales reveal the wholly different depths from which Tolstoy drew his power. In these writings the last remnants of esthetic attitudes have been burned away by the fire of Christianity. Their utter, shaming simplicity lifts them entirely above the category of literature. The folk tales could only be written by a man who was prepared to lose the most precious element of his life—his art—for the sake of Christ, and who in so doing found it again. These works no longer have the stark quality of *The Kreutzer Sonata*, where everything is stripped naked. Rather, the components of religion and art have fused in wonderful union. These stories are illuminated by the white radiance of Russian religiosity; they deserve a place close to the Gospels themselves. Anyone who could describe religious reality with such plainness and profundity had thrown himself open to divinity. In the face of these holy folk tales, the most glorious of all the glorious works created by this Russian heretic, who can continue to speak slightingly of Tolstoy's rationalistic Christianity? The man of Yasnaya Polyana must be counted among the few really Christian writers the nineteenth century produced. These tales glow with the eternal truth: Where love is, God is.

We have spoken several times of the madness which overcame Tolstoy and which he himself portrayed in the "Memoirs of a Madman." It was not the sort of madness which falls within the province of medicine, but that which had seized Paul when he spoke to Agrippa and the king said to him: "Paul, you are mad, your great learning is turning you mad." [1] This Eastern heretic had accesses of holy madness. The Tolstoy who turned against art, and to the consternation of all lovers of literature condemned his own works, burned with the fire of primitive Christianity. He

[1] Acts xxvi, 24.

represented, in the first place, Russian Christianity as it might have developed had it not been for the rigid cast given to it by Byzantinism. In the second place he exemplified that genuine Christian radicalism which consists in the imitation of Christ, which refuses to make compromises with civilization and opposes the most dangerous threat to all self-complacent finiteness. It is the same divine madness which provoked a St. Francis to challenge medieval civilization. In Tolstoy its sudden, powerful flare-up terrified a good many of his contemporaries.

Faced with this primitive Christian anarchism, we can only say of Tolstoy what he himself says of the "three hermits" in his folk tale of that name. The bishop, it will be remembered, tried to teach them the Lord's Prayer, but when he had sailed away they came after him, gliding along upon the water to tell him: "We have forgotten your teaching, servant of God. As long as we kept repeating it, we remembered, but when we stopped saying it for a time, a word dropped out and then another, and now it is all gone to pieces. We can remember nothing of it. Teach us again." [5]

[5] Tolstoy: "The Three Hermits," in *Twenty-three Tales by Tolstoy* (London: Oxford University Press; 1906), p. 181.

+   +

22

Tentative Conclusion

+   +

The Heretic's Homecoming

The situation of the heretic has changed fundamentally in modern times. People are no longer, as in earlier centuries, expelled from the church for deviant religious views. On the contrary, hordes of church members turn from her of their own accord. This flight from the church has become a general experience, conditioned not so much by religious causes as, in most cases, by the changed psychology of modern man. From decade to decade the number of Christians who do not feel comfortable in the bosom of the church has been growing. In our day, the movement represents a mass flight, and there may be more persons outside than inside the fold. We might say that the heretics, not the church, seem to have conquered. At any rate, the church has been driven on the defensive. The result has been the virtual extinction of the concept of heresy. If everyone has become heretical, how can this or that individual be branded a heretic? The man of today has left the house of the church and slammed the door behind him.

It is appropriate to point out, first of all, the historical factors which led to the modern attitude. The birth of the modern world was neither an act of arbitrary will, nor did it take place overnight. The roots of the change reach back into the Middle Ages. Yet so radical has the upheaval been that a student of history may well be baffled and cry out: "What contrasts! What transformations! Hierarchy, discipline, an order maintained by authority, dogmas firmly controlling life—these were precious to the men of the seventeenth century. Coercion, authority, dogmas—these were what the men of the eighteenth century, their immediate successors, found most obnoxious!" [1]

Since the century of the Enlightenment there has taken place a radical shift in men's concerns from the transcendental to the purely secular. The whole of existence has taken on another aspect because of this fundamental displacement; "above" and "below" have been reversed. The tissue of men's souls has undergone a profound transformation, which Christians in general are too little aware of. This reorientation has been most vividly described by Bernhard Groethuysen in his instructive book, *Die Entstehung der bürgerlichen Welt- und Lebensanschauung in Frankreich* ("The Origins of Bourgeois Views and Attitudes in France"). His conclusion can be summed up as follows: "The importance of faith as an experience has steadily diminished for the bourgeois, and at the same time the world of religion has been confined within constantly narrowing limits. Or to put it another way: Religion is changing both as to its extent and its experiential quality." [2]

[1] P. Hazard: *Die Krisis des europäischen Geistes* (1939), p. 19.
[2] Groethuysen: *Die Entstehung der bürgerlichen Welt- und Lebensanschauung in Frankreich* (1927), I, 70.

The rebellion against authority is a dominant theme of our time. One of the essential marks of the widespread modern heresy is the disdain for anything claiming spiritual authority. Whatever prestige any given authority may enjoy, however venerable it may be, modern man feels it as a shackle upon him and thrusts it from him. Autonomy has replaced authority. Modern man acknowledges only what springs from himself, not what is imposed upon him by outside forces.

But emancipation from authority is only one side of the total issue, which is freedom. The principle of freedom has become the real theme of modern history. Without freedom modern man cannot live a dignified life. He venerates freedom, he regards it as the essential component of life. Whether freedom has been actually achieved in modern times, or only replaced by a more cleverly disguised servitude, is a question into which we cannot enter here. Nor shall we discuss whether modern man may not have too superficial a view of freedom. That is a matter for another book. In this connection it is only important to observe that the idea of freedom is inseparable from the existence of modern man.

Of no less importance to him is reason. The man of the present day considers *ratio* the surest guide in life. He instinctively draws back from ideas which are expressly proclaimed as contrary to reason—despite the fact that he frequently falls prey to irrationalism. Nowadays a proof must be logical if it is to have any effect upon men's minds. Once again, we must acknowledge the nobility of this attitude. The dignity of man does consist in thinking. And we must likewise pay tribute to the passionate insistence on truth which also is manifest in the modern worldview. Modern man wants truth, no matter what the cost. Even if its effects are ugly and disillusioning, he continues to crave it. He prefers truth at any price to a pious fraud. He has what might be called a religious fervor for the truth and will often voice this belief in enthusiastic words. This craving for truth in the modern man must be lauded for the great thing it is.

And yet, closely linked with the undeniable nobility of the

modern sensibility, is the misery that follows in its train. Modern consciousness, pursued to the end in a straight line, has led to nihilism. And nihilism is far removed from all heresy, which was always focused upon religious concerns. Nihilism is an intellectual disease; it takes a frivolous attitude toward any and all philosophical questions, and consequently renounces all answers in advance. Life loses all deeper meaning and recognizes no goal that is worth sacrificing for. In nihilism, the destructive forces win the upper hand completely, and the result is a breakdown of all standards. The surrogates which replaced the genuine values of religion, such as national honor, love of sports, etc., have succeeded only temporarily in filling the spiritual vacuum. Today their inadequacy has already become plain. The complete nihilism of the present day is a confrontation with nothingness, which inevitably leads to desperation. Nihilism is a modern mutation of the medieval plague; spiritually, as many are dying of it as perished from the Black Death. Many young people have already succumbed to it; that is evident from their instability, indifference, and cynicism. They can only be regarded as pitiable victims of the spirit of the age. For abysses open before the man who has subscribed to the creed of nothingness. The consequence of nihilism is that tormenting anxiety which, if we follow the poignant accounts of Julian Green, distresses the man of today. Thus the terminus of the modern consciousness is a fearful thing. An impenetrable darkness is beginning to enshroud the Occident. No one has any idea of how to deal with the encroaching deluge. Every slogan is already outmoded before it is pronounced; the chaos is beyond managing. Nor does anyone know how to vanquish nihilism, which throws into question the whole being of man. Such is the dreadful outcome of modern heresy.

It is part and parcel of the truthfulness of the modern sensibility that people can bear the sight of the monstrous abyss, and not try to prettify it. In place of the optimistic faith in progress which dominated nineteenth-century Christendom, we live in a time of the dark night of the soul. The horsemen of the Apocalypse have ridden forth over the West. The Deluge of the twentieth century can only be regarded in eschatological terms. A world-wide tempest, with prodigious flashes of lightning and crashes of thunder, has burst upon the earth, and the unleashed elements are threatening to destroy all man has built up through the ages. Repeated crises disintegrate the political entities of the West, and shatter the churches. After almost two thousand years Europe is on the verge of taking leave of Christianity and degrading itself to the status of a peninsula of Asia. Nor can this inexorable process be halted unless some change of heart should take place at the last moment.

Whereas people of other centuries were shaken by nightmarish deliriums during times of upheaval, contemporary man seems curiously unaware of the plight of Christianity. He scarcely observes what is happening to the very basis of Western culture. Political events and economic changes claim his entire attention, and he imagines that this or that measure will fend off the dangers that beset the West. Yet the Christian heritage is being wiped out as much by capitalist commercialism as by communism when it comes to power. For each, in its own fashion, kills the soul of man. Totalitarianism abolishes the individuality of man and converts him into a cog in machinery grown vast beyond understanding. The specter of a human ant-state draws alarmingly close.

It is a curious fact that, along with this development, heresy has been more and more displaced into the political realm. The struggles which used to take place within the churches between orthodoxy and opposition are being repeated in the field of politics under different names but with astonishing similarities. Within the "Marxist church" there are orthodox and heretics; the party congresses become councils in which anathemas are hurled at minorities representing divergent opinions.

To further carry out the analogy, political orthodoxy deals with its heretics in the same manner as the Christian church once did. The repressive measures are just as brutal. Since the ideological struggles are actually a struggle for power, all dissidents are liquidated. It may be added that the study of church history should be of interest to the political rulers—for from it they can see who won out in the end! But the political orthodoxies can no more tolerate opposition than the church could, in its period of dynamic growth.

But the unexpected is already happening! When the typhoon reaches its height, its end is already predictable. At the extreme pole, negation becomes affirmation. To the perceptive eye it must become evident that something of fundamental importance has taken place in our era. The two world wars have produced a fundamental change in the spiritual outlook of Western man. Dostoevsky's and Nietzsche's somber prophecies of doom have already been fulfilled. The dreadful hour in which the West was reduced to a heap of rubble has come and gone. Such jeremiads can therefore not be repeated. The pronouncements of a last judgment must cease, and a new set of tidings drafted. It is urgently necessary to recognize that the situation has changed. Another direction must be sought. This is the decisive problem confronting man at the present time.

It cannot be a question of prophesying. Nothing is so misplaced as prophecy by one whom the Lord of history has not appointed to the office of prophet. The professional historian, too, must feel that he is poorly qualified to act as a soothsayer. But in the present critical moment, he feels compelled to take a role other than that of the impartial observer. He cannot prophesy, it is true, but surely he can make some sort of profession of faith— even though he bear in mind the warning of Kierkegaard: "A single man cannot help his age."

In fact all stabs at salvation have proved to be helpless gestures; nihilism cannot be battled directly because it is a "nothing." In the face of global disasters all efforts at local reform are bound to fail. For what are these but an attempt to guide history, and how can man presume to do this? This is not to preach a quietistic passivity. The spiritual man can only take a negative attitude toward the present age; inwardly, he must repel it. This repulsion constitutes the heretic's homecoming. The matter cannot be described in scholarly and scientific terms because it belongs entirely to the sphere of religion. By a conscious decision the modern heretic turns away from contemporary events and sets out on the homeward road. In Goethe's metaphor, he descends to the "Mothers" once more.

But this remarkable process takes place in utter stillness. The general public has not yet realized that it is necessary. Our existence within the social framework bars the way to this insight, as does the egocentricity of the individualist. But the single man, to use Kierkegaard's terminology, has already set out. He longs to have a native place again, where he feels at home; he wishes soil in which he can strike root. Nietzsche had already felt a racking need for some such anchorage and harbor. How moving is the cry from the lips of that modern heretic: "This search for my home, O Zarathustra, this search and travel toward it, you know it well; this travel was my travail; it consumes me. Where is my home? I ask and seek and sought and found it not. O eternal everywhere, O eternal nowhere, O eternal In vain." [3] And the dying Van Gogh—who set down upon canvas the sensibility of modern man as has no other painter—uttered the last words: "Now I would like to go home."

Modern man can no longer shut his ears to the message of these prophetic figures. It is his task to accomplish the heretic's homecoming, for the alternative to this is senseless self-destruction. The shades of an evening of history close in; all ideas that mankind is on the threshold of a new dawn have proved illusory. And in the evening one returns home because one does not wish to be overtaken by the darkness of night.

The heretic's homecoming, understood as a task and not as a completed solution, is an extremely complicated process. It has nothing to do with a return to primitivism. Homer has shown that homecoming is the most difficult undertaking a human being can assume. His *Odyssey* presents the eternal symbol of homecoming man; it shows the manifold dangers that threaten such a project. With all the strength of his heart Odysseus strives to reach his home port, and ever and again is led astray into new wanderings. The nymph Calypso tempts him with sweet allurements to give

[3] Nietzsche: *Werke*, VI, 398.

up all thought of his homeward journey, and he must use all his wits to steer between Scylla and Charybdis. The fruits of the Lotus-eaters which induce forgetfulness of home are a perennial symbol of that temptation to which countless men have succumbed in modern times: modern comforts have driven everything else out of their minds. With the wonderful music of its verse, Homer's epic is the eternally truthful song of man's homecoming. Whether Odysseus will reach his destination remains in doubt to the last moment. It is a weary road that the homeward-bound heretic must tread, and he will need his sharpest faculties not to stray from it.

This new homecoming has the distinctive quality that modern man sets out for home as a conscious heretic. He does not consider everything that has happened in modern times wrong, and he is by no means ready for a general indictment of the modern sensibility. The modern Odysseus, then, has the problem of distinguishing. There are a great many achievements of the modern spirit which can never again be renounced. The homecoming heretic does not deny his past. Neither does he break faith with the heretics who lived before him, whom he loves as kindred spirits. He abides by the magnificent perceptions which these witnesses to the truth won by unspeakable suffering. Returning, the contemporary heretic takes the modern sensibility home with him. This is neither inconsistency nor halfheartedness. Nor is the modern sensibility a unitary thing, containing as it does both grandeur and misery. These elements must be carefully thought through and separated. The extraordinary achievements of the modern sensibility must not be prematurely thrown over in the hour of peril.

It is not easy to formulate how the heretic's homecoming must take place, for the process is only beginning and has not yet assumed tangible form. There is not even any proper name for it; only the outlines of the new mood are as yet visible. Modern man does not yet possess the new religious language to replace phrases which have become outworn—and enable him again to speak in adequate terms of the Eternal. There is little value in supplying the lack by fabricating a philosophical secret language which only a few people can with difficulty understand, and which will soon be worn out in its turn. The new words can emerge only out of a new experience with the divine. Until that experience has taken form, Christian speech will be a helpless babble. It will be well, therefore, not to speak of religious matters with assertive self-assurance.

Stammering inadequately, then, we must suggest that the homecoming of the heretic will consist first and foremost in a new encounter with the metaphysical powers. It has come as a terrible shock to modern man's mind to discover how utterly insufficient are all attitudes rooted wholly in this world. He has found that life on this basis loses all its depth. He has therefore learned that this so-called "solid earth" is no longer the sole reality. From the very impoverishment of the materialistic consciousness, the modern heretic has discovered that new dimension of reality which passes into the transcendental realm. A mighty craving has been born in him for a true relationship to those eternal powers which permit a new striking of roots in the soil of religion. Only a metaphysical anchorage gives man that stability which makes him able to bear all tempests. The homecoming heretic has formed ties once again with the metaphysical powers. He has struck a new link with the ground of the universe—without which there is no lasting life. There is no cure for the disease of nihilism without this renewed experiencing of the eternal powers which surround man on all sides. Only by turning again to the Essential and the Substantial can man recover that indispensable knowledge of the center and the periphery, of the divine and the diabolic, which alone confer eternal values upon all of existence. Only in this way does man arrive at a supportable relationship with God, which is quite another thing from mere intellectual discussions of the concept of God.

The religious reality to which the homecoming heretic must find his way can, for Occidental man, only be Christianity. It is toward this that the modern heretic bends his steps. It is senseless to wait for a new religion, or to found a new one. Religions are not made by men; they crash down upon men "from above." Christianity came to Occidental man and gave him the means for most deeply penetrating the ground of the cosmos. The Gospel is destiny; with the existence of Christianity, Europe stands and falls. But the Christian values must be seen in new terms. Tradition, it is true, must be respected and cannot be renounced. Man must turn back to it again and again, if he is not to hang in a void. Nevertheless, the homecoming heretic can accept only a transformed tradition which frees him finally from all sterile apologetics—which have never truly helped Christianity. A new coinage of Christianity is needed, one which condenses and does not adulterate the Gospel. The homecoming to the Christian realm consists not in any trimming down of Christianity—the elimination, for example, of the mythic framework which offends the rationalistic mind—but in an intensification of the divine elements. The heretic of our day is seeking a radical renewal of Christianity, a renewal at the root. The history of heresy has shown that Christianity is richer in content than its ecclesiastical embodiment; the Gospel holds potentialities which have not yet come to the surface.

The new coinage of Christianity will also recognize the writings of the Eastern Church as "varieties of a different revelation," as Leopold Ziegler has put it.[4] The modern heretic strives for a newly experienced Christianity, which is no longer the same as that of the past. Only by grace of such a doctrine can the man caught up in nihilism possibly come home at all to the Christian realm. The followers of nihilism have hitherto been offered a Christianity denuded in the main of its deepest essence. The new view of Christianity will comprehend even nihilistic destruction, seeing it as the lowest stage of truth, from which it is possible for man to ascend.

One cannot speak of a return to the Christian realm without considering the figure of Christ who stands at the heart of the Gospel. Like no other personality in world history, the original Jesus has been buried under the rubble of words and pictures,

[4] Leopold Ziegler: *Überlieferung* (1926), p. 443.

and his image distorted almost beyond recognition. Any return to Christianity depends upon whether or not the essential Christ can be seen plain, freed from the endless moribund formulas which have always proved a fatal obstruction to a living relationship.

One of the most unfathomable mysteries of the Founder of the New Covenant consists in just this, that no formula can do justice to him. Whatever may be said about him—as Messiah, Exemplar, Redeemer, etc.—these are all only partial aspects which present themselves to the worshipper, but which cannot contain his whole essence. But what does the inscrutable Christ have to do with those who profess themselves heretics? Are they not detestable to him, as the church has always held?

How could they be, since during his lifetime he himself appeared in the same light and suffered the same accusation? Nor was it an unjust charge. Toward the Old Testament Jesus took the position of a heretic—although Christendom has understandably enough always said as little as possible about the rebellious aspects of Jesus' ministry. To the pious ears of the Jews the words of the Sermon on the Mount had an altogether heretical sound: "You have heard that it was said to the men of old . . . but I say to you." [5] With all the intrepidity of the heretic, Jesus appealed from the traditional law to a higher court. He took precisely the same point of view again when he asked the Pharisees and scribes: "Why do you transgress the commandment of God for the sake of your tradition?" [6] This turning from human commandments to God's is the very attitude we have encountered again and again among the heretics; in this, Jesus was the timeless exemplar. It involved him in a life-and-death struggle with the men of the synagogue. His conflict with the representatives of the Jewish church came to a climax in his militant sermon: "Woe to you, scribes and Pharisees, hypocrites! because you shut the kingdom of heaven against men; for you neither enter yourselves, nor allow those who would enter to go in." [7] To this day the denunciations of the "whited sepulchers," as Jesus called the ecclesiastical leaders of his people, ring in the ears of those who

[5] Matt. v, 21–2.   [6] Matt. xv, 3.   [7] Matt. xxiii, 13.

read the Gospels. Here is evidence of a militant figure of quite another stripe from the person with the beautifully curled hair, the parted beard, and the insipid features whose image has been built up over many centuries. This essential belligerence of Jesus led him, with the utmost consistency, before the Sanhedrin where the high priest himself cried the verdict: "You have now heard his blasphemy." [8] It is impossible to read the interrogation of Jesus without seeing in it the prototype of all heresy trials! In this light it becomes clear why Dostoevsky has his Grand Inquisitor say to Christ: "Tomorrow I shall condemn Thee and burn Thee at the stake as the worst of heretics."

The word makes us start. But in fear and trembling we must ask ourselves: Is it not true? Was not Jesus in fact the "worst of heretics"? Is it mere chance that his name has cropped up in every chapter of the story of heretics, that all heretics spoke in his name?

It is to this Christ, the heretic in the eyes of his people, to whom modern man comes home. Not that the epithet "worst of heretics" even begins to include all the aspects of Christ. It places too one-sided an emphasis upon his rebellion against a calcified tradition. But it does cast new light upon one hitherto overlooked aspect of Jesus. And here is the path by which modern man can come to a fresh understanding of him. With the revelation of Jesus as a heretic, we have at least made a beginning in the hard task of speaking about him in other than the hackneyed phrases which have lost all affective power. Such a beginning is essential for preparing the epiphany of the inexplicable Christ. A mysterious emanation from this eternal Christ creates the atmosphere in which the homecoming heretic approaches the divine. In no other personality of history is the divine so vividly, so tangibly embodied. To say this is not to comprehend his whole mystery, which cannot be plumbed by any man. Nevertheless, this is one way to project the grandeur of the Christian realm to modern man. Christ must be experienced not only as the Way which leads out of all impasses; in him can also be felt the unique pres-

[8] Matt. xxvi, 63–5.

ence of God. Only by rediscovering this can man regain his health. And when this has come to pass, it shall be for the home-coming heretic as it was in Jesus' parable of the Prodigal Son: "And they began to make merry . . ." [9]

[9] Fëdor Dostoevsky: *The Brothers Karamazov* (New York: Modern Library; no date), p. 310.

Index

i

Index

A Note about the Author

Walter Georg Nigg was born in Gersau on the Lake of Lucerne, Switzerland, on January 6, 1903. After being graduated from a *Gymnasium*, he continued his studies at the Universities of Göttingen, Leipzig, and Zurich. He received an honorary doctorate from the University of Marburg in 1949. The author of many books, Dr. Nigg is an ordained minister and an associate professor at the University of Zurich. He is married, and lives with his wife and two children at Dällikon (Zurich). He is a regular contributor of book reviews and articles to the *Neue Zürcher Zeitung* and the monthly *Du*.

A Note on the Type

The text of this book is set in Caledonia, a Linotype face designed by W. A. Dwiggins (1880–1956), the man responsible for so much that is good in contemporary book design and typography. Caledonia belongs to the family of printing types called "modern face" by printers—a term used to mark the change in style of type-letters that occurred about 1800. Caledonia borders on the general design of Scotch Modern but is more freely drawn than that letter.